O Maidens in your Savage Season

4

Story by **Mari Okada**
Art by **Nao Emoto**

【 *Contents* 】

Meeting 13

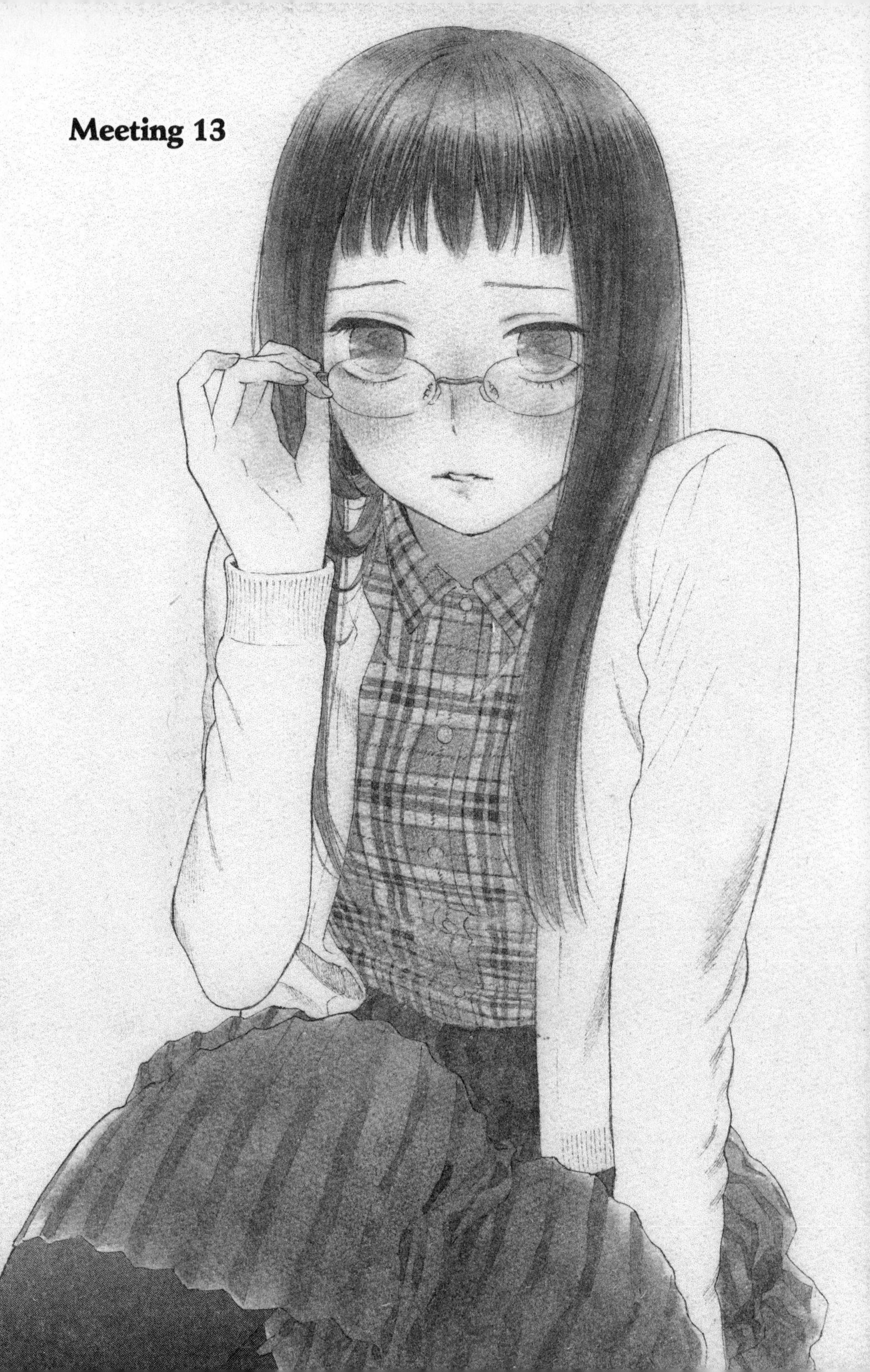

O Maidens
in
your Savage
Season

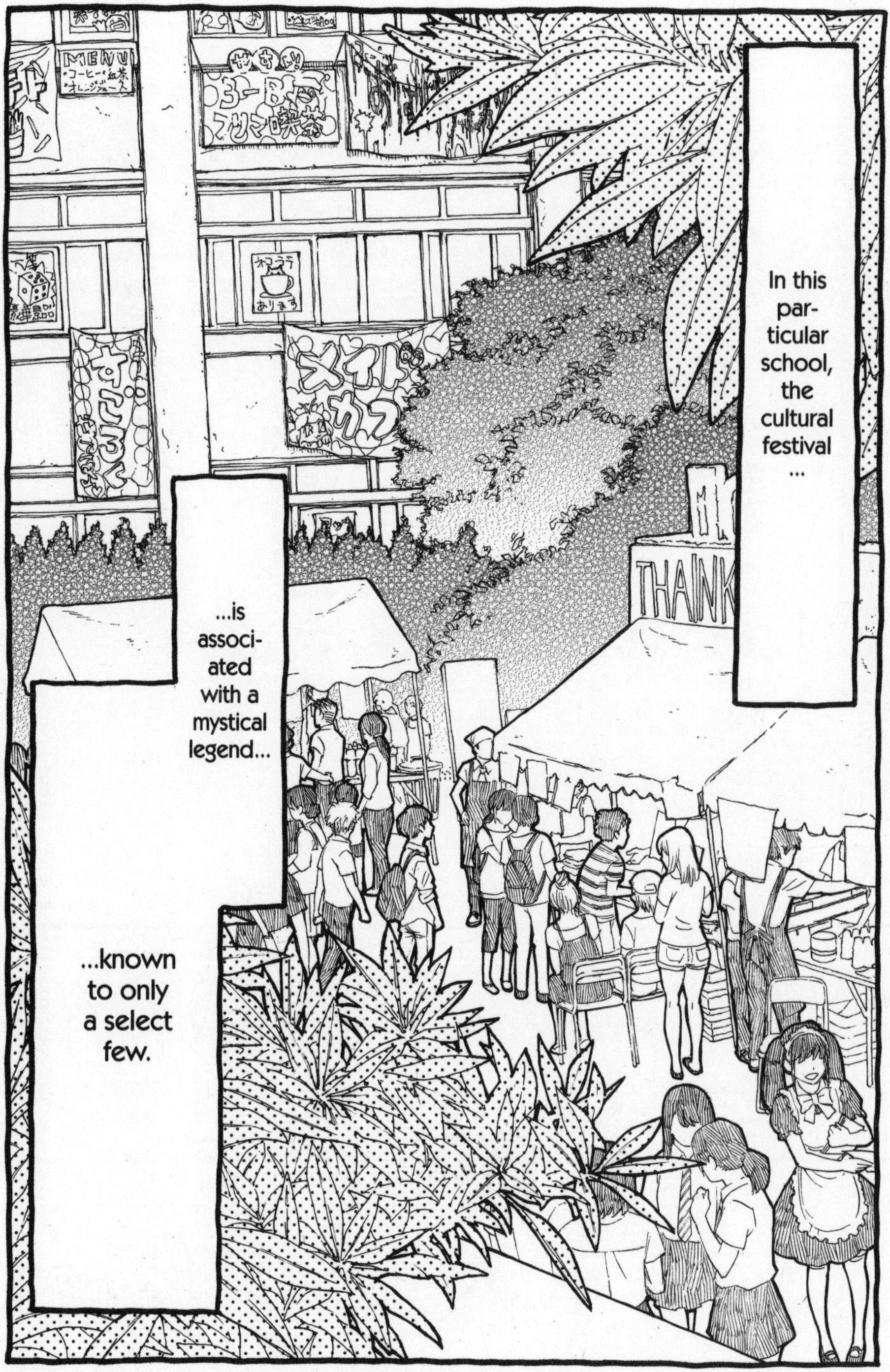
In this particular school, the cultural festival ...
...is associated with a mystical legend...
...known to only a select few.

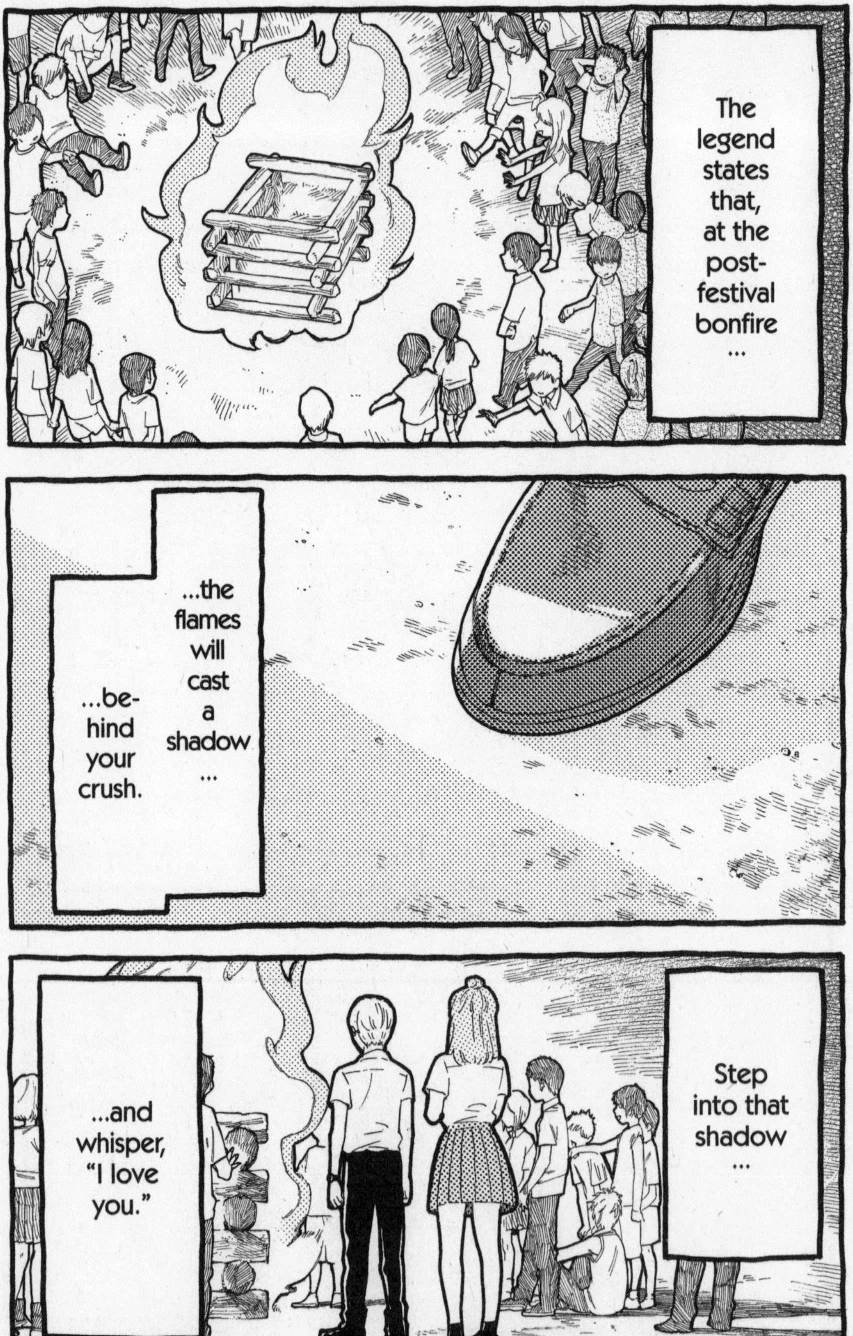
The legend states that, at the post-festival bonfire...
...the flames will cast a shadow...
...be-hind your crush.
Step into that shadow...
...and whisper, "I love you."

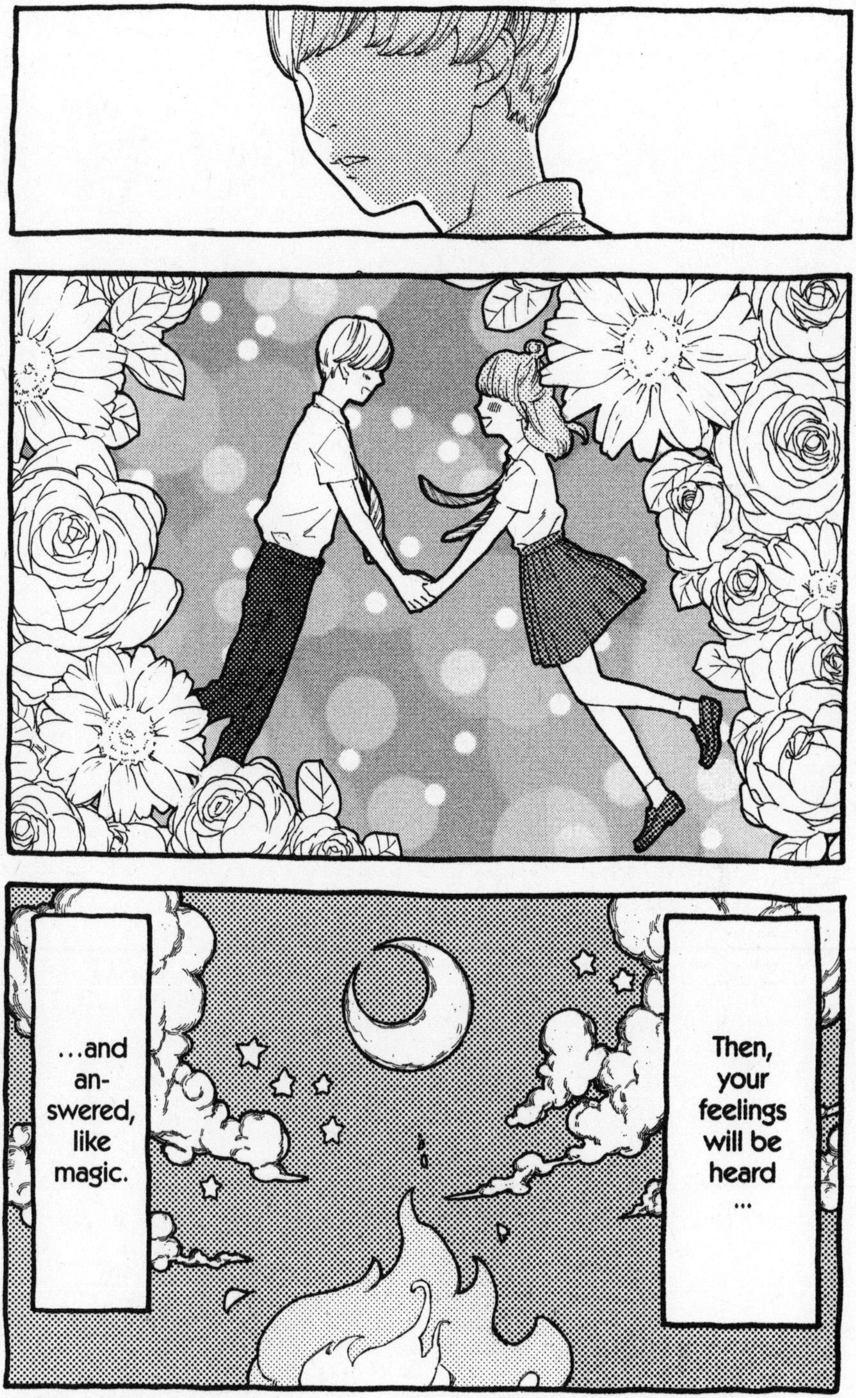
Then, your feelings will be heard ...
...and an-swered, like magic.

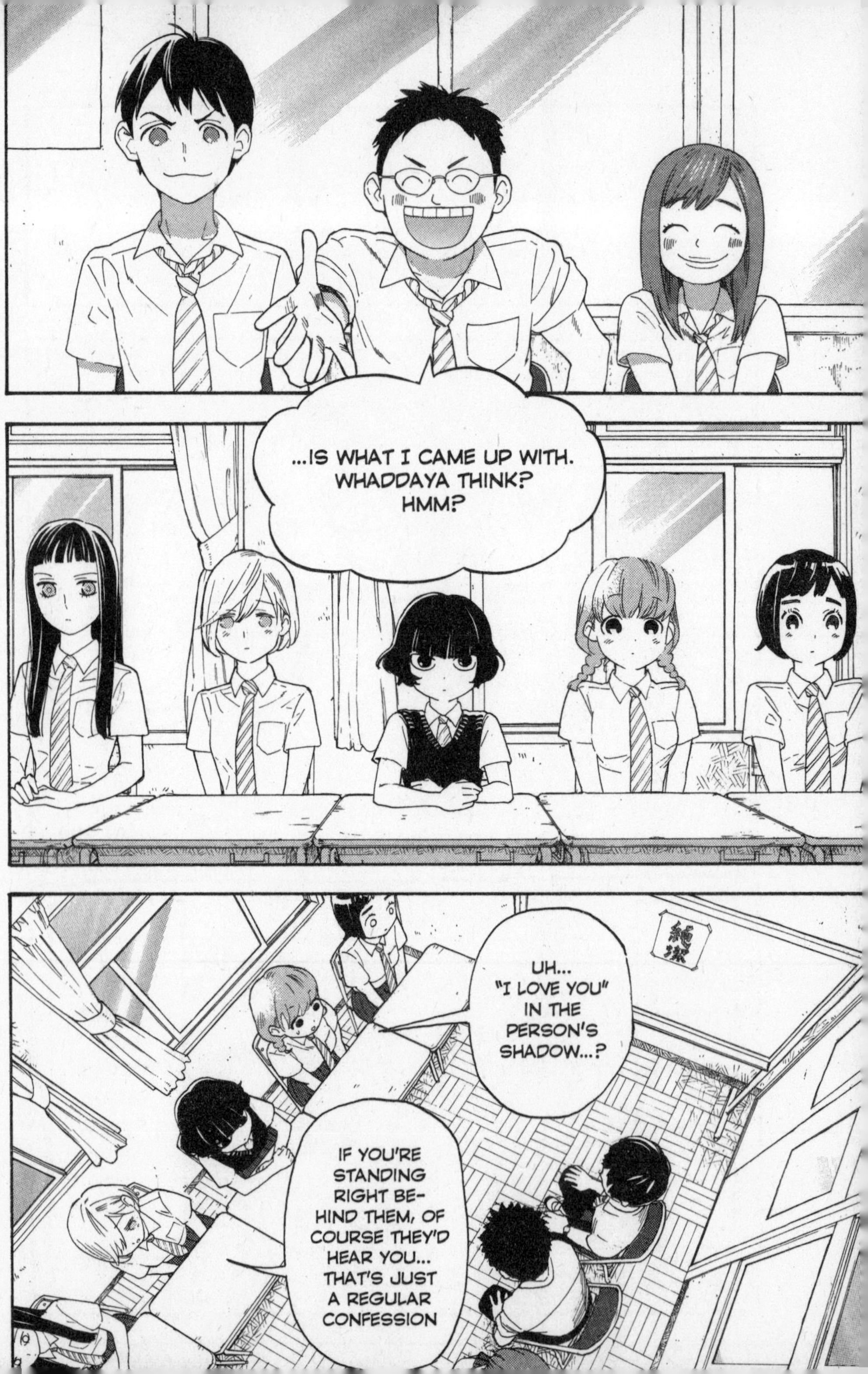
...IS WHAT I CAME UP WITH. WHADDAYA THINK? HMM?
純潔
UH... "I LOVE YOU" IN THE PERSON'S SHADOW...?
IF YOU'RE STANDING RIGHT BE-HIND THEM, OF COURSE THEY'D HEAR YOU... THAT'S JUST A REGULAR CONFESSION

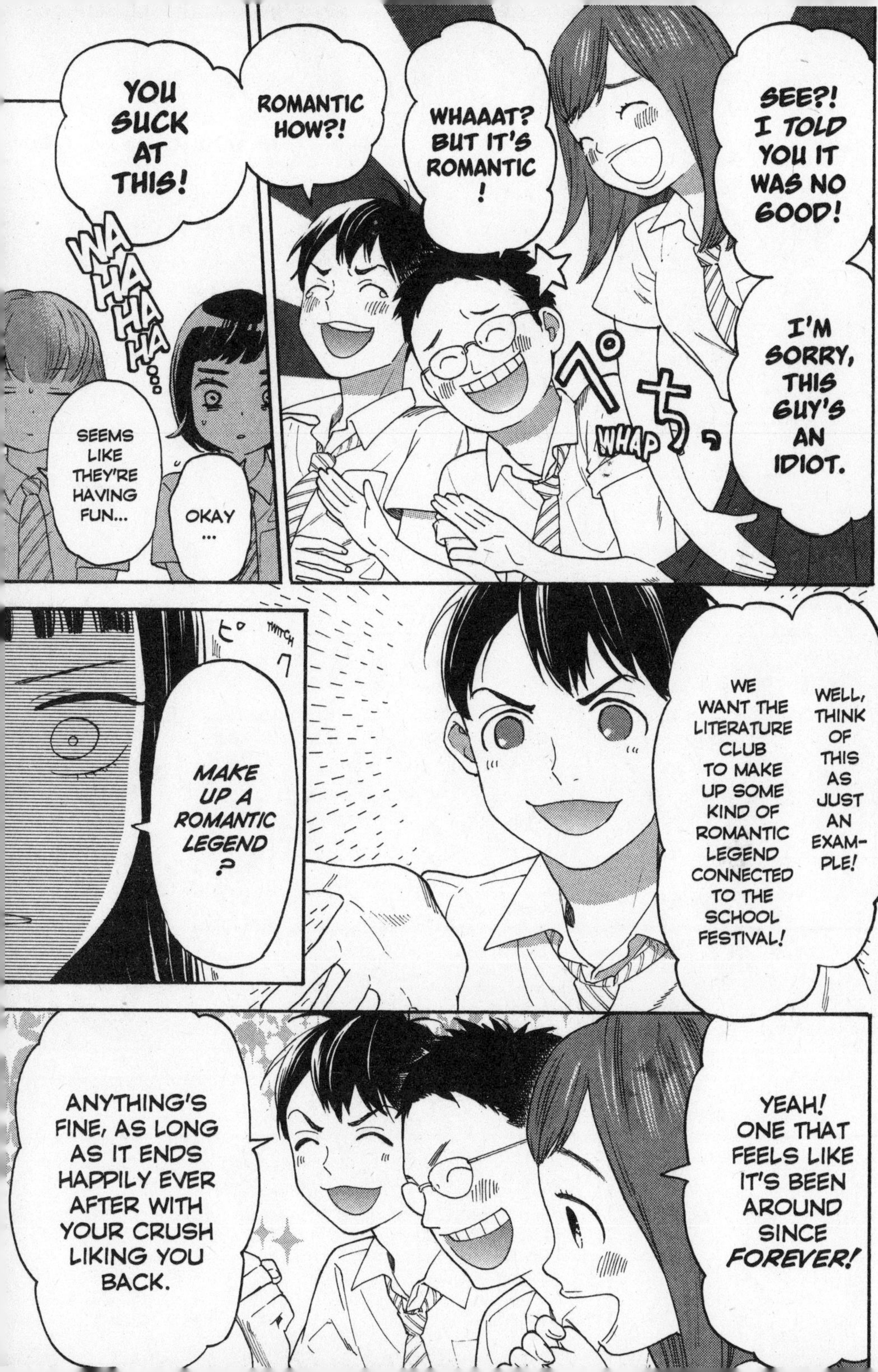
SEE?! I *TOLD* YOU IT WAS NO GOOD!
I'M SORRY, THIS GUY'S AN IDIOT.
WHAAAT? BUT IT'S ROMANTIC!
WHAP
ROMANTIC HOW?!
YOU SUCK AT THIS!
WA HA HA HA HA...
SEEMS LIKE THEY'RE HAVING FUN...
OKAY...
WELL, THINK OF THIS AS JUST AN EXAMPLE!
WE WANT THE LITERATURE CLUB TO MAKE UP SOME KIND OF ROMANTIC LEGEND CONNECTED TO THE SCHOOL FESTIVAL!
TWITCH
MAKE UP A ROMANTIC LEGEND?
YEAH! ONE THAT FEELS LIKE IT'S BEEN AROUND SINCE *FOREVER!*
ANYTHING'S FINE, AS LONG AS IT ENDS HAPPILY EVER AFTER WITH YOUR CRUSH LIKING YOU BACK.

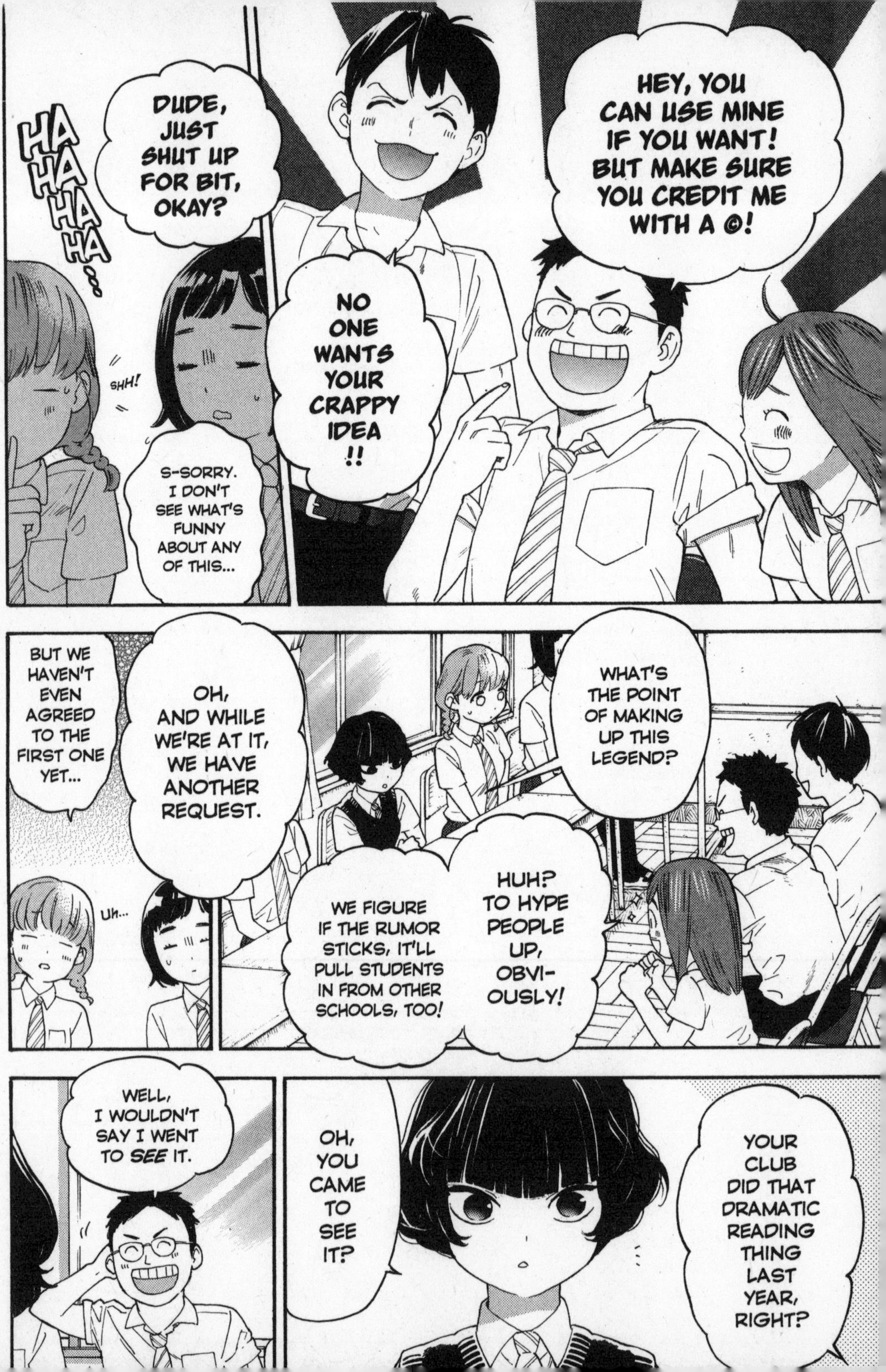
HEY, YOU CAN USE MINE IF YOU WANT! BUT MAKE SURE YOU CREDIT ME WITH A ©!
DUDE, JUST SHUT UP FOR BIT, OKAY?
HA HA HA HA HA...
NO ONE WANTS YOUR CRAPPY IDEA !!
SHH!
S-SORRY. I DON'T SEE WHAT'S FUNNY ABOUT ANY OF THIS...
WHAT'S THE POINT OF MAKING UP THIS LEGEND?
HUH? TO HYPE PEOPLE UP, OBVI-OUSLY!
WE FIGURE IF THE RUMOR STICKS, IT'LL PULL STUDENTS IN FROM OTHER SCHOOLS, TOO!
OH, AND WHILE WE'RE AT IT, WE HAVE ANOTHER REQUEST.
BUT WE HAVEN'T EVEN AGREED TO THE FIRST ONE YET...
Uh...
YOUR CLUB DID THAT DRAMATIC READING THING LAST YEAR, RIGHT?
OH, YOU CAME TO SEE IT?
WELL, I WOULDN'T SAY I WENT TO *SEE* IT.

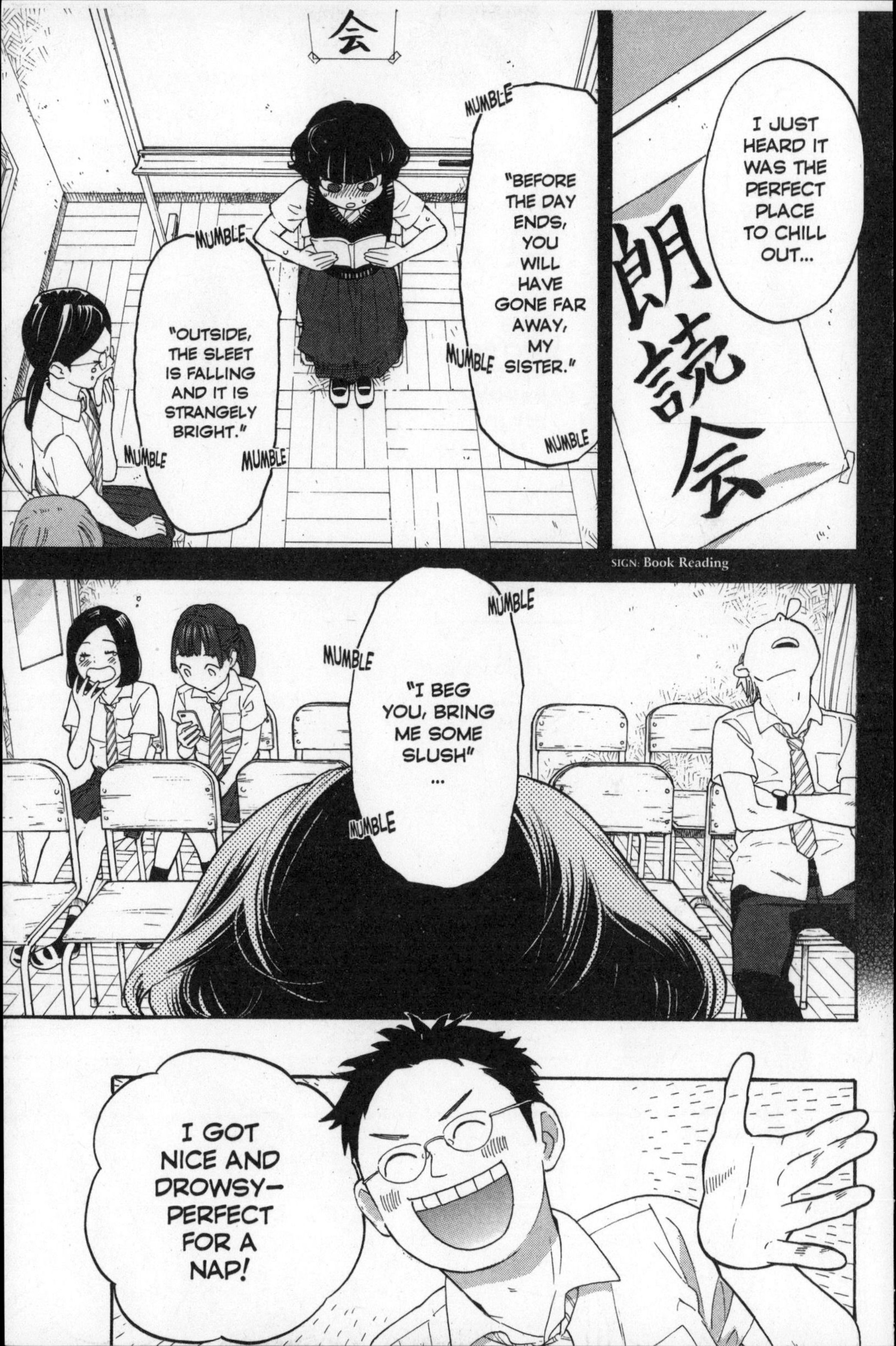
I JUST HEARD IT WAS THE PERFECT PLACE TO CHILL OUT...
朗読会
会
MUMBLE
"BEFORE THE DAY ENDS, YOU WILL HAVE GONE FAR AWAY, MY SISTER."
MUMBLE
MUMBLE
MUMBLE
"OUTSIDE, THE SLEET IS FALLING AND IT IS STRANGELY BRIGHT."
MUMBLE
MUMBLE
MUMBLE
MUMBLE
"I BEG YOU, BRING ME SOME SLUSH" ...
MUMBLE
I GOT NICE AND DROWSY—PERFECT FOR A NAP!
SIGN: Book Reading

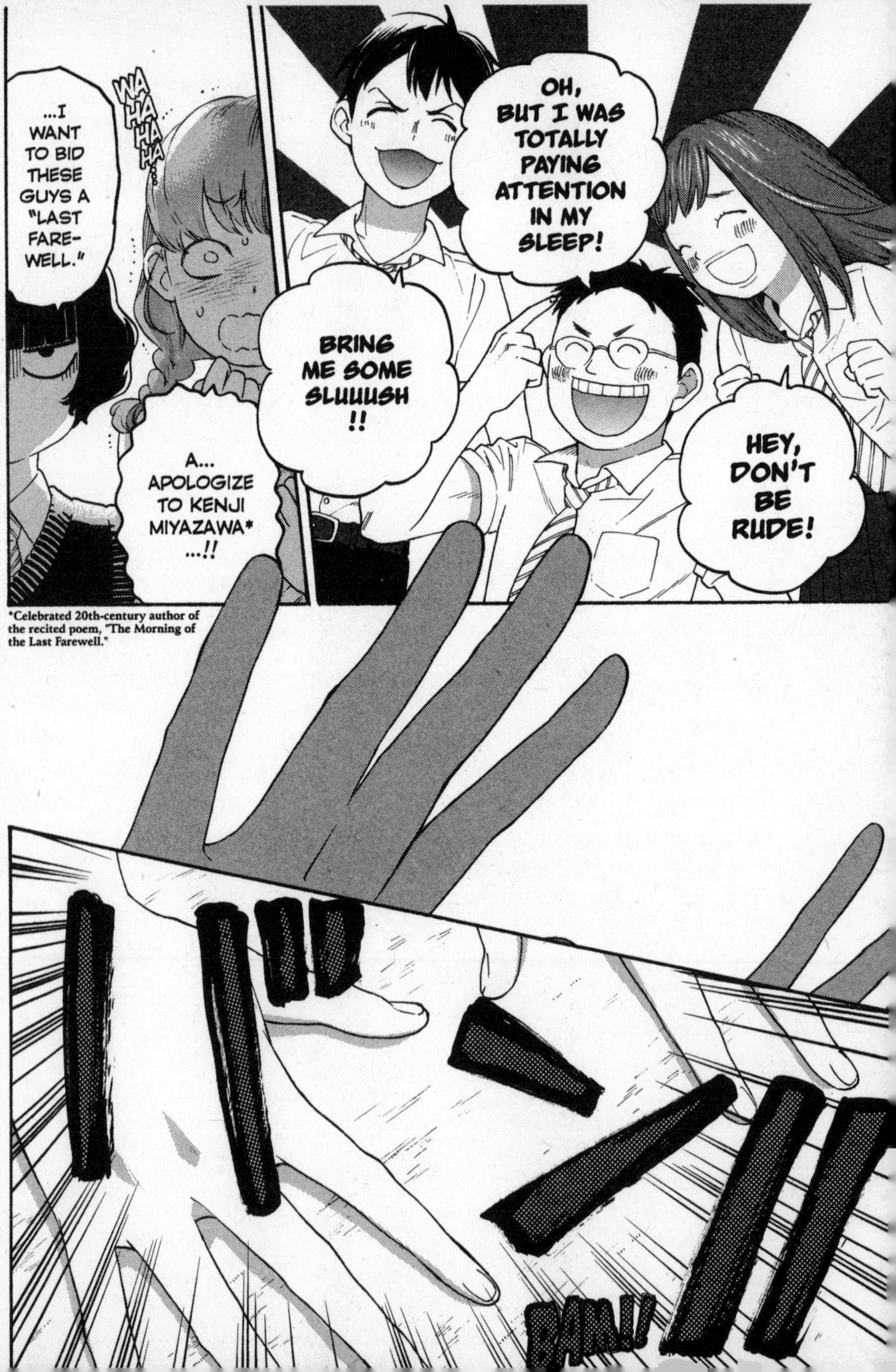
OH, BUT I WAS TOTALLY PAYING ATTENTION IN MY SLEEP!
HEY, DON'T BE RUDE!
BRING ME SOME SLUUUSH!!
WA HA HA HA HA
...I WANT TO BID THESE GUYS A "LAST FARE-WELL."
A... APOLOGIZE TO KENJI MIYAZAWA* ...!!
BAM!

*Celebrated 20th-century author of the recited poem, "The Morning of the Last Farewell."

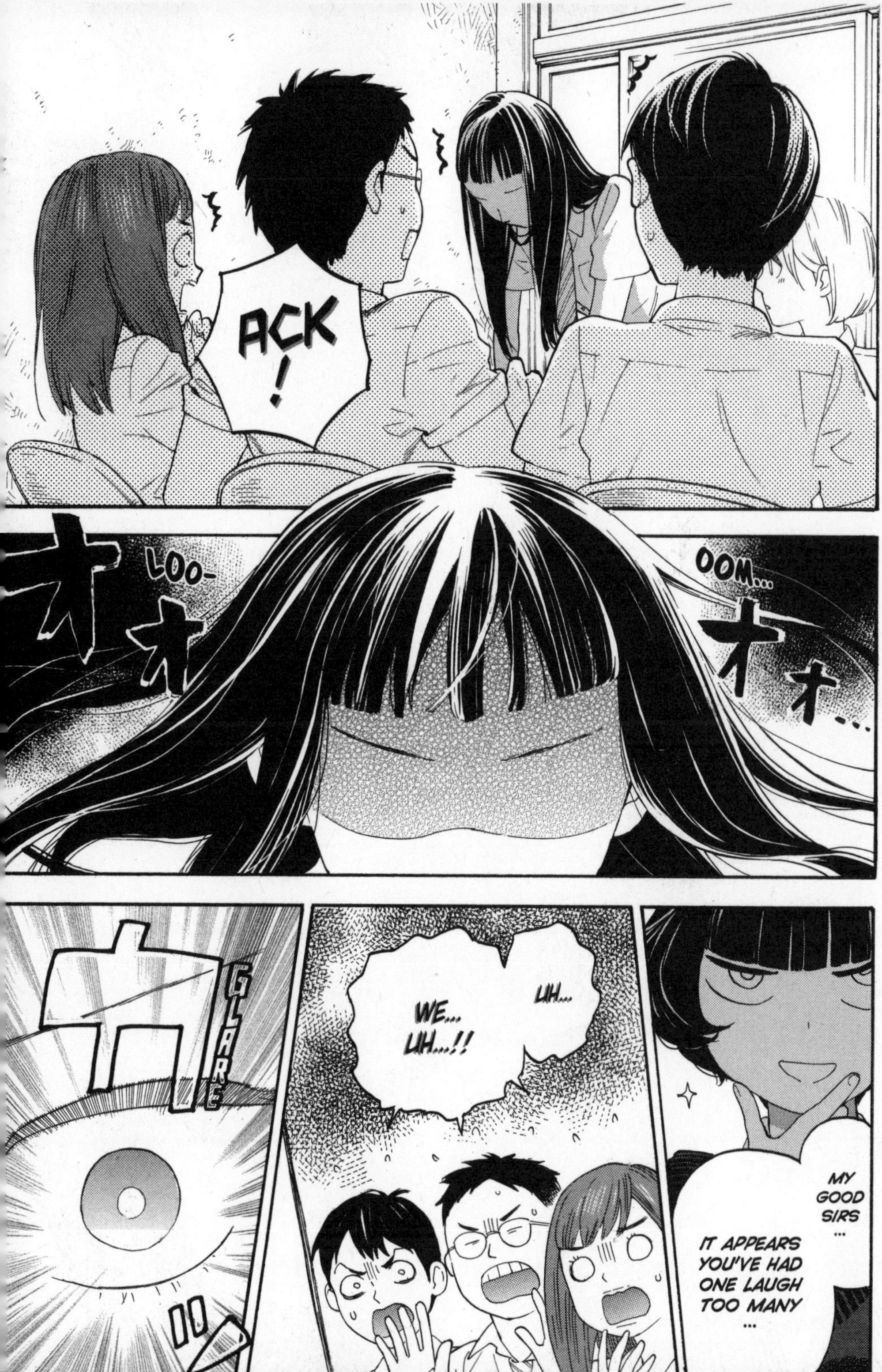
ACK !
LOO-
OOM...
MY GOOD SIRS ...
IT APPEARS YOU'VE HAD ONE LAUGH TOO MANY ...
UH...
WE... UH...!!
GLARE

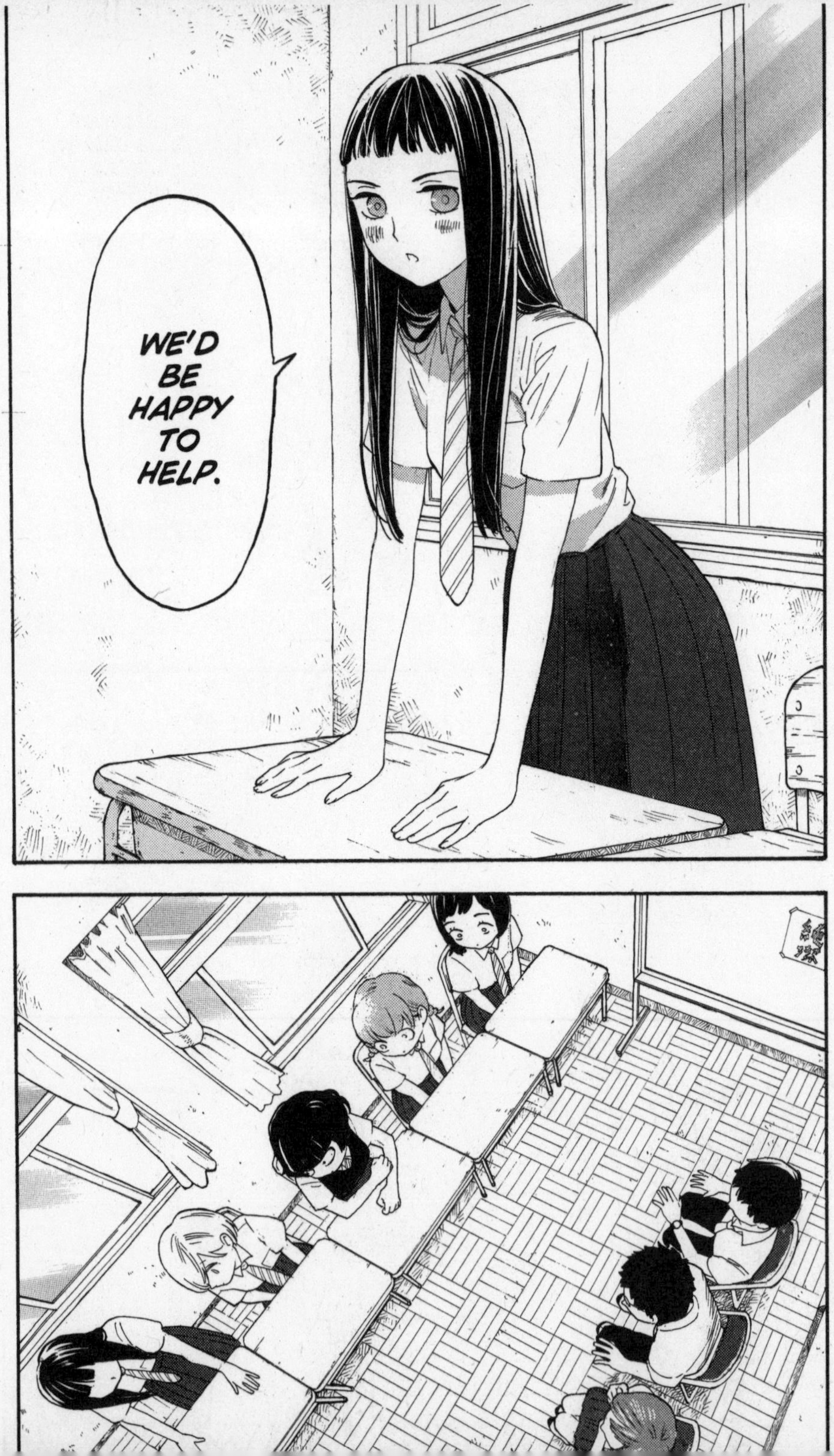
WE'D BE HAPPY TO HELP.

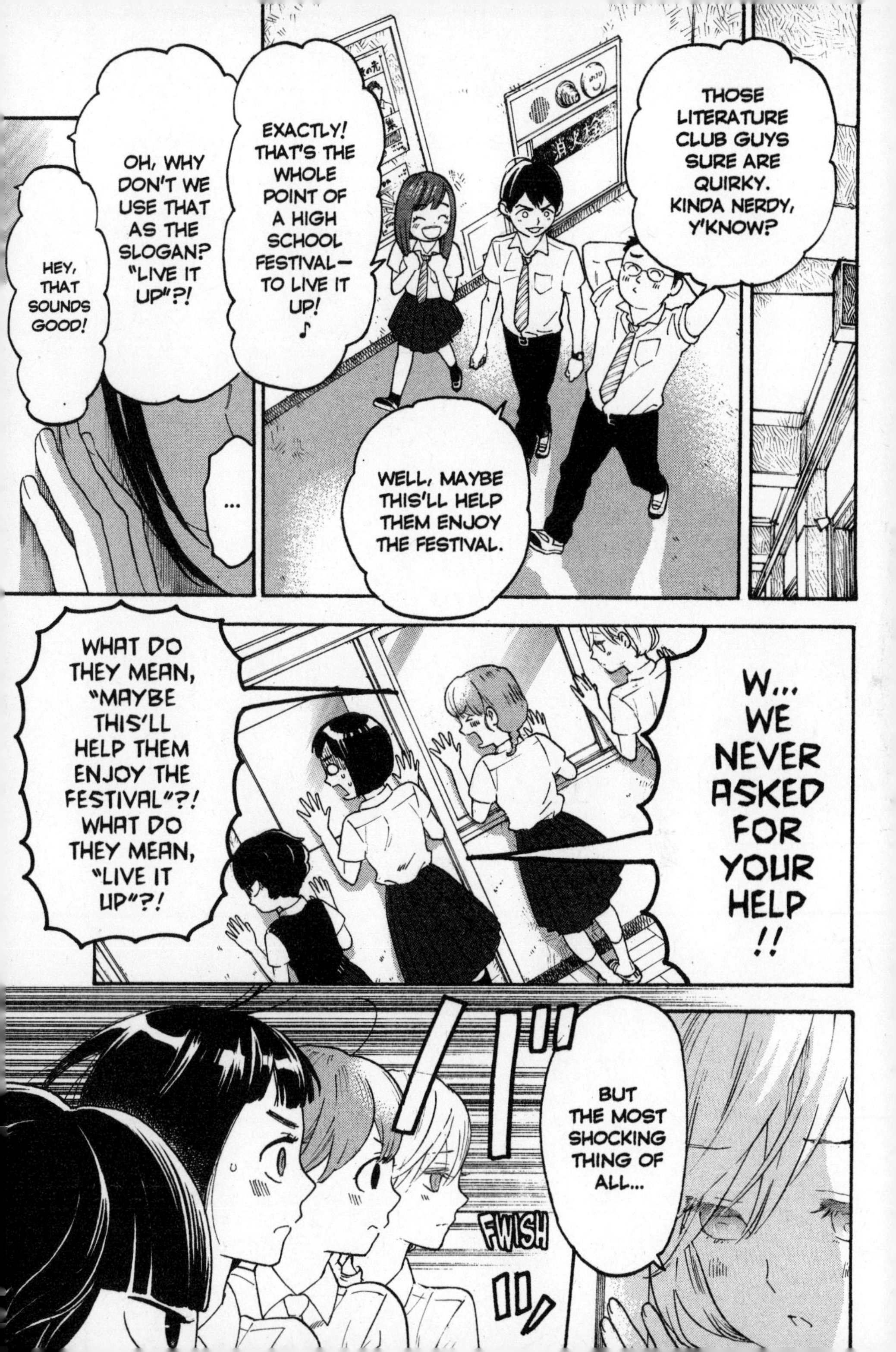
THOSE LITERATURE CLUB GUYS SURE ARE QUIRKY. KINDA NERDY, Y'KNOW?
EXACTLY! THAT'S THE WHOLE POINT OF A HIGH SCHOOL FESTIVAL— TO LIVE IT UP! ♪
OH, WHY DON'T WE USE THAT AS THE SLOGAN? "LIVE IT UP"?!
HEY, THAT SOUNDS GOOD!
WELL, MAYBE THIS'LL HELP THEM ENJOY THE FESTIVAL.
...
W... WE NEVER ASKED FOR YOUR HELP !!
WHAT DO THEY MEAN, "MAYBE THIS'LL HELP THEM ENJOY THE FESTIVAL"?! WHAT DO THEY MEAN, "LIVE IT UP"?!
BUT THE MOST SHOCKING THING OF ALL...
FWISH

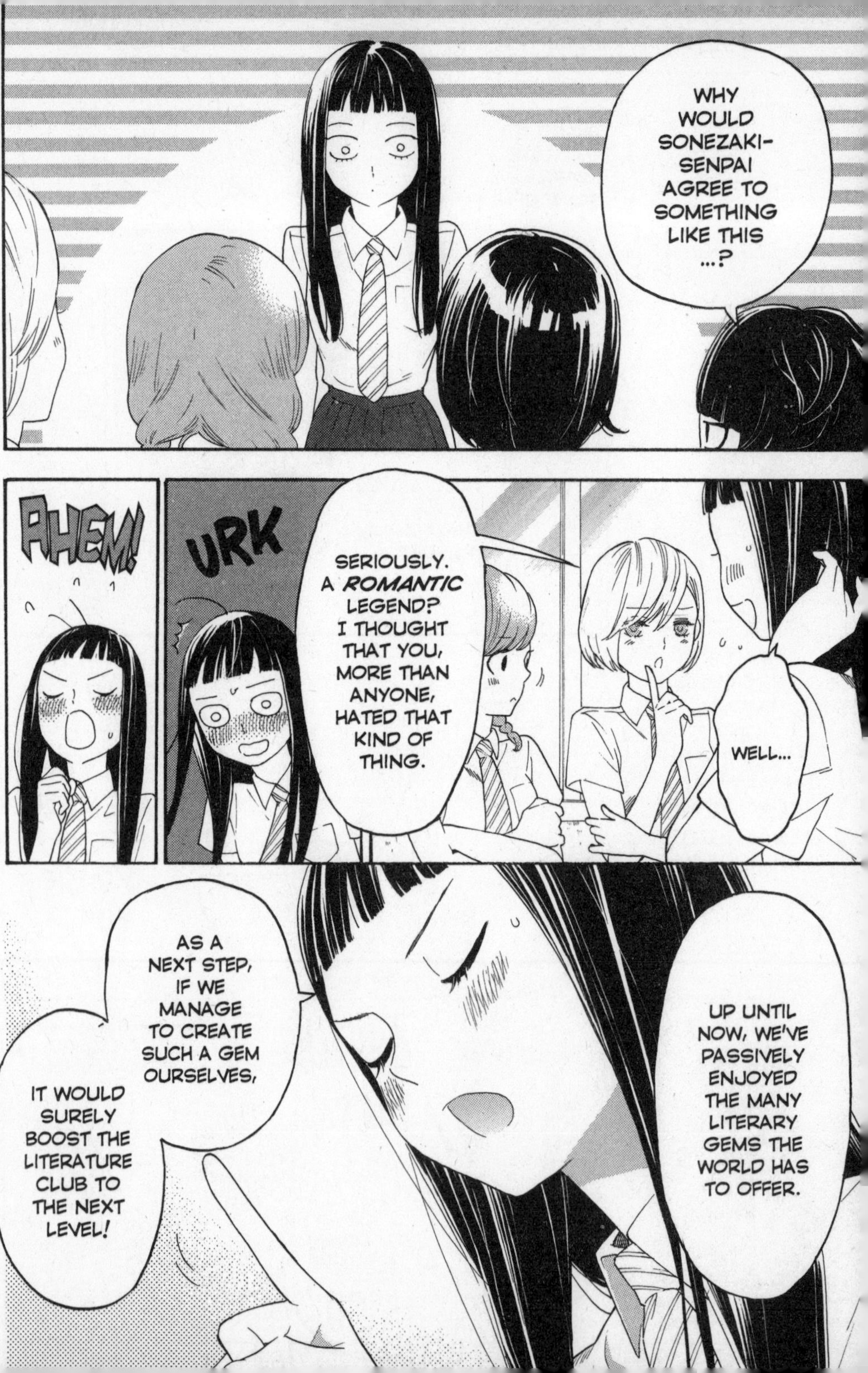
WHY WOULD SONEZAKI-SENPAI AGREE TO SOMETHING LIKE THIS ...?
WELL...
SERIOUSLY. A *ROMANTIC* LEGEND? I THOUGHT THAT YOU, MORE THAN ANYONE, HATED THAT KIND OF THING.
URK
AHEM!
UP UNTIL NOW, WE'VE PASSIVELY ENJOYED THE MANY LITERARY GEMS THE WORLD HAS TO OFFER.
AS A NEXT STEP, IF WE MANAGE TO CREATE SUCH A GEM OURSELVES,
IT WOULD SURELY BOOST THE LITERATURE CLUB TO THE NEXT LEVEL!

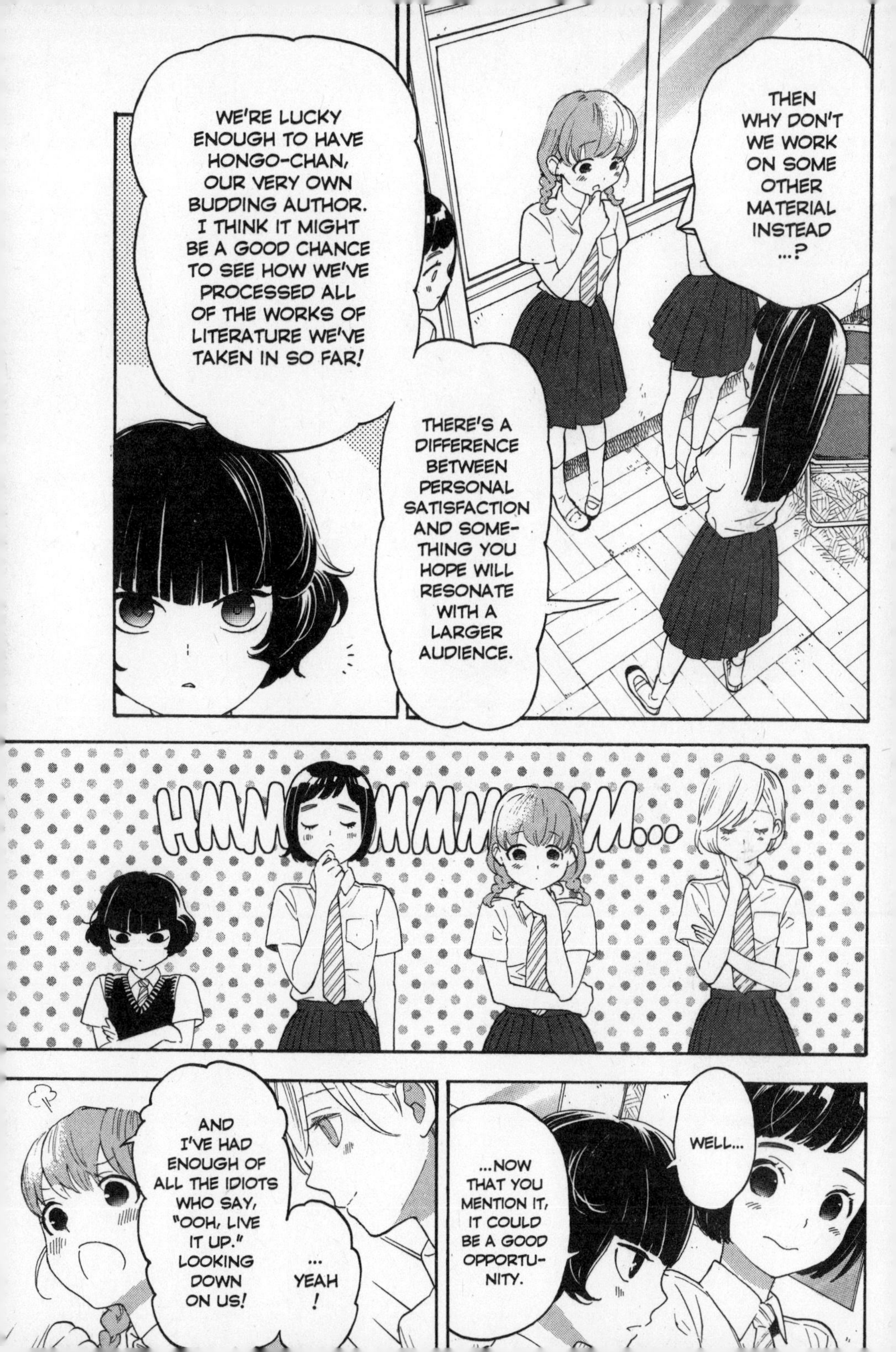
WE'RE LUCKY ENOUGH TO HAVE HONGO-CHAN, OUR VERY OWN BUDDING AUTHOR. I THINK IT MIGHT BE A GOOD CHANCE TO SEE HOW WE'VE PROCESSED ALL OF THE WORKS OF LITERATURE WE'VE TAKEN IN SO FAR!
THEN WHY DON'T WE WORK ON SOME OTHER MATERIAL INSTEAD ...?
THERE'S A DIFFERENCE BETWEEN PERSONAL SATISFACTION AND SOME-THING YOU HOPE WILL RESONATE WITH A LARGER AUDIENCE.
HMMMMMMMMM...
WELL...
...NOW THAT YOU MENTION IT, IT COULD BE A GOOD OPPORTU-NITY.
AND I'VE HAD ENOUGH OF ALL THE IDIOTS WHO SAY, "OOH, LIVE IT UP." LOOKING DOWN ON US!
...YEAH!

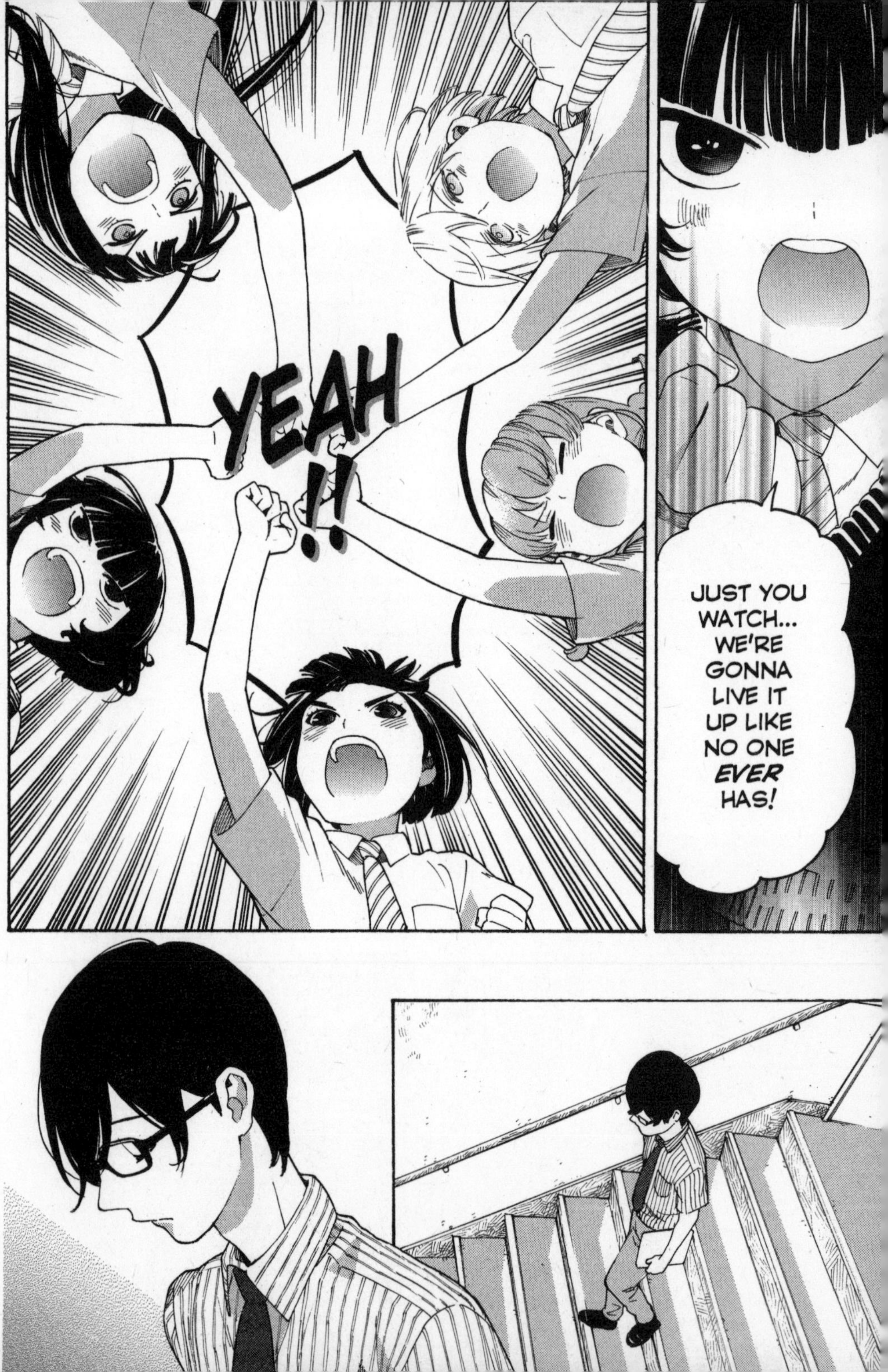
JUST YOU WATCH... WE'RE GONNA LIVE IT UP LIKE NO ONE EVER HAS!
YEAH!!

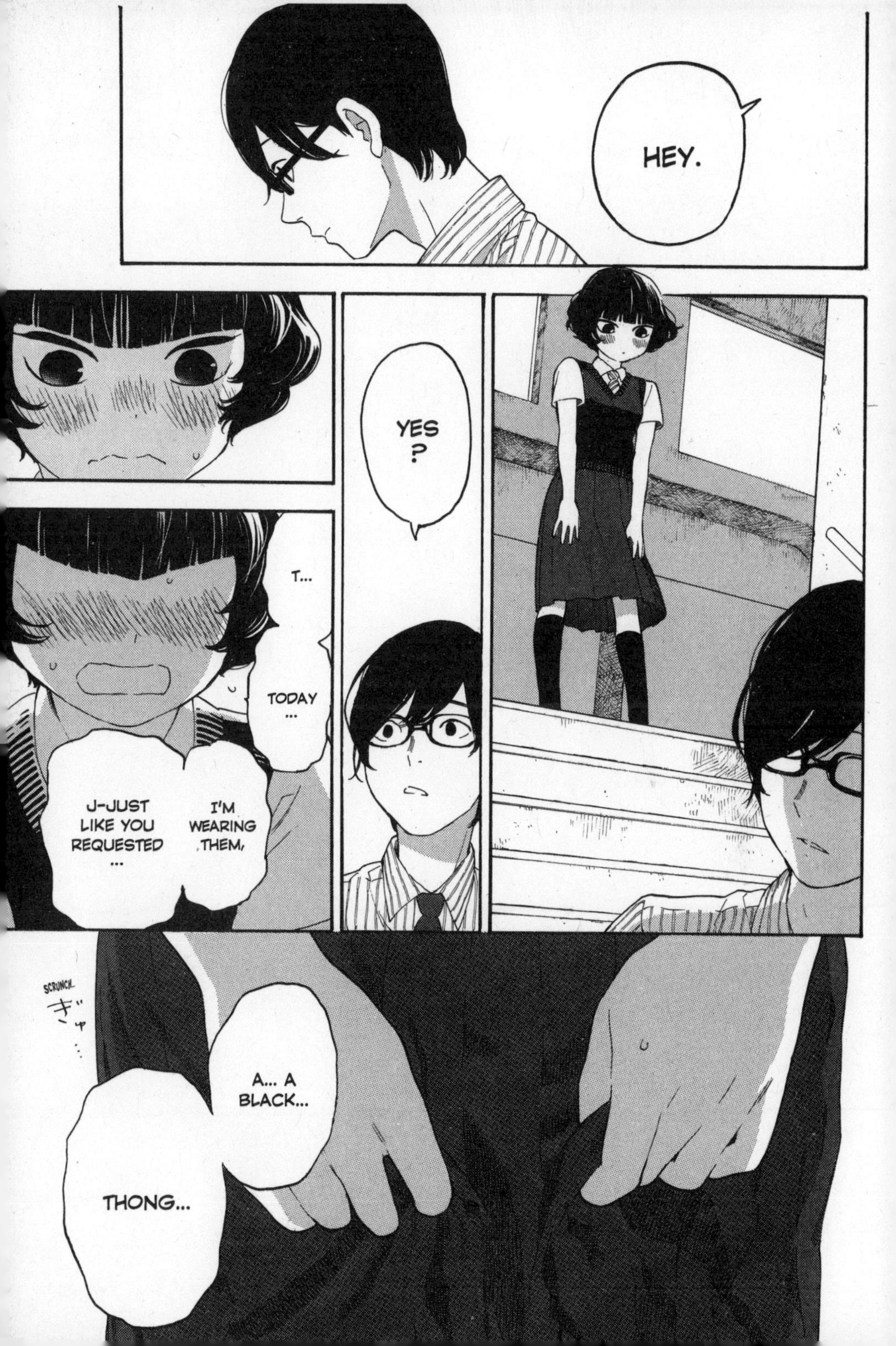
HEY.
YES?
T...
TODAY...
I'M WEARING THEM,
J-JUST LIKE YOU REQUESTED...
A... A BLACK...
SCRUNCH
ぎゅ…
THONG...

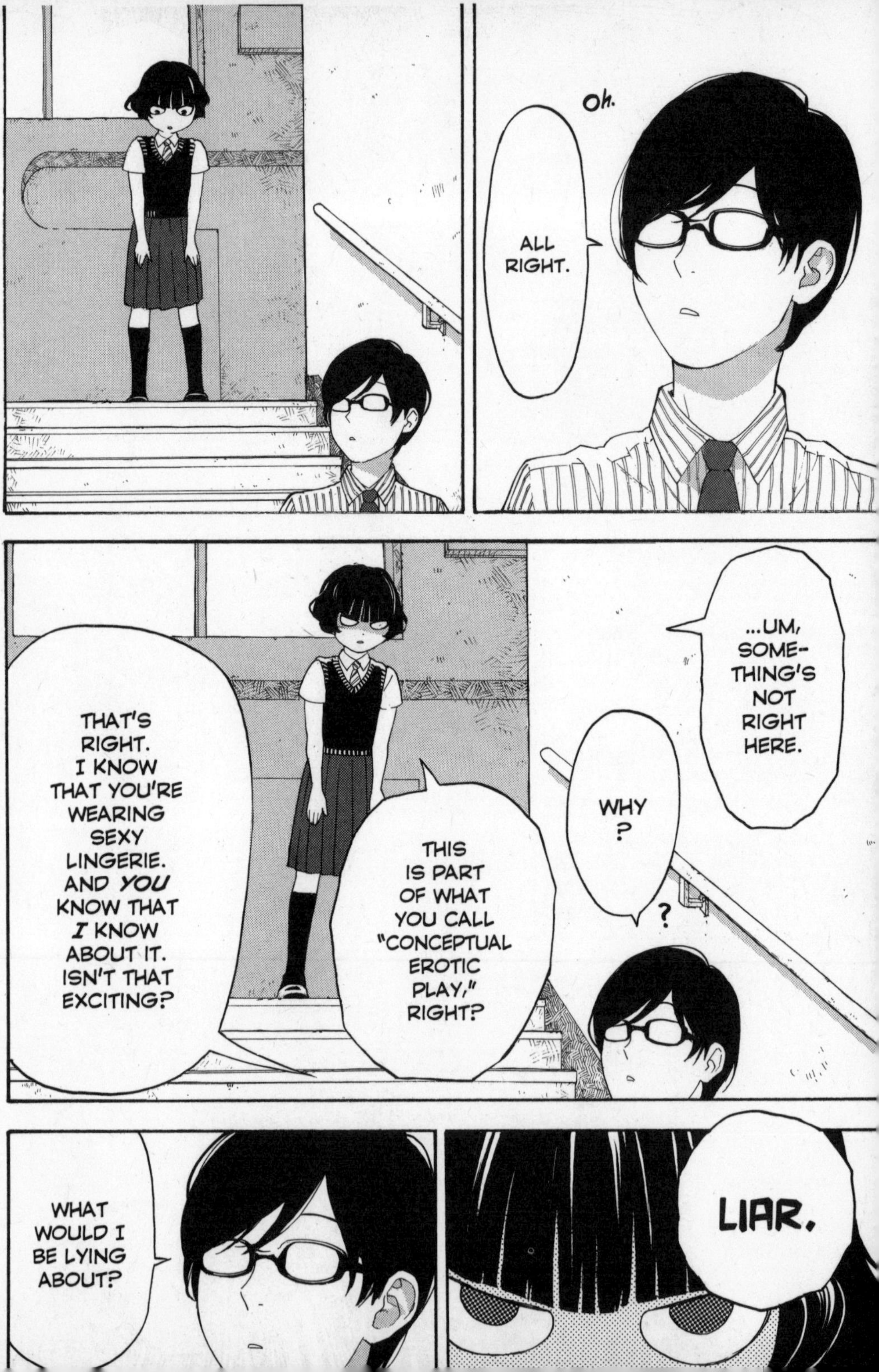
Oh.
ALL RIGHT.
...UM, SOME-THING'S NOT RIGHT HERE.
WHY?
?
THIS IS PART OF WHAT YOU CALL "CONCEPTUAL EROTIC PLAY," RIGHT?
THAT'S RIGHT. I KNOW THAT YOU'RE WEARING SEXY LINGERIE. AND *YOU* KNOW THAT *I* KNOW ABOUT IT. ISN'T THAT EXCITING?
LIAR.
WHAT WOULD I BE LYING ABOUT?

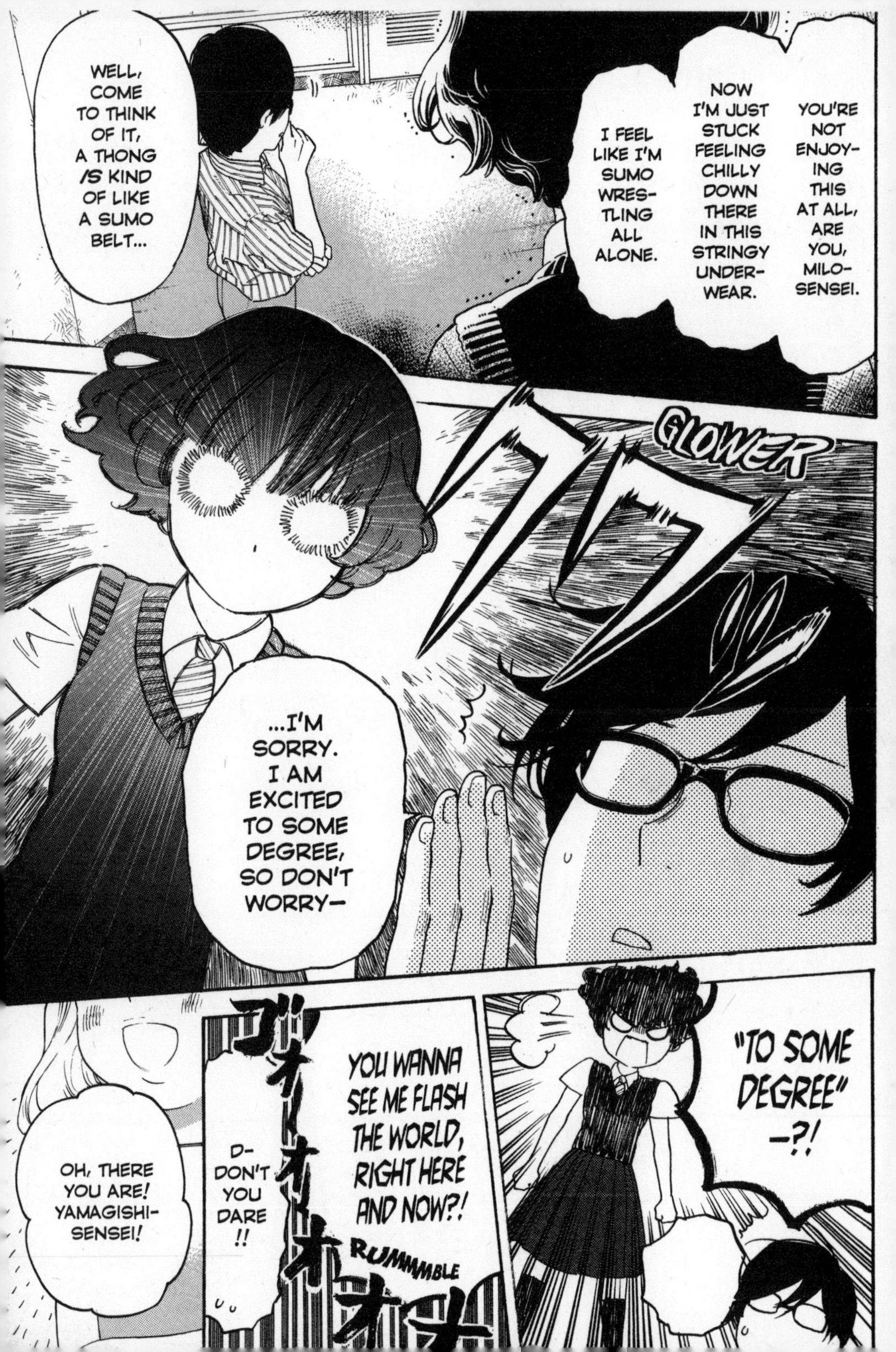
YOU'RE NOT ENJOYING THIS AT ALL, ARE YOU, MILO-SENSEI.
NOW I'M JUST STUCK FEELING CHILLY DOWN THERE IN THIS STRINGY UNDERWEAR.
I FEEL LIKE I'M SUMO WRESTLING ALL ALONE.
WELL, COME TO THINK OF IT, A THONG *IS* KIND OF LIKE A SUMO BELT...
GLOWER
...I'M SORRY. I AM EXCITED TO SOME DEGREE, SO DON'T WORRY—
"TO SOME DEGREE"—?!
YOU WANNA SEE ME FLASH THE WORLD, RIGHT HERE AND NOW?!
RUMMMBLE
D-DON'T YOU DARE!!
OH, THERE YOU ARE! YAMAGISHI-SENSEI!

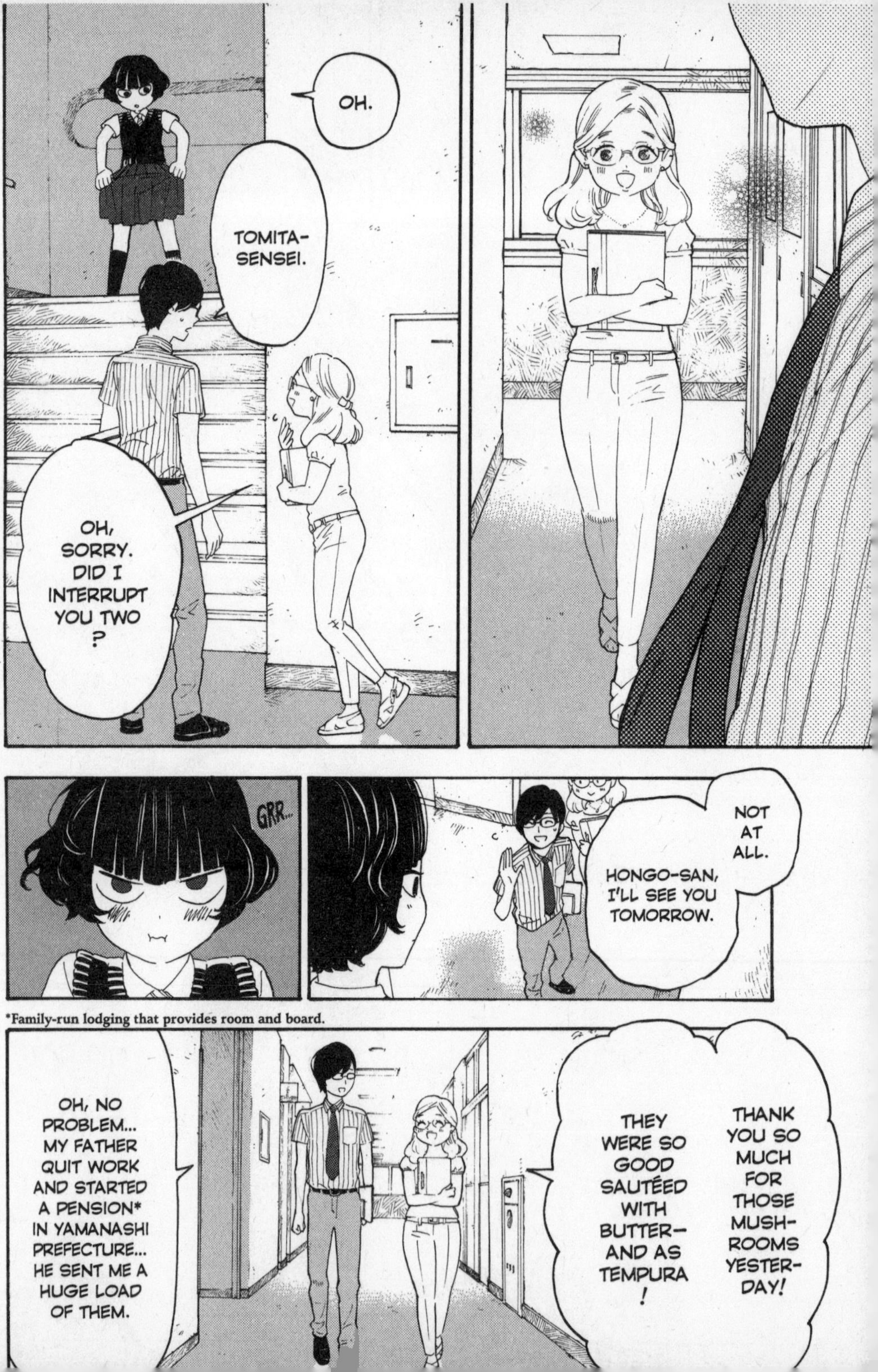
OH.
TOMITA-SENSEI.
OH, SORRY. DID I INTERRUPT YOU TWO?
NOT AT ALL.
HONGO-SAN, I'LL SEE YOU TOMORROW.
GRR...
THANK YOU SO MUCH FOR THOSE MUSH-ROOMS YESTER-DAY!
THEY WERE SO GOOD SAUTÉED WITH BUTTER—AND AS TEMPURA!
OH, NO PROBLEM... MY FATHER QUIT WORK AND STARTED A PENSION* IN YAMANASHI PREFECTURE... HE SENT ME A HUGE LOAD OF THEM.

*Family-run lodging that provides room and board.

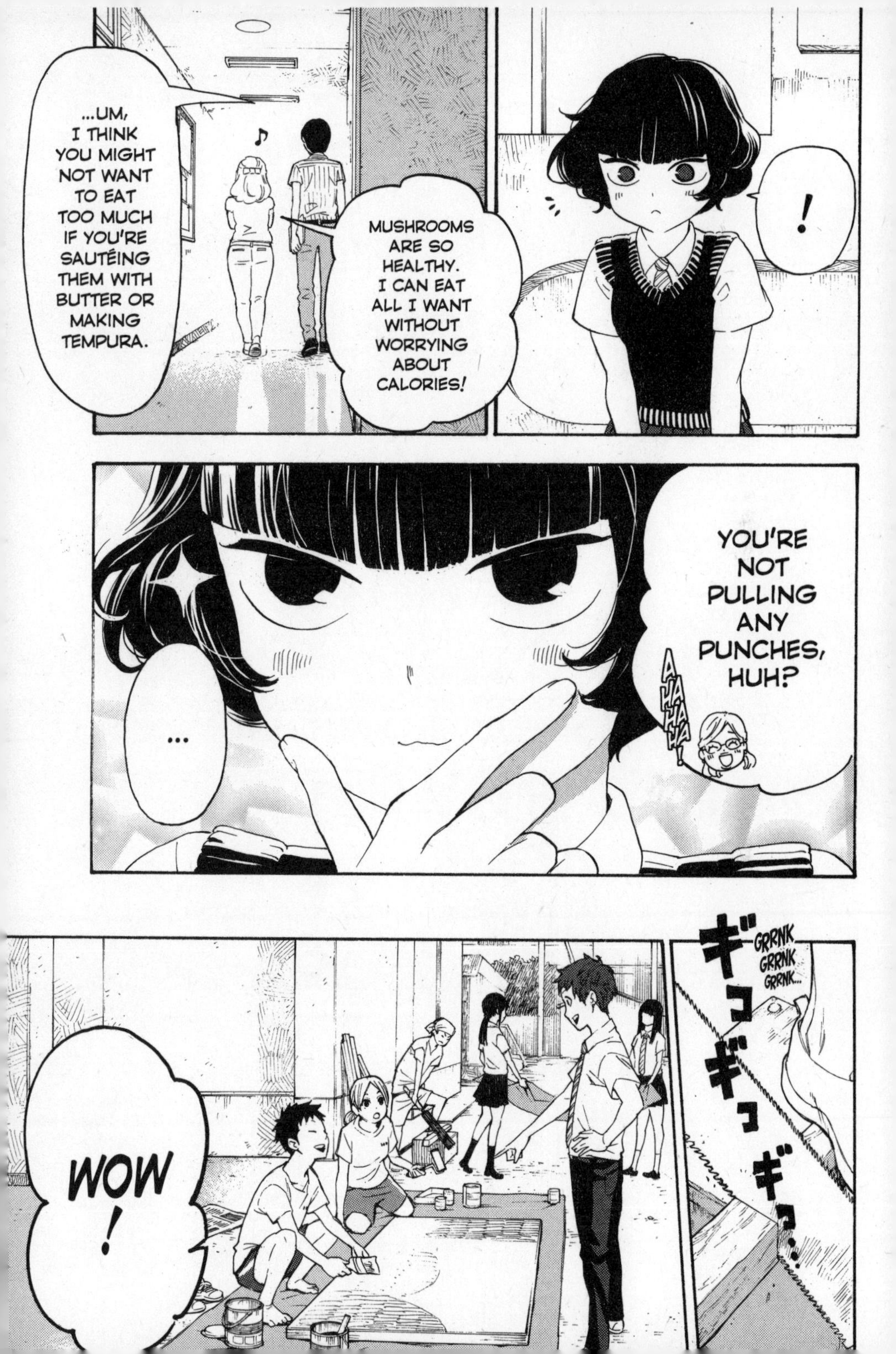
!
MUSHROOMS ARE SO HEALTHY. I CAN EAT ALL I WANT WITHOUT WORRYING ABOUT CALORIES!
...UM, I THINK YOU MIGHT NOT WANT TO EAT TOO MUCH IF YOU'RE SAUTÉING THEM WITH BUTTER OR MAKING TEMPURA.
YOU'RE NOT PULLING ANY PUNCHES, HUH?
AHAHAHA!
...
GRRNK GRRNK GRRNK...
ギコギッギ ギコ...
WOW!

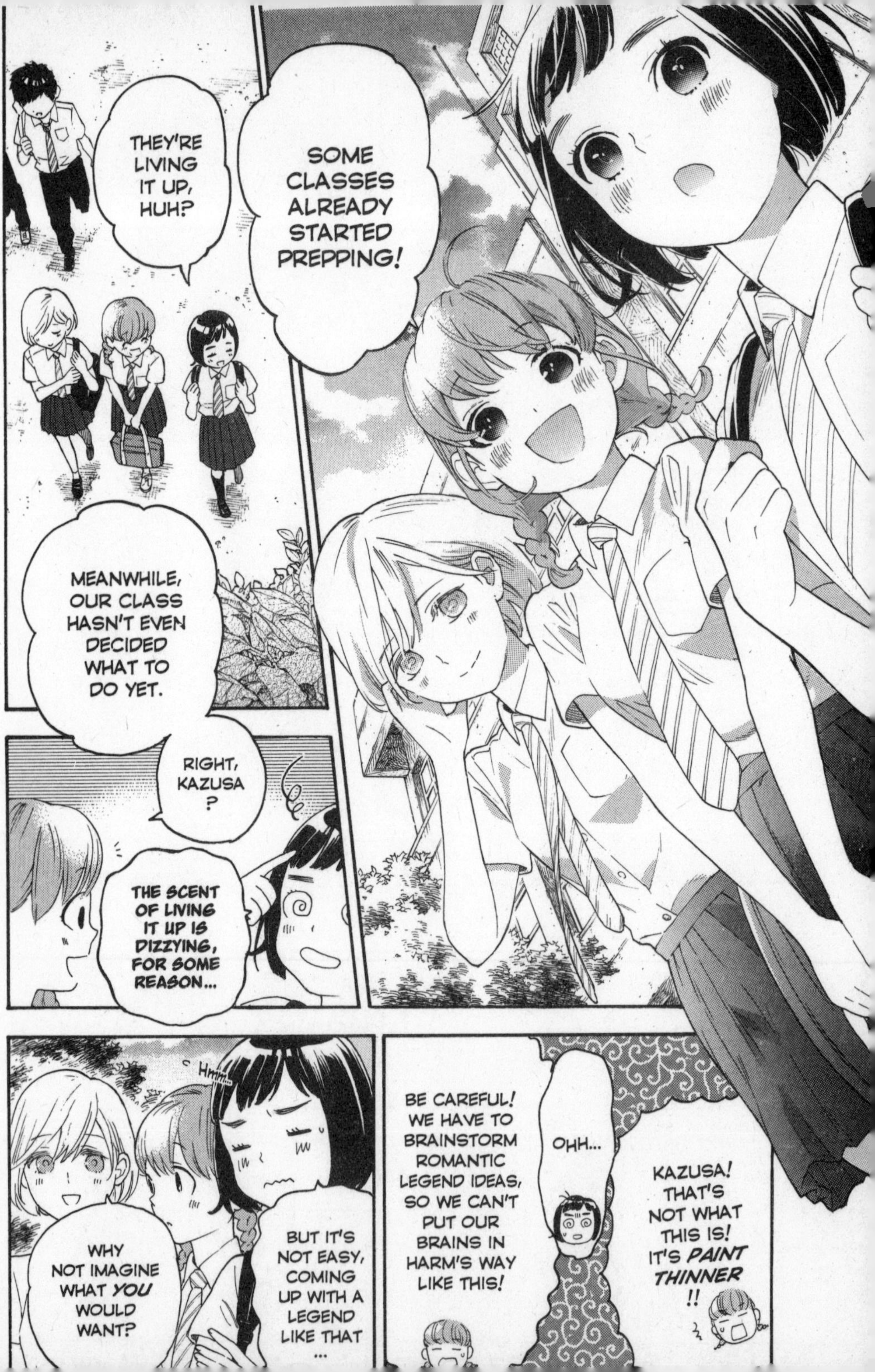
SOME CLASSES ALREADY STARTED PREPPING!
THEY'RE LIVING IT UP, HUH?
MEANWHILE, OUR CLASS HASN'T EVEN DECIDED WHAT TO DO YET.
RIGHT, KAZUSA?
THE SCENT OF LIVING IT UP IS DIZZYING, FOR SOME REASON...
KAZUSA! THAT'S NOT WHAT THIS IS! IT'S *PAINT THINNER*!!
OHH...
BE CAREFUL! WE HAVE TO BRAINSTORM ROMANTIC LEGEND IDEAS, SO WE CAN'T PUT OUR BRAINS IN HARM'S WAY LIKE THIS!
Hmmm
BUT IT'S NOT EASY, COMING UP WITH A LEGEND LIKE THAT...
WHY NOT IMAGINE WHAT *YOU* WOULD WANT?

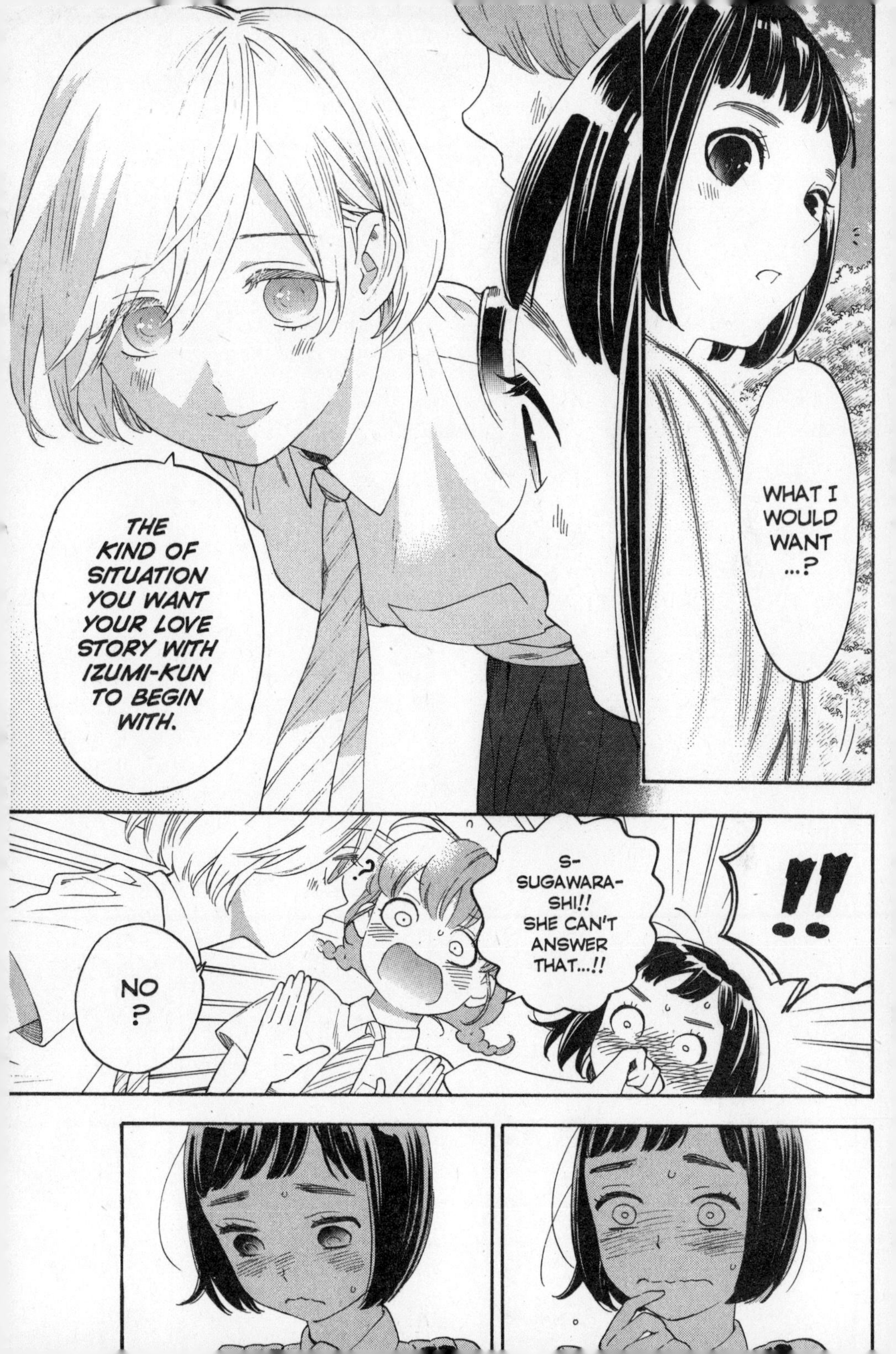

WHAT I WOULD WANT ...?
THE KIND OF SITUATION YOU WANT YOUR LOVE STORY WITH IZUMI-KUN TO BEGIN WITH.
!!
S-SUGAWARA-SHI!! SHE CAN'T ANSWER THAT...!!
?
NO ?

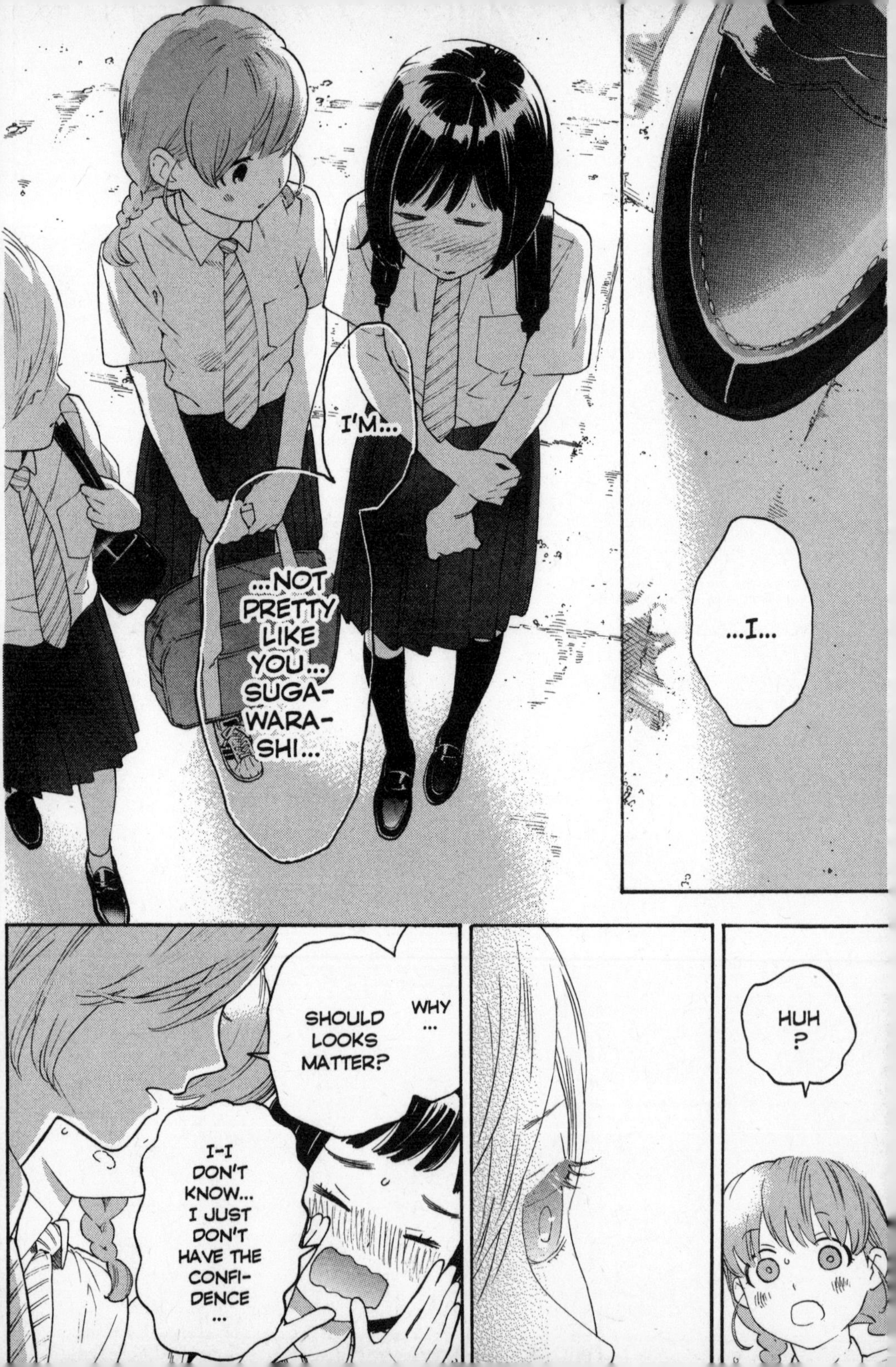
...I...
I'M...
...NOT PRETTY LIKE YOU... SUGAWARA-SHI...
HUH?
WHY... SHOULD LOOKS MATTER?
I-I DON'T KNOW... I JUST DON'T HAVE THE CONFIDENCE...

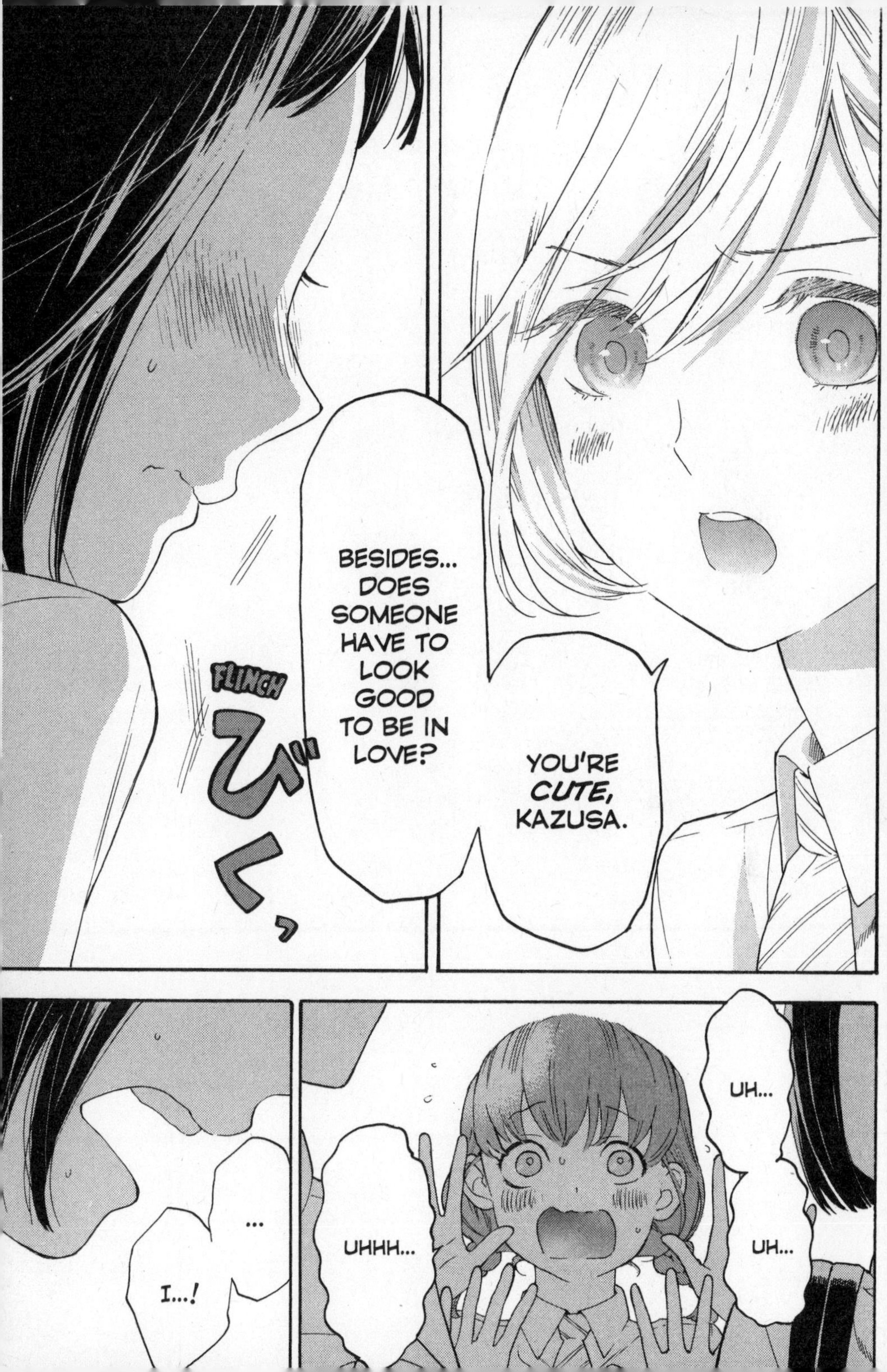
YOU'RE *CUTE*, KAZUSA.
BESIDES... DOES SOMEONE HAVE TO LOOK GOOD TO BE IN LOVE?
FLINCH
びくっ
UH...
UH...
UHHH...
...
I...!

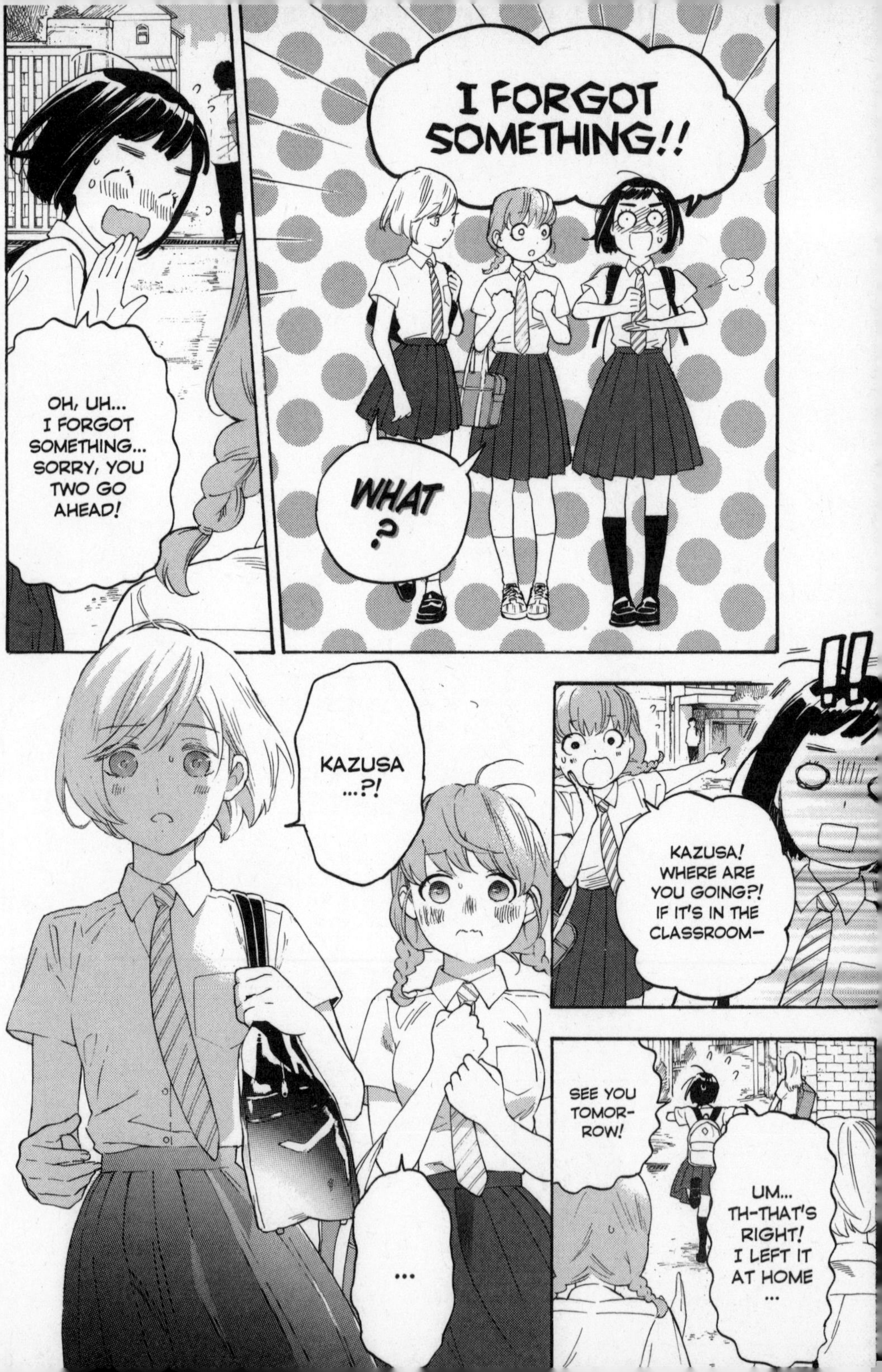
I FORGOT SOMETHING!!
WHAT?
OH, UH... I FORGOT SOMETHING... SORRY, YOU TWO GO AHEAD!
!!
KAZUSA! WHERE ARE YOU GOING?! IF IT'S IN THE CLASSROOM—
UM... TH-THAT'S RIGHT! I LEFT IT AT HOME...
SEE YOU TOMOR-ROW!
KAZUSA...?!
...

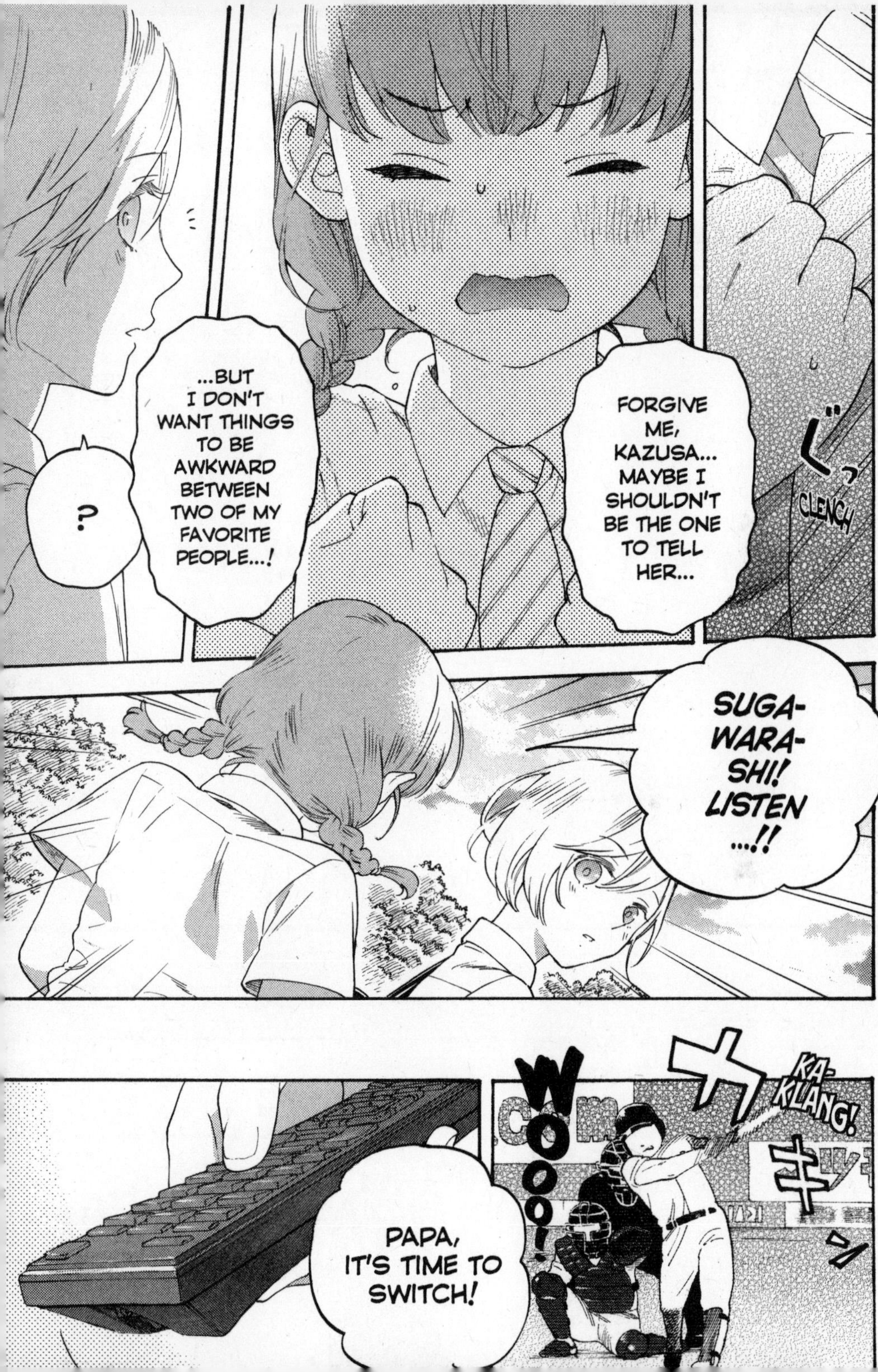
CLENCH
FORGIVE ME, KAZUSA... MAYBE I SHOULDN'T BE THE ONE TO TELL HER...
...BUT I DON'T WANT THINGS TO BE AWKWARD BETWEEN TWO OF MY FAVORITE PEOPLE...!
?
SUGA-WARA-SHI! LISTEN ...!!
KA-KLANG!
WOOO!
PAPA, IT'S TIME TO SWITCH!

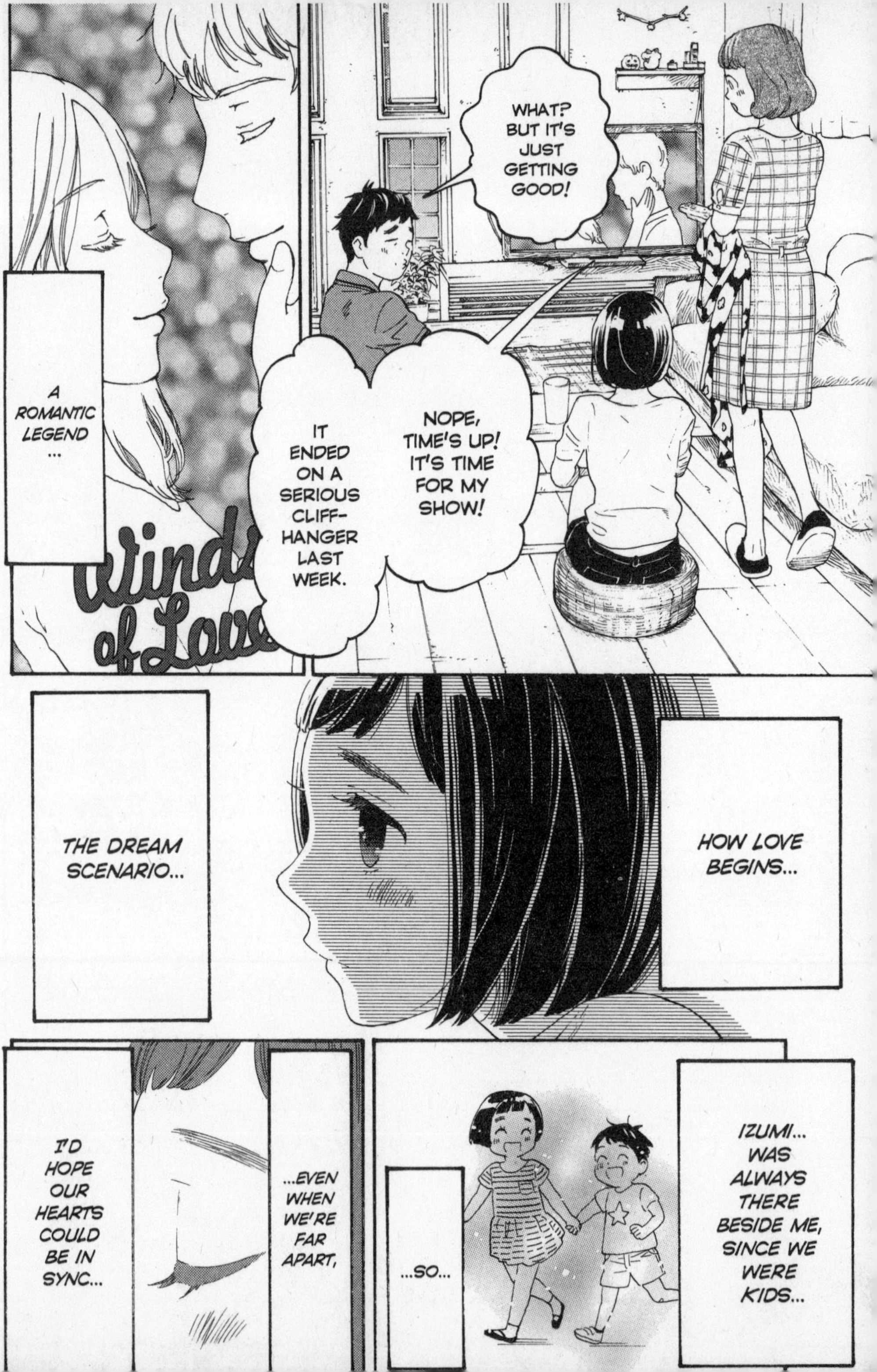
WHAT? BUT IT'S JUST GETTING GOOD!
NOPE, TIME'S UP! IT'S TIME FOR MY SHOW!
IT ENDED ON A SERIOUS CLIFF-HANGER LAST WEEK.
A ROMANTIC LEGEND ...
HOW LOVE BEGINS...
THE DREAM SCENARIO...
IZUMI... WAS ALWAYS THERE BESIDE ME, SINCE WE WERE KIDS...
...SO...
...EVEN WHEN WE'RE FAR APART,
I'D HOPE OUR HEARTS COULD BE IN SYNC...

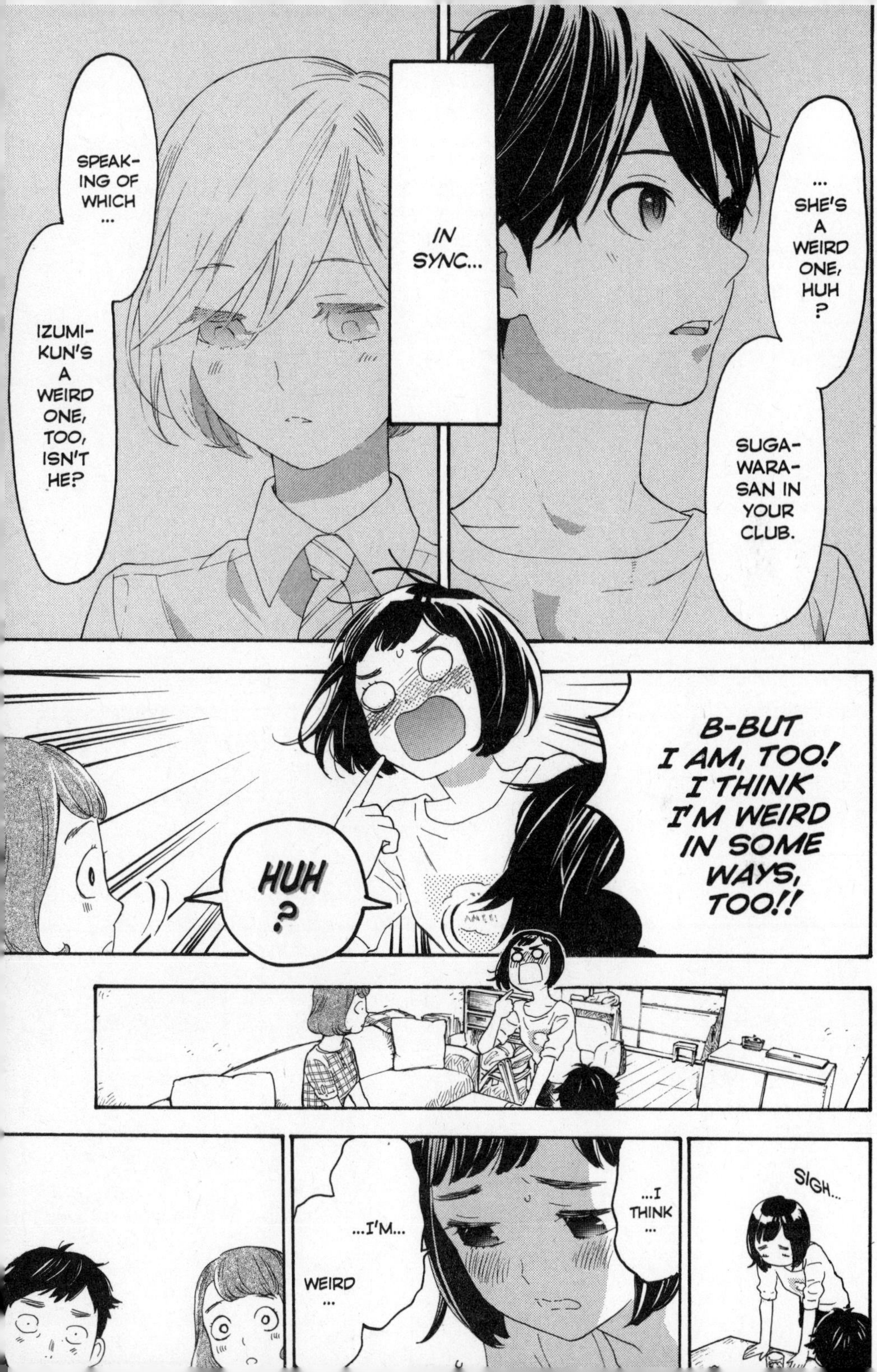

...SHE'S A WEIRD ONE, HUH?
SUGAWARA-SAN IN YOUR CLUB.
IN SYNC...
SPEAKING OF WHICH...
IZUMI-KUN'S A WEIRD ONE, TOO, ISN'T HE?
B-BUT I AM, TOO! I THINK I'M WEIRD IN SOME WAYS, TOO!!
HUH?
SIGH...
...I THINK...
...I'M...
WEIRD...

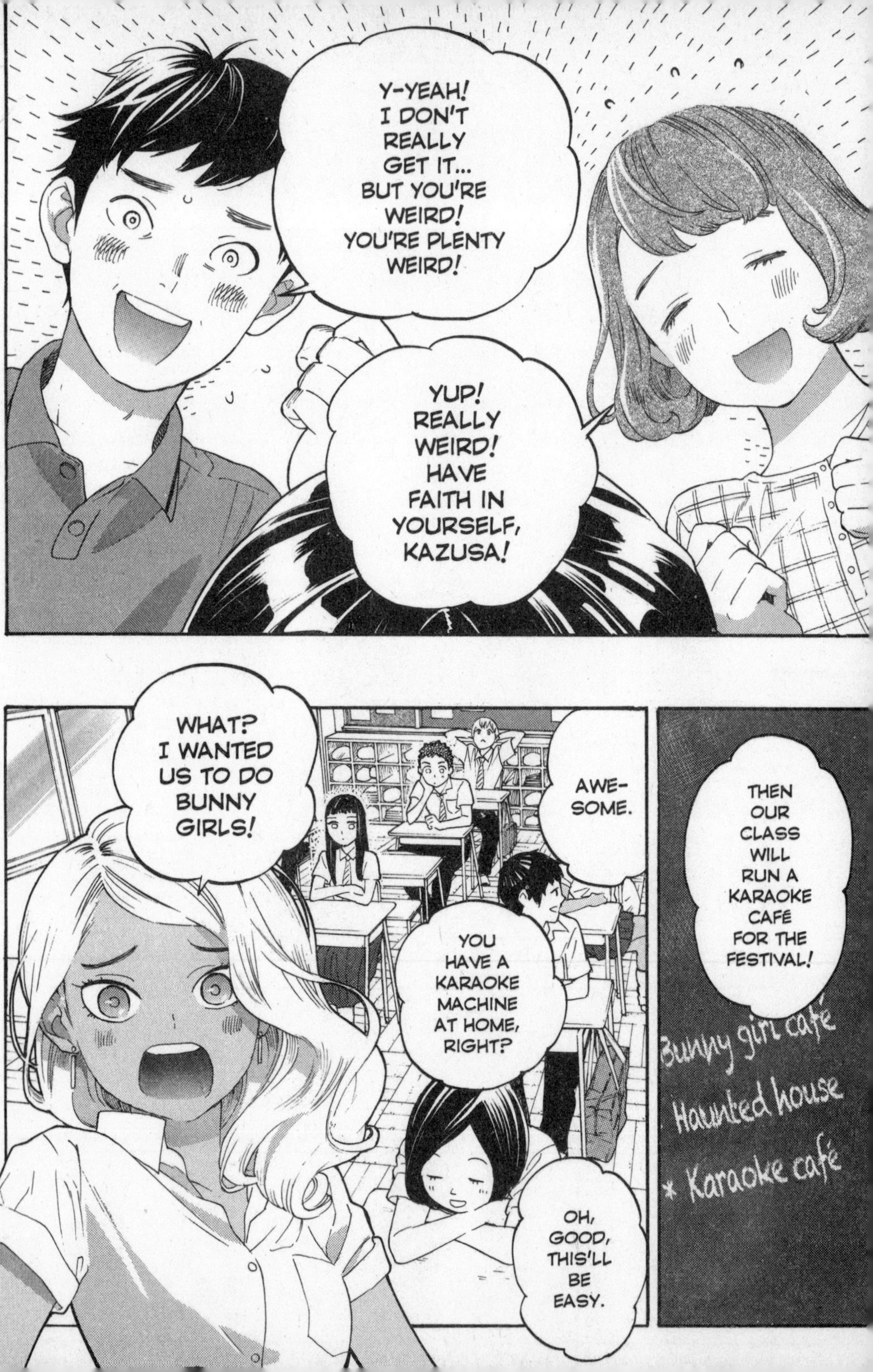
Y-YEAH! I DON'T REALLY GET IT... BUT YOU'RE WEIRD! YOU'RE PLENTY WEIRD!
YUP! REALLY WEIRD! HAVE FAITH IN YOURSELF, KAZUSA!
THEN OUR CLASS WILL RUN A KARAOKE CAFÉ FOR THE FESTIVAL!
Bunny girl café
Haunted house
* Karaoke café
AWE-SOME.
WHAT? I WANTED US TO DO BUNNY GIRLS!
YOU HAVE A KARAOKE MACHINE AT HOME, RIGHT?
OH, GOOD, THIS'LL BE EASY.

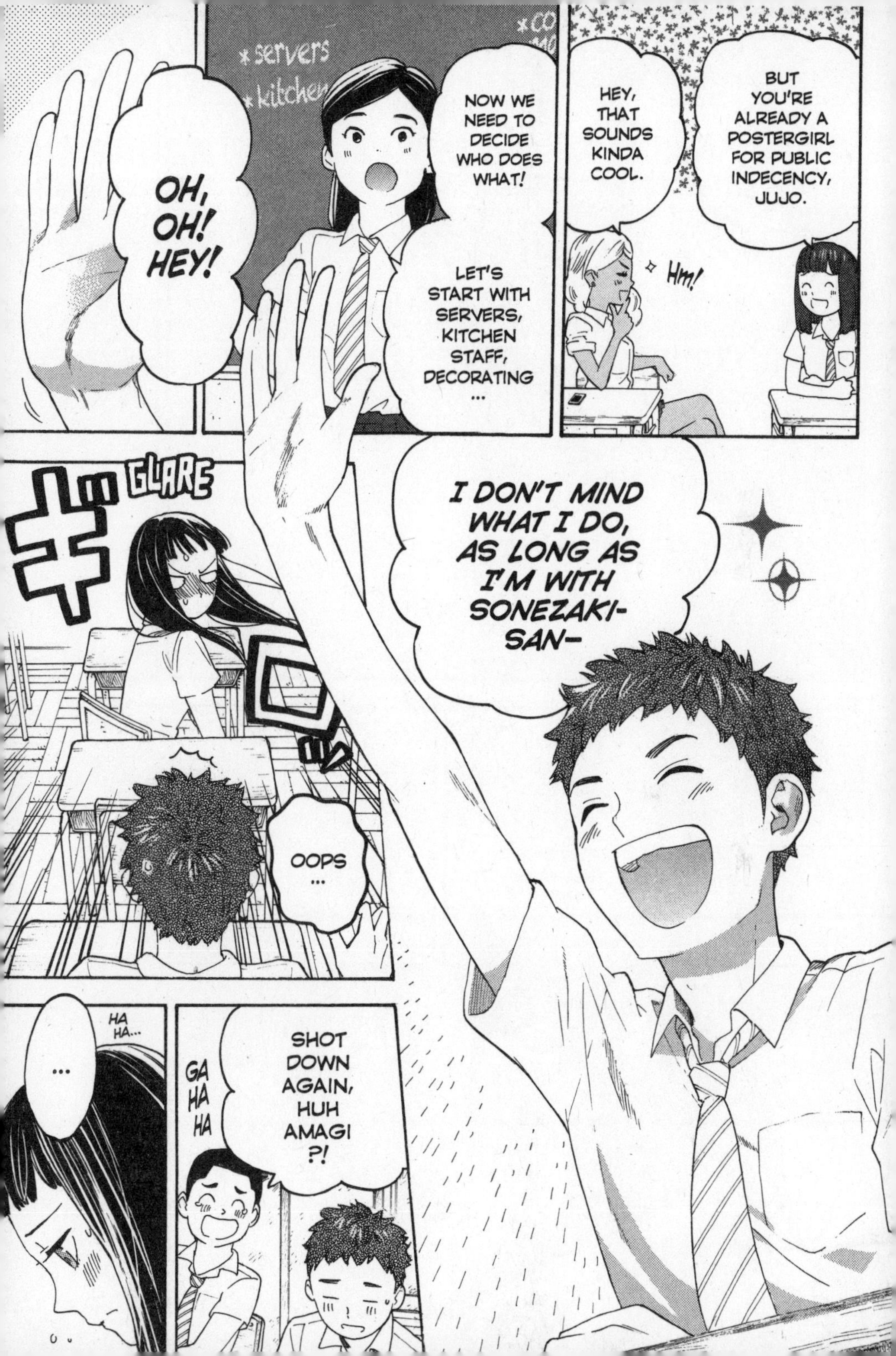
HEY, THAT SOUNDS KINDA COOL.
BUT YOU'RE ALREADY A POSTERGIRL FOR PUBLIC INDECENCY, JUJO.
Hm!
*servers
*kitchen
NOW WE NEED TO DECIDE WHO DOES WHAT!
LET'S START WITH SERVERS, KITCHEN STAFF, DECORATING ...
OH, OH! HEY!
I DON'T MIND WHAT I DO, AS LONG AS I'M WITH SONEZAKI-SAN-
GLARE
OOPS ...
SHOT DOWN AGAIN, HUH AMAGI ?!
GA HA HA
HA HA...
...

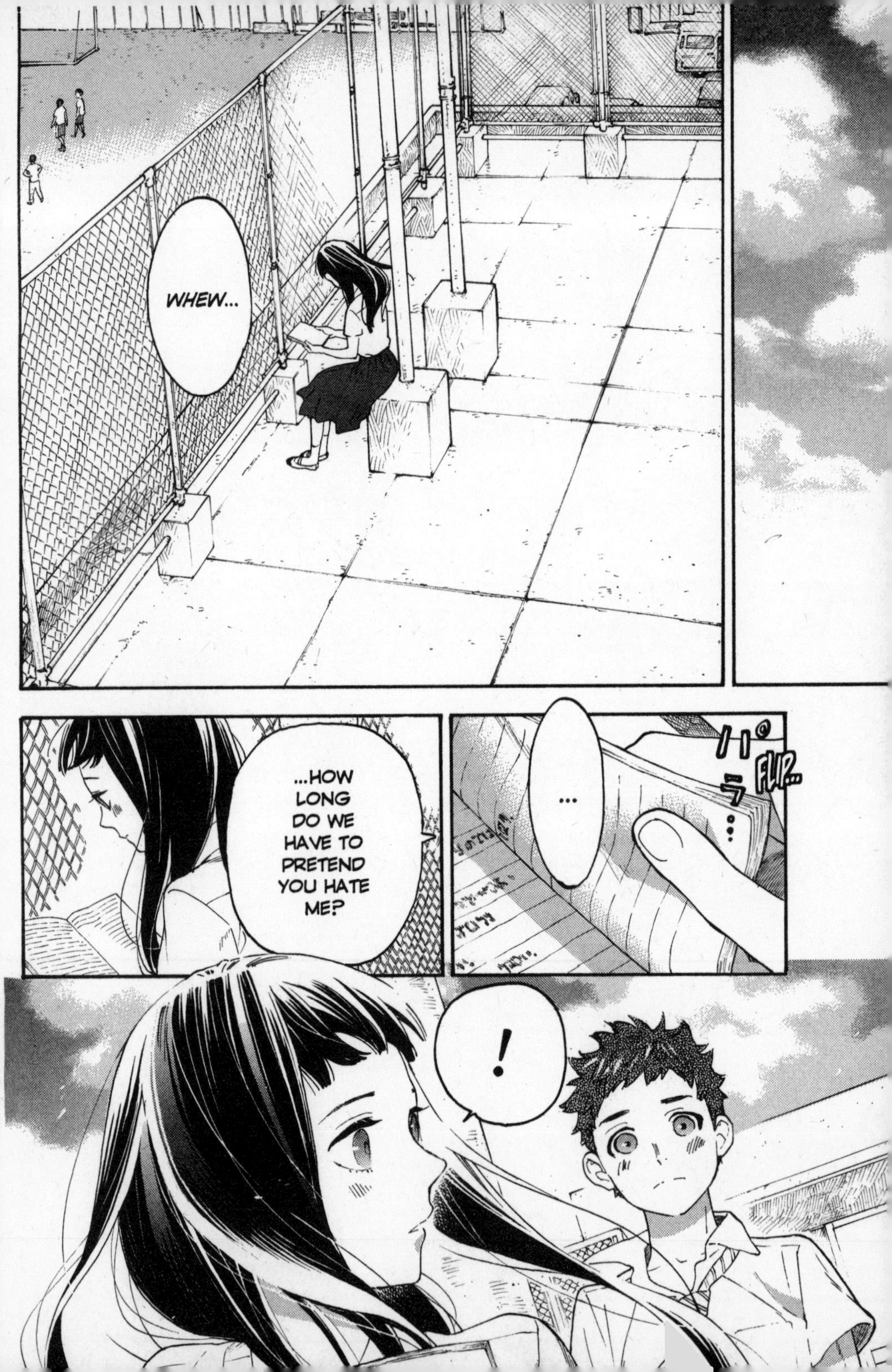
WHEW...
...
パラ
FLIP...
...HOW LONG DO WE HAVE TO PRETEND YOU HATE ME?
!

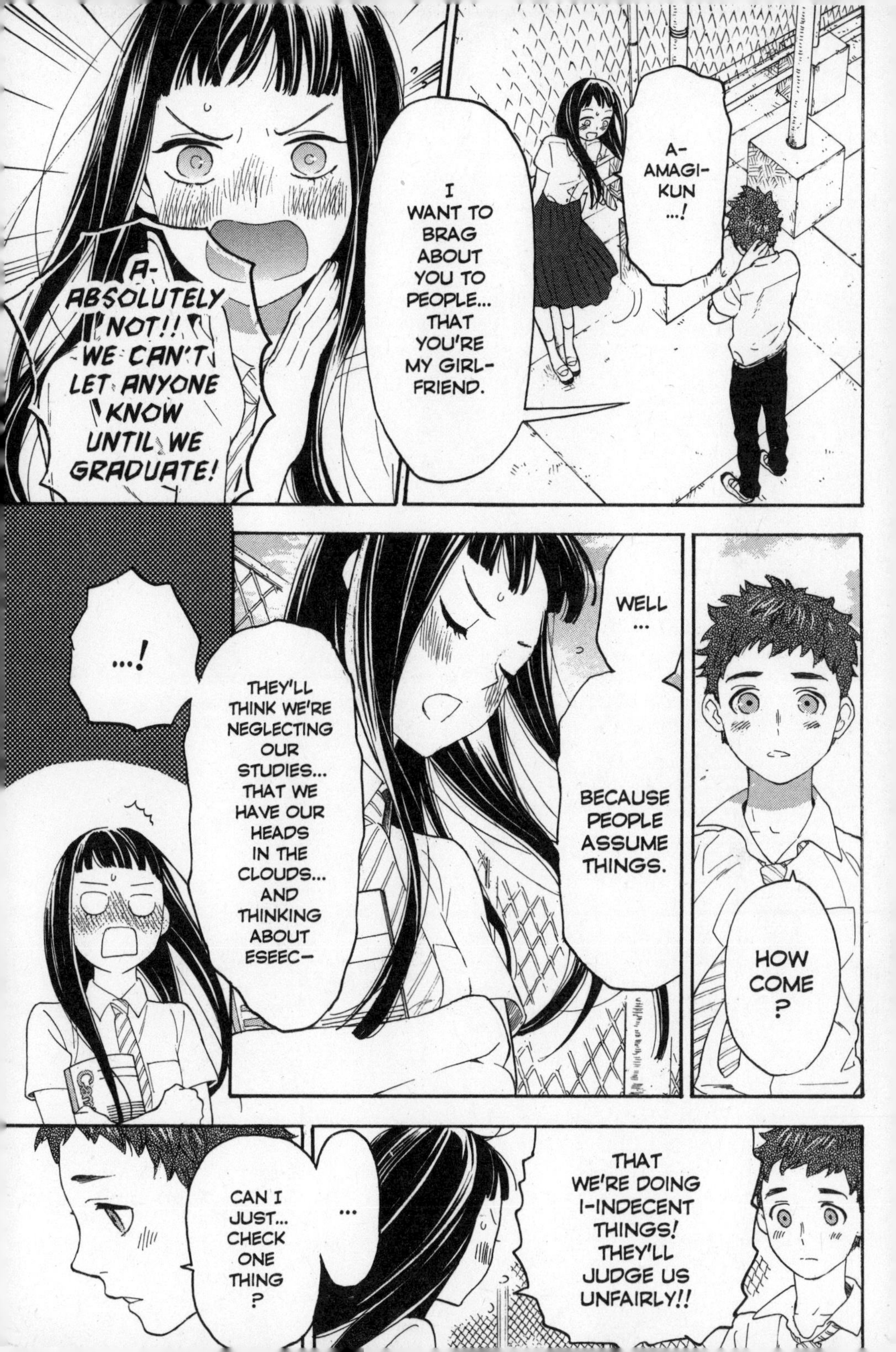
A-AMAGI-KUN ...!
I WANT TO BRAG ABOUT YOU TO PEOPLE... THAT YOU'RE MY GIRLFRIEND.
A-ABSOLUTELY NOT!! WE CAN'T LET ANYONE KNOW UNTIL WE GRADUATE!
HOW COME?
WELL ...
BECAUSE PEOPLE ASSUME THINGS.
THEY'LL THINK WE'RE NEGLECTING OUR STUDIES... THAT WE HAVE OUR HEADS IN THE CLOUDS... AND THINKING ABOUT ESEEC—
...!
THAT WE'RE DOING I-INDECENT THINGS! THEY'LL JUDGE US UNFAIRLY!!
...
CAN I JUST... CHECK ONE THING?

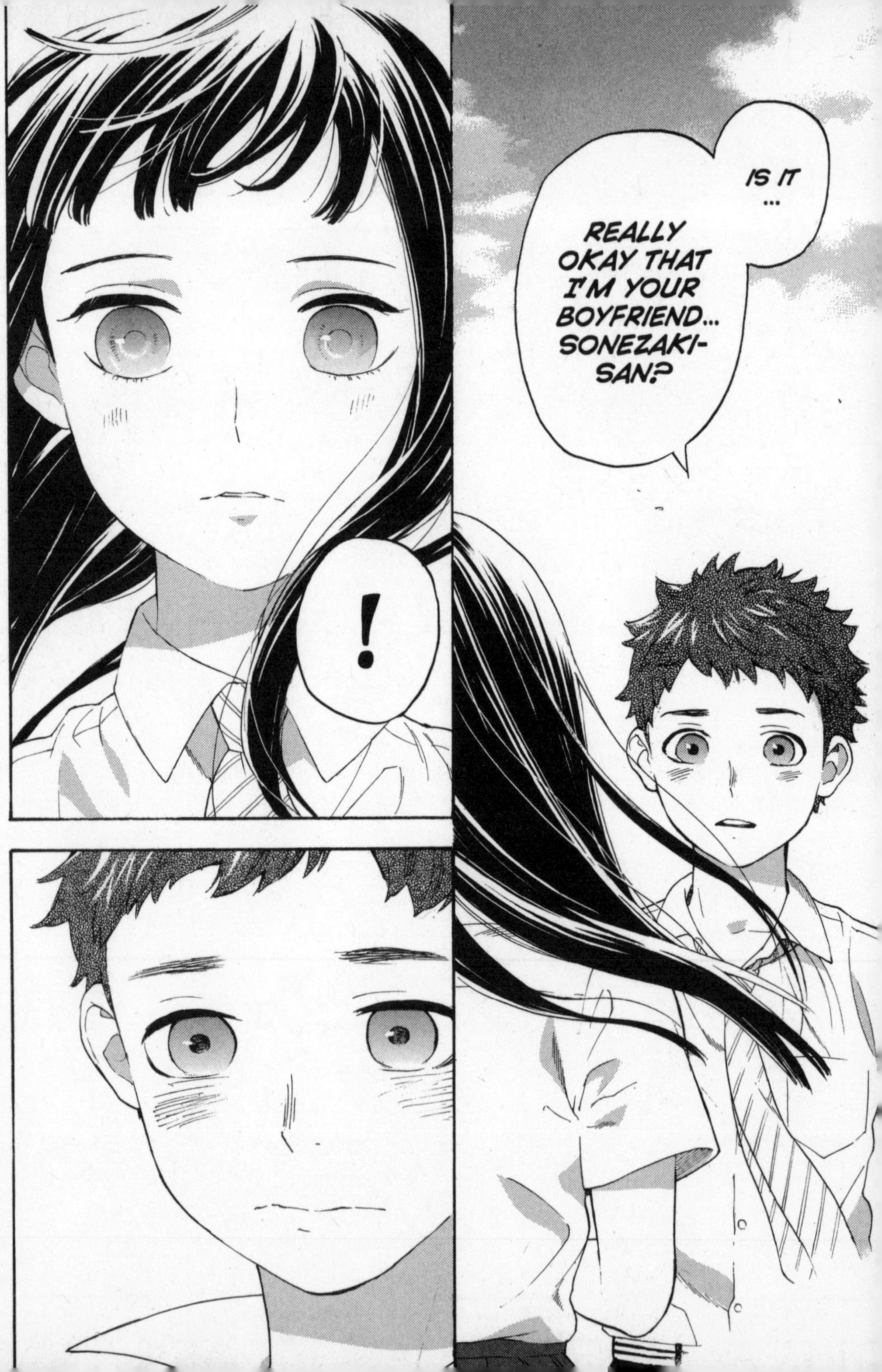
IS IT ...
REALLY OKAY THAT I'M YOUR BOYFRIEND... SONEZAKI-SAN?
!

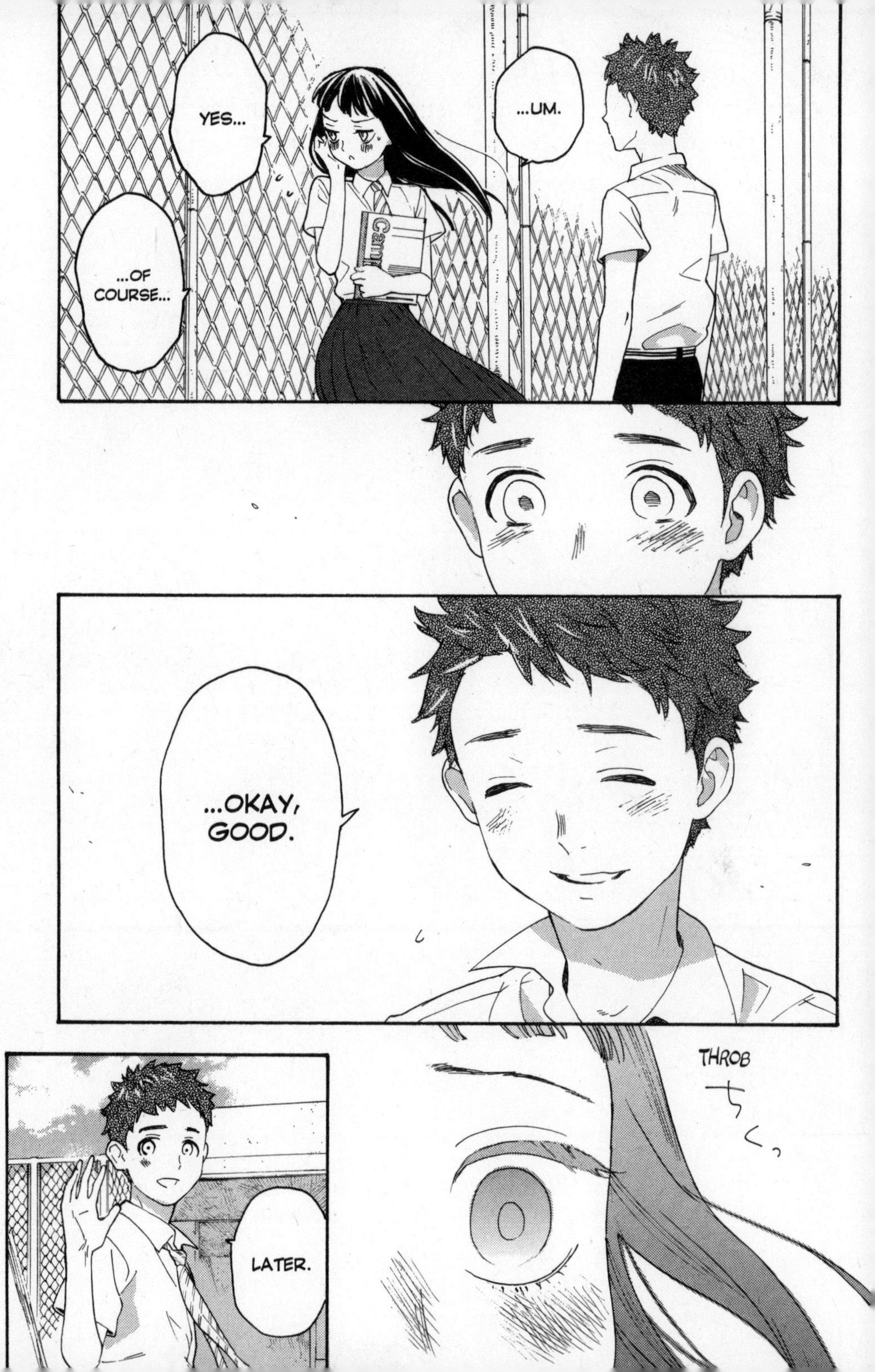
...UM.
YES...
...OF COURSE...
...OKAY, GOOD.
THROB
ちくっ
LATER.

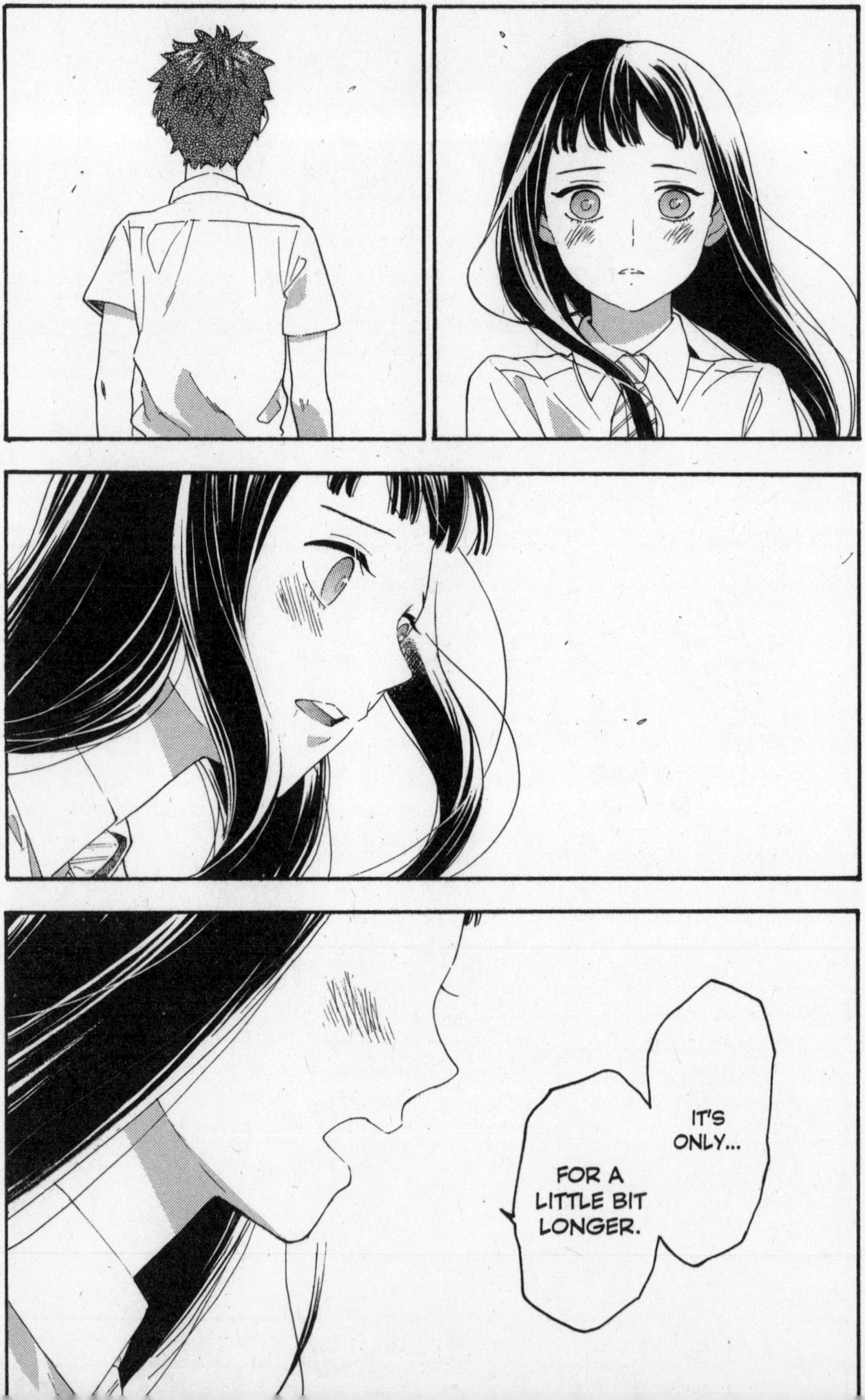
IT'S ONLY...
FOR A LITTLE BIT LONGER.

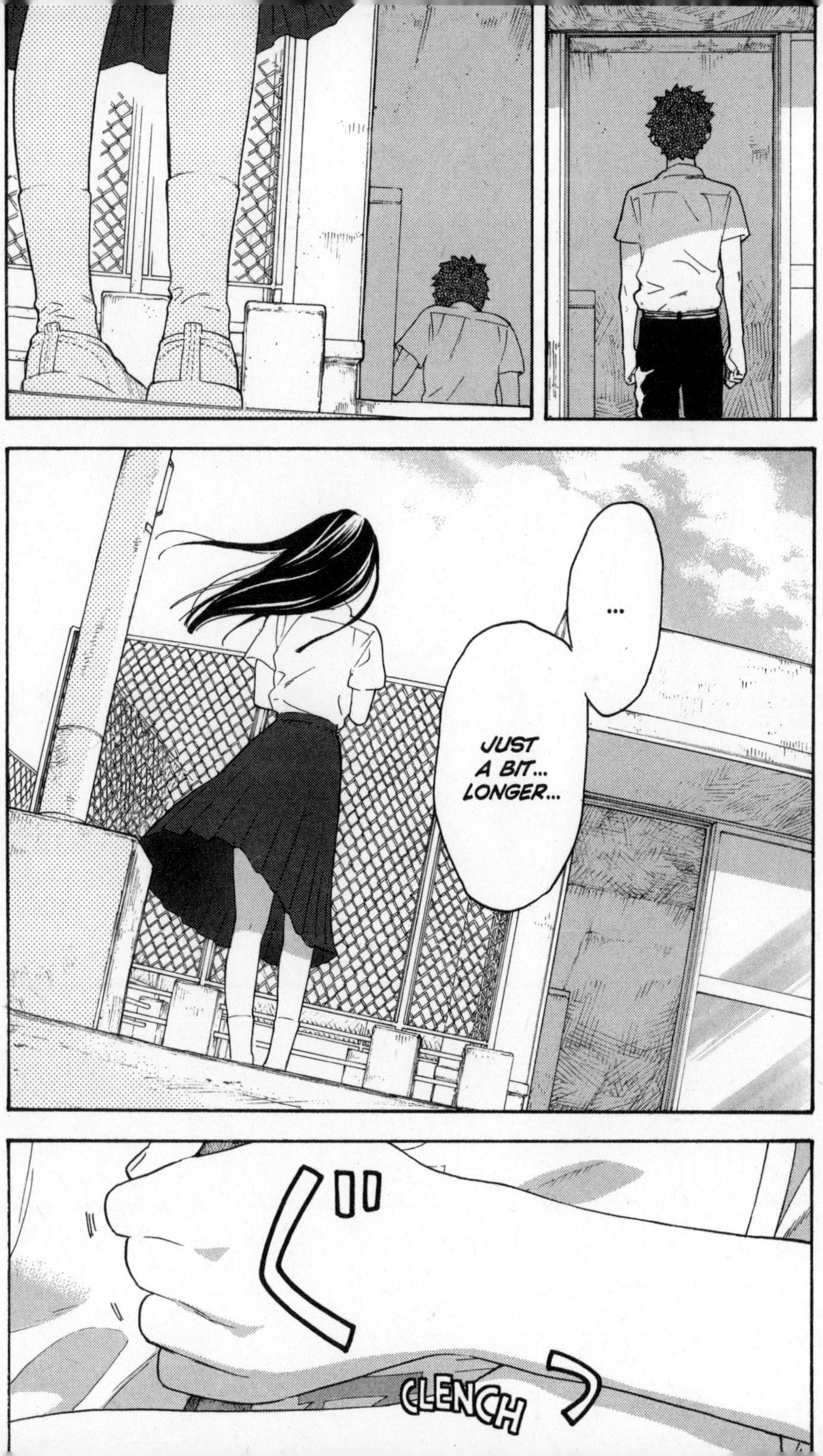
...
JUST A BIT... LONGER...
CLENCH

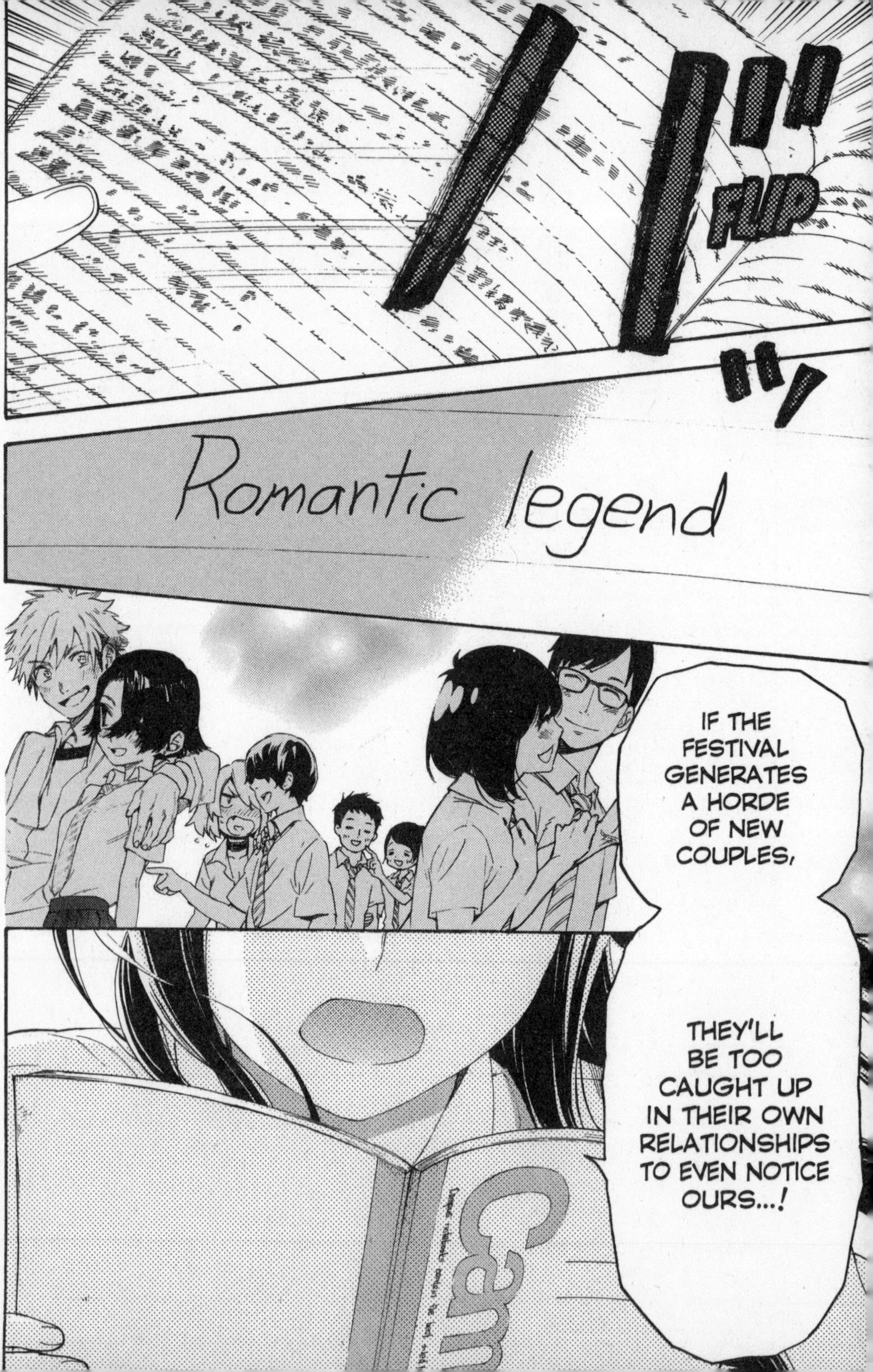
FLIP
Romantic legend
IF THE FESTIVAL GENERATES A HORDE OF NEW COUPLES,
THEY'LL BE TOO CAUGHT UP IN THEIR OWN RELATIONSHIPS TO EVEN NOTICE OURS...!

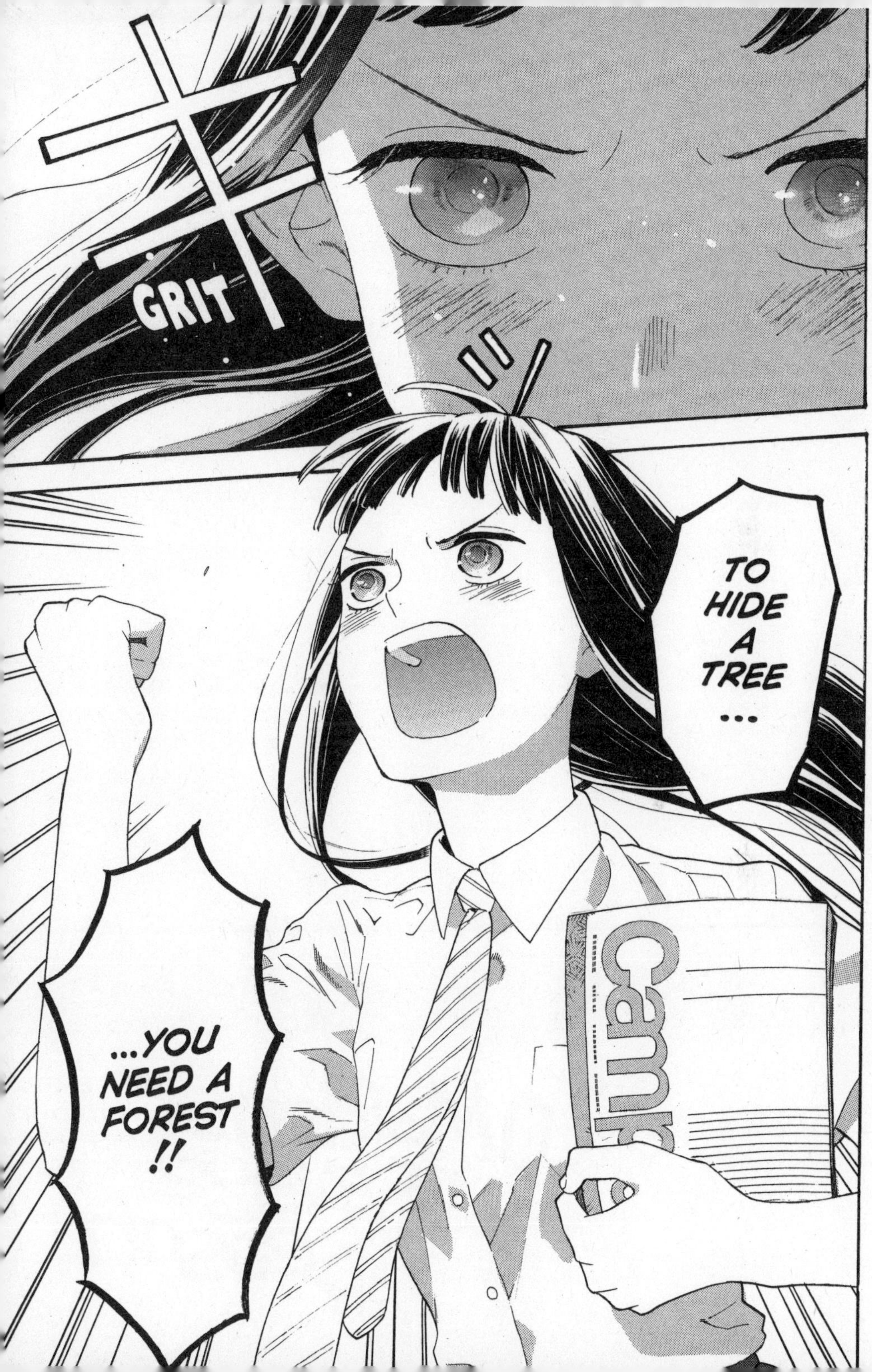
GRIT
TO HIDE A TREE ...
...YOU NEED A FOREST !!

O Maidens
in your Savage
your Season

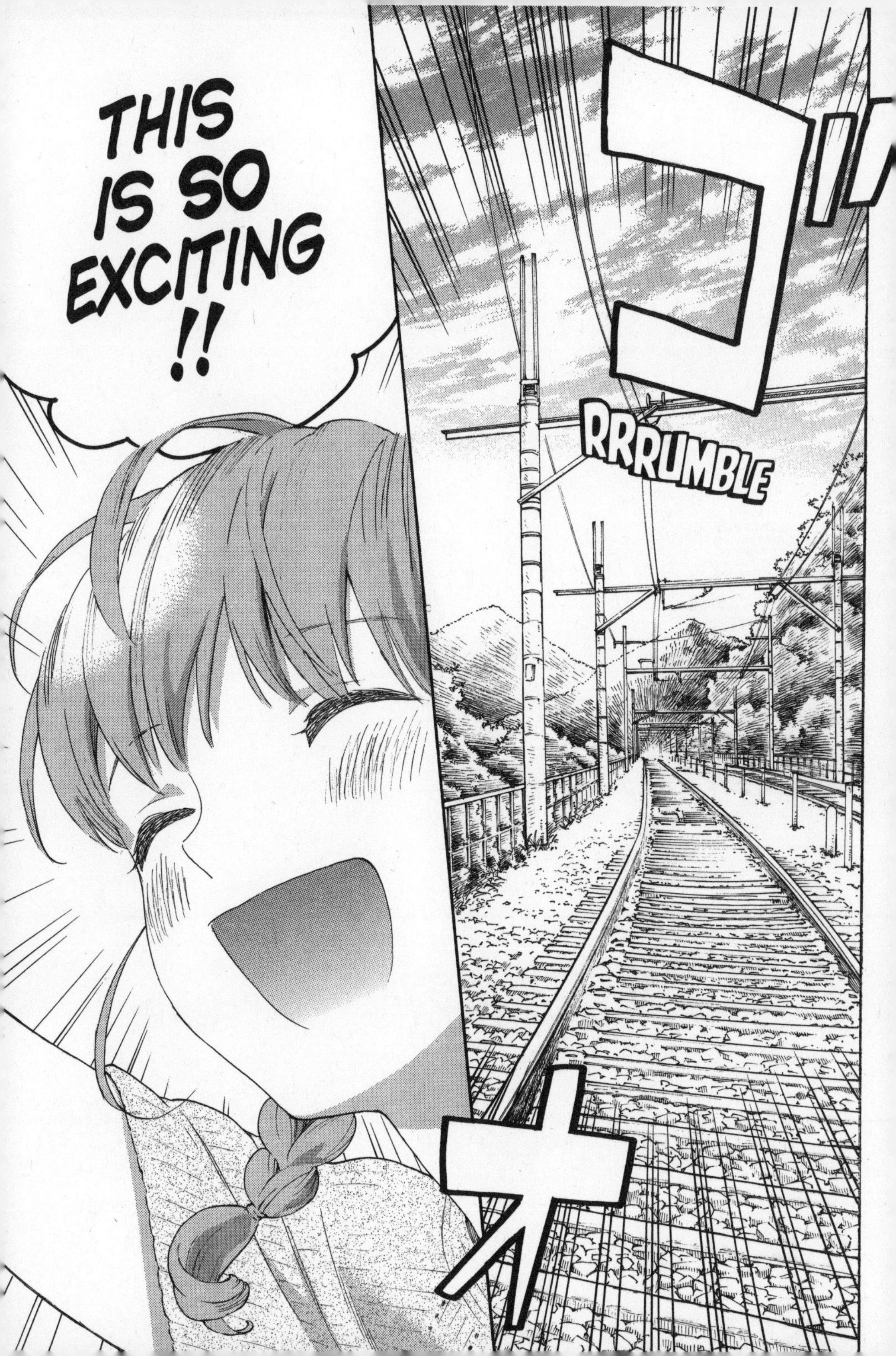
RRRUMBLE
THIS IS SO EXCITING!!

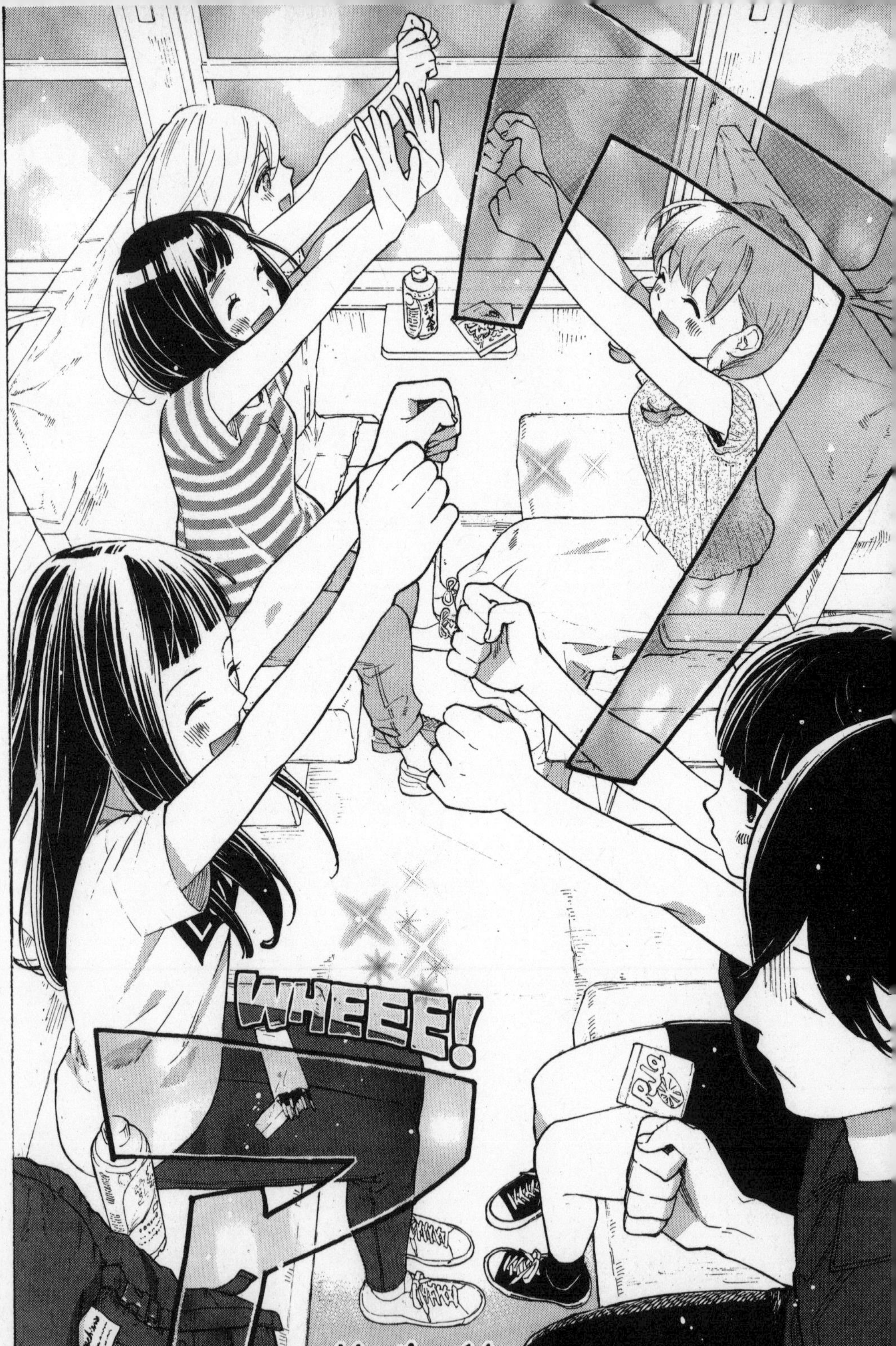
WHEEE!

Meeting 14

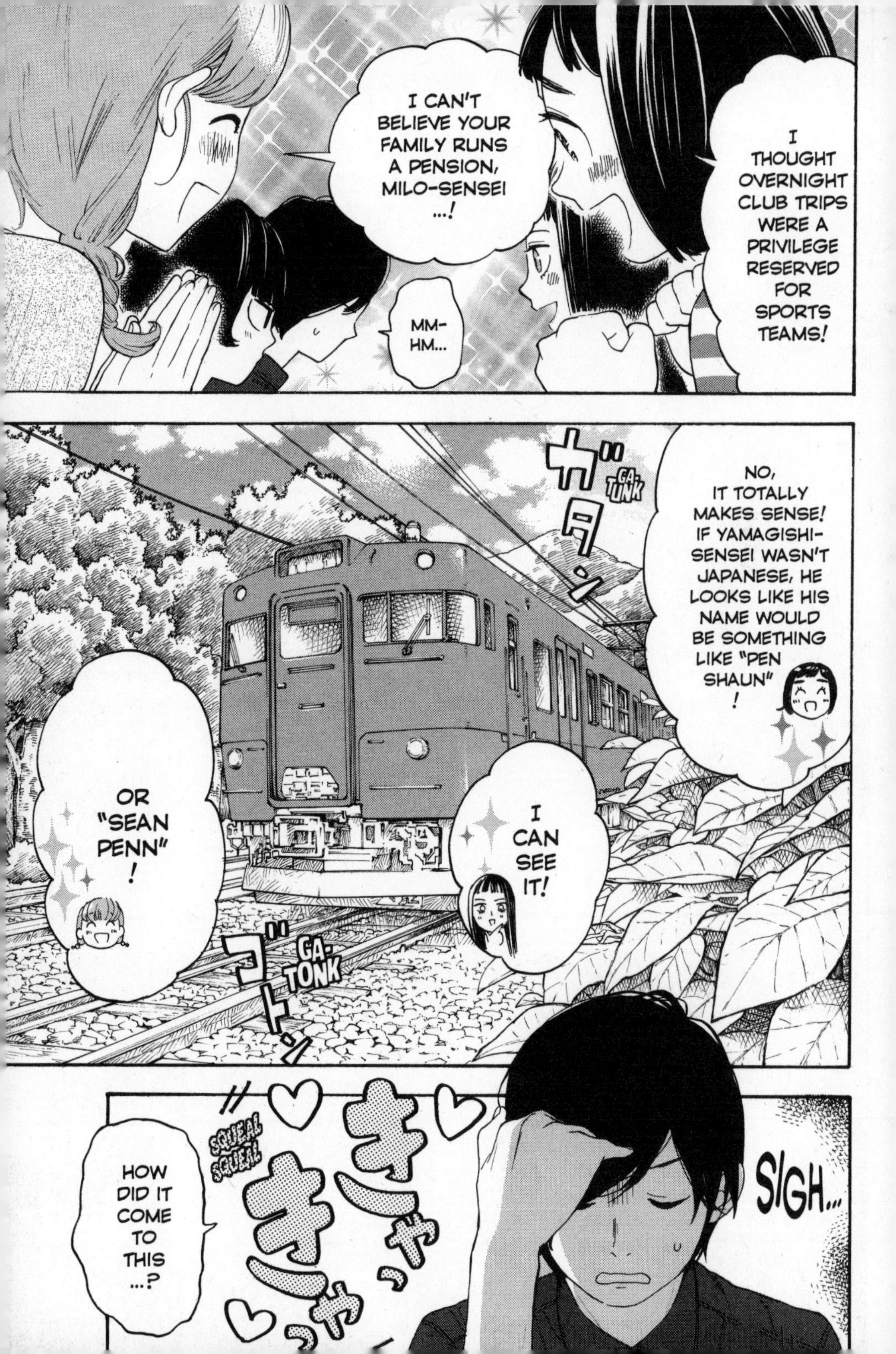
I THOUGHT OVERNIGHT CLUB TRIPS WERE A PRIVILEGE RESERVED FOR SPORTS TEAMS!
I CAN'T BELIEVE YOUR FAMILY RUNS A PENSION, MILO-SENSEI ...!
MM-HM...
GA-TONK
NO, IT TOTALLY MAKES SENSE! IF YAMAGISHI-SENSEI WASN'T JAPANESE, HE LOOKS LIKE HIS NAME WOULD BE SOMETHING LIKE "PEN SHAUN"!
I CAN SEE IT!
OR "SEAN PENN"!
GA-TONK
SIGH...
SQUEAL SQUEAL
HOW DID IT COME TO THIS ...?

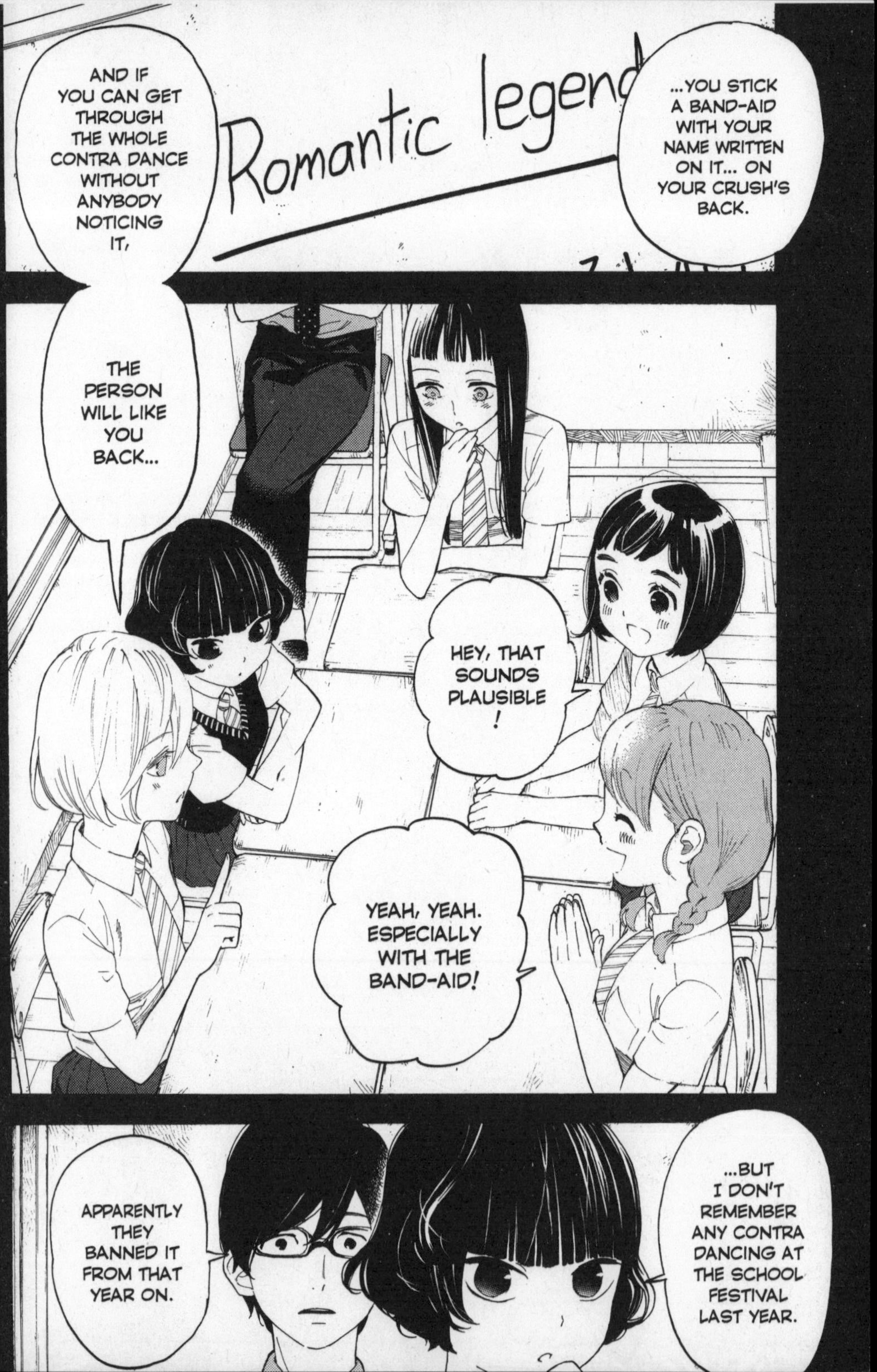
...YOU STICK A BAND-AID WITH YOUR NAME WRITTEN ON IT... ON YOUR CRUSH'S BACK.
Romantic legend
AND IF YOU CAN GET THROUGH THE WHOLE CONTRA DANCE WITHOUT ANYBODY NOTICING IT,
THE PERSON WILL LIKE YOU BACK...
HEY, THAT SOUNDS PLAUSIBLE!
YEAH, YEAH. ESPECIALLY WITH THE BAND-AID!
...BUT I DON'T REMEMBER ANY CONTRA DANCING AT THE SCHOOL FESTIVAL LAST YEAR.
APPARENTLY THEY BANNED IT FROM THAT YEAR ON.

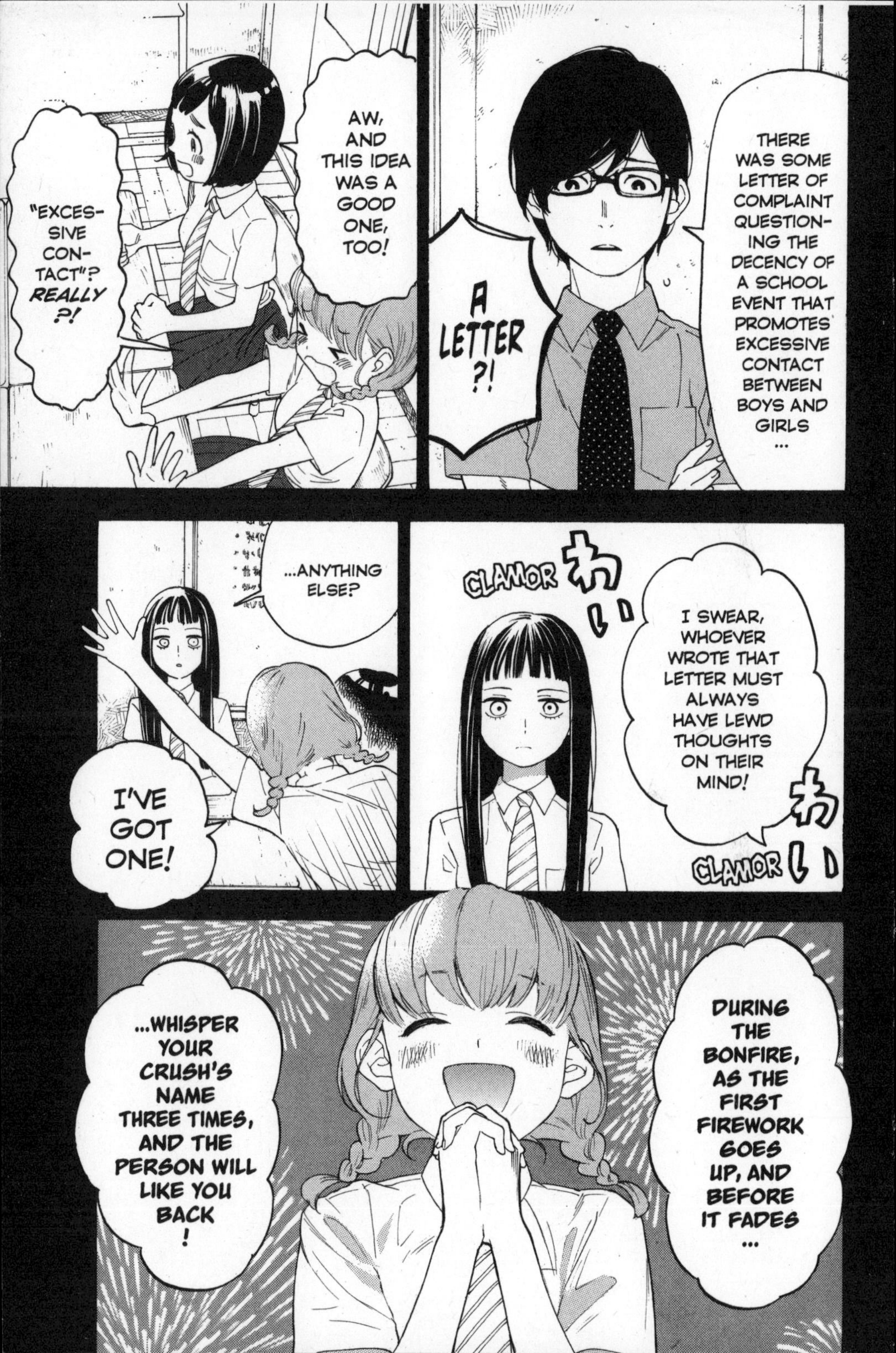
THERE WAS SOME LETTER OF COMPLAINT QUESTIONING THE DECENCY OF A SCHOOL EVENT THAT PROMOTES EXCESSIVE CONTACT BETWEEN BOYS AND GIRLS ...
A LETTER ?!
AW, AND THIS IDEA WAS A GOOD ONE, TOO!
"EXCESSIVE CONTACT"? *REALLY* ?!
CLAMOR わい
I SWEAR, WHOEVER WROTE THAT LETTER MUST ALWAYS HAVE LEWD THOUGHTS ON THEIR MIND!
CLAMOR わい
...ANYTHING ELSE?
I'VE GOT ONE!
DURING THE BONFIRE, AS THE FIRST FIREWORK GOES UP, AND BEFORE IT FADES ...
...WHISPER YOUR CRUSH'S NAME THREE TIMES, AND THE PERSON WILL LIKE YOU BACK !

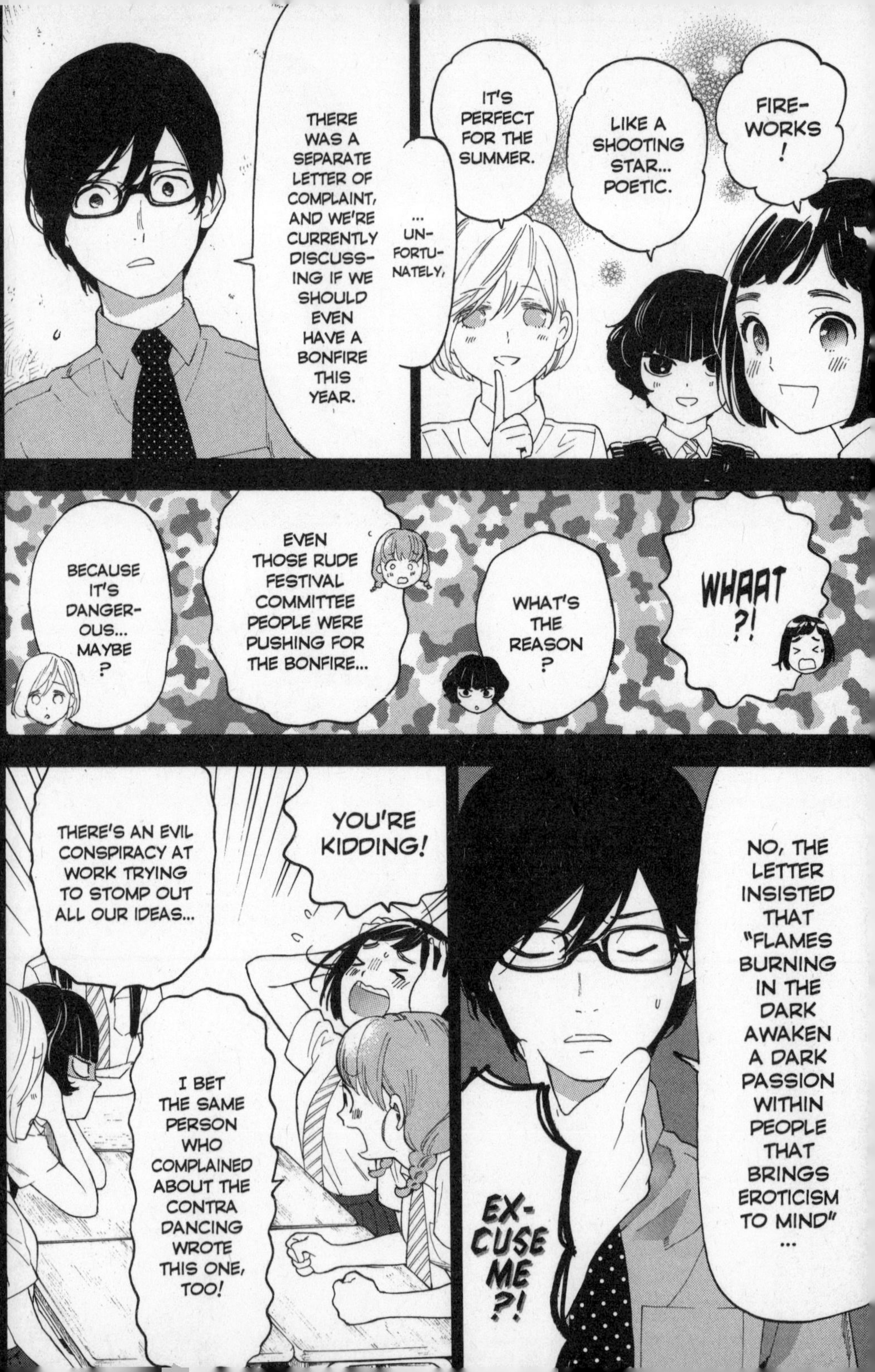
FIRE-WORKS!
LIKE A SHOOTING STAR... POETIC.
IT'S PERFECT FOR THE SUMMER.
... UN-FORTU-NATELY,
THERE WAS A SEPARATE LETTER OF COMPLAINT, AND WE'RE CURRENTLY DISCUSS-ING IF WE SHOULD EVEN HAVE A BONFIRE THIS YEAR.
WHAAT?!
WHAT'S THE REASON?
EVEN THOSE RUDE FESTIVAL COMMITTEE PEOPLE WERE PUSHING FOR THE BONFIRE...
BECAUSE IT'S DANGER-OUS... MAYBE?
NO, THE LETTER INSISTED THAT "FLAMES BURNING IN THE DARK AWAKEN A DARK PASSION WITHIN PEOPLE THAT BRINGS EROTICISM TO MIND" ...
EX-CUSE ME?!
YOU'RE KIDDING!
THERE'S AN EVIL CONSPIRACY AT WORK TRYING TO STOMP OUT ALL OUR IDEAS...
I BET THE SAME PERSON WHO COMPLAINED ABOUT THE CONTRA DANCING WROTE THIS ONE, TOO!

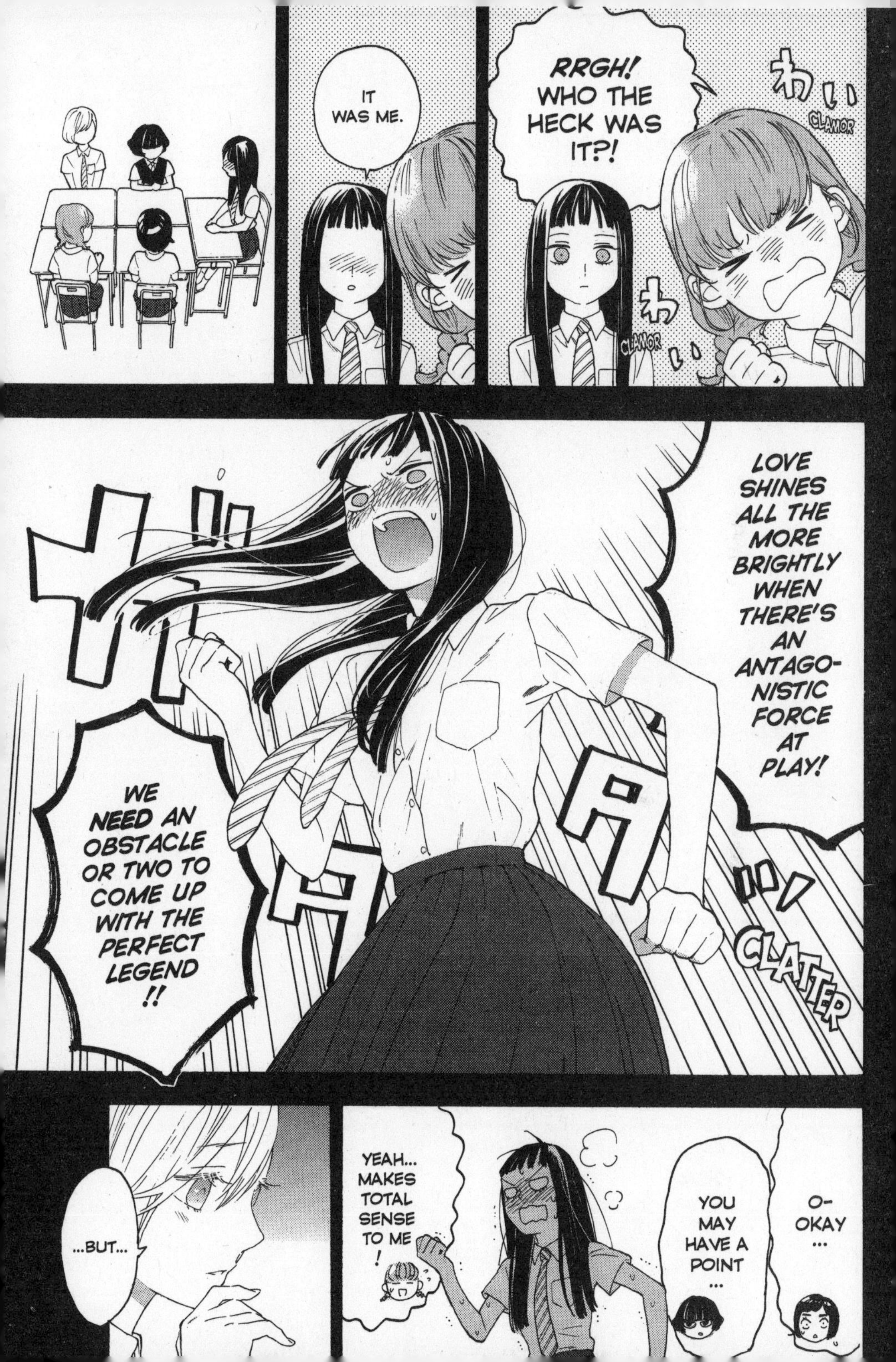
RRGH! WHO THE HECK WAS IT?!
CLAMOR
CLAMOR
IT WAS ME.
LOVE SHINES ALL THE MORE BRIGHTLY WHEN THERE'S AN ANTAGO-NISTIC FORCE AT PLAY!
WE NEED AN OBSTACLE OR TWO TO COME UP WITH THE PERFECT LEGEND!!
CLATTER
O-OKAY...
YOU MAY HAVE A POINT...
YEAH... MAKES TOTAL SENSE TO ME!
...BUT...

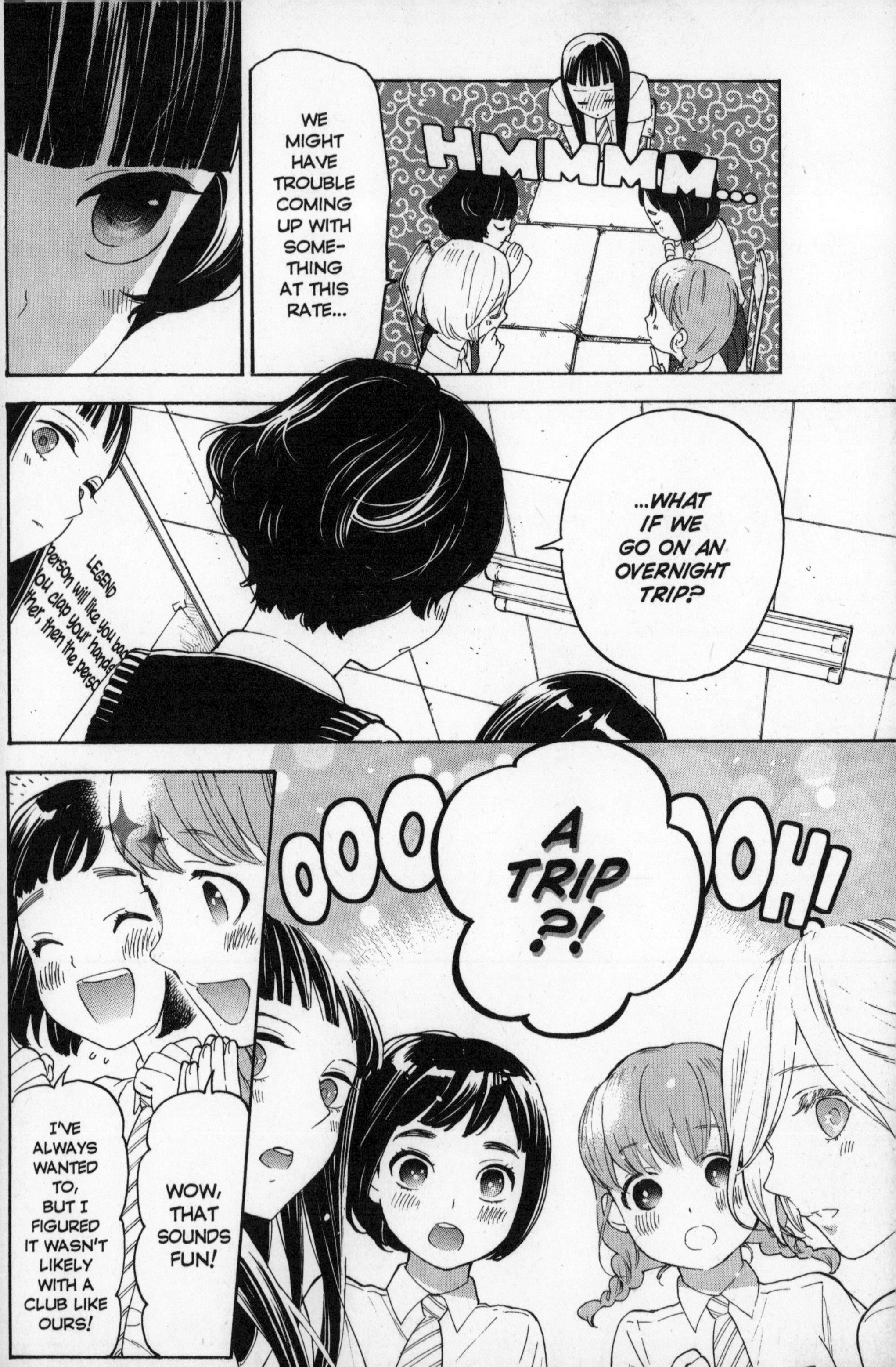
HMMMM...
WE MIGHT HAVE TROUBLE COMING UP WITH SOME-THING AT THIS RATE...
...WHAT IF WE GO ON AN OVERNIGHT TRIP?
LEGEND
OOOOOOH!
A TRIP?!
WOW, THAT SOUNDS FUN!
I'VE ALWAYS WANTED TO, BUT I FIGURED IT WASN'T LIKELY WITH A CLUB LIKE OURS!

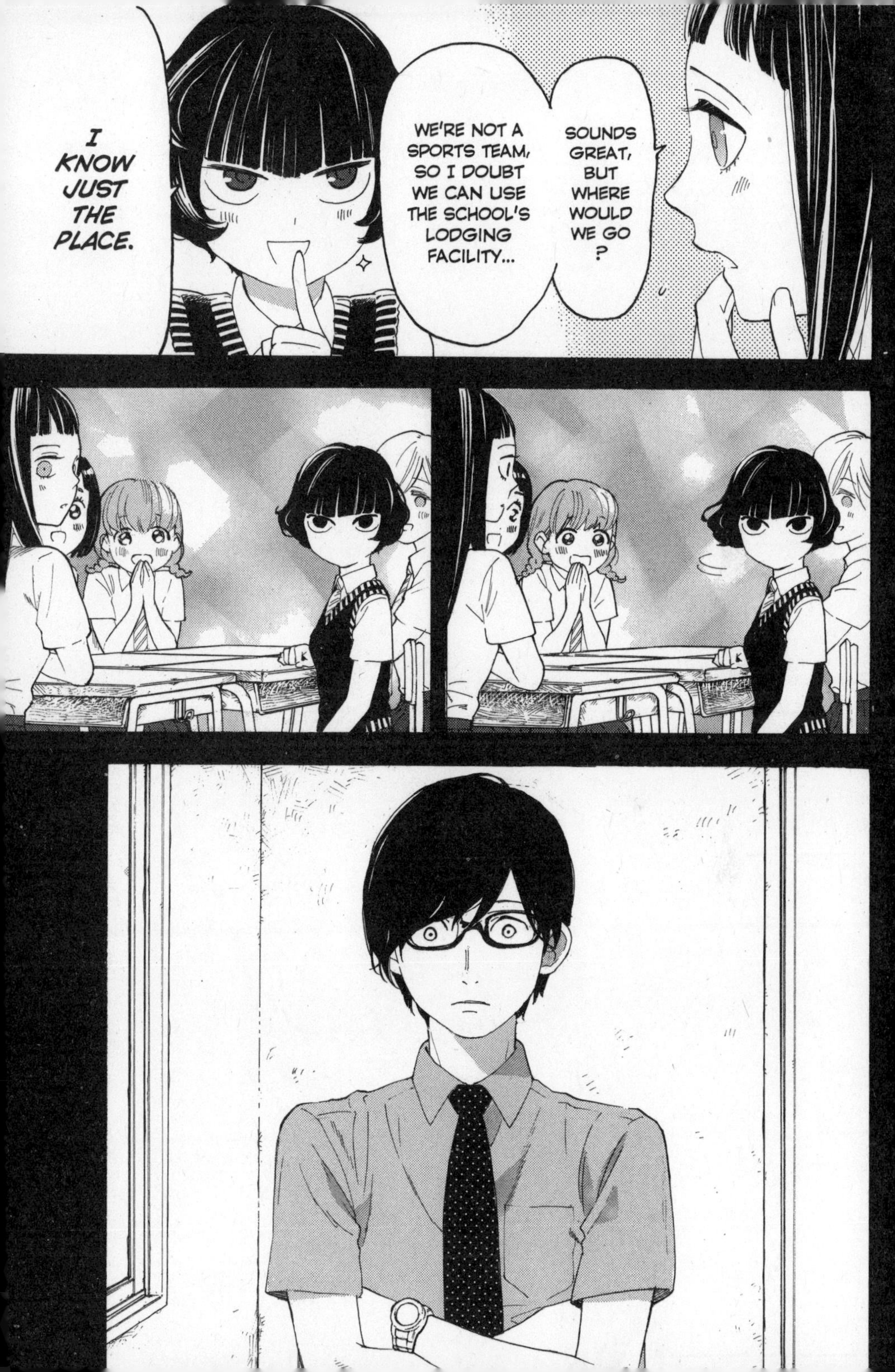
SOUNDS GREAT, BUT WHERE WOULD WE GO?
WE'RE NOT A SPORTS TEAM, SO I DOUBT WE CAN USE THE SCHOOL'S LODGING FACILITY...
I KNOW JUST THE PLACE.

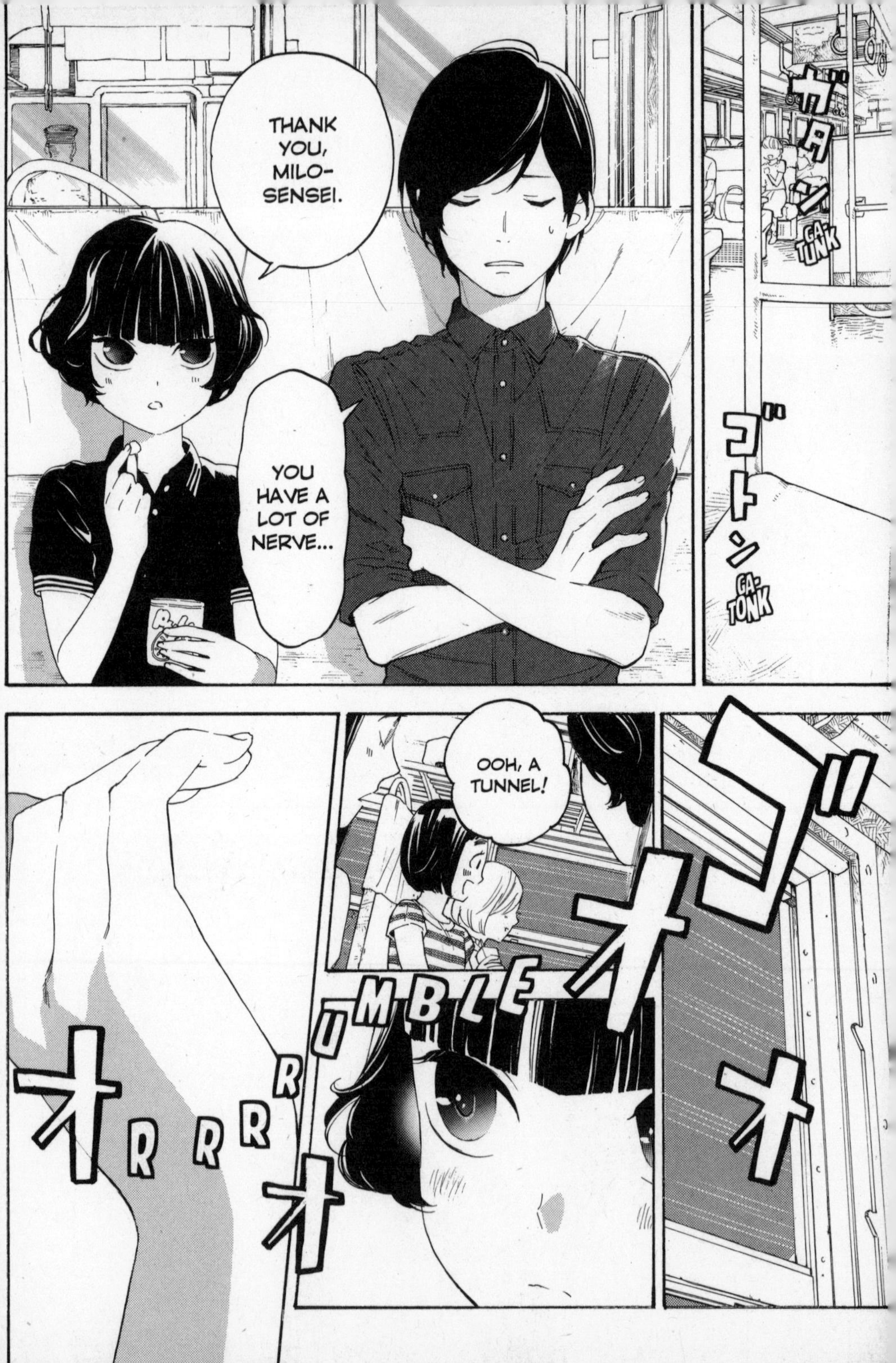
ガタン
GA-TONK
ゴトン
GA-TONK
THANK YOU, MILO-SENSEI.
YOU HAVE A LOT OF NERVE...
OOH, A TUNNEL!
ゴオオオ
RRRRUMBLE

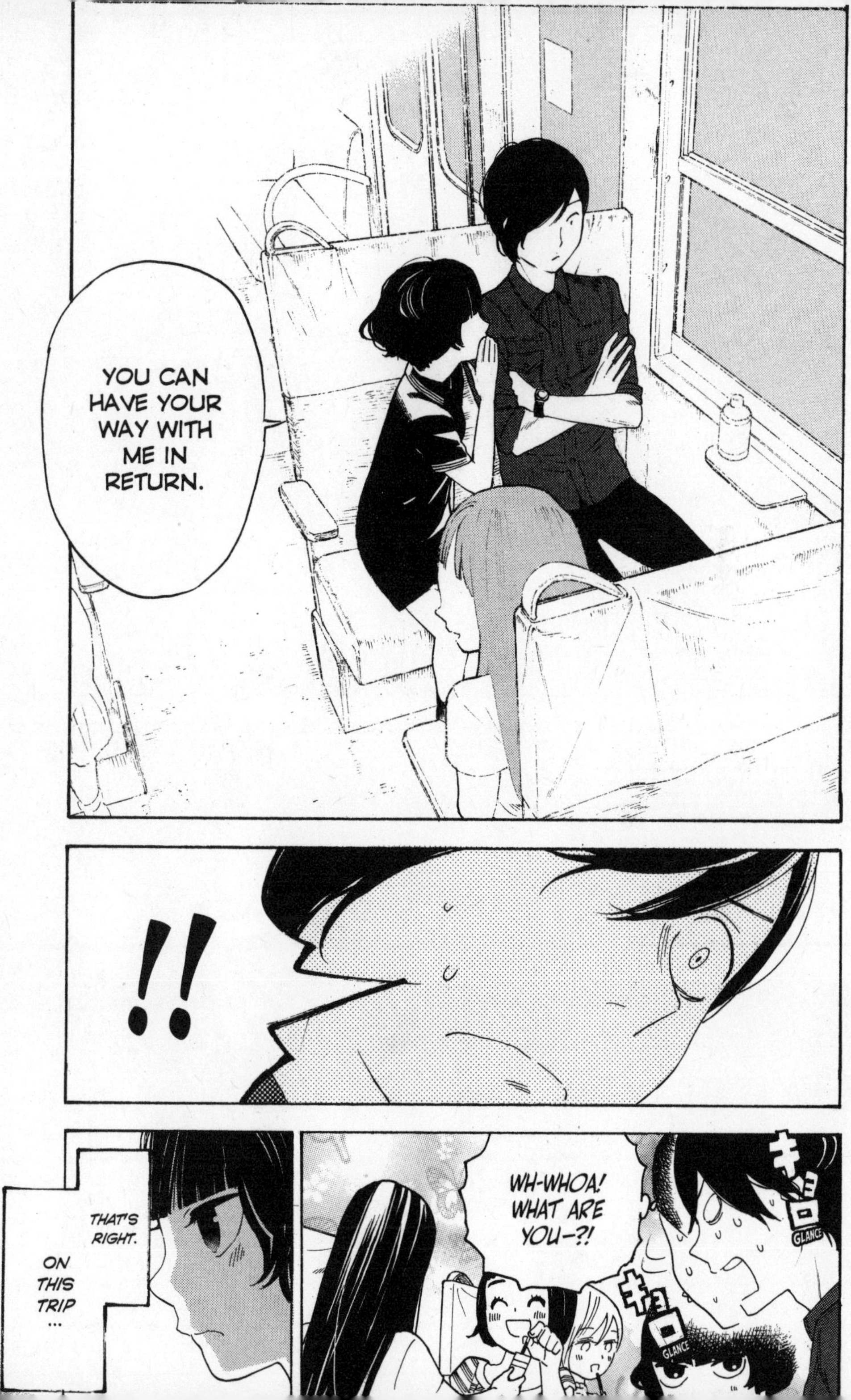
YOU CAN HAVE YOUR WAY WITH ME IN RETURN.
!!
キョロ
GLANCE
WH-WHOA! WHAT ARE YOU-?!
キョロ
GLANCE
THAT'S RIGHT.
ON THIS TRIP ...

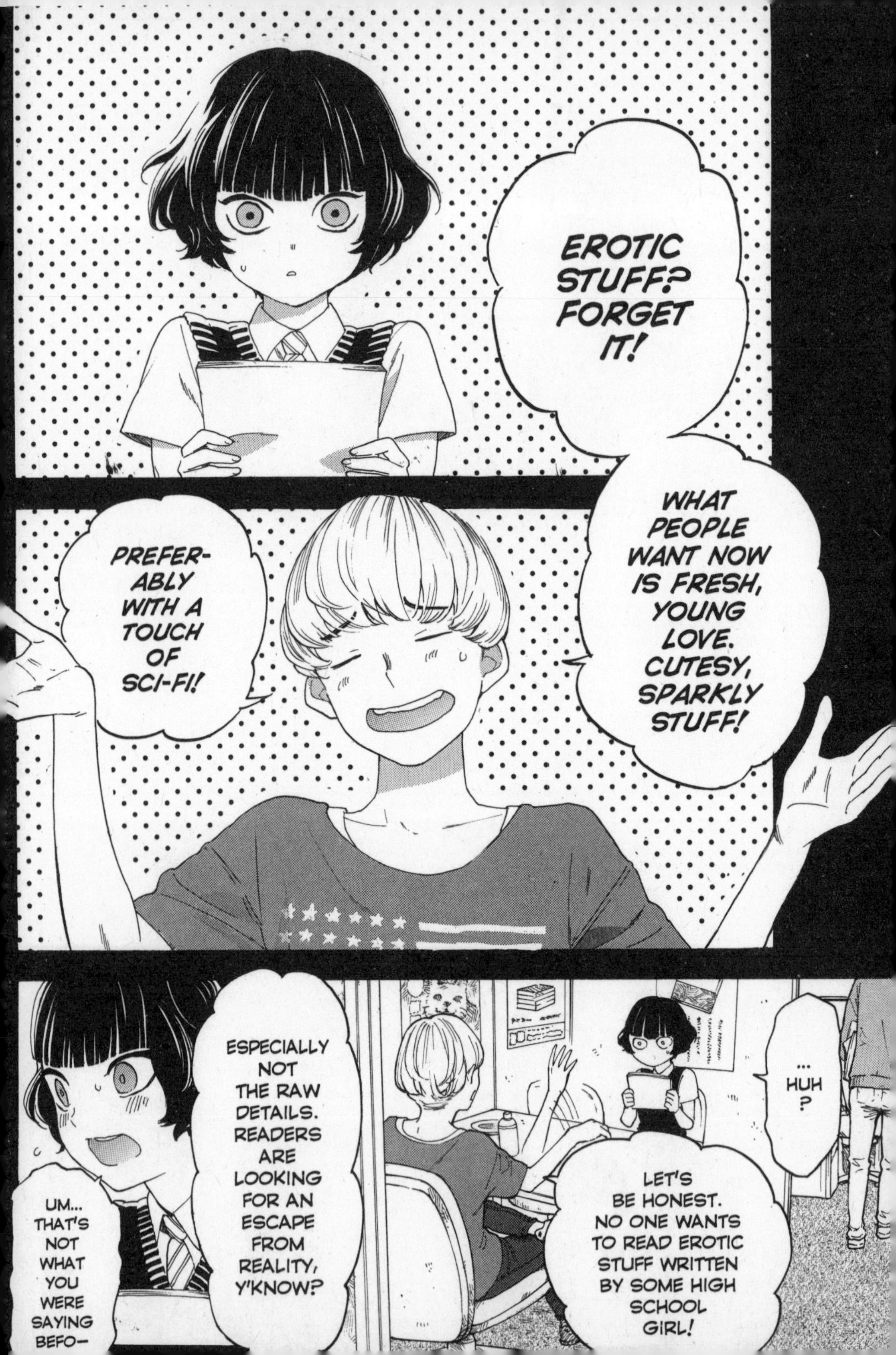
EROTIC STUFF? FORGET IT!
WHAT PEOPLE WANT NOW IS FRESH, YOUNG LOVE. CUTESY, SPARKLY STUFF!
PREFER-ABLY WITH A TOUCH OF SCI-FI!
... HUH?
LET'S BE HONEST. NO ONE WANTS TO READ EROTIC STUFF WRITTEN BY SOME HIGH SCHOOL GIRL!
ESPECIALLY NOT THE RAW DETAILS. READERS ARE LOOKING FOR AN ESCAPE FROM REALITY, Y'KNOW?
UM... THAT'S NOT WHAT YOU WERE SAYING BEFO—

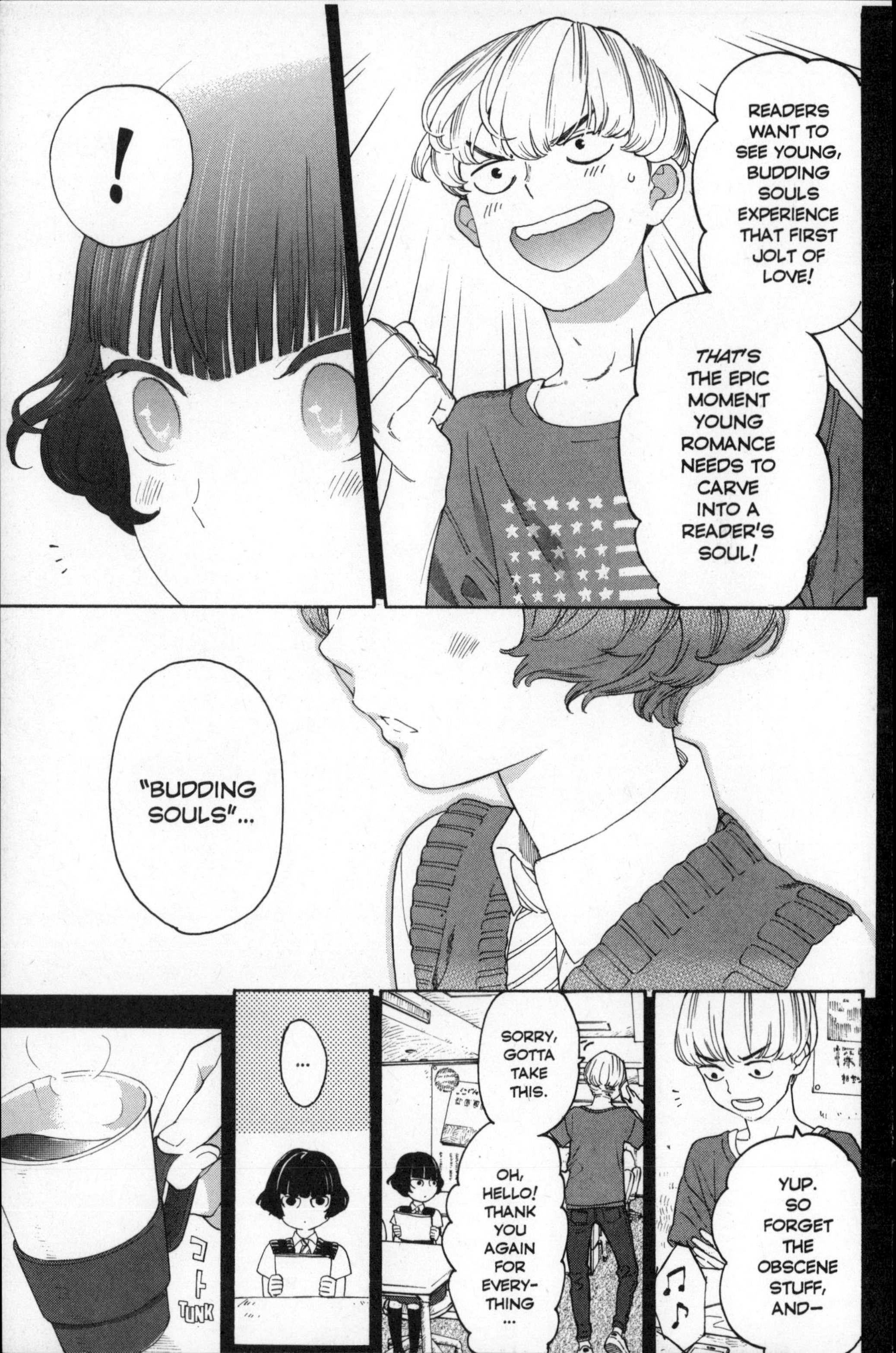
READERS WANT TO SEE YOUNG, BUDDING SOULS EXPERIENCE THAT FIRST JOLT OF LOVE!
THAT'S THE EPIC MOMENT YOUNG ROMANCE NEEDS TO CARVE INTO A READER'S SOUL!
!
"BUDDING SOULS"...
YUP. SO FORGET THE OBSCENE STUFF, AND—
SORRY, GOTTA TAKE THIS.
OH, HELLO! THANK YOU AGAIN FOR EVERY-THING...
...
コト
TUNK

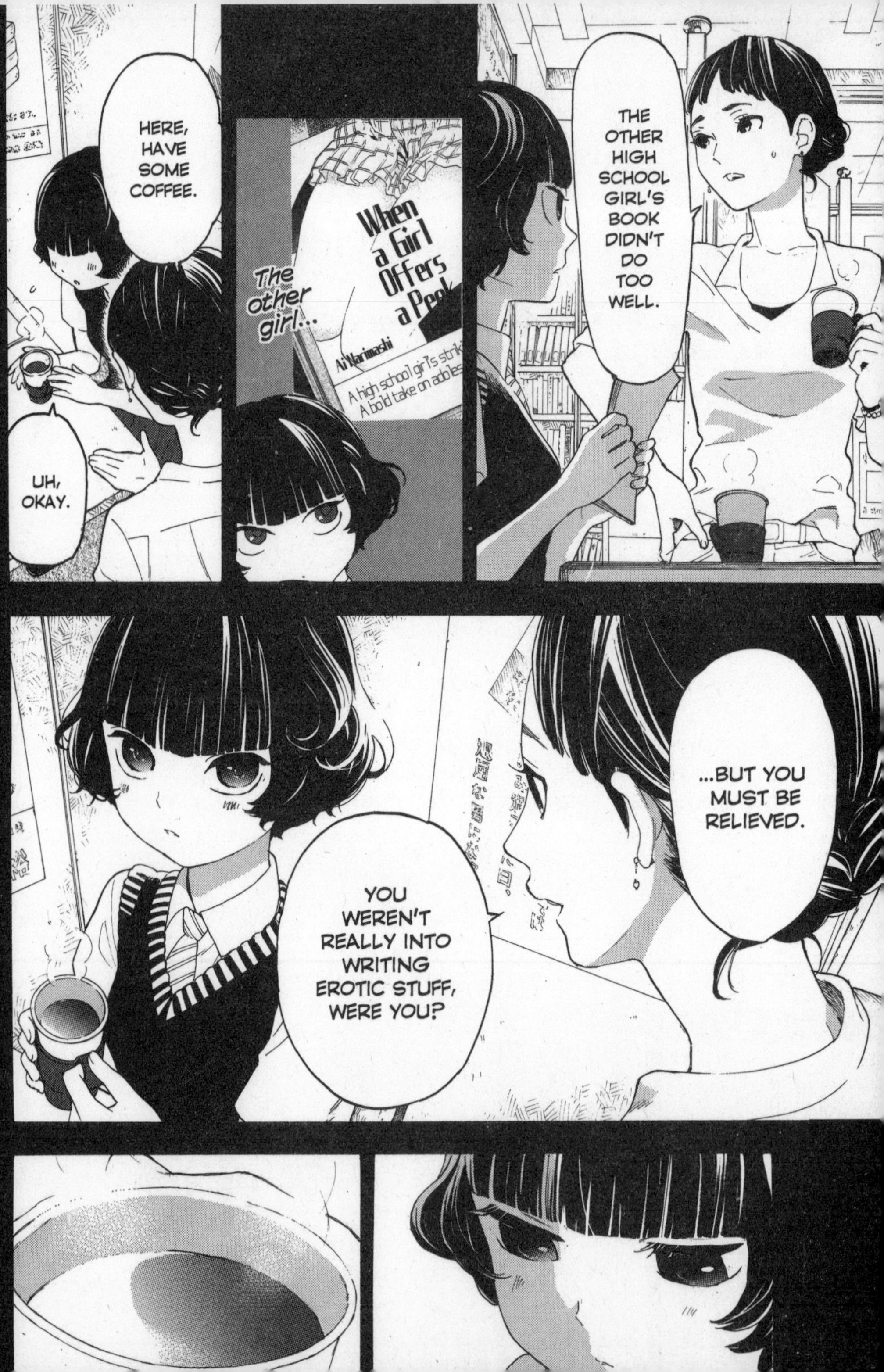
THE OTHER HIGH SCHOOL GIRL'S BOOK DIDN'T DO TOO WELL.
When a Girl Offers a Peek
Ai Narimashi
The other girl...
HERE, HAVE SOME COFFEE.
UH, OKAY.
...BUT YOU MUST BE RELIEVED.
YOU WEREN'T REALLY INTO WRITING EROTIC STUFF, WERE YOU?

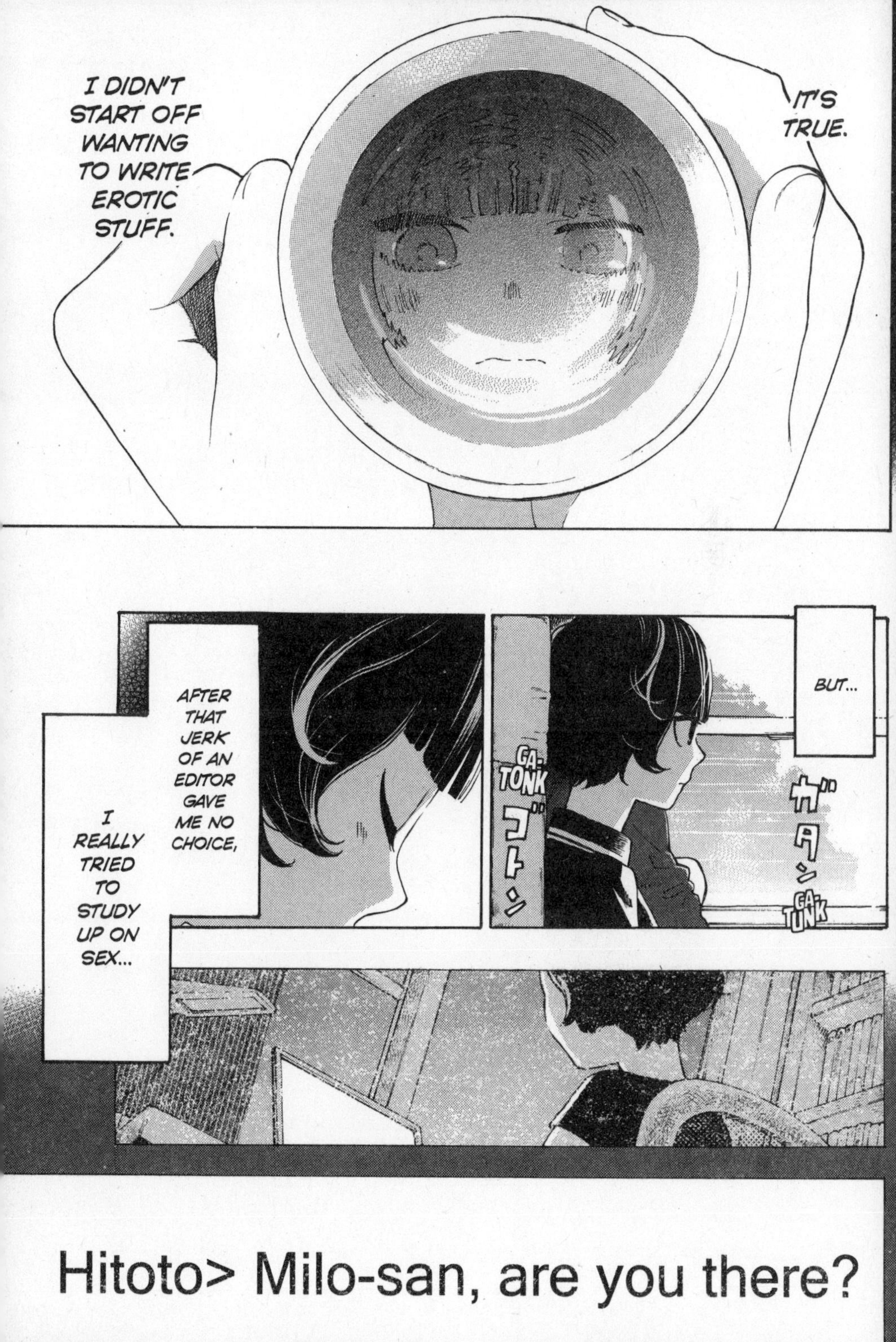
IT'S TRUE.
I DIDN'T START OFF WANTING TO WRITE EROTIC STUFF.
BUT...
ガタン
GA-TUNK
ゴトン
GA-TONK
AFTER THAT JERK OF AN EDITOR GAVE ME NO CHOICE,
I REALLY TRIED TO STUDY UP ON SEX...
Hitoto> Milo-san, are you there?

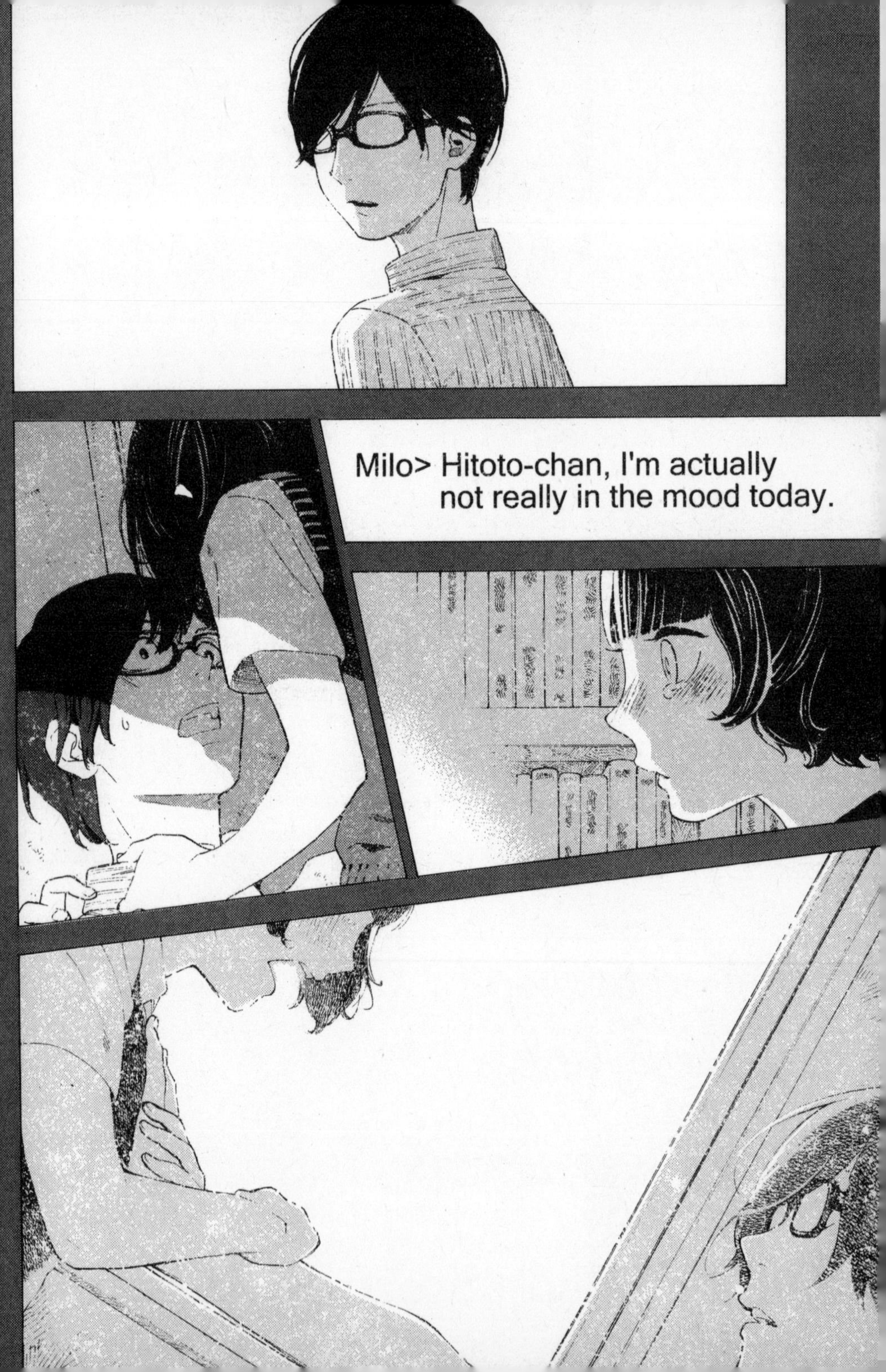
Milo> Hitoto-chan, I'm actually not really in the mood today.

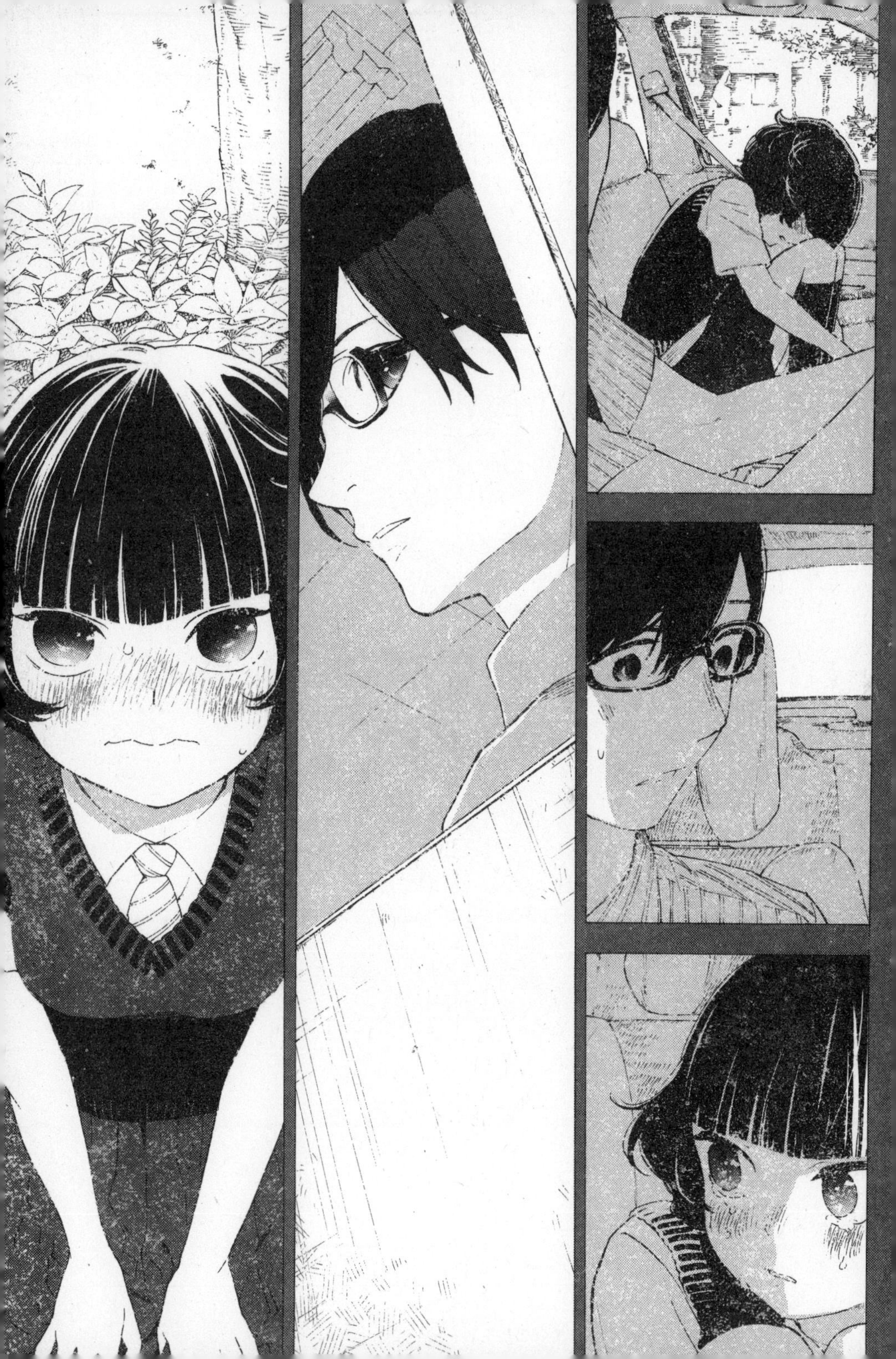

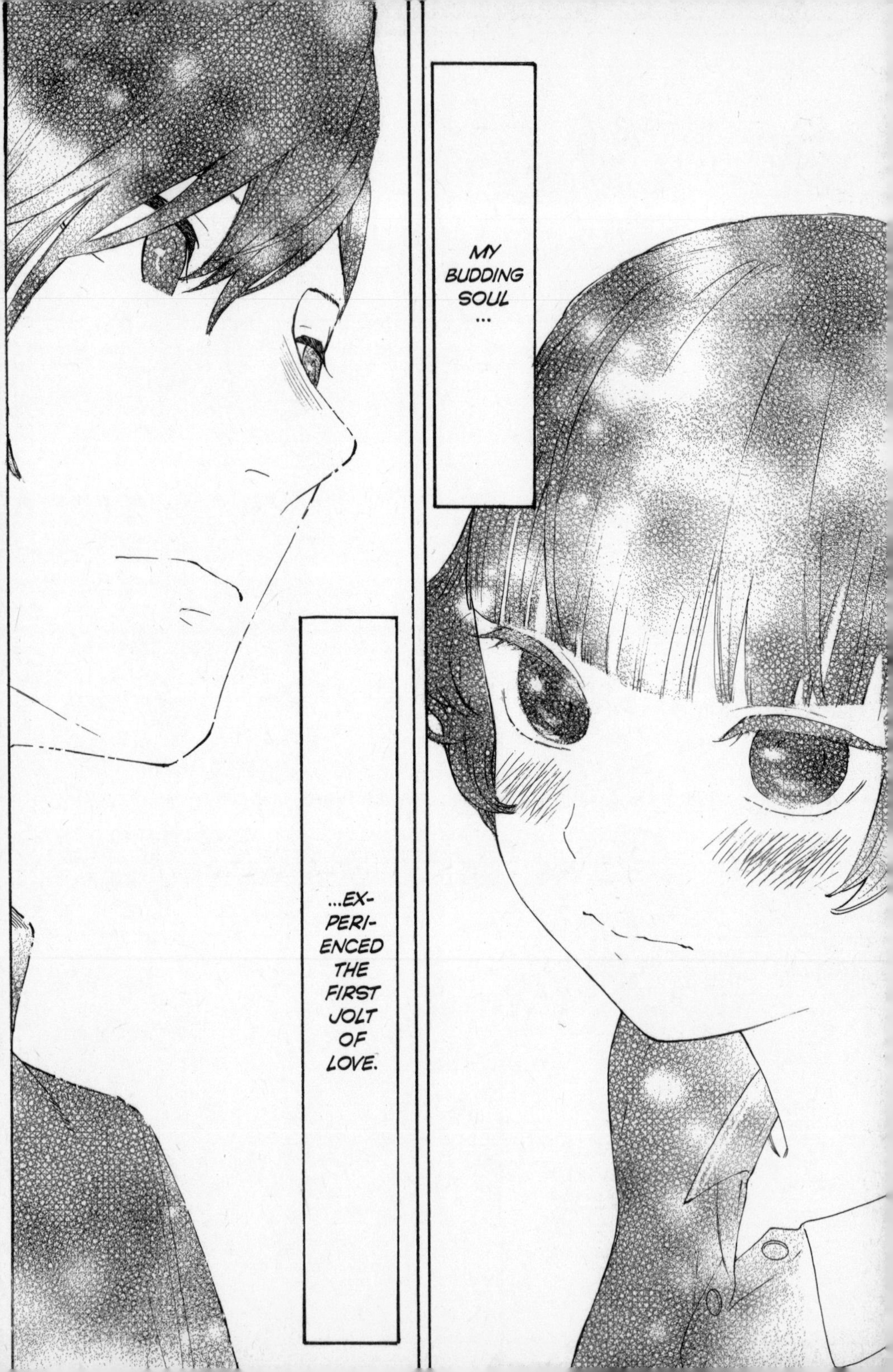
MY BUDDING SOUL ...
...EX-PERI-ENCED THE FIRST JOLT OF LOVE.

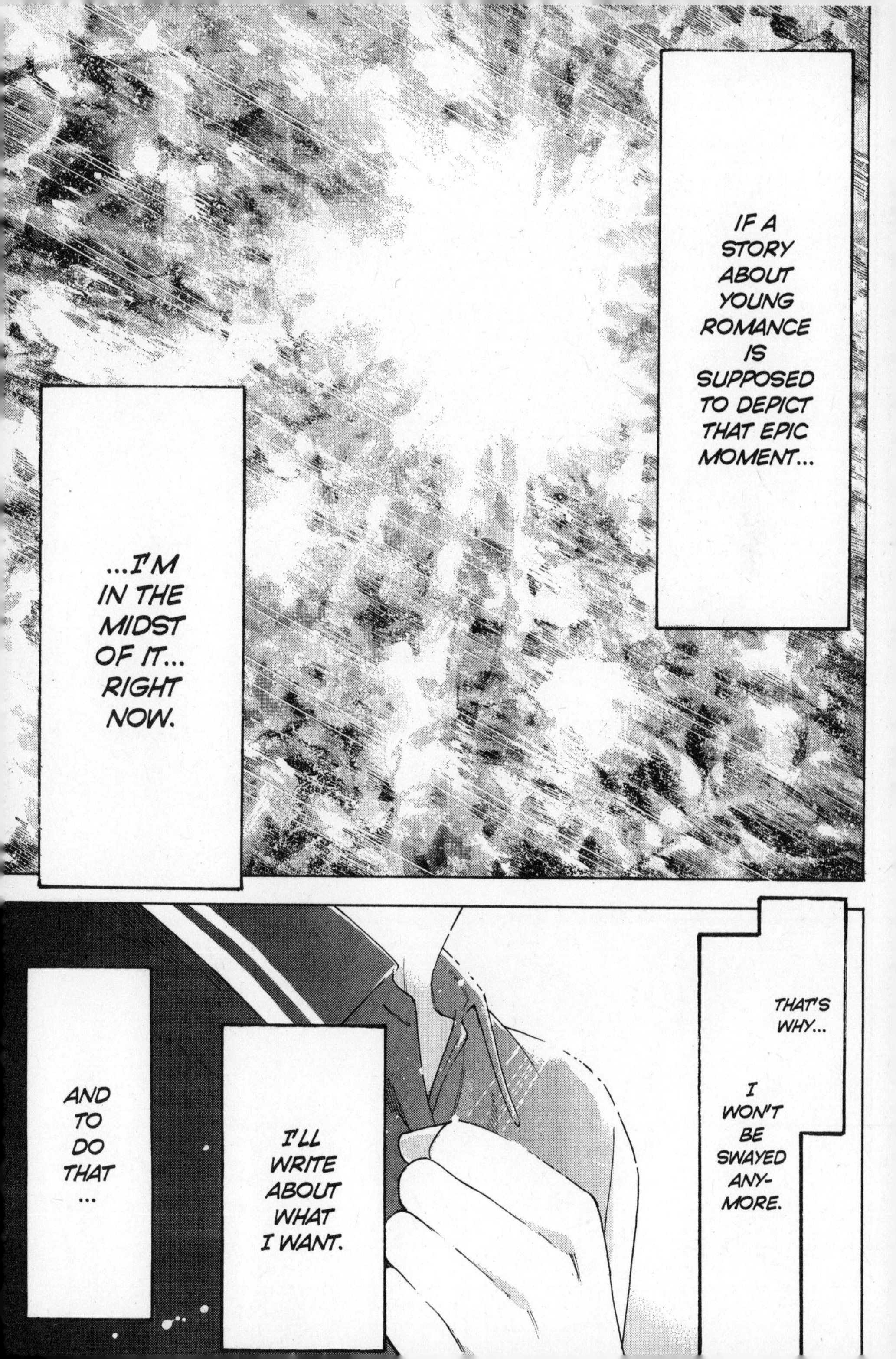
IF A STORY ABOUT YOUNG ROMANCE IS SUPPOSED TO DEPICT THAT EPIC MOMENT...
...I'M IN THE MIDST OF IT... RIGHT NOW.
THAT'S WHY...
I WON'T BE SWAYED ANY-MORE.
I'LL WRITE ABOUT WHAT I WANT.
AND TO DO THAT ...

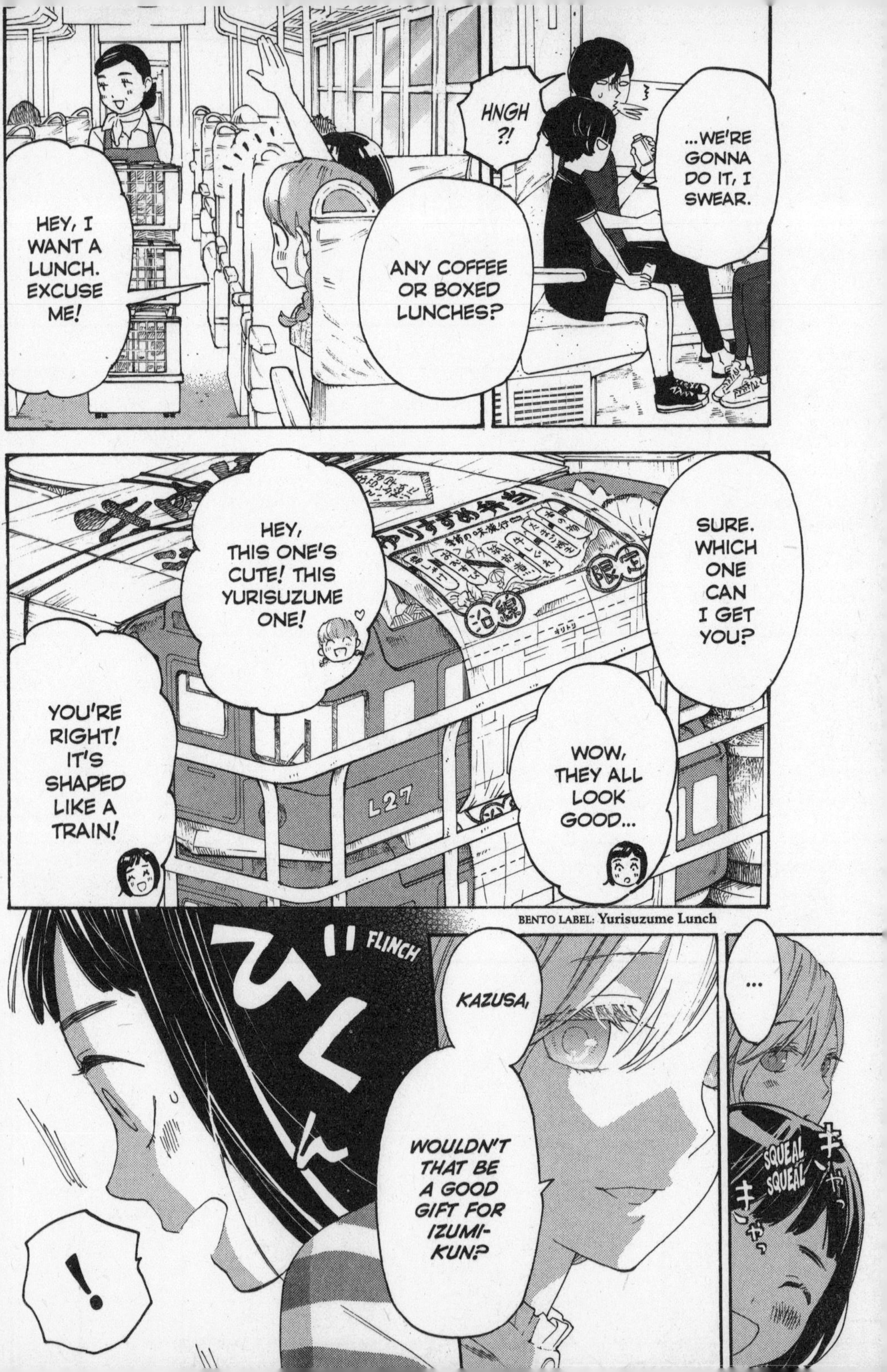
...WE'RE GONNA DO IT, I SWEAR.
HNGH ?!
ANY COFFEE OR BOXED LUNCHES?
HEY, I WANT A LUNCH. EXCUSE ME!
SURE. WHICH ONE CAN I GET YOU?
HEY, THIS ONE'S CUTE! THIS YURISUZUME ONE!
WOW, THEY ALL LOOK GOOD...
YOU'RE RIGHT! IT'S SHAPED LIKE A TRAIN!
...
SQUEAL SQUEAL
KAZUSA,
WOULDN'T THAT BE A GOOD GIFT FOR IZUMI-KUN?
FLINCH
!

BENTO LABEL: Yurisuzume Lunch

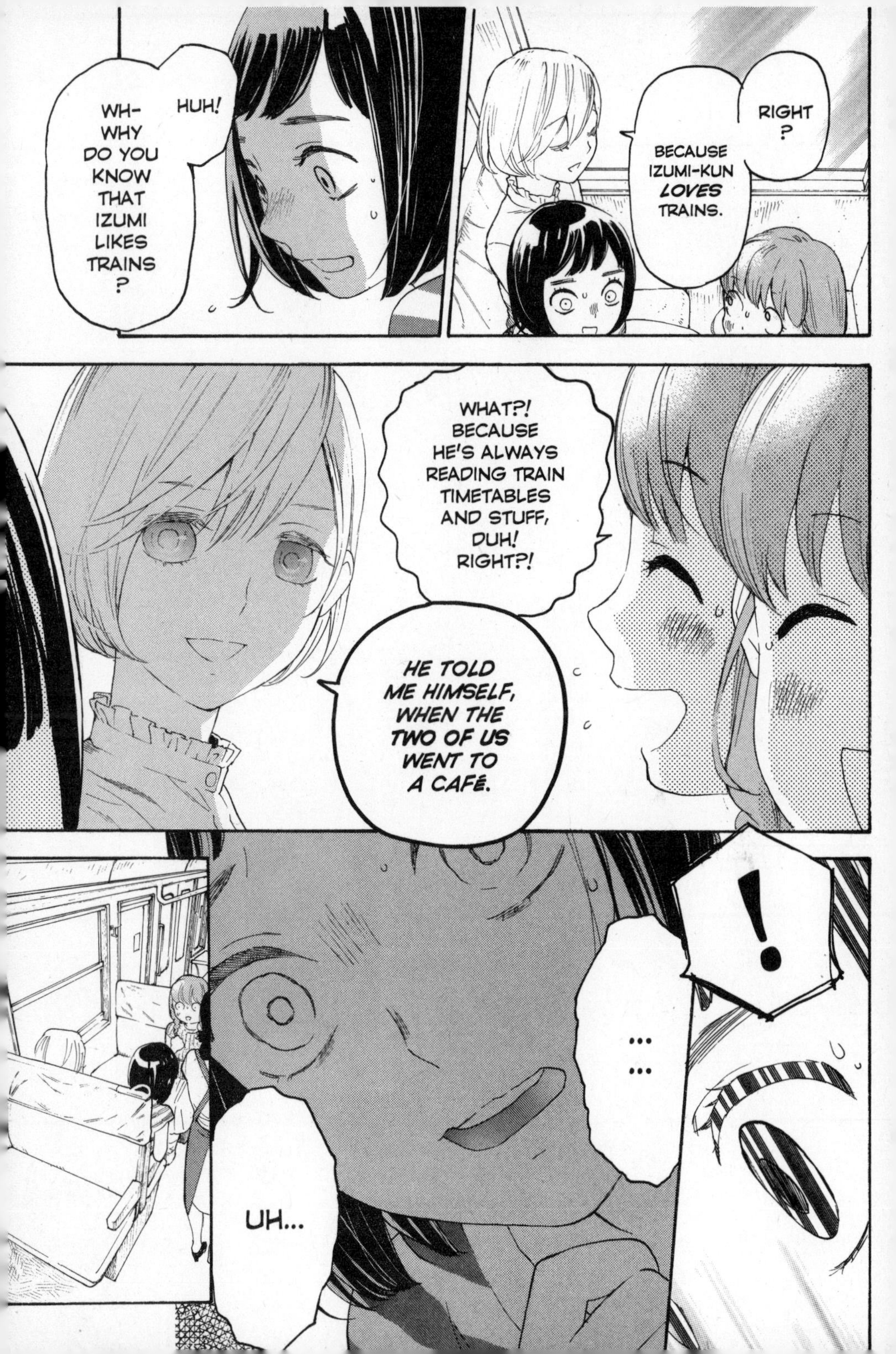
RIGHT?
BECAUSE IZUMI-KUN *LOVES* TRAINS.
HUH!
WH- WHY DO YOU KNOW THAT IZUMI LIKES TRAINS?
WHAT?! BECAUSE HE'S ALWAYS READING TRAIN TIMETABLES AND STUFF, DUH! RIGHT?!
HE TOLD ME HIMSELF, WHEN THE TWO OF US WENT TO A CAFÉ.
!
… …
UH...

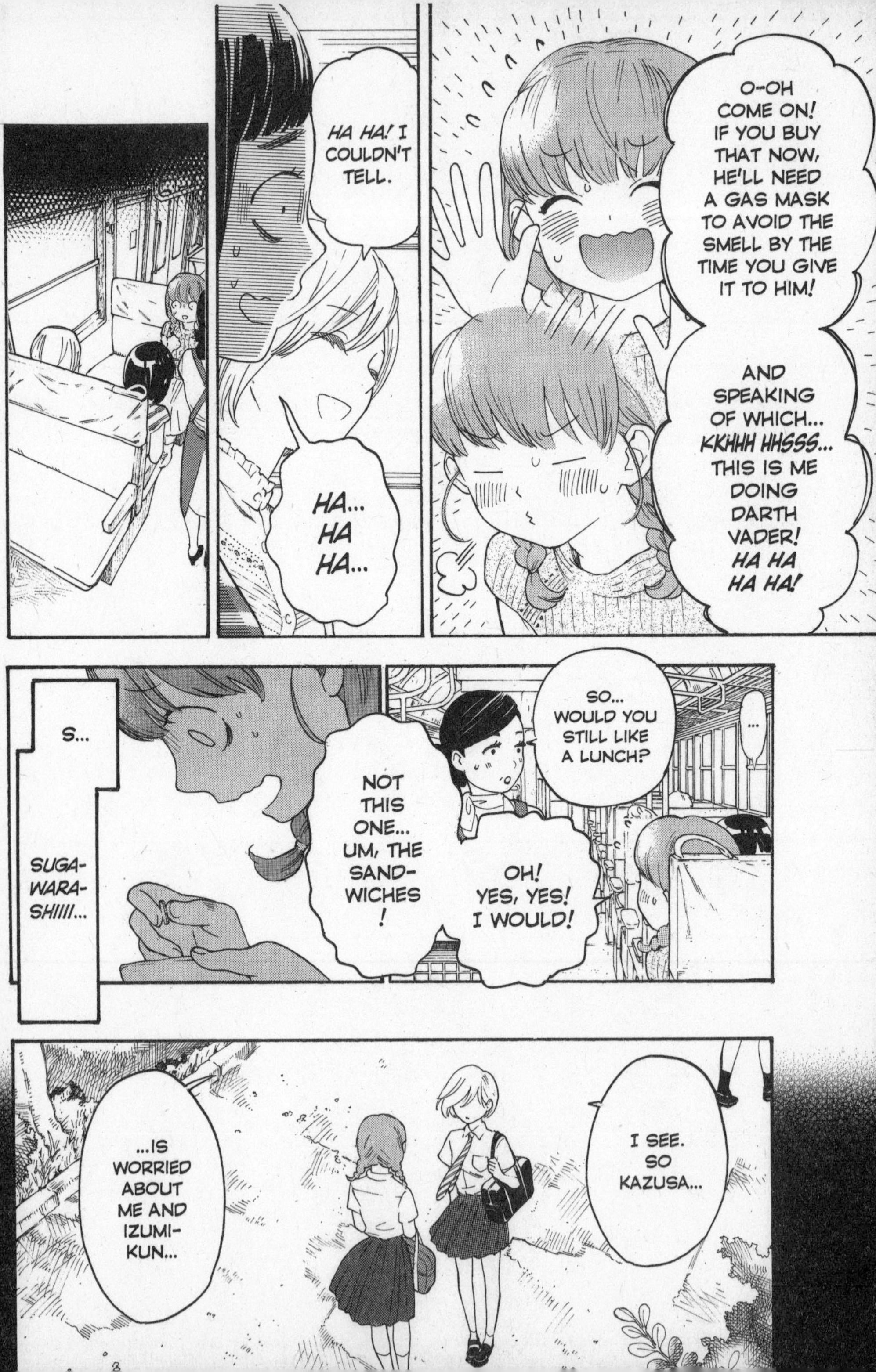
O-OH COME ON! IF YOU BUY THAT NOW, HE'LL NEED A GAS MASK TO AVOID THE SMELL BY THE TIME YOU GIVE IT TO HIM!
AND SPEAKING OF WHICH... KKHHH HHSSS... THIS IS ME DOING DARTH VADER! HA HA HA HA!
HA HA! I COULDN'T TELL.
HA... HA HA...
...
SO... WOULD YOU STILL LIKE A LUNCH?
OH! YES, YES! I WOULD!
NOT THIS ONE... UM, THE SAND-WICHES!
S...
SUGA-WARA-SHIIII...
I SEE. SO KAZUSA...
...IS WORRIED ABOUT ME AND IZUMI-KUN...

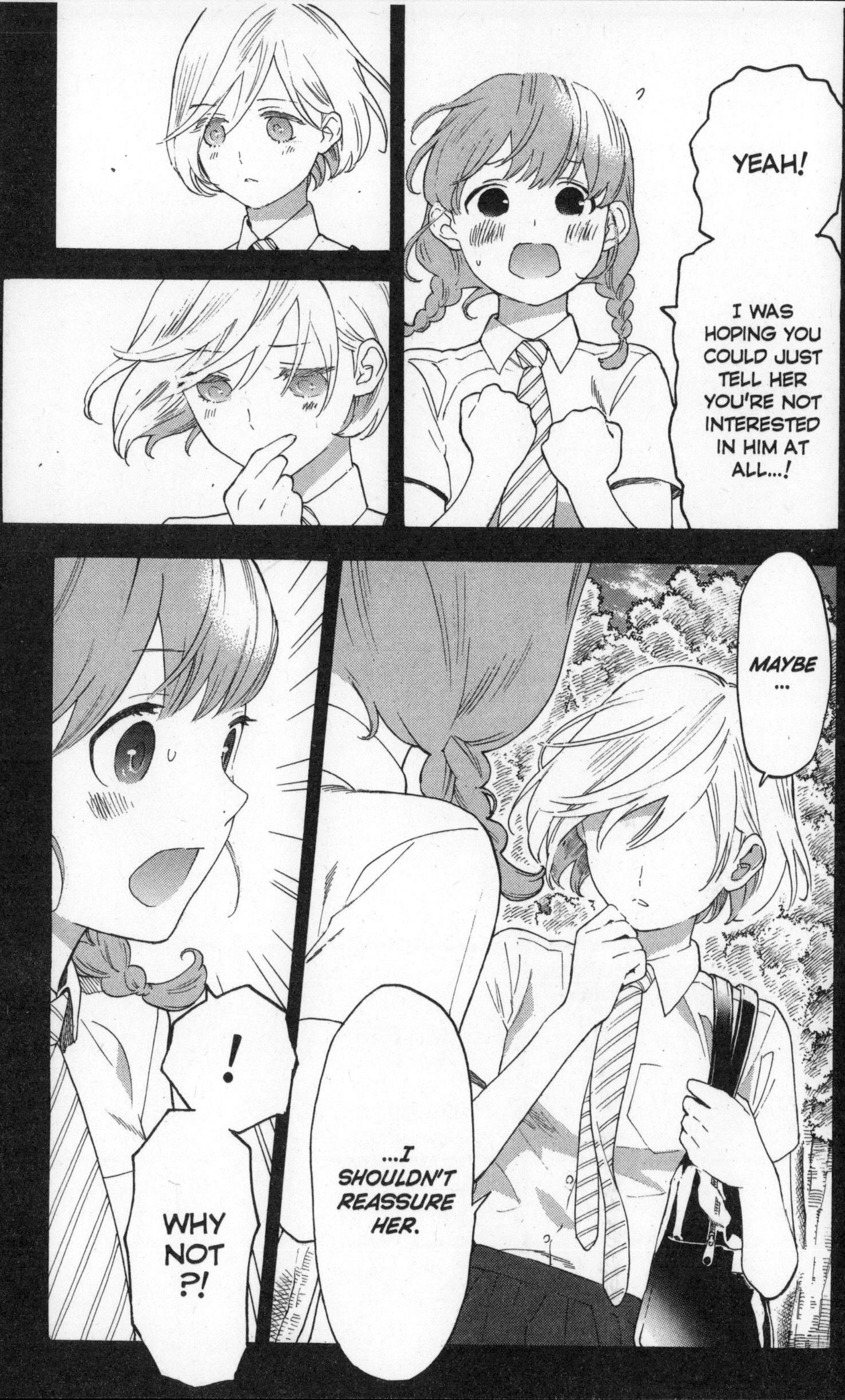
YEAH!
I WAS HOPING YOU COULD JUST TELL HER YOU'RE NOT INTERESTED IN HIM AT ALL...!
MAYBE...
...I SHOULDN'T REASSURE HER.
!
WHY NOT?!

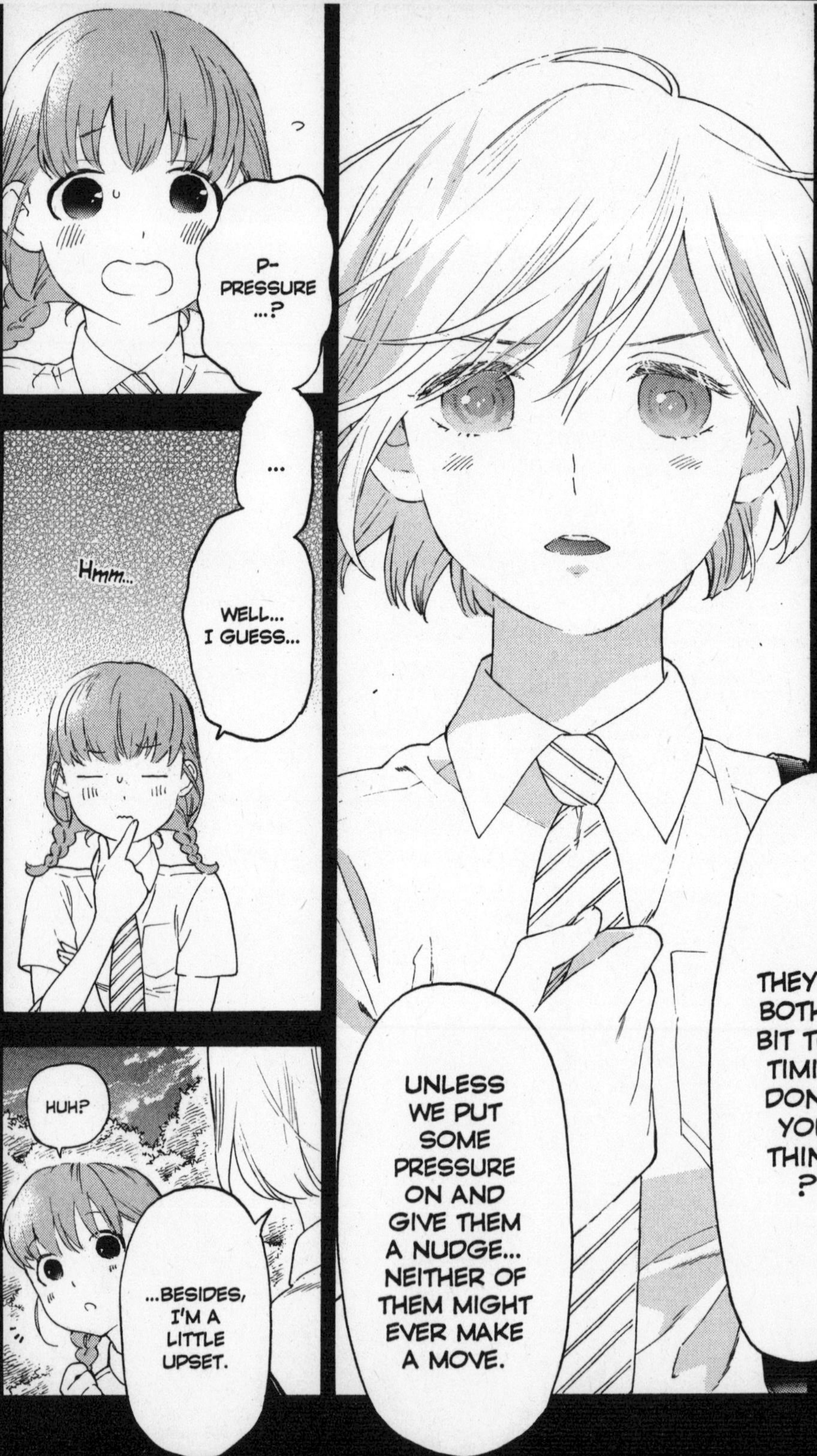

THEY'RE BOTH A BIT TOO TIMID, DON'T YOU THINK?
UNLESS WE PUT SOME PRESSURE ON AND GIVE THEM A NUDGE... NEITHER OF THEM MIGHT EVER MAKE A MOVE.
P-PRESSURE ...?
...
Hmm...
WELL... I GUESS...
HUH?
...BESIDES, I'M A LITTLE UPSET.

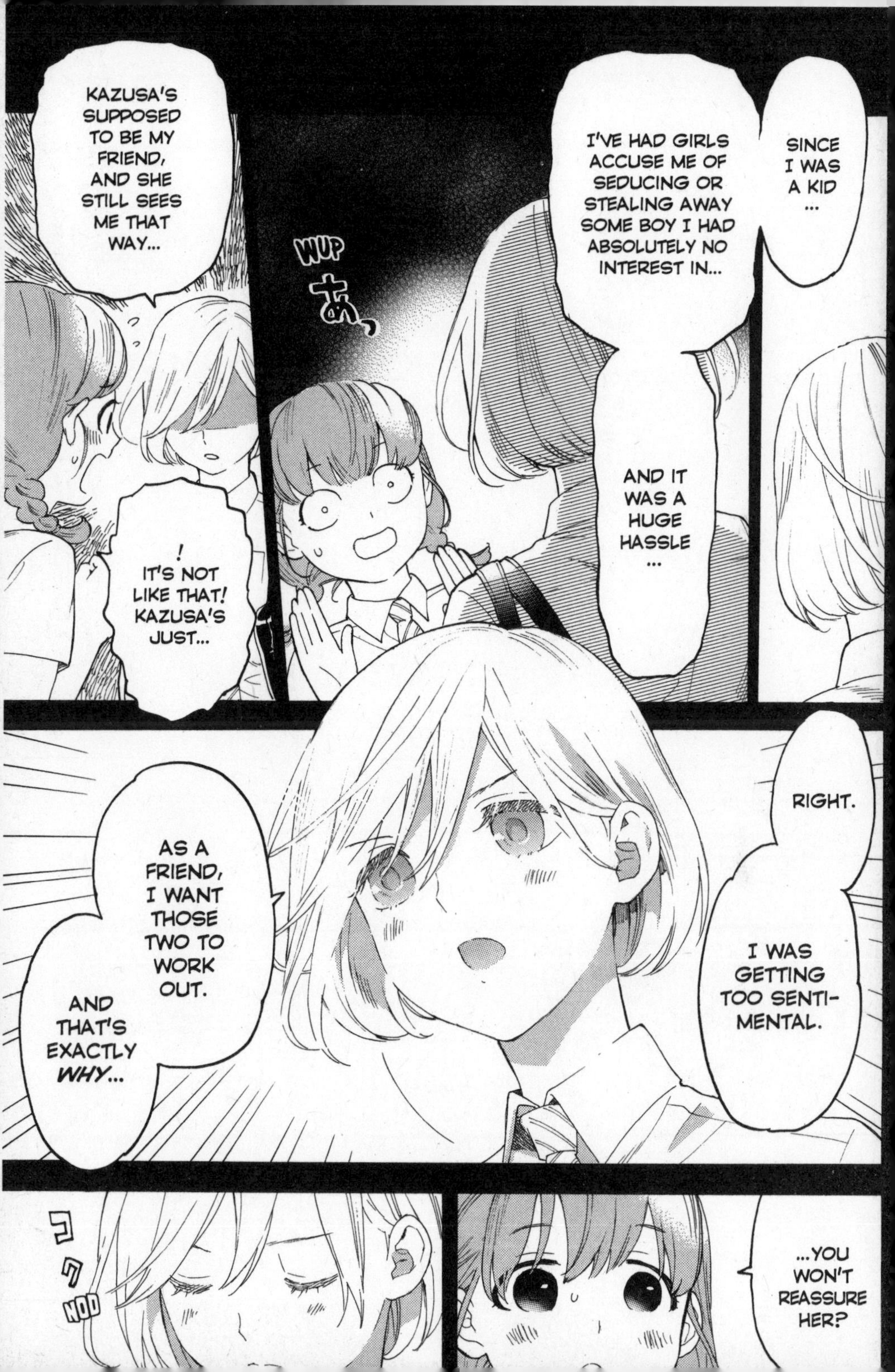
SINCE I WAS A KID ...
I'VE HAD GIRLS ACCUSE ME OF SEDUCING OR STEALING AWAY SOME BOY I HAD ABSOLUTELY NO INTEREST IN...
AND IT WAS A HUGE HASSLE ...
WUP
あ、
KAZUSA'S SUPPOSED TO BE MY FRIEND, AND SHE STILL SEES ME THAT WAY...
! IT'S NOT LIKE THAT! KAZUSA'S JUST...
RIGHT.
I WAS GETTING TOO SENTI-MENTAL.
AS A FRIEND, I WANT THOSE TWO TO WORK OUT.
AND THAT'S EXACTLY *WHY*...
...YOU WON'T REASSURE HER?
コク
NOD

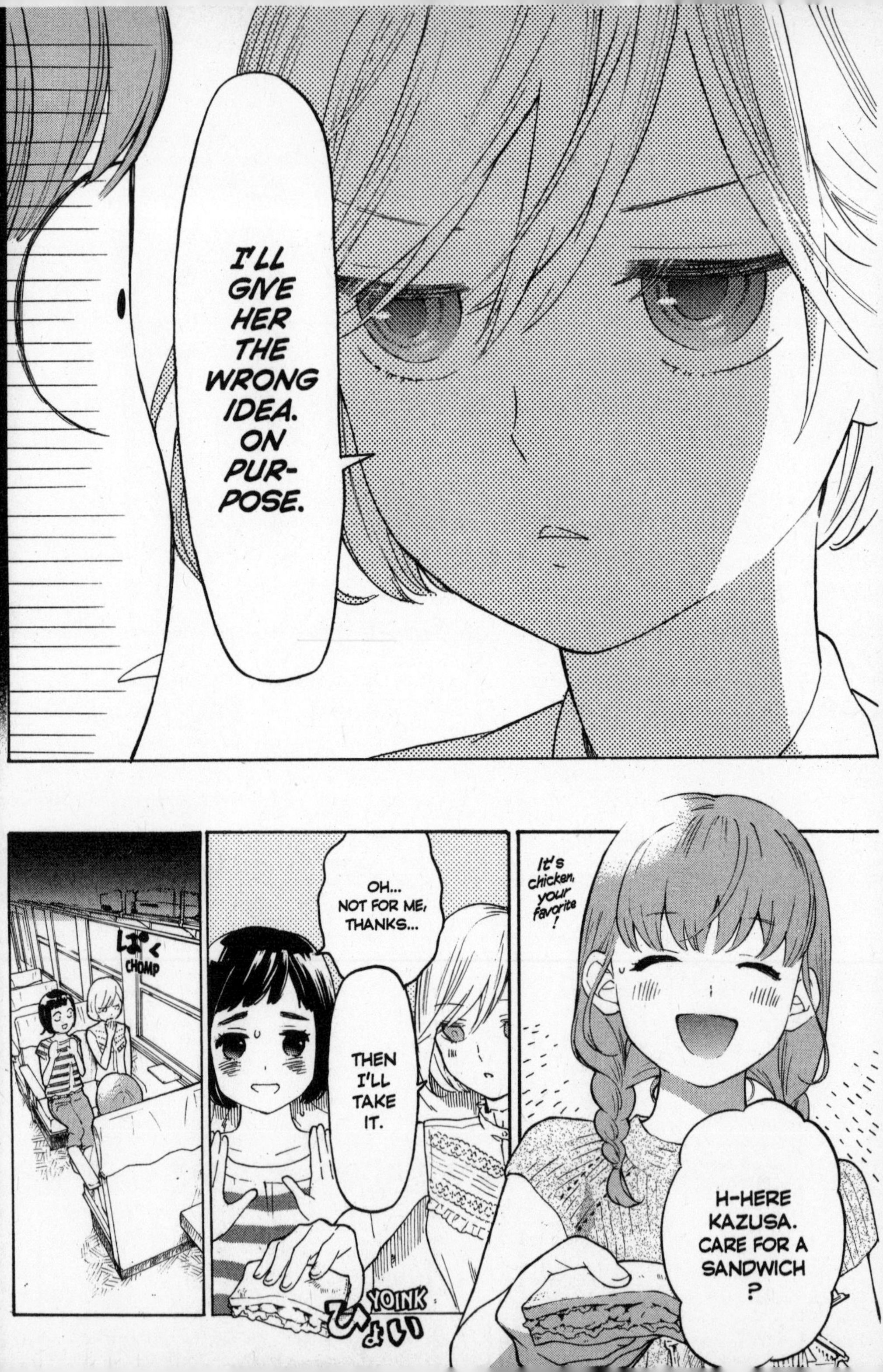
I'LL GIVE HER THE WRONG IDEA. ON PURPOSE.
H-HERE KAZUSA. CARE FOR A SANDWICH?
It's chicken, your favorite!
OH... NOT FOR ME, THANKS...
THEN I'LL TAKE IT.
ひょい
YOINK
ぱく
CHOMP

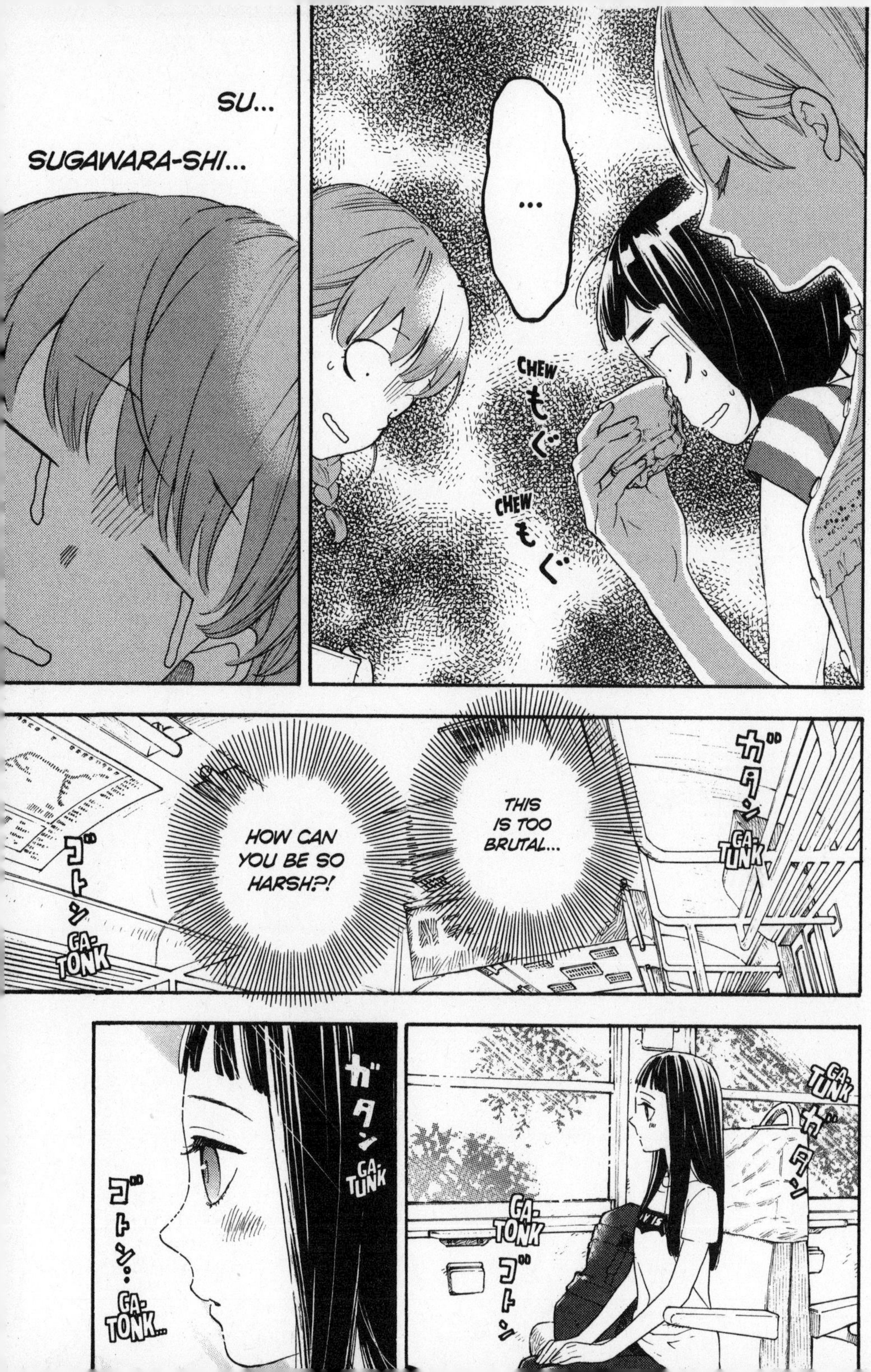
...
CHEW もぐ
CHEW もぐ
SU...
SUGAWARA-SHI...
ガタン GA-TUNK
THIS IS TOO BRUTAL...
HOW CAN YOU BE SO HARSH?!
ゴトン GA-TONK
GA-TUNK ガタン
GA-TONK ゴトン
ガタン GA-TUNK
ゴトン・・ GA-TONK...

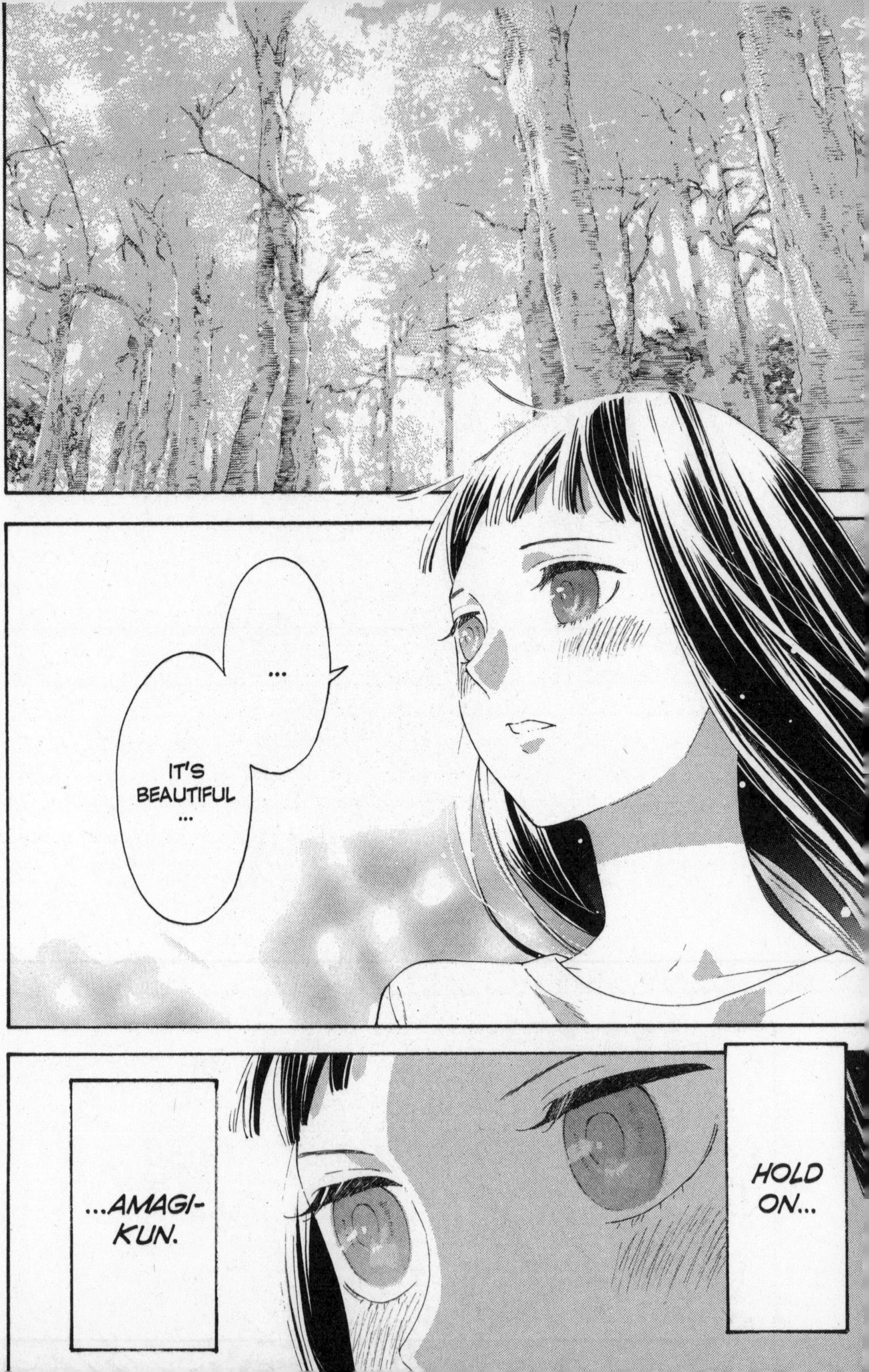
...
IT'S BEAUTIFUL ...
HOLD ON...
...AMAGI-KUN.

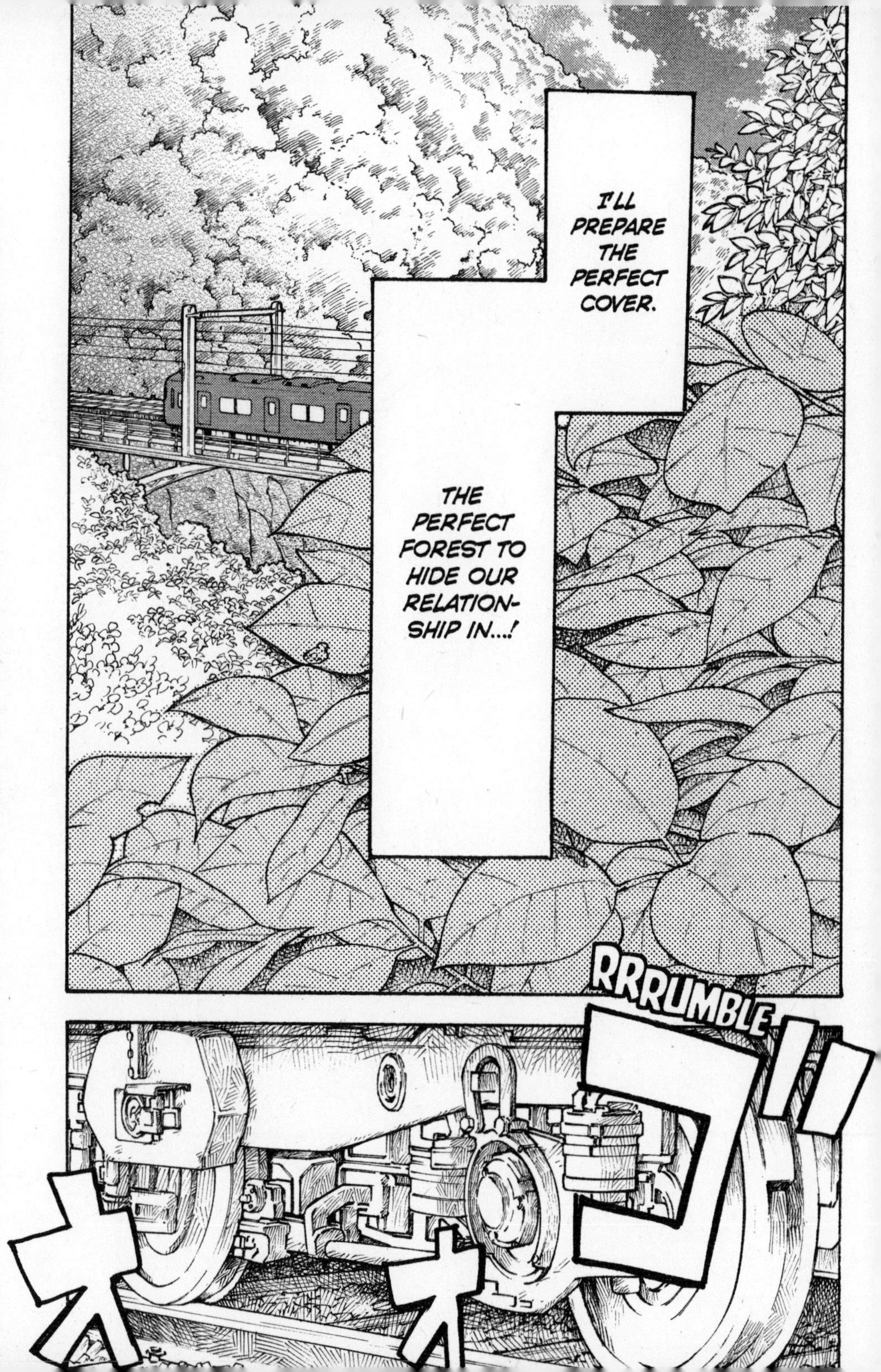
I'LL PREPARE THE PERFECT COVER.
THE PERFECT FOREST TO HIDE OUR RELATION-SHIP IN...!
RRRUMBLE
ゴ゛
オ
オ

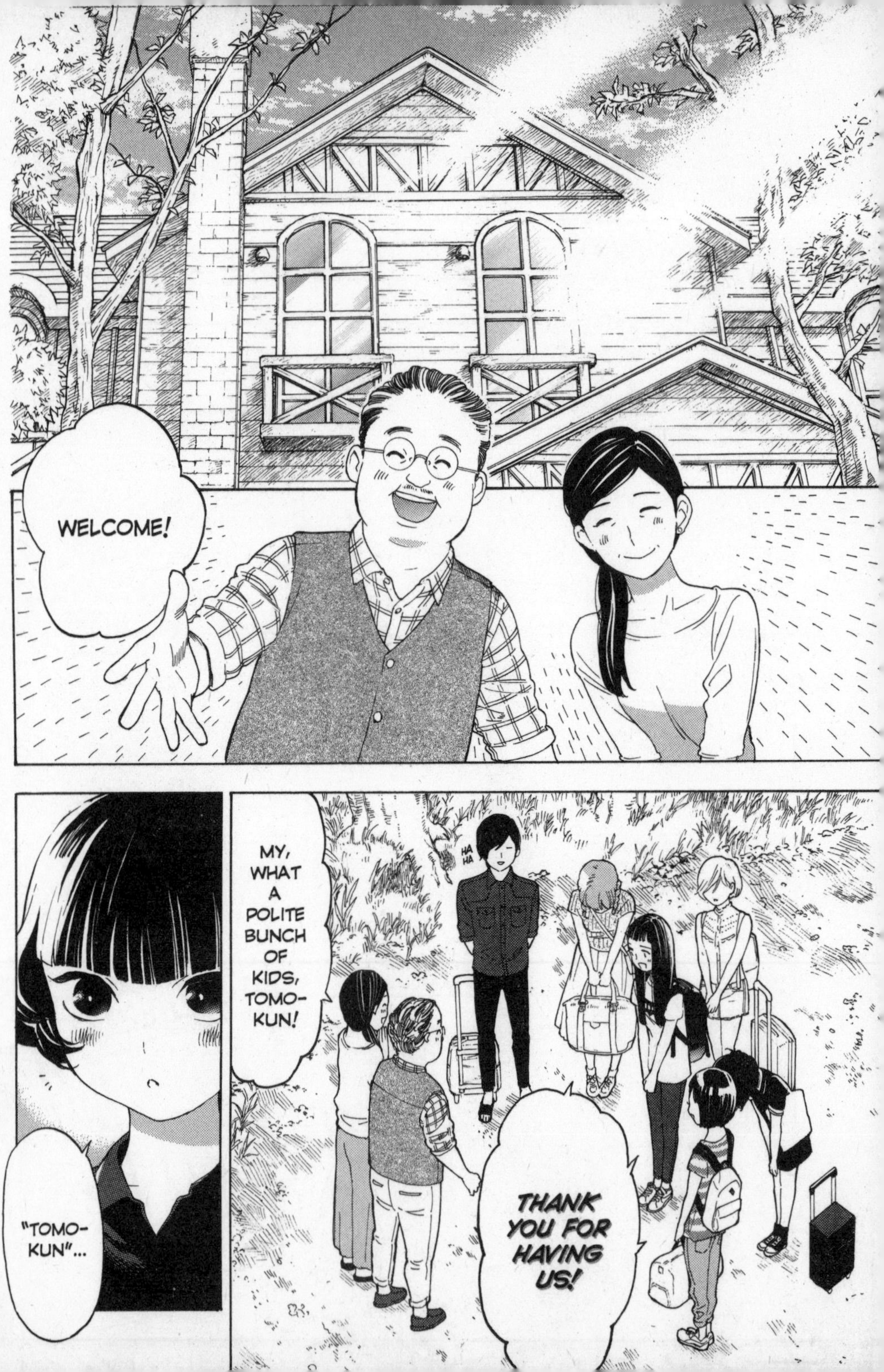
WELCOME!
HA HA
MY, WHAT A POLITE BUNCH OF KIDS, TOMO-KUN!
THANK YOU FOR HAVING US!
"TOMO-KUN"...

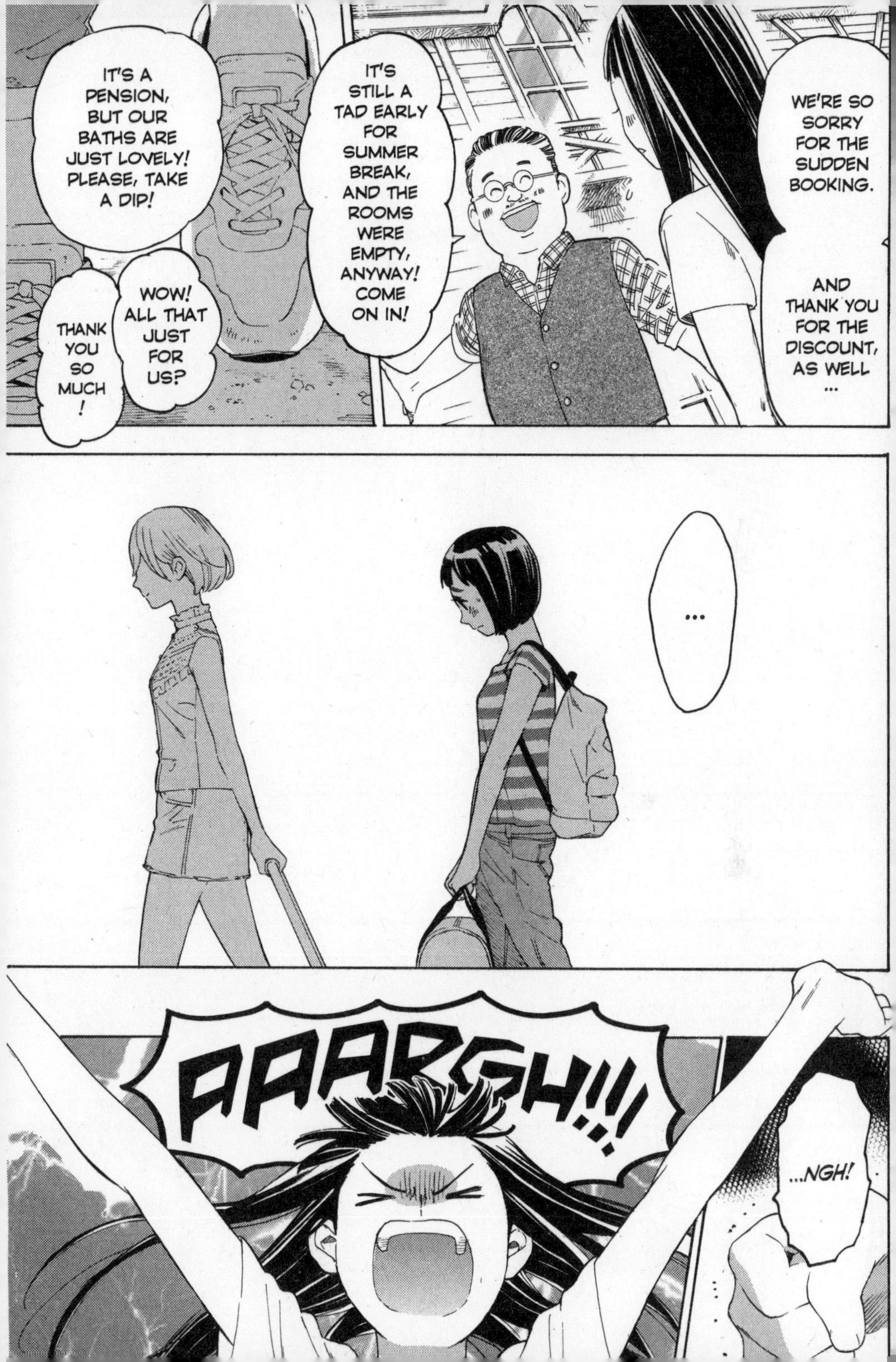
WE'RE SO SORRY FOR THE SUDDEN BOOKING.
AND THANK YOU FOR THE DISCOUNT, AS WELL ...
IT'S STILL A TAD EARLY FOR SUMMER BREAK, AND THE ROOMS WERE EMPTY, ANYWAY! COME ON IN!
IT'S A PENSION, BUT OUR BATHS ARE JUST LOVELY! PLEASE, TAKE A DIP!
WOW! ALL THAT JUST FOR US?
THANK YOU SO MUCH!
...
AAARGH!!!
...NGH!

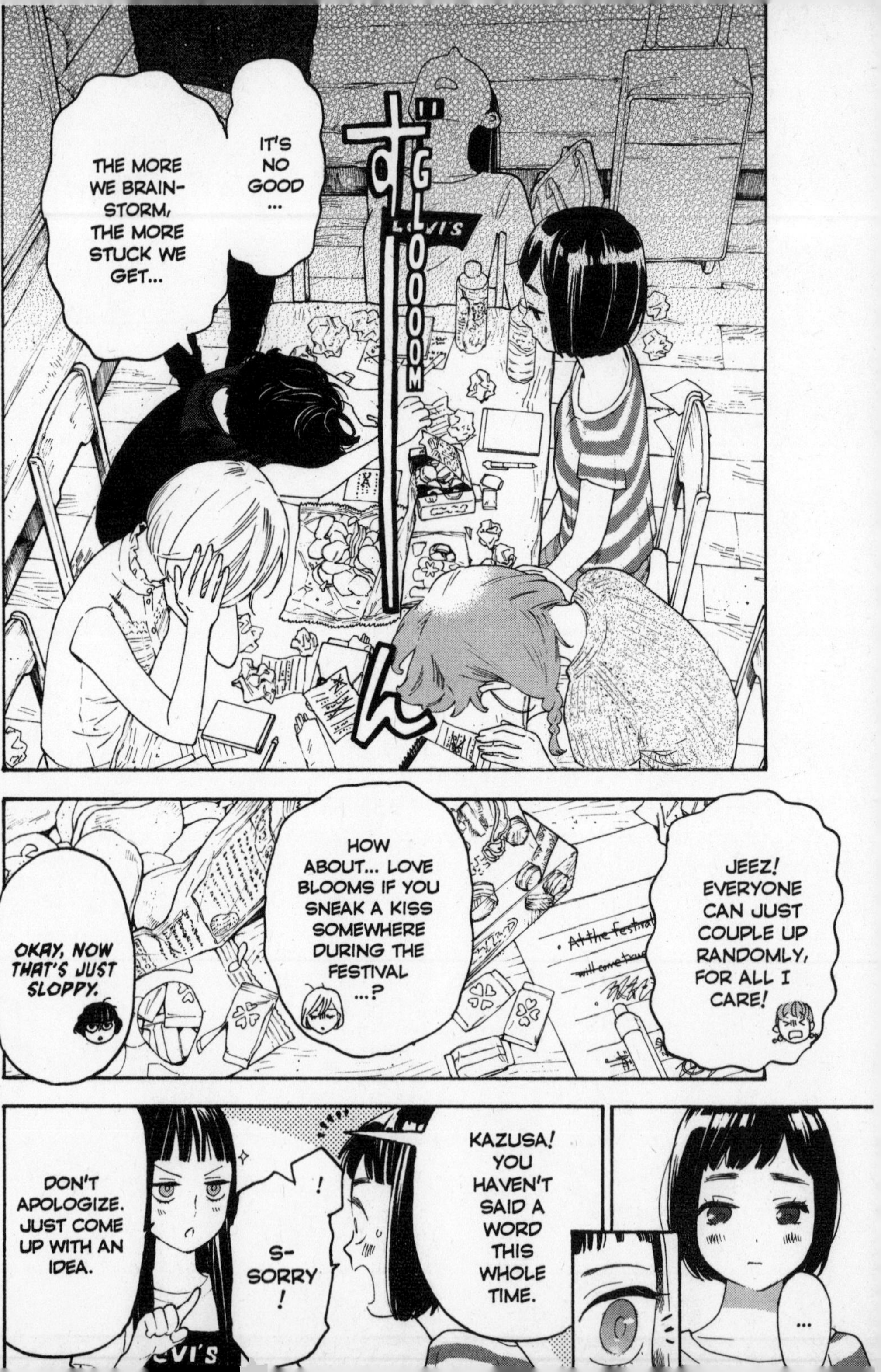
IT'S NO GOOD...
THE MORE WE BRAIN-STORM, THE MORE STUCK WE GET...
GLOOOOOM
JEEZ! EVERYONE CAN JUST COUPLE UP RANDOMLY, FOR ALL I CARE!
HOW ABOUT... LOVE BLOOMS IF YOU SNEAK A KISS SOMEWHERE DURING THE FESTIVAL ...?
OKAY, NOW THAT'S JUST SLOPPY.
...
KAZUSA! YOU HAVEN'T SAID A WORD THIS WHOLE TIME.
!
S-SORRY!
DON'T APOLOGIZE. JUST COME UP WITH AN IDEA.

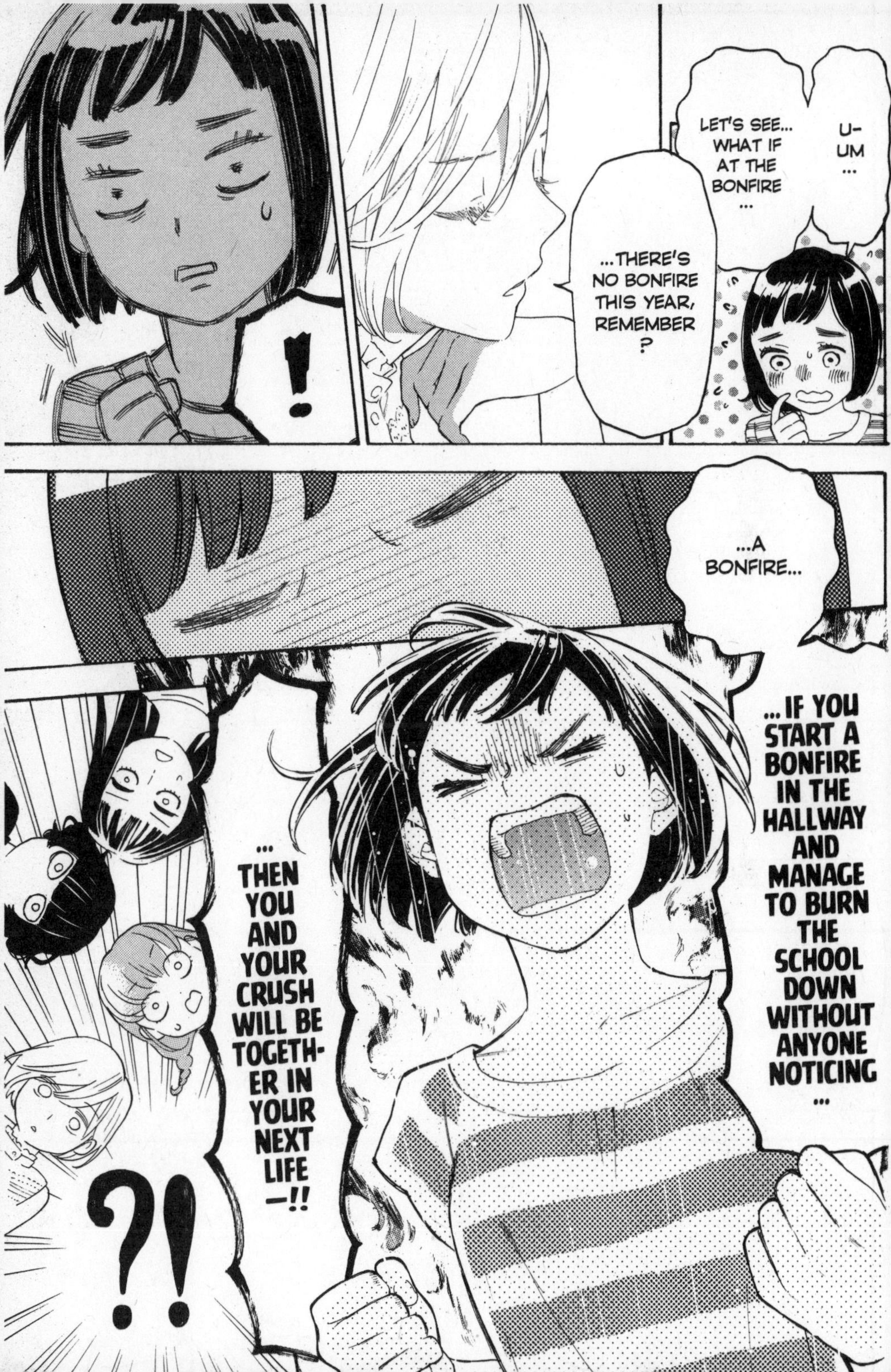
U-UM...
LET'S SEE... WHAT IF AT THE BONFIRE...
...THERE'S NO BONFIRE THIS YEAR, REMEMBER?
!
...A BONFIRE...
...IF YOU START A BONFIRE IN THE HALLWAY AND MANAGE TO BURN THE SCHOOL DOWN WITHOUT ANYONE NOTICING...
...THEN YOU AND YOUR CRUSH WILL BE TOGETH-ER IN YOUR NEXT LIFE—!!
?!

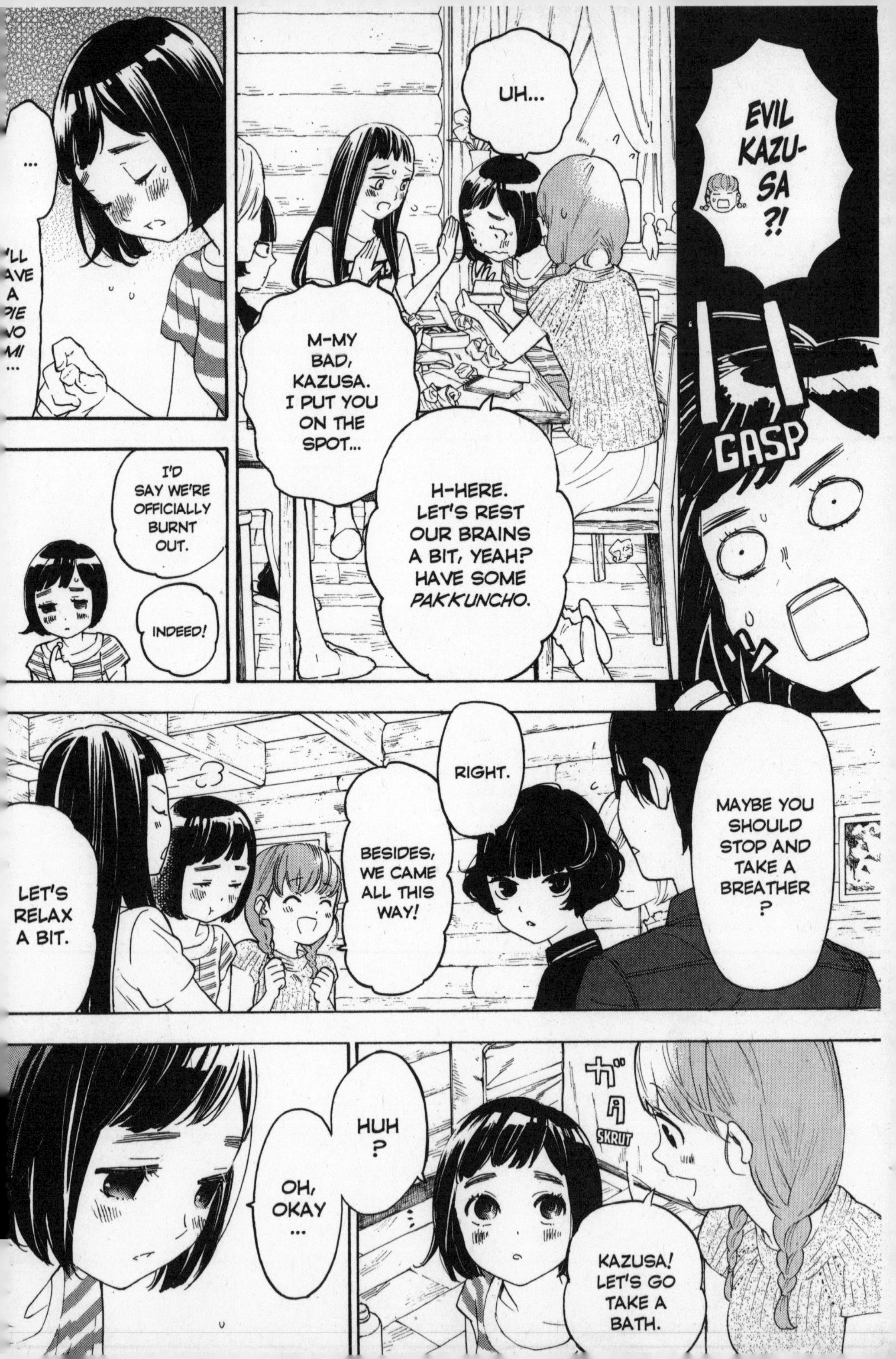

EVIL KAZUSA?!
GASP
UH...
M-MY BAD, KAZUSA. I PUT YOU ON THE SPOT...
H-HERE. LET'S REST OUR BRAINS A BIT, YEAH? HAVE SOME *PAKKUNCHO*.
...
'LL AVE A PIE NO MI ...
I'D SAY WE'RE OFFICIALLY BURNT OUT.
INDEED!
MAYBE YOU SHOULD STOP AND TAKE A BREATHER?
RIGHT.
BESIDES, WE CAME ALL THIS WAY!
LET'S RELAX A BIT.
ガタ
SKRUT
KAZUSA! LET'S GO TAKE A BATH.
HUH?
OH, OKAY...

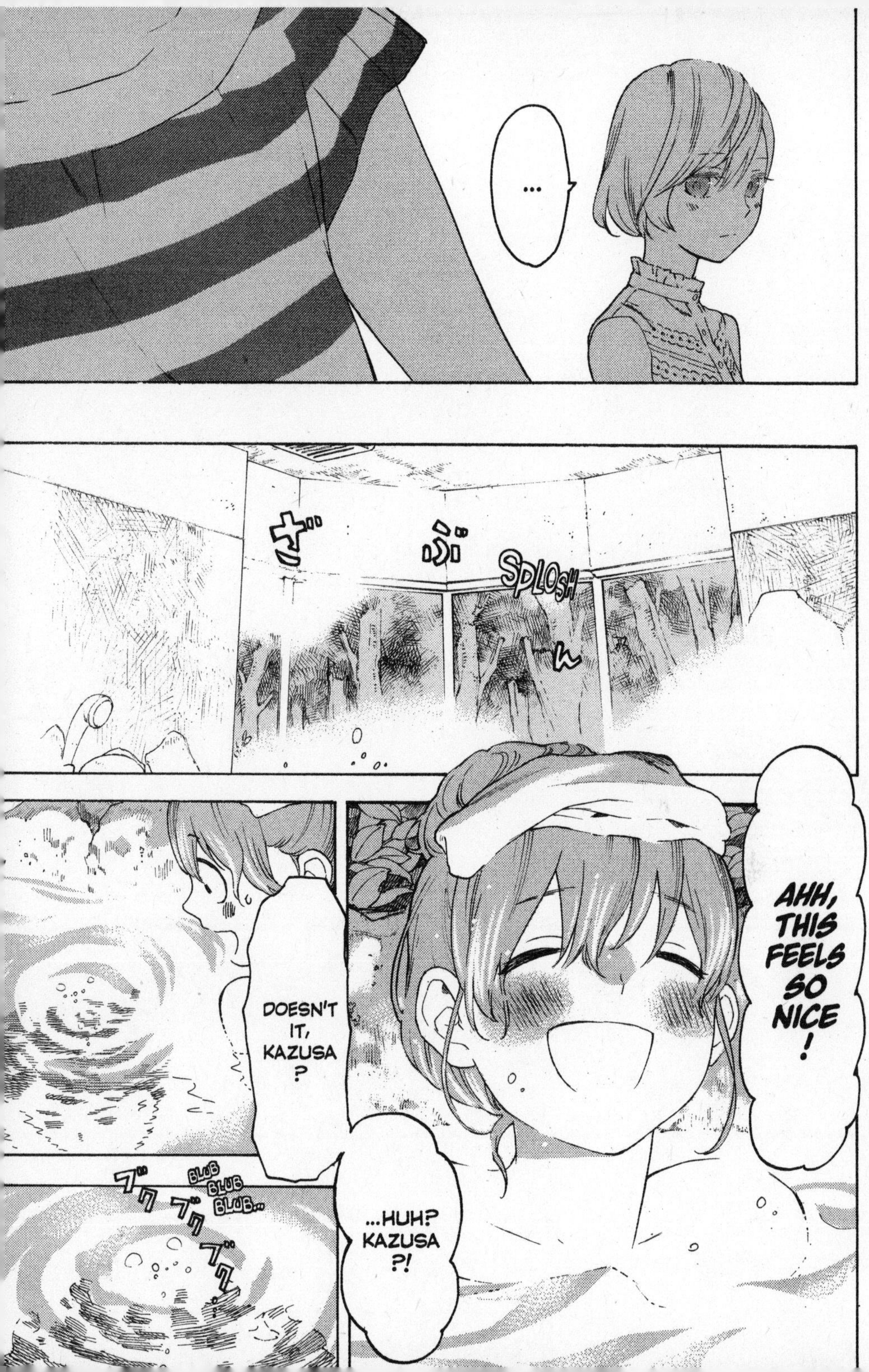
...
ざぶ
SPLOSH
ん
AHH, THIS FEELS SO NICE!
DOESN'T IT, KAZUSA?
...HUH? KAZUSA?!
ブクブクブク
BLUB BLUB BLUB...

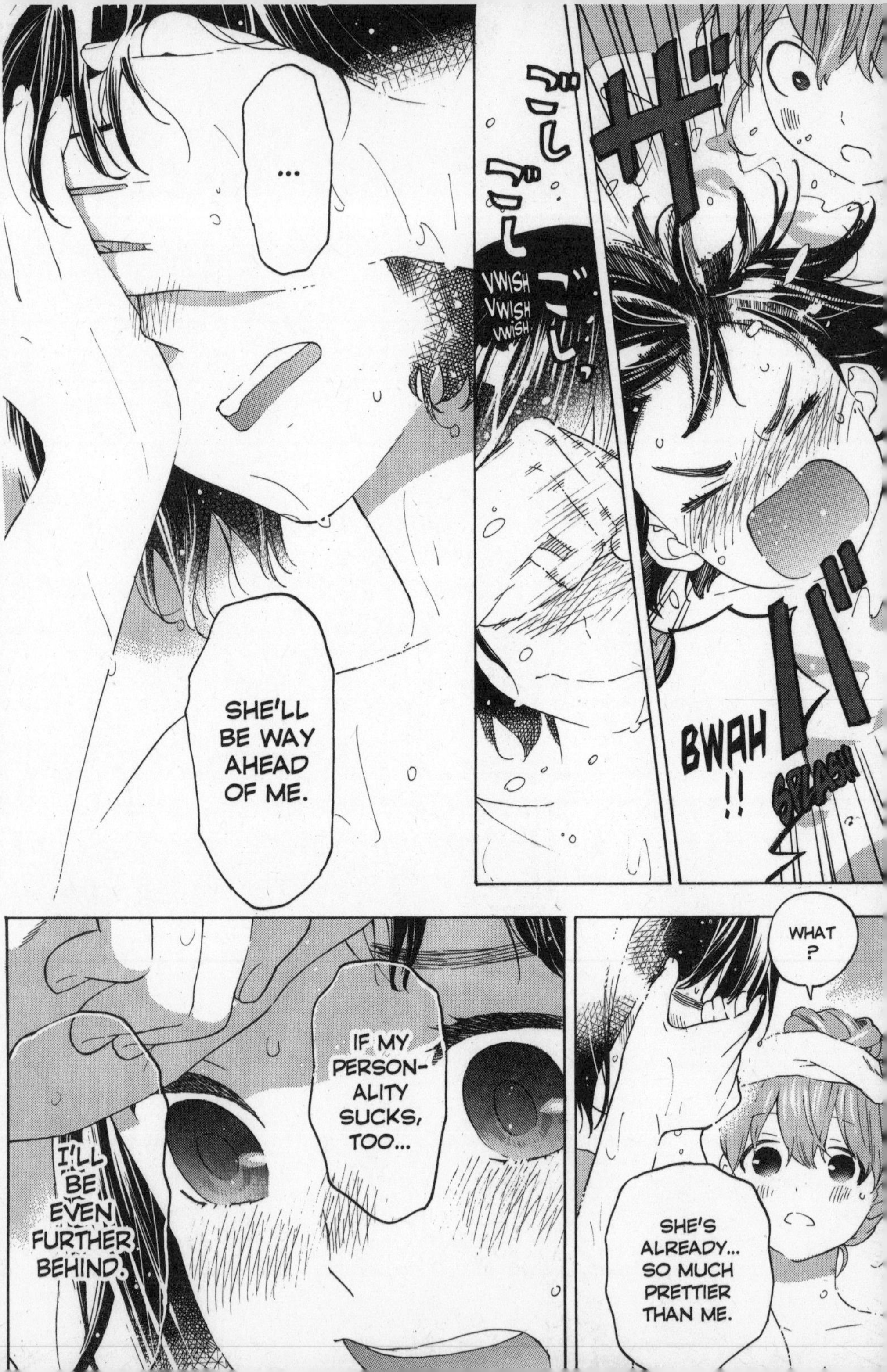
ザ
BWAH!!
バ
SPLASH
ごしごしごし
VWISH
VWISH
VWISH
...
SHE'LL BE WAY AHEAD OF ME.
WHAT?
SHE'S ALREADY... SO MUCH PRETTIER THAN ME.
IF MY PERSON-ALITY SUCKS, TOO...
I'LL BE EVEN FURTHER BEHIND.

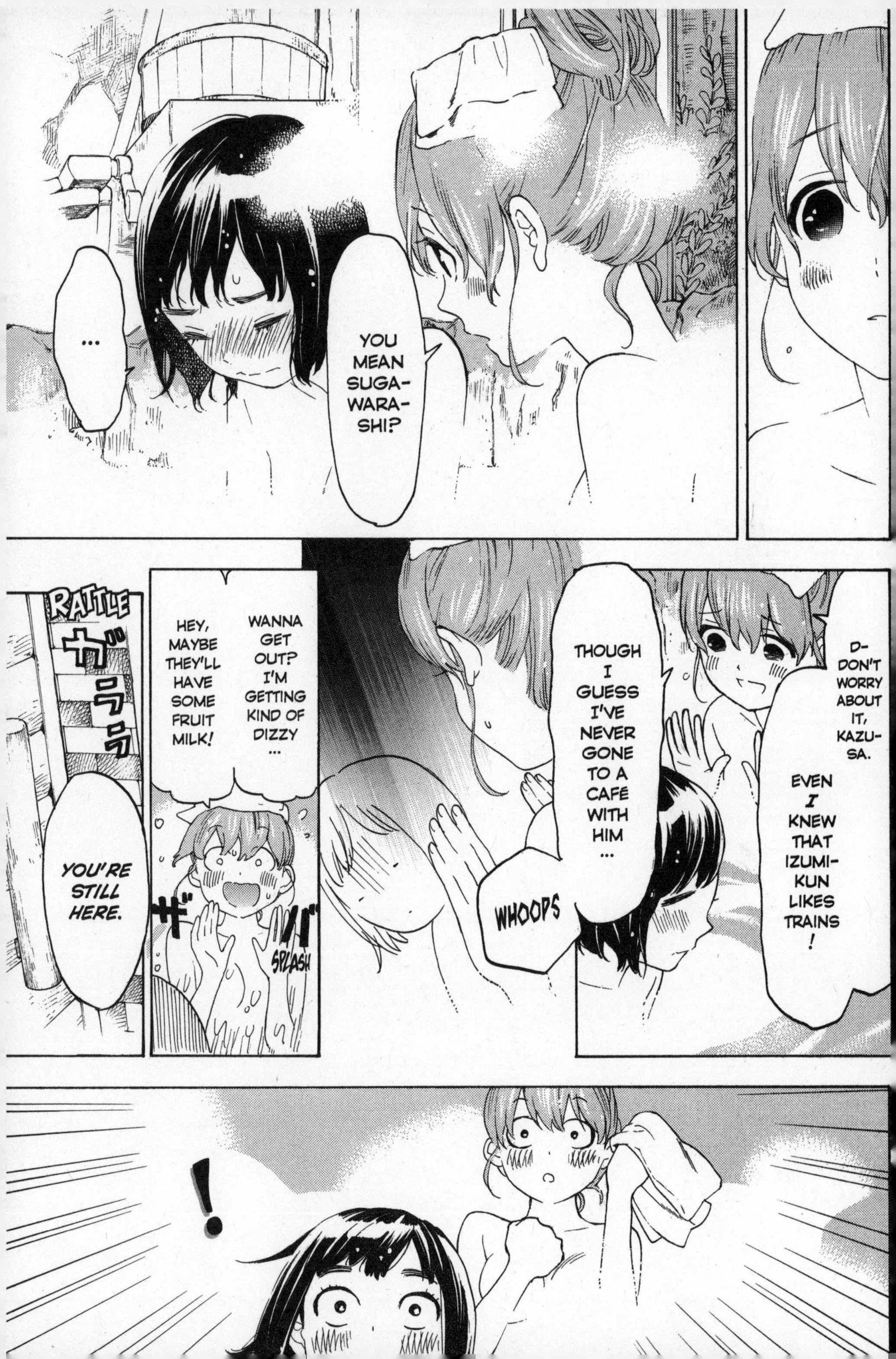
YOU MEAN SUGA-WARA-SHI?
...
D-DON'T WORRY ABOUT IT, KAZU-SA.
EVEN I KNEW THAT IZUMI-KUN LIKES TRAINS!
THOUGH I GUESS I'VE NEVER GONE TO A CAFÉ WITH HIM...
WHOOPS
WANNA GET OUT? I'M GETTING KIND OF DIZZY...
HEY, MAYBE THEY'LL HAVE SOME FRUIT MILK!
ザバ
SPLASH
RATTLE
ガラララ
YOU'RE STILL HERE.
!

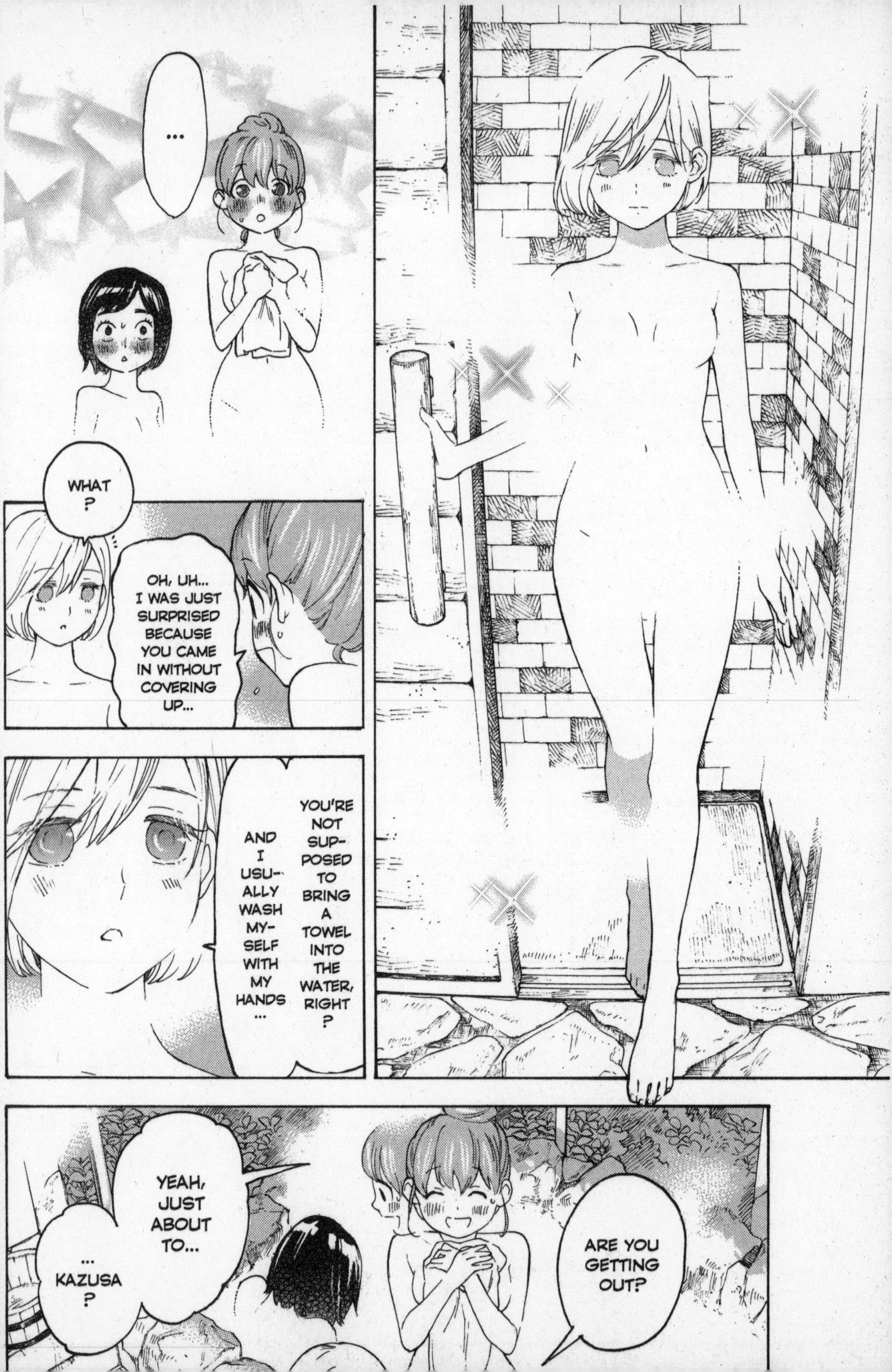
...
WHAT?
OH, UH... I WAS JUST SURPRISED BECAUSE YOU CAME IN WITHOUT COVERING UP...
YOU'RE NOT SUP-POSED TO BRING A TOWEL INTO THE WATER, RIGHT?
AND I USU-ALLY WASH MY-SELF WITH MY HANDS...
ARE YOU GETTING OUT?
YEAH, JUST ABOUT TO...
... KAZUSA?

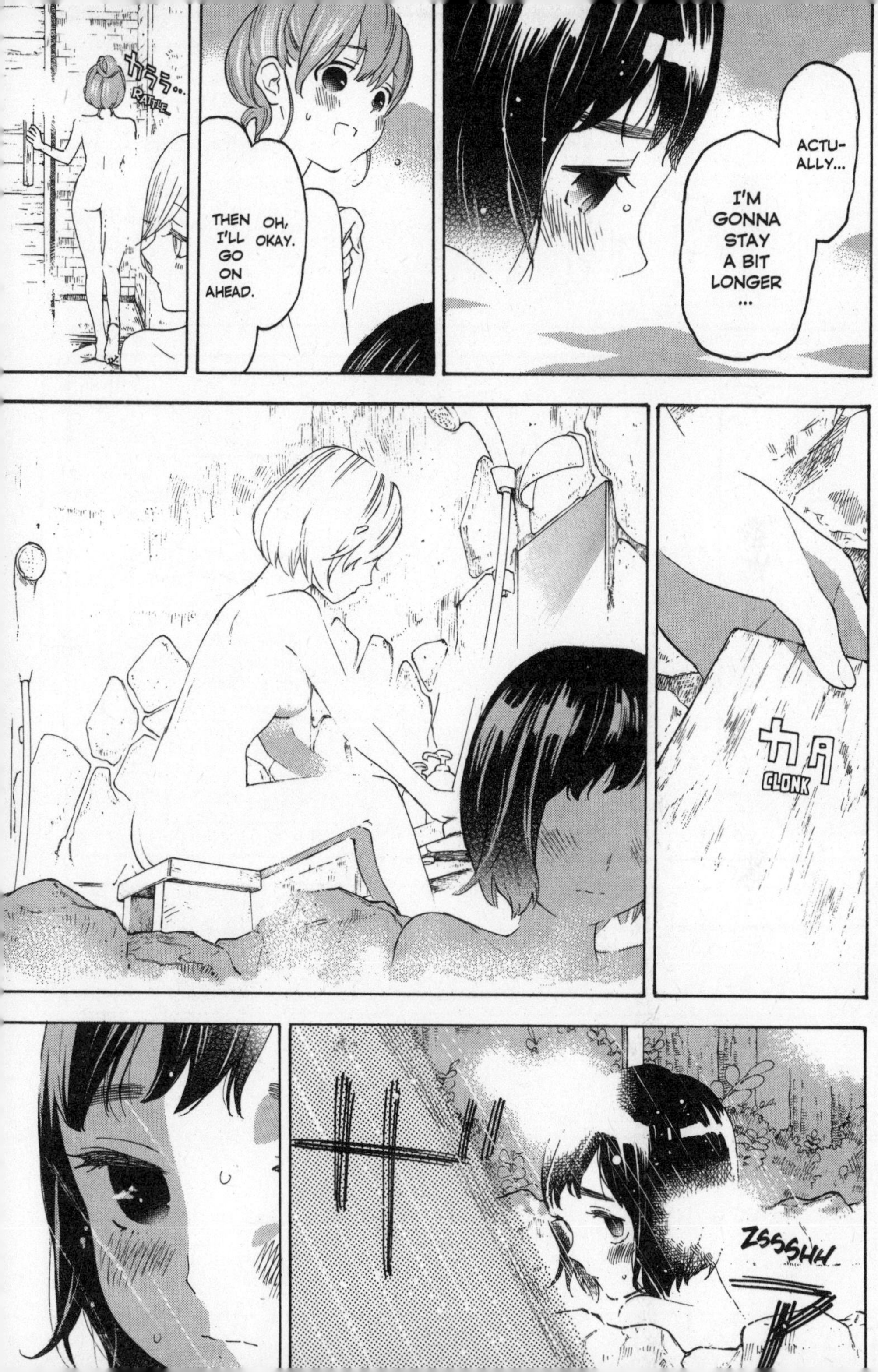
ACTU-ALLY...
I'M GONNA STAY A BIT LONGER ...
OH, OKAY.
THEN I'LL GO ON AHEAD.
カララ..
RATTLE
カタ
CLONK
ZSSSHH

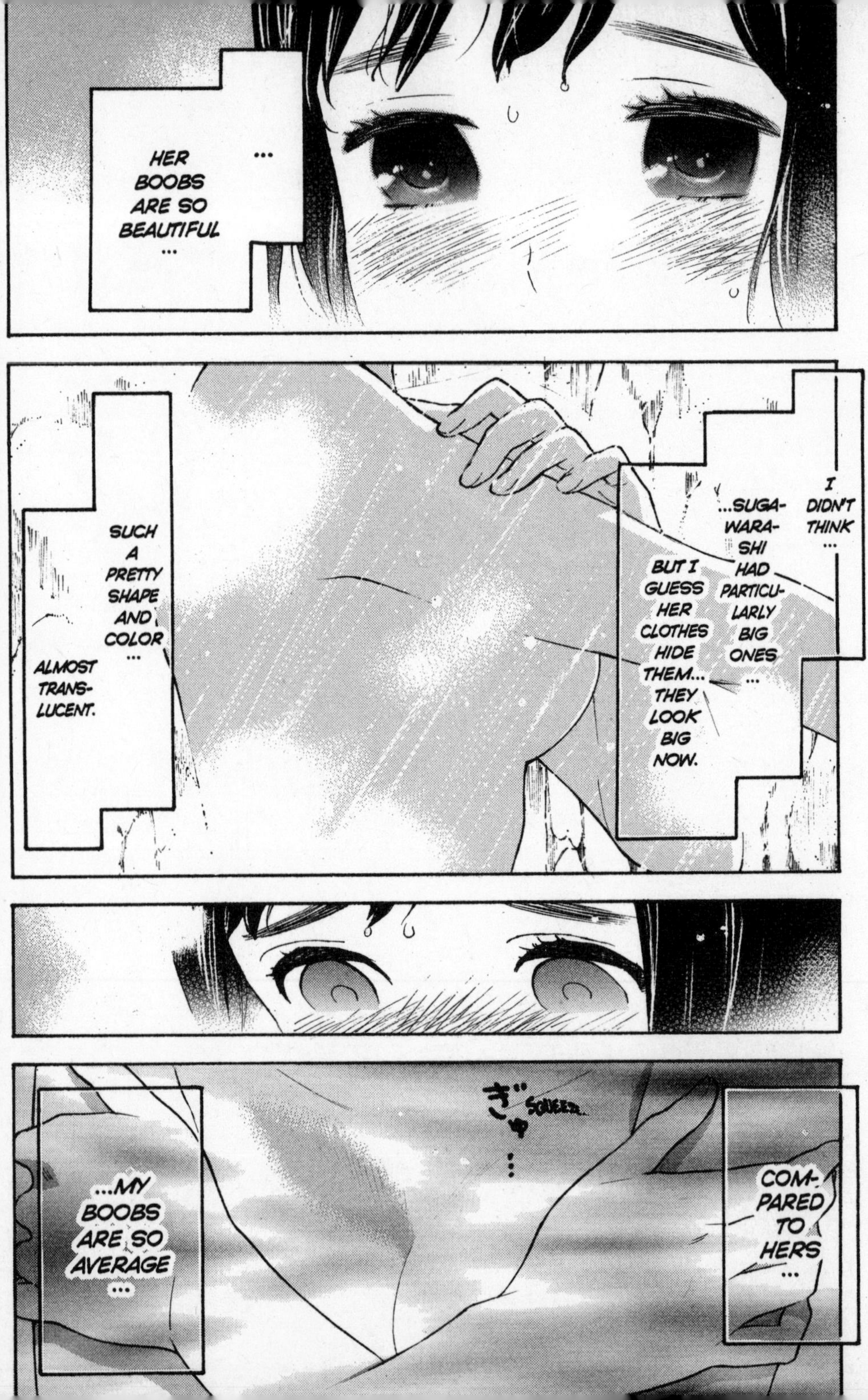
...
HER BOOBS ARE SO BEAUTIFUL...
I DIDN'T THINK...
...SUGAWARA-SHI HAD PARTICULARLY BIG ONES...
BUT I GUESS HER CLOTHES HIDE THEM... THEY LOOK BIG NOW.
SUCH A PRETTY SHAPE AND COLOR...
ALMOST TRANSLUCENT.
ぎゅ SQUEEZE...
COMPARED TO HERS...
...MY BOOBS ARE SO AVERAGE...

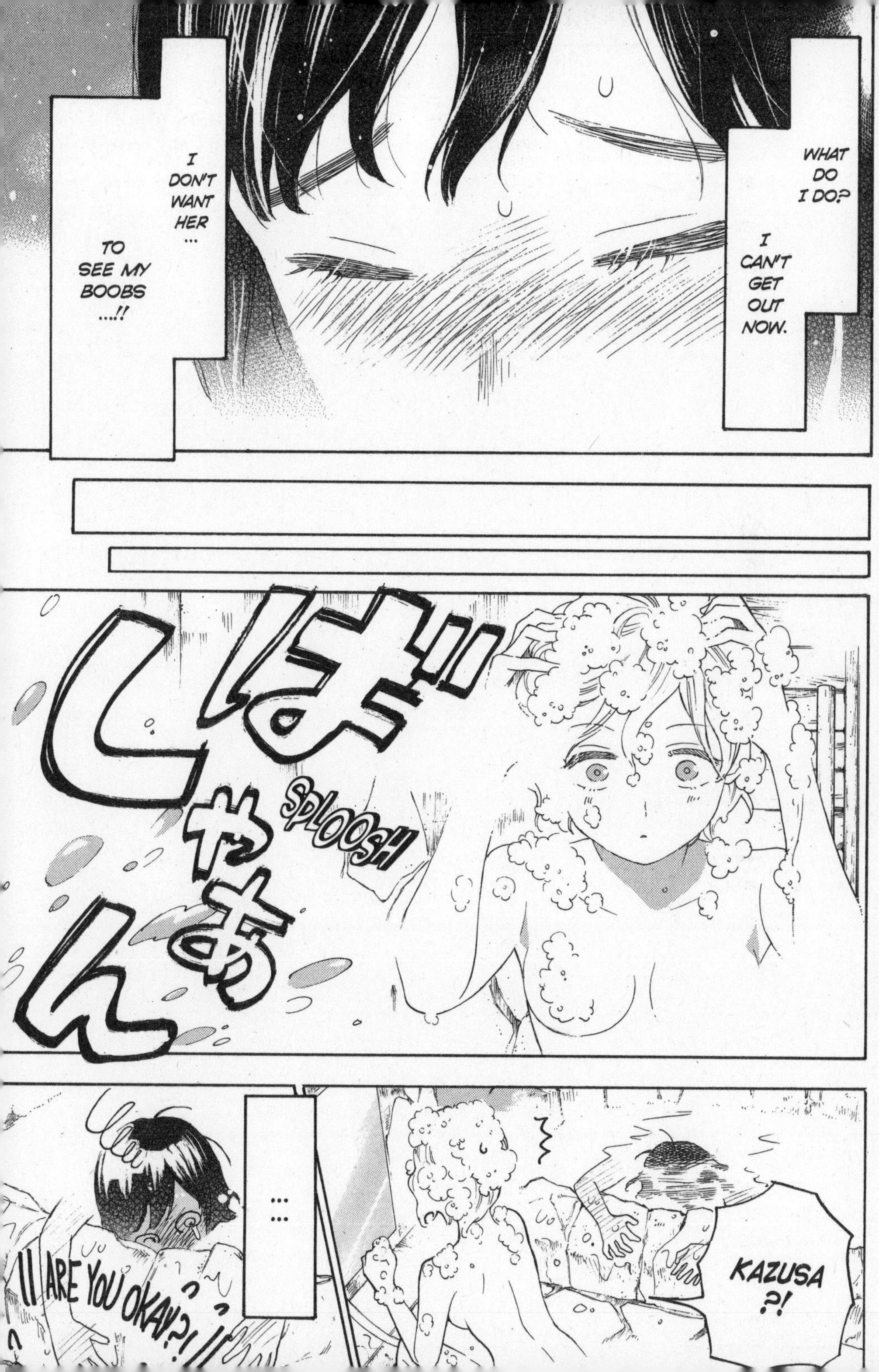
WHAT DO I DO?
I CAN'T GET OUT NOW.
I DON'T WANT HER...
TO SEE MY BOOBS...!!
ばしゃあん
SPLOOSH
KAZUSA?!
......
ARE YOU OKAY?!

O Maidens
in your Savage
your Season

Meeting 15

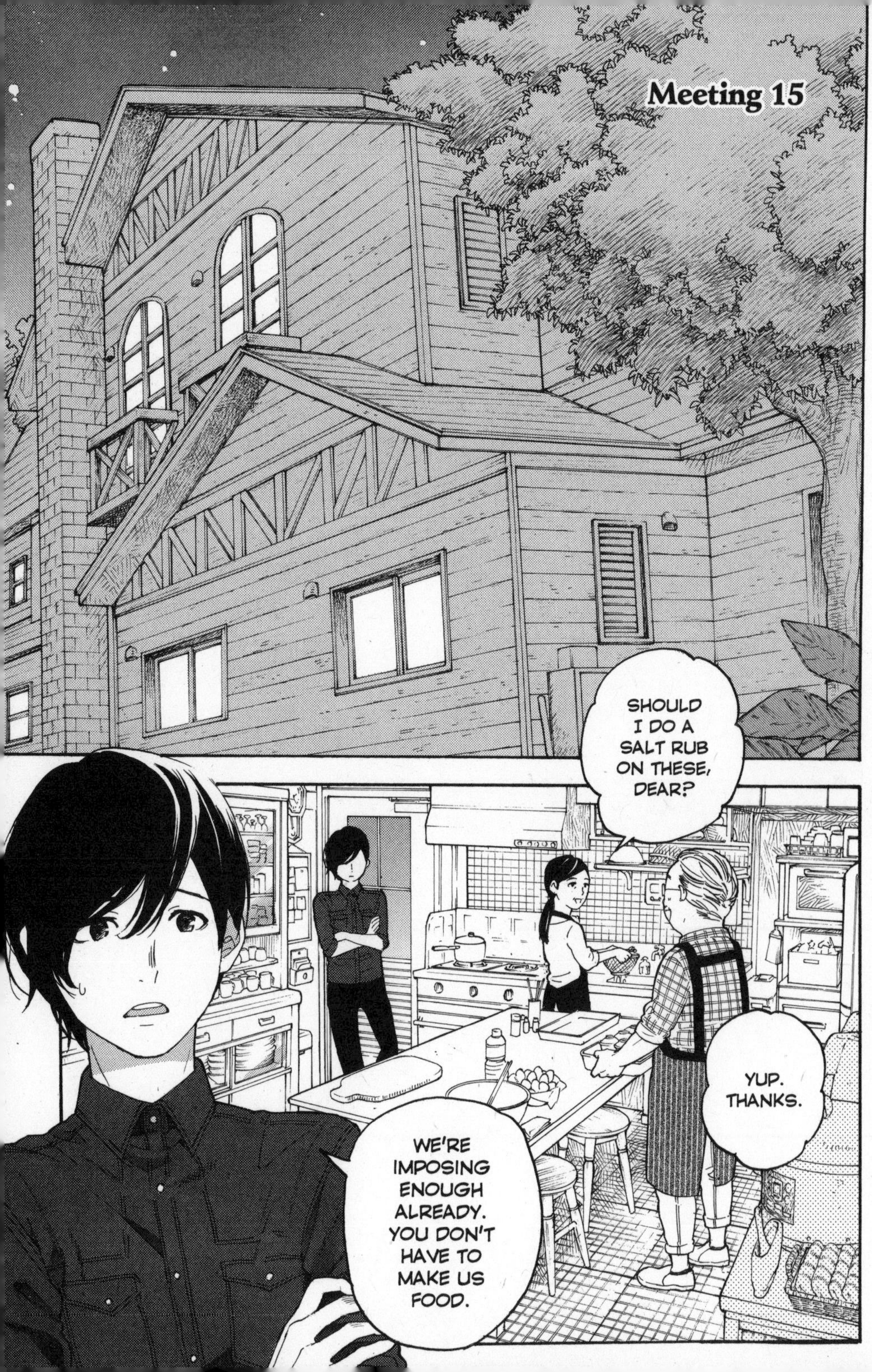
SHOULD I DO A SALT RUB ON THESE, DEAR?
YUP. THANKS.
WE'RE IMPOSING ENOUGH ALREADY. YOU DON'T HAVE TO MAKE US FOOD.

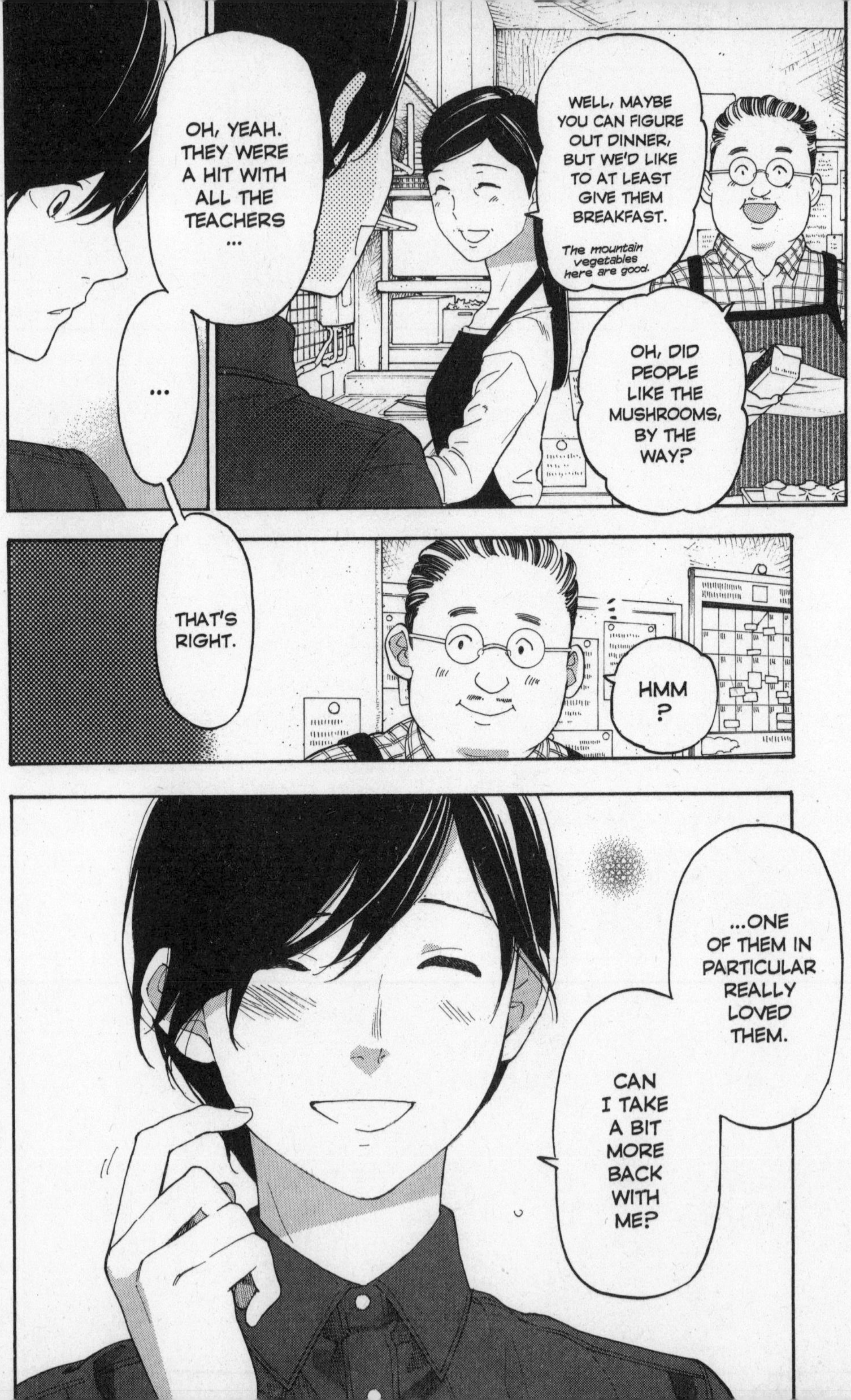
WELL, MAYBE YOU CAN FIGURE OUT DINNER, BUT WE'D LIKE TO AT LEAST GIVE THEM BREAKFAST.
The mountain vegetables here are good.
OH, DID PEOPLE LIKE THE MUSHROOMS, BY THE WAY?
OH, YEAH. THEY WERE A HIT WITH ALL THE TEACHERS ...
...
THAT'S RIGHT.
HMM ?
...ONE OF THEM IN PARTICULAR REALLY LOVED THEM.
CAN I TAKE A BIT MORE BACK WITH ME?

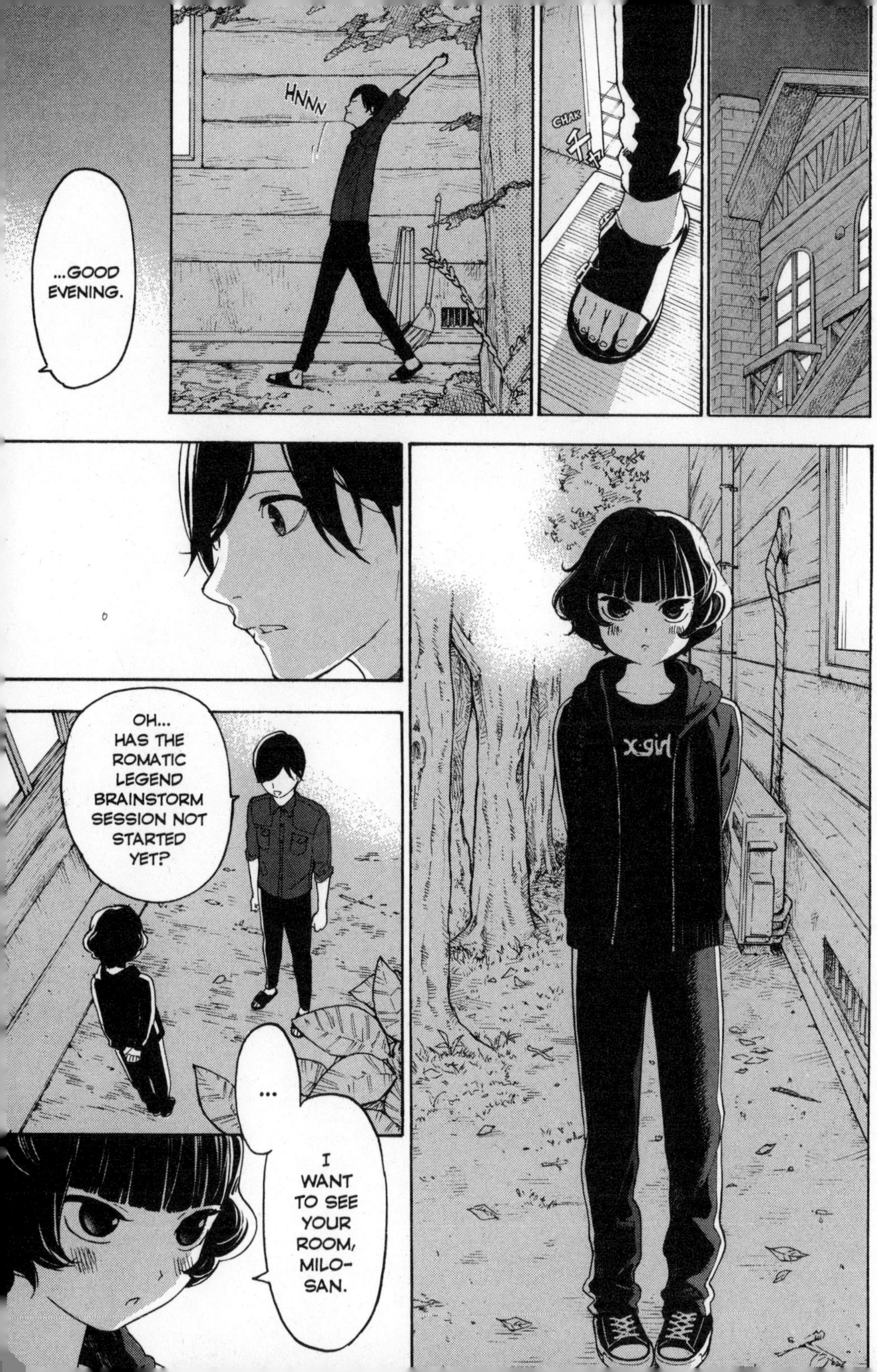
CHAK
HNNN
...GOOD EVENING.
x-girl
OH... HAS THE ROMATIC LEGEND BRAINSTORM SESSION NOT STARTED YET?
...
I WANT TO SEE YOUR ROOM, MILO-SAN.

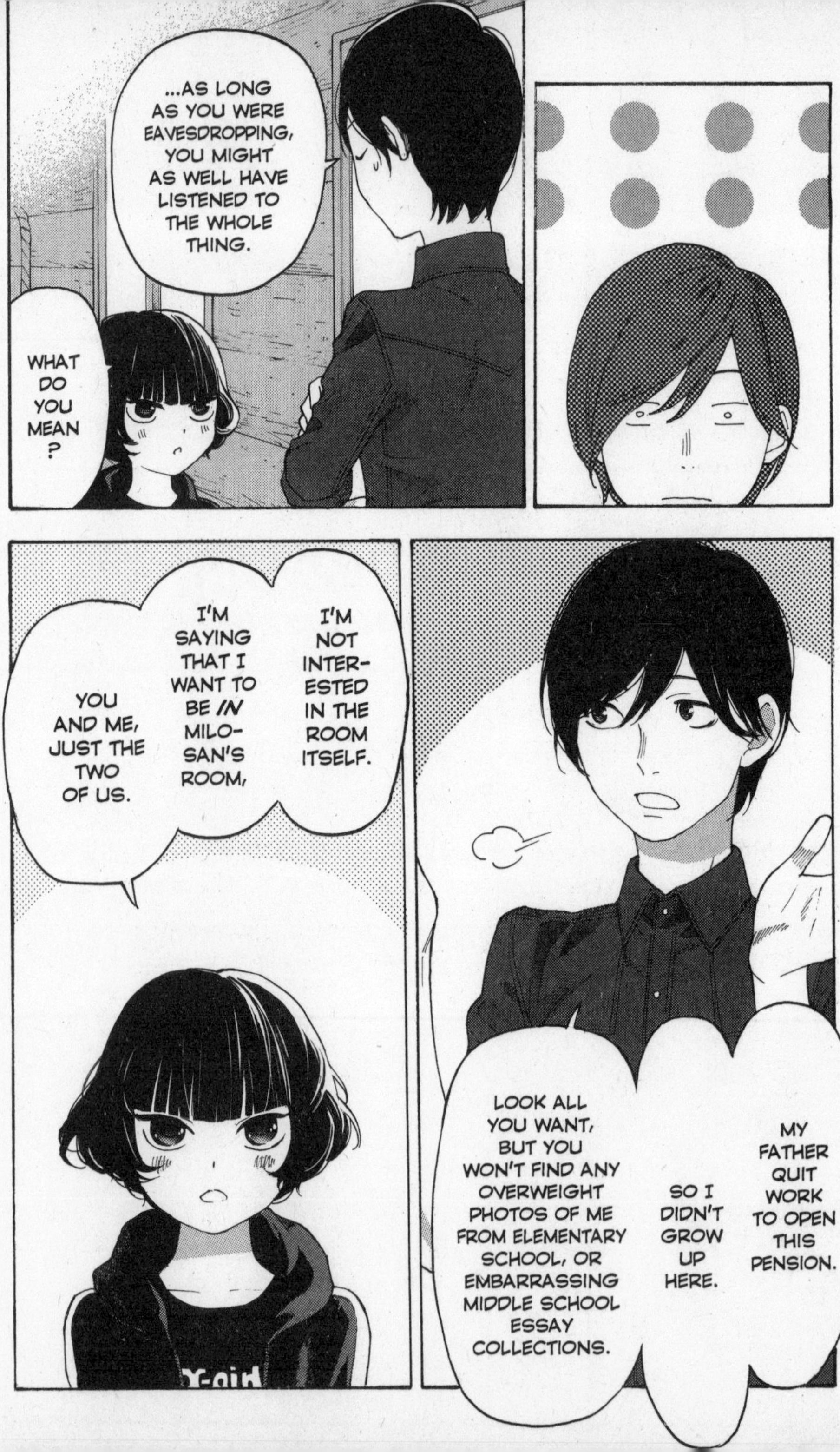
...AS LONG AS YOU WERE EAVESDROPPING, YOU MIGHT AS WELL HAVE LISTENED TO THE WHOLE THING.
WHAT DO YOU MEAN?
MY FATHER QUIT WORK TO OPEN THIS PENSION.
SO I DIDN'T GROW UP HERE.
LOOK ALL YOU WANT, BUT YOU WON'T FIND ANY OVERWEIGHT PHOTOS OF ME FROM ELEMENTARY SCHOOL, OR EMBARRASSING MIDDLE SCHOOL ESSAY COLLECTIONS.
I'M NOT INTER-ESTED IN THE ROOM ITSELF.
I'M SAYING THAT I WANT TO BE *IN* MILO-SAN'S ROOM,
YOU AND ME, JUST THE TWO OF US.

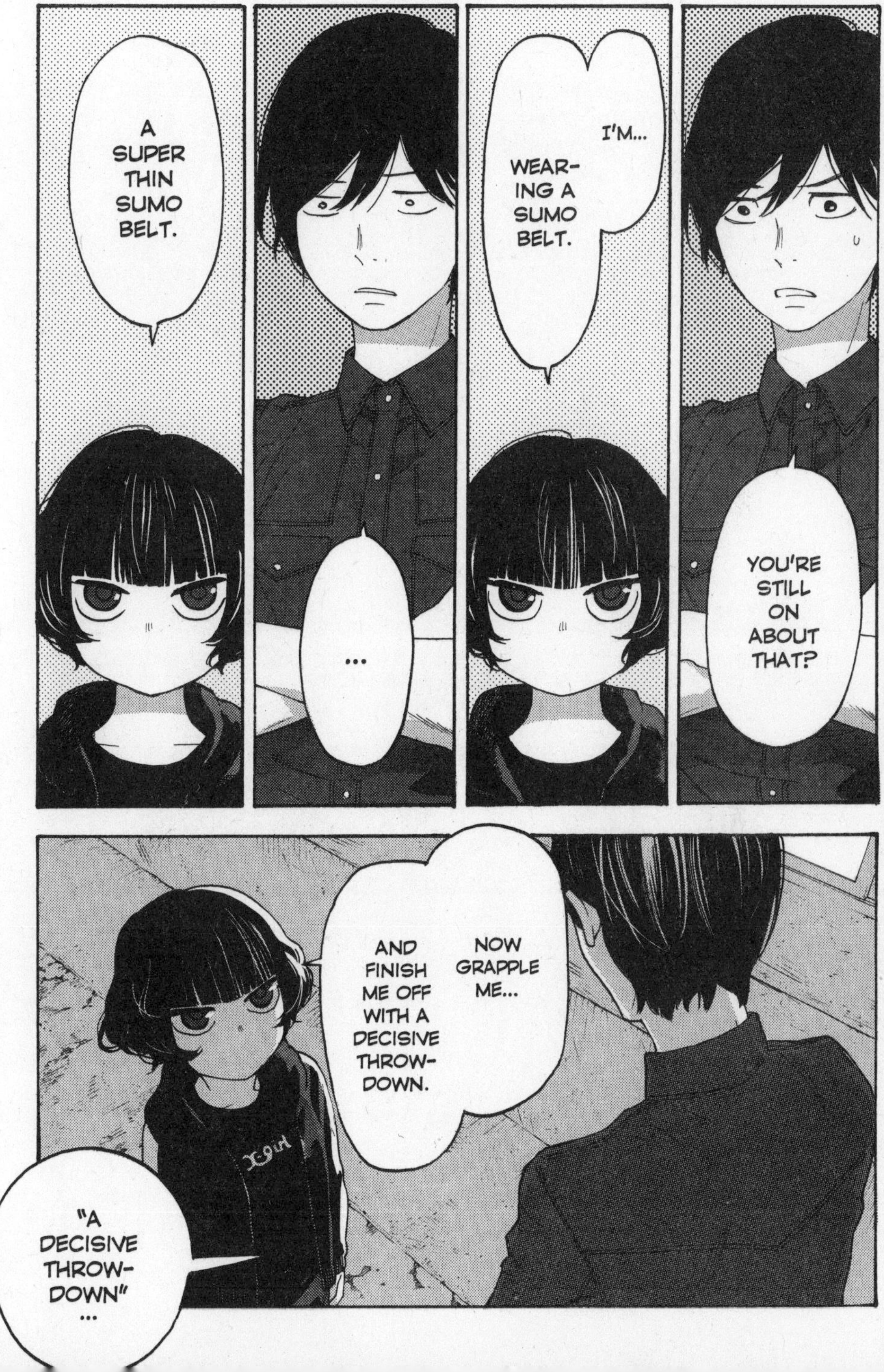
YOU'RE STILL ON ABOUT THAT?
I'M... WEARING A SUMO BELT.
...
A SUPER THIN SUMO BELT.
NOW GRAPPLE ME...
AND FINISH ME OFF WITH A DECISIVE THROW-DOWN.
"A DECISIVE THROW-DOWN"...

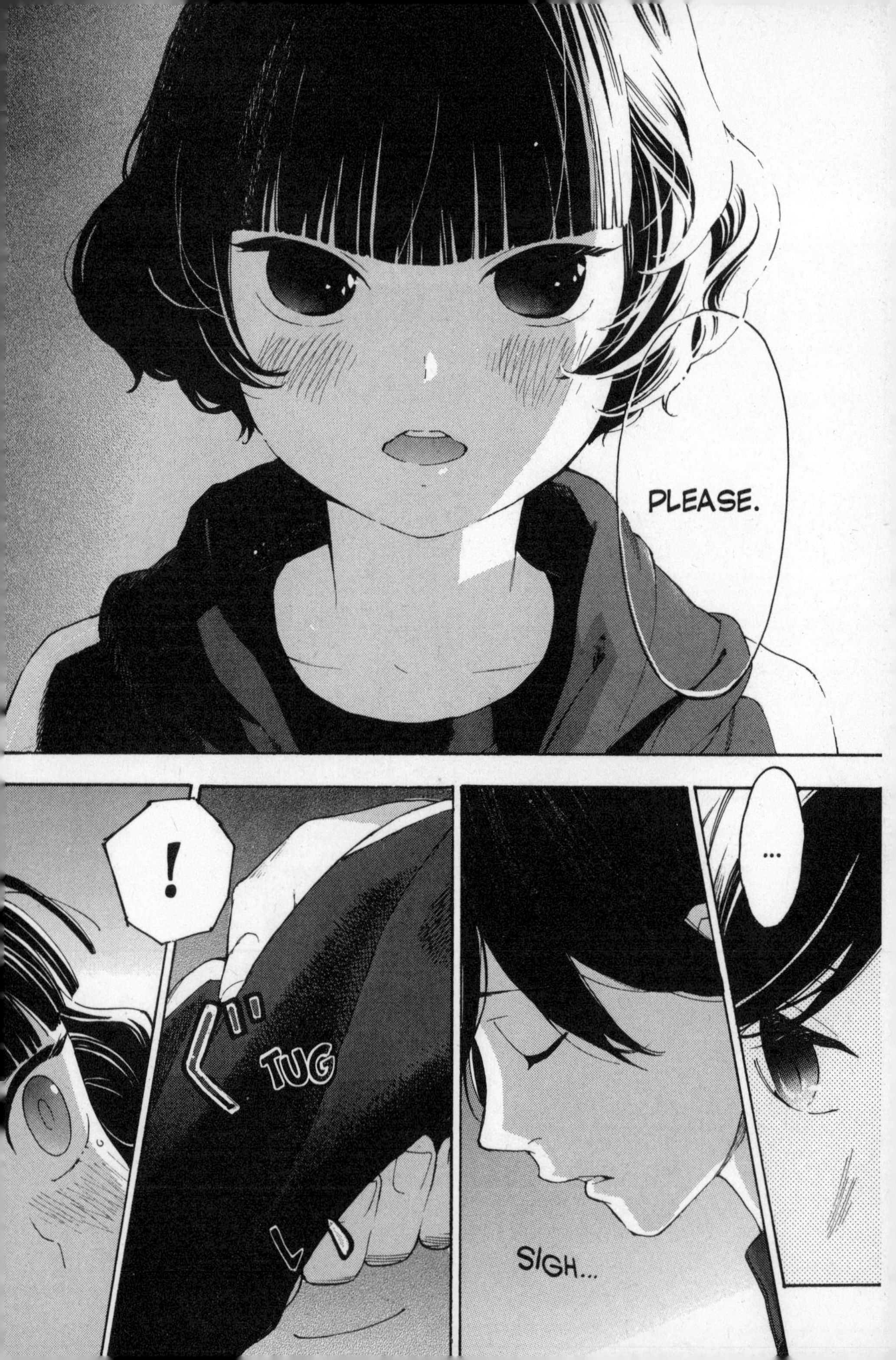
PLEASE.
...
SIGH...
TUG
!

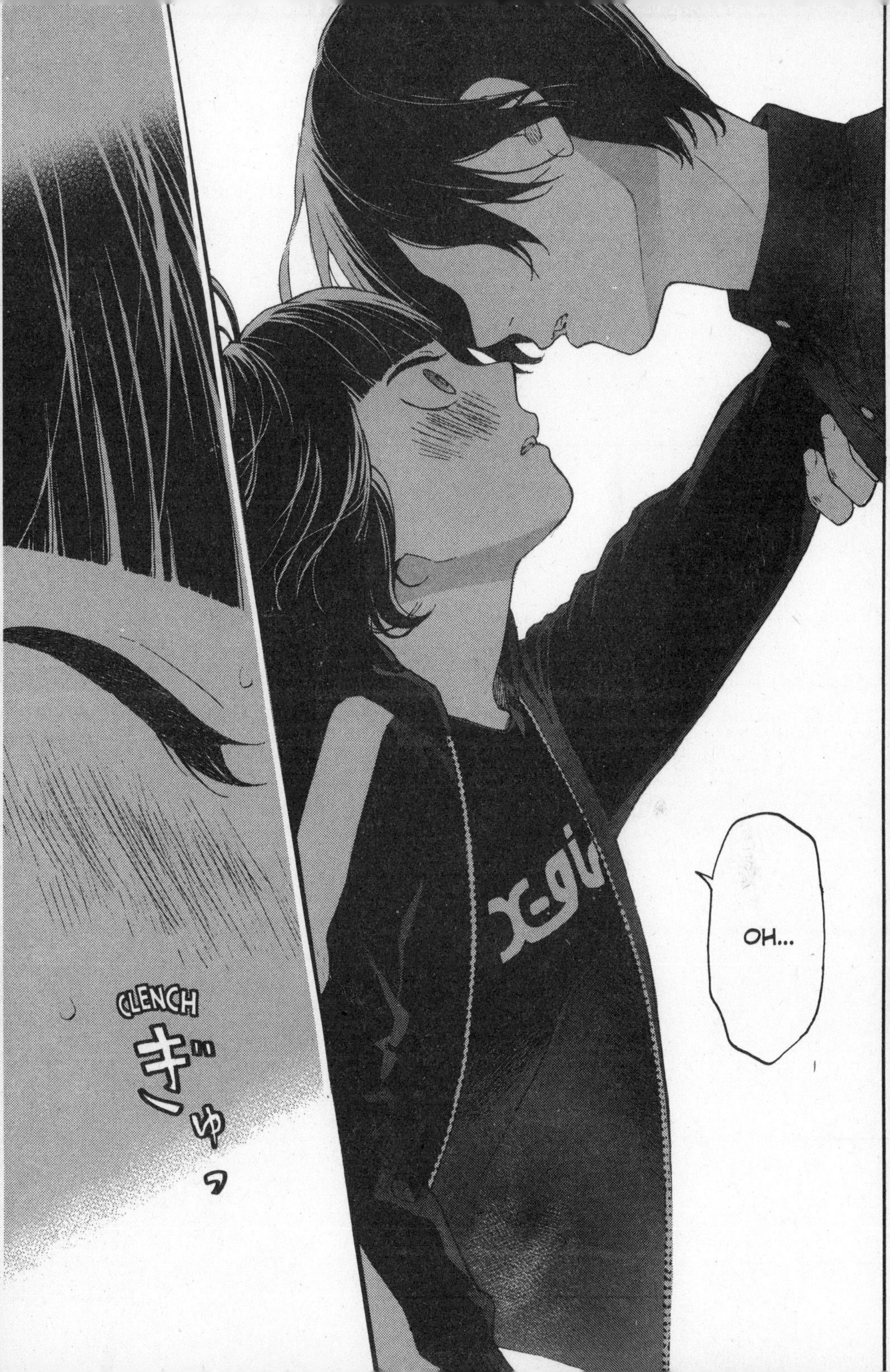
OH...
CLENCH
ぎゅっ

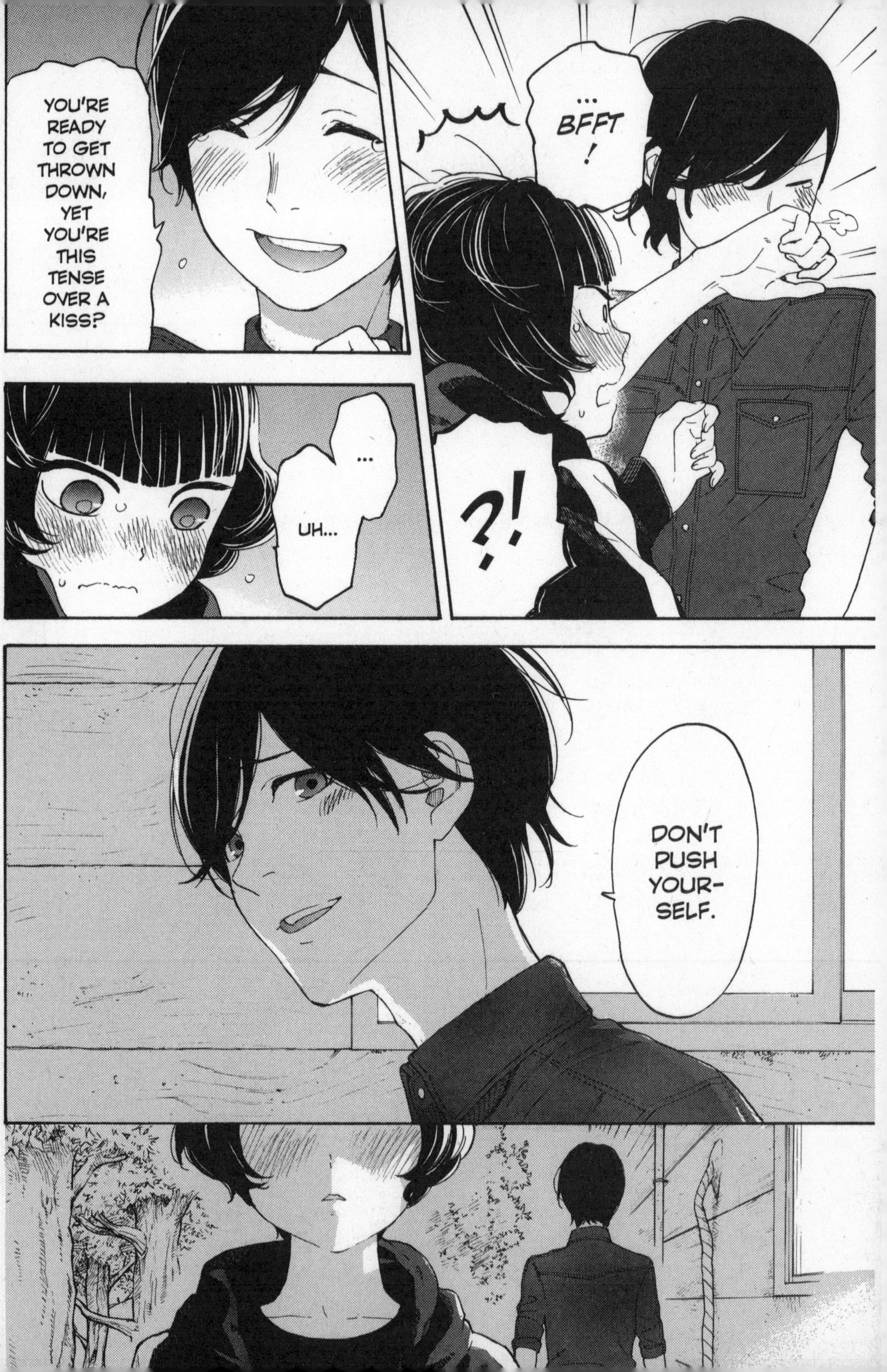
... BFFT!
?!
YOU'RE READY TO GET THROWN DOWN, YET YOU'RE THIS TENSE OVER A KISS?
... UH...
DON'T PUSH YOURSELF.

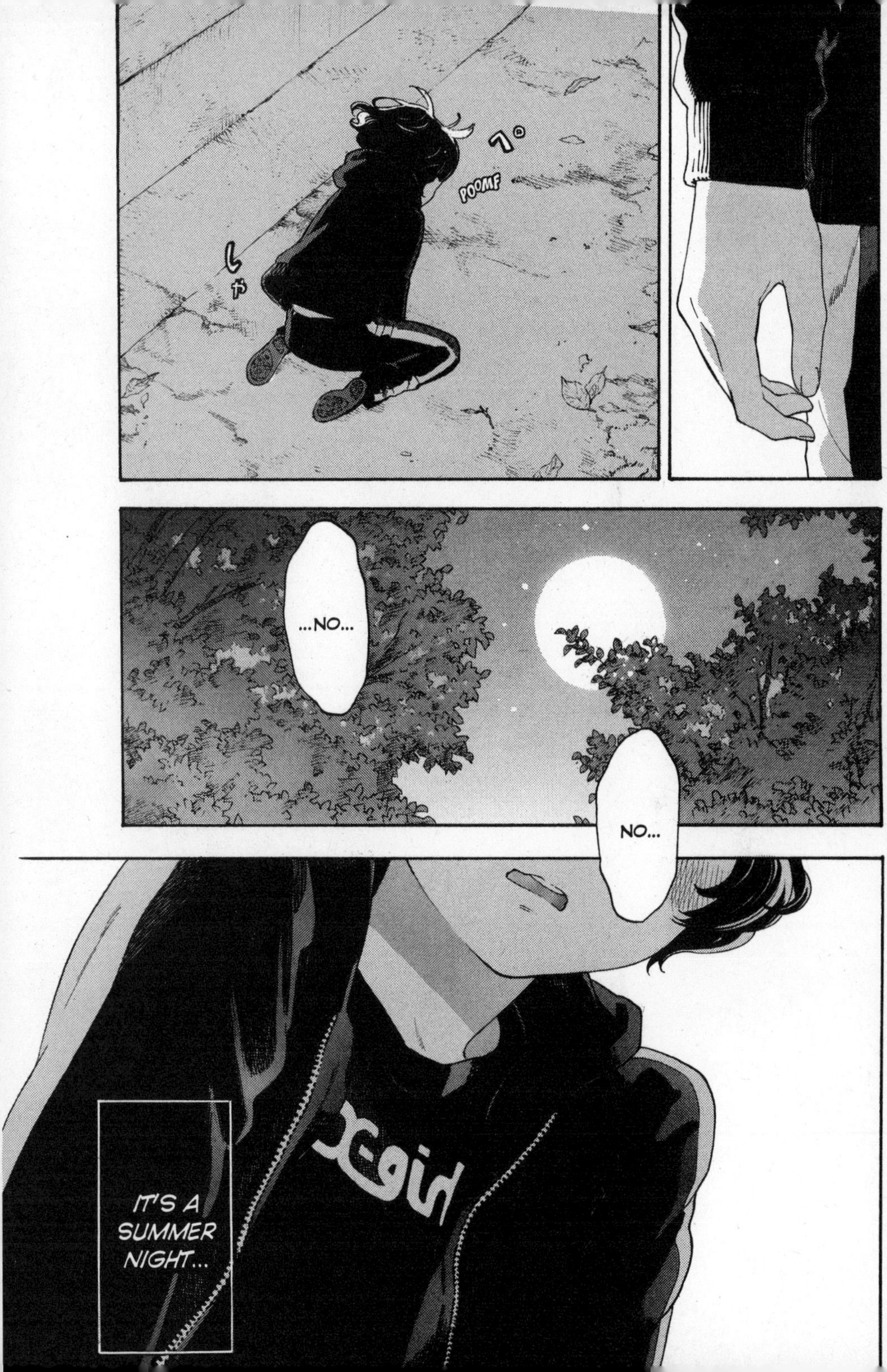
POOMF
...NO...
NO...
IT'S A SUMMER NIGHT...

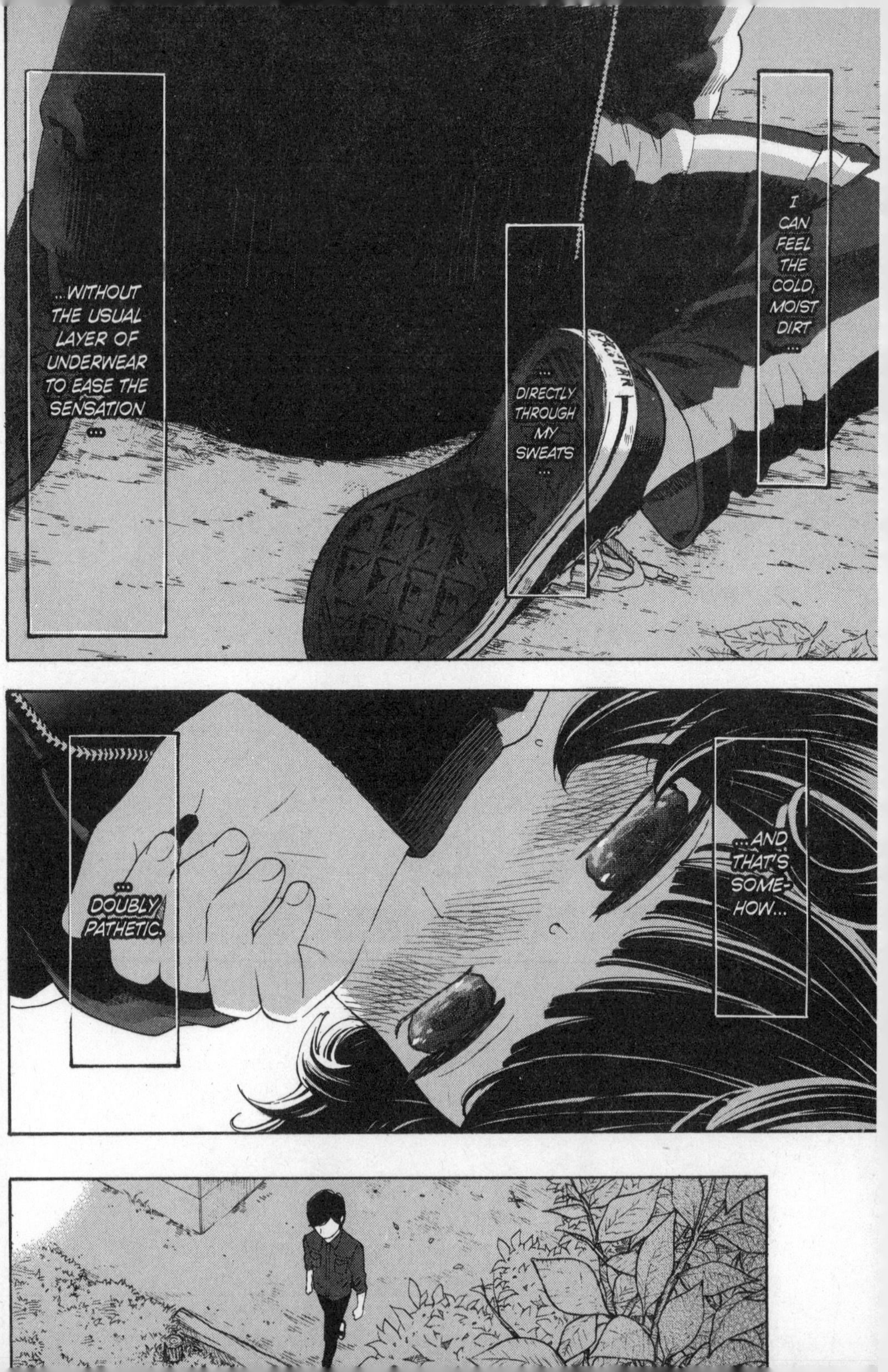
I CAN FEEL THE COLD, MOIST DIRT...
...DIRECTLY THROUGH MY SWEATS...
...WITHOUT THE USUAL LAYER OF UNDERWEAR TO EASE THE SENSATION...
...AND THAT'S SOME-HOW...
...DOUBLY PATHETIC.

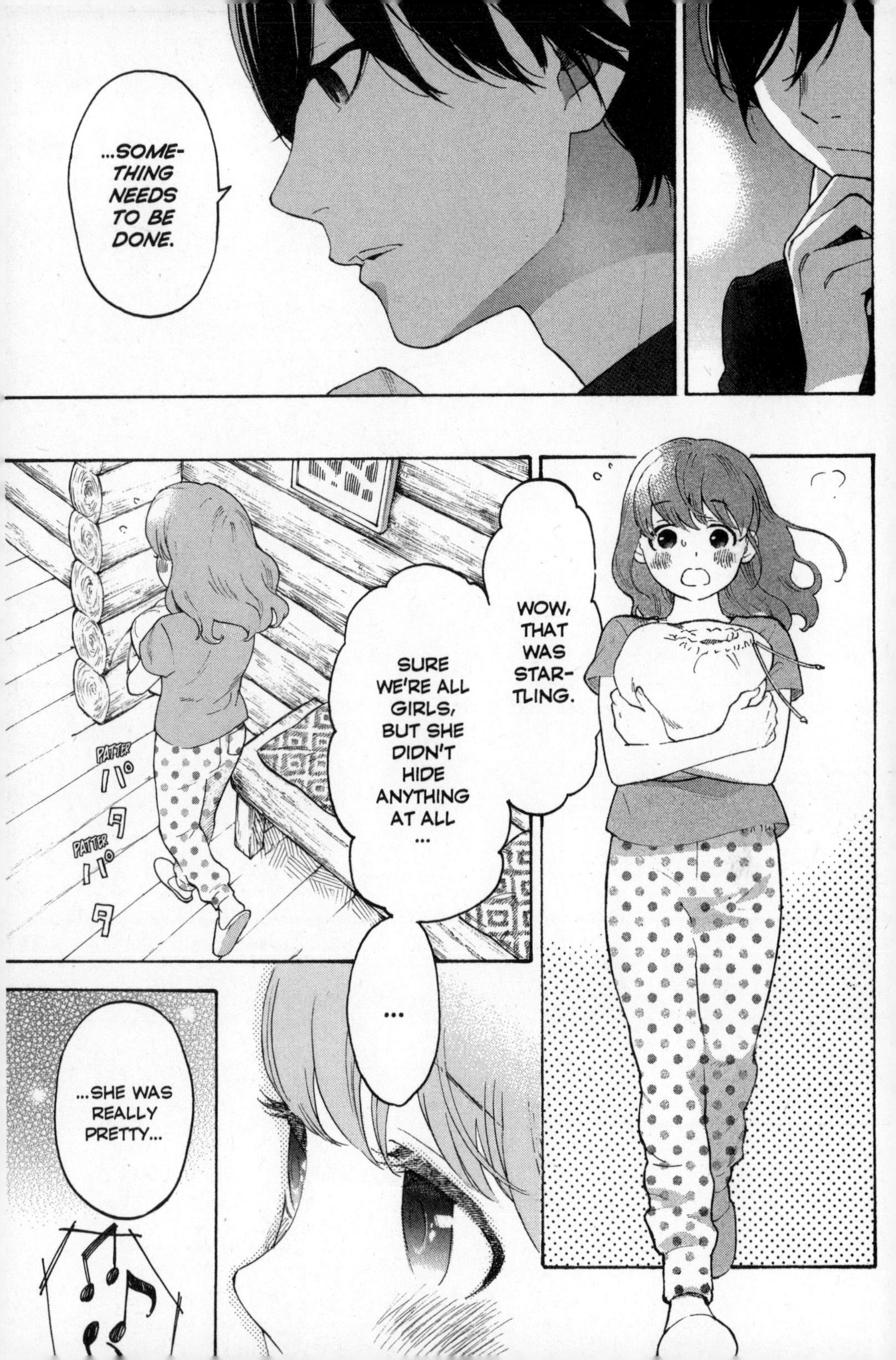
...SOME-THING NEEDS TO BE DONE.
WOW, THAT WAS STAR-TLING.
SURE WE'RE ALL GIRLS, BUT SHE DIDN'T HIDE ANYTHING AT ALL ...
PATTER
パタ
PATTER
パタ
...
...SHE WAS REALLY PRETTY...

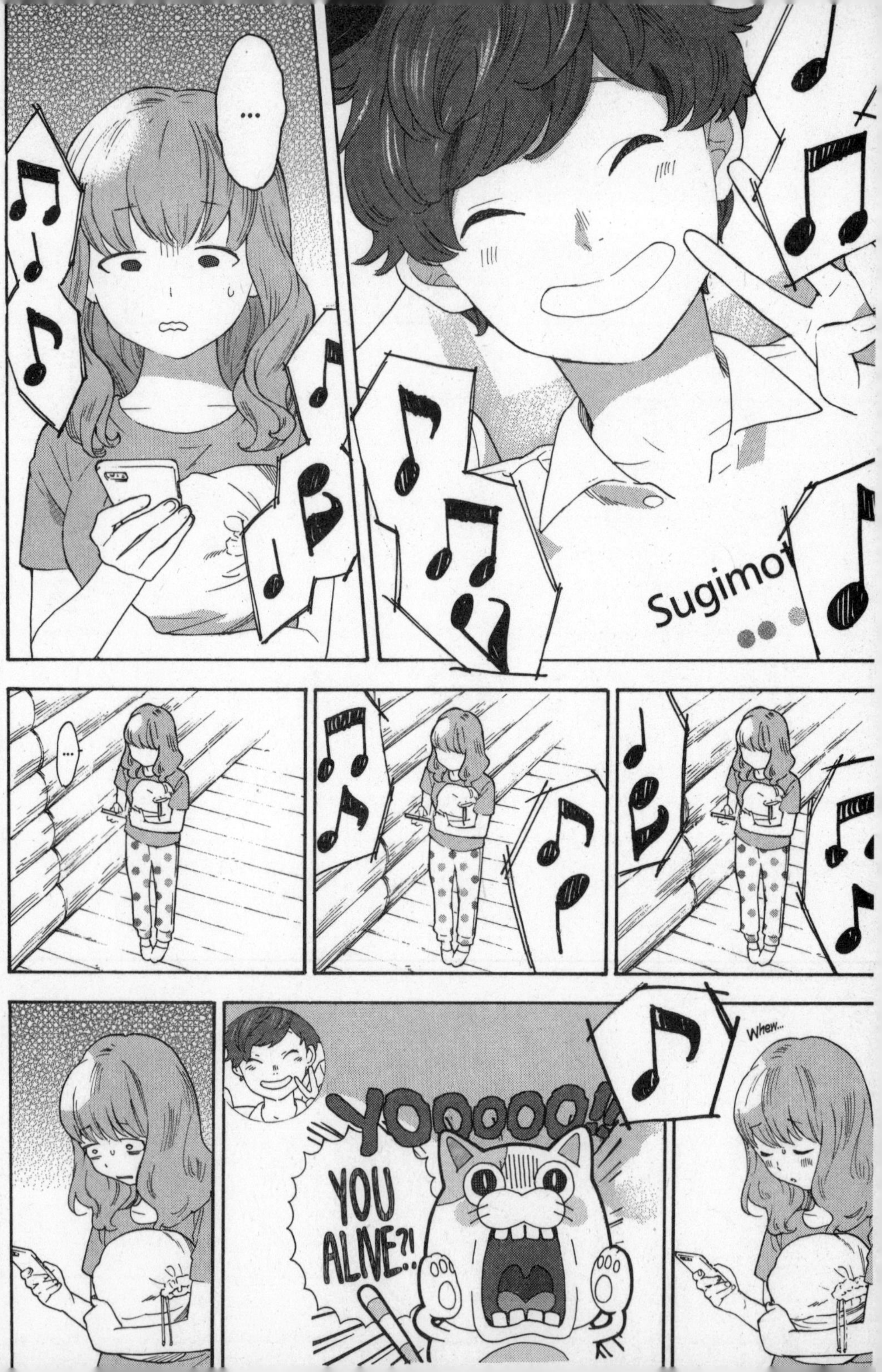
Sugimot
...
...
Whew...
YOOOOO!!
YOU ALIVE?!

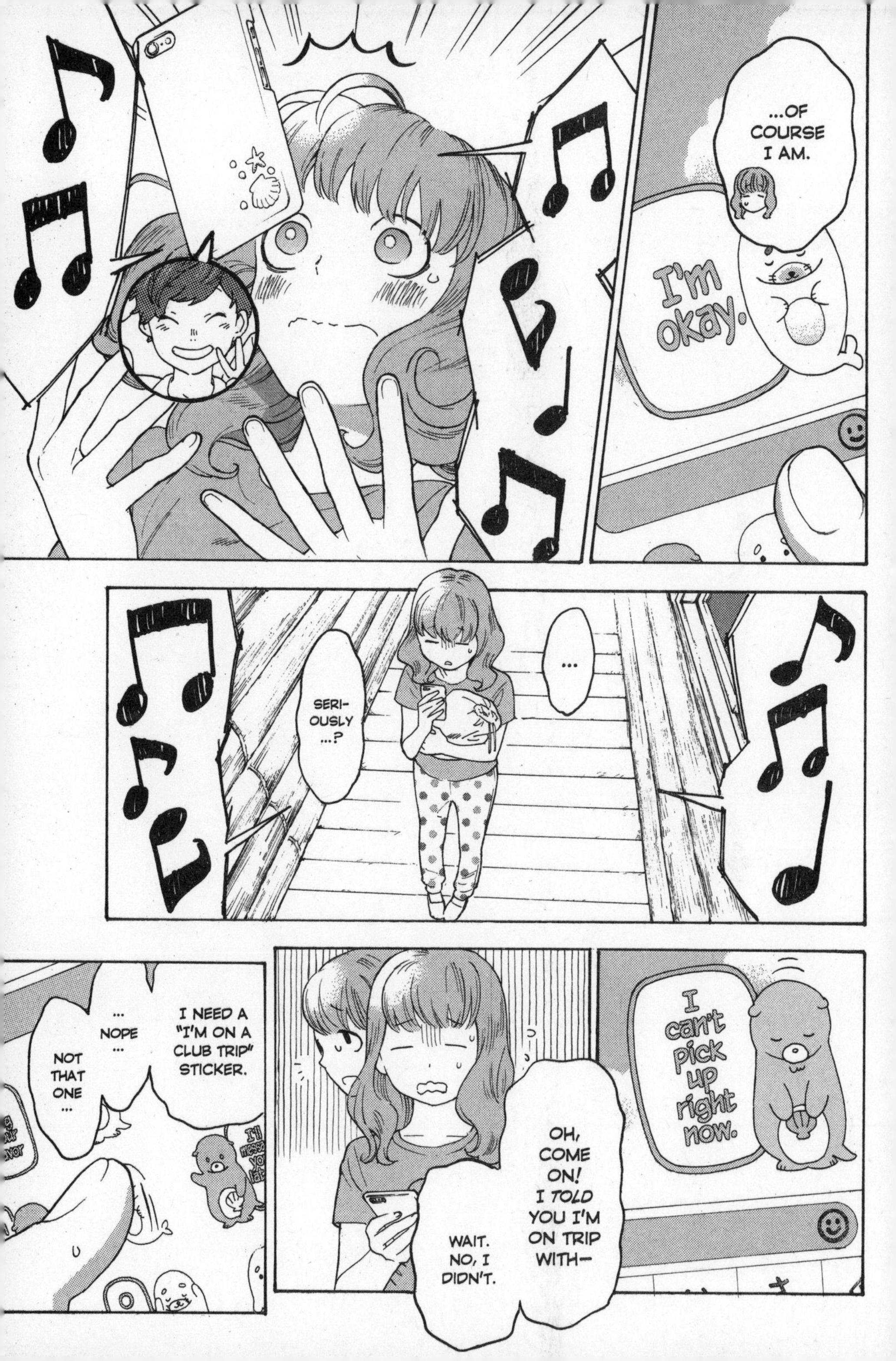

...OF COURSE I AM.
I'm okay.
...
SERIOUSLY ...?
I can't pick up right now.
OH, COME ON! I *TOLD* YOU I'M ON TRIP WITH—
WAIT. NO, I DIDN'T.
I NEED A "I'M ON A CLUB TRIP" STICKER.
... NOPE ...
NOT THAT ONE ...

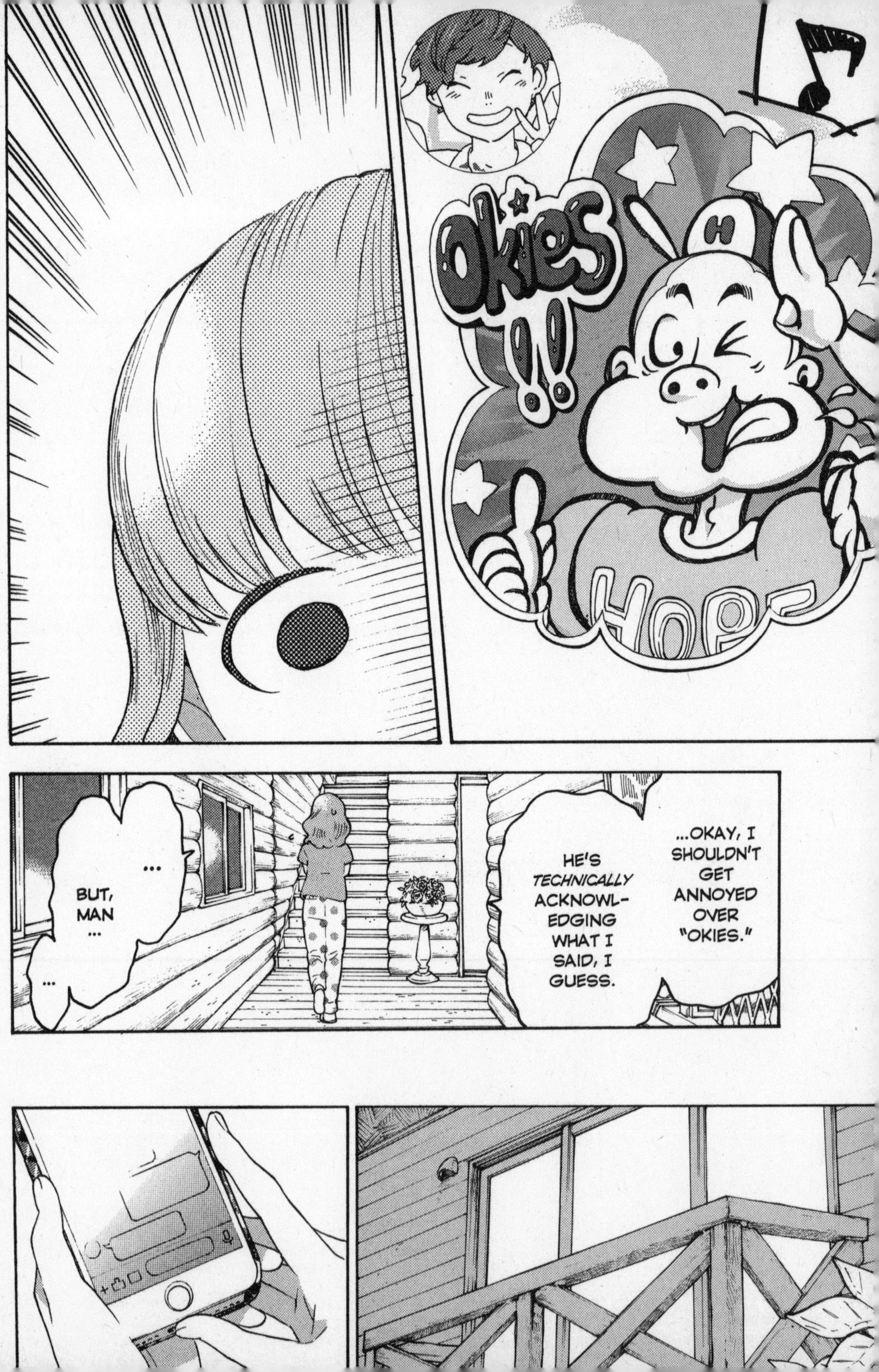

OKIES!!
HOPE
...OKAY, I SHOULDN'T GET ANNOYED OVER "OKIES."
HE'S *TECHNICALLY* ACKNOWLEDGING WHAT I SAID, I GUESS.
...
BUT, MAN ...
...

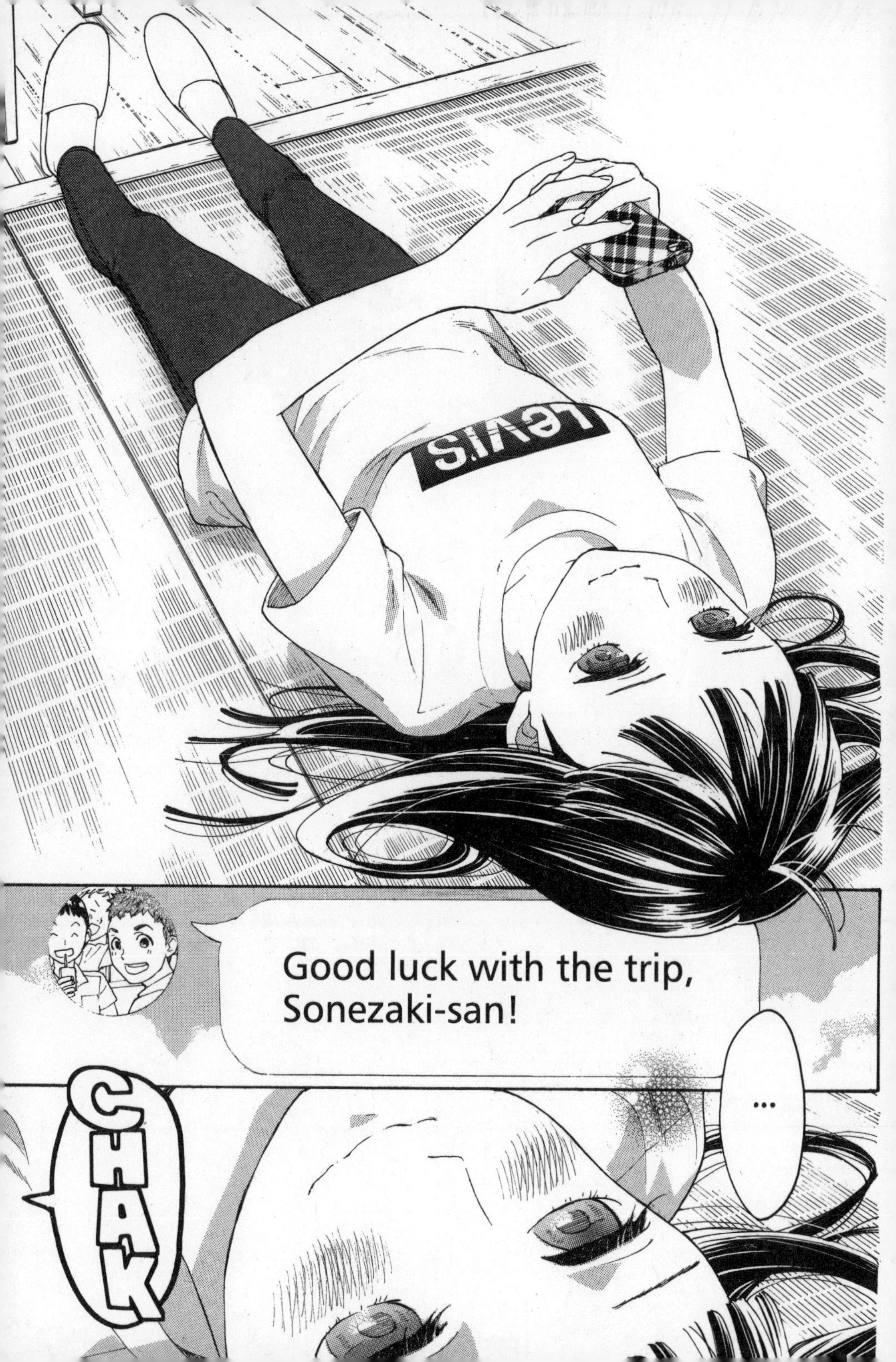
Good luck with the trip, Sonezaki-san!
...
CHAK

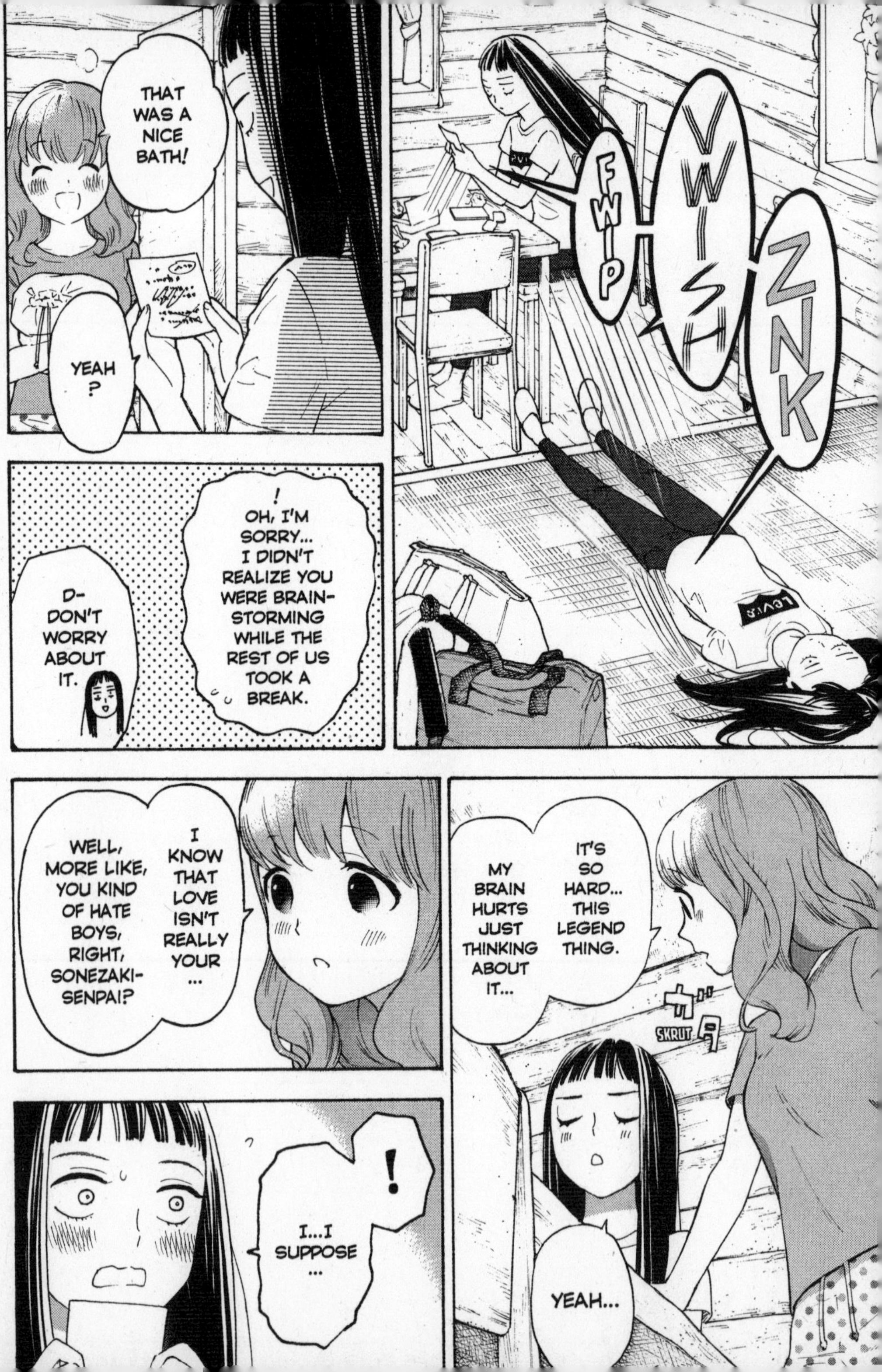
FWIP
VWISH
ZNK
THAT WAS A NICE BATH!
YEAH?
! OH, I'M SORRY... I DIDN'T REALIZE YOU WERE BRAIN-STORMING WHILE THE REST OF US TOOK A BREAK.
D-DON'T WORRY ABOUT IT.
IT'S SO HARD... THIS LEGEND THING.
MY BRAIN HURTS JUST THINKING ABOUT IT...
SKRUT
YEAH...
I KNOW THAT LOVE ISN'T REALLY YOUR...
WELL, MORE LIKE, YOU KIND OF HATE BOYS, RIGHT, SONEZAKI-SENPAI?
!
I...I SUPPOSE...

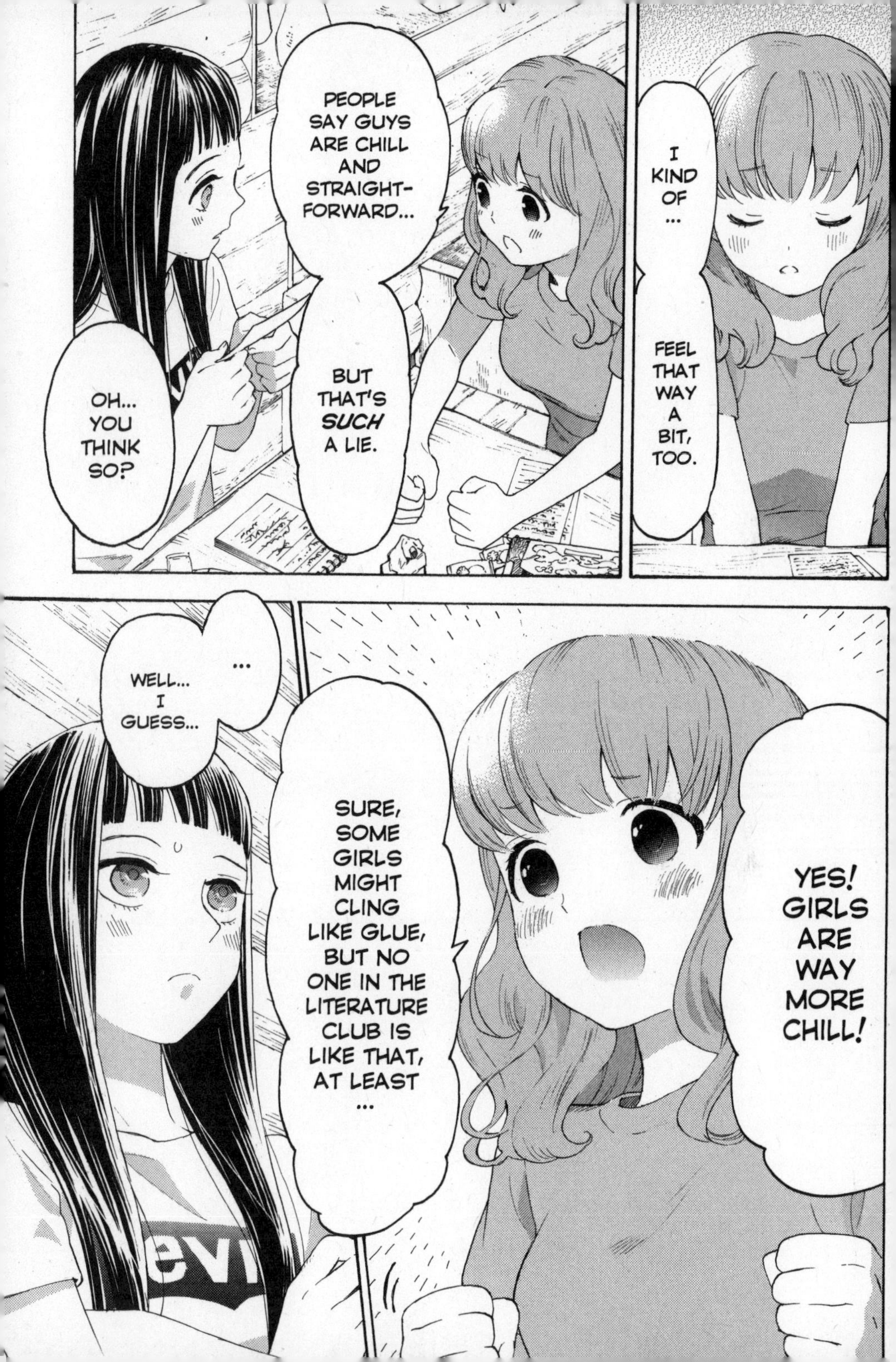
I KIND OF ... FEEL THAT WAY A BIT, TOO.
PEOPLE SAY GUYS ARE CHILL AND STRAIGHT-FORWARD... BUT THAT'S *SUCH* A LIE.
OH... YOU THINK SO?
YES! GIRLS ARE WAY MORE CHILL!
SURE, SOME GIRLS MIGHT CLING LIKE GLUE, BUT NO ONE IN THE LITERATURE CLUB IS LIKE THAT, AT LEAST ...
... WELL... I GUESS...

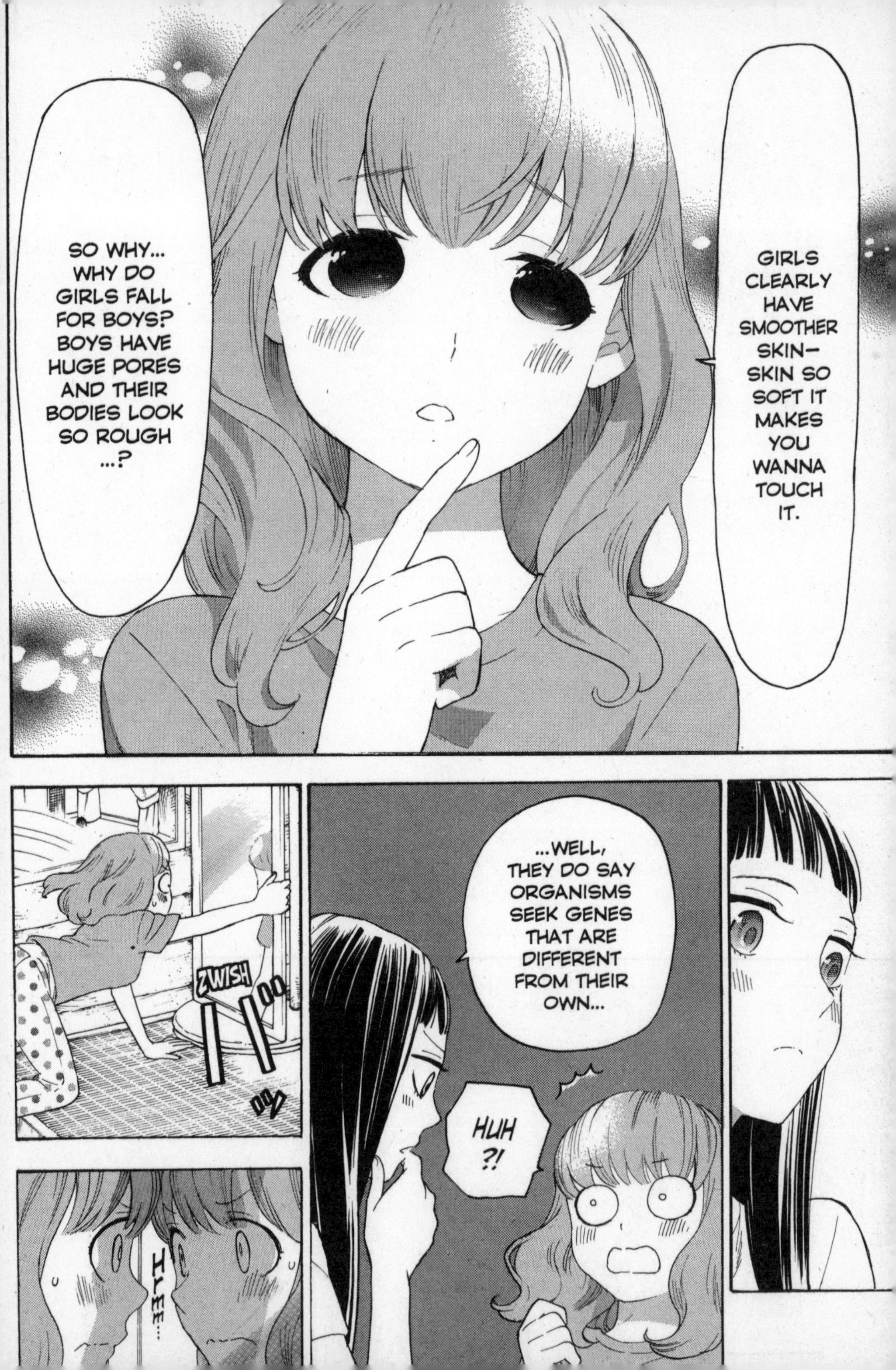
GIRLS CLEARLY HAVE SMOOTHER SKIN—SKIN SO SOFT IT MAKES YOU WANNA TOUCH IT.
SO WHY... WHY DO GIRLS FALL FOR BOYS? BOYS HAVE HUGE PORES AND THEIR BODIES LOOK SO ROUGH ...?
...WELL, THEY DO SAY ORGANISMS SEEK GENES THAT ARE DIFFERENT FROM THEIR OWN...
HUH ?!
ZWISH
Hrmm...

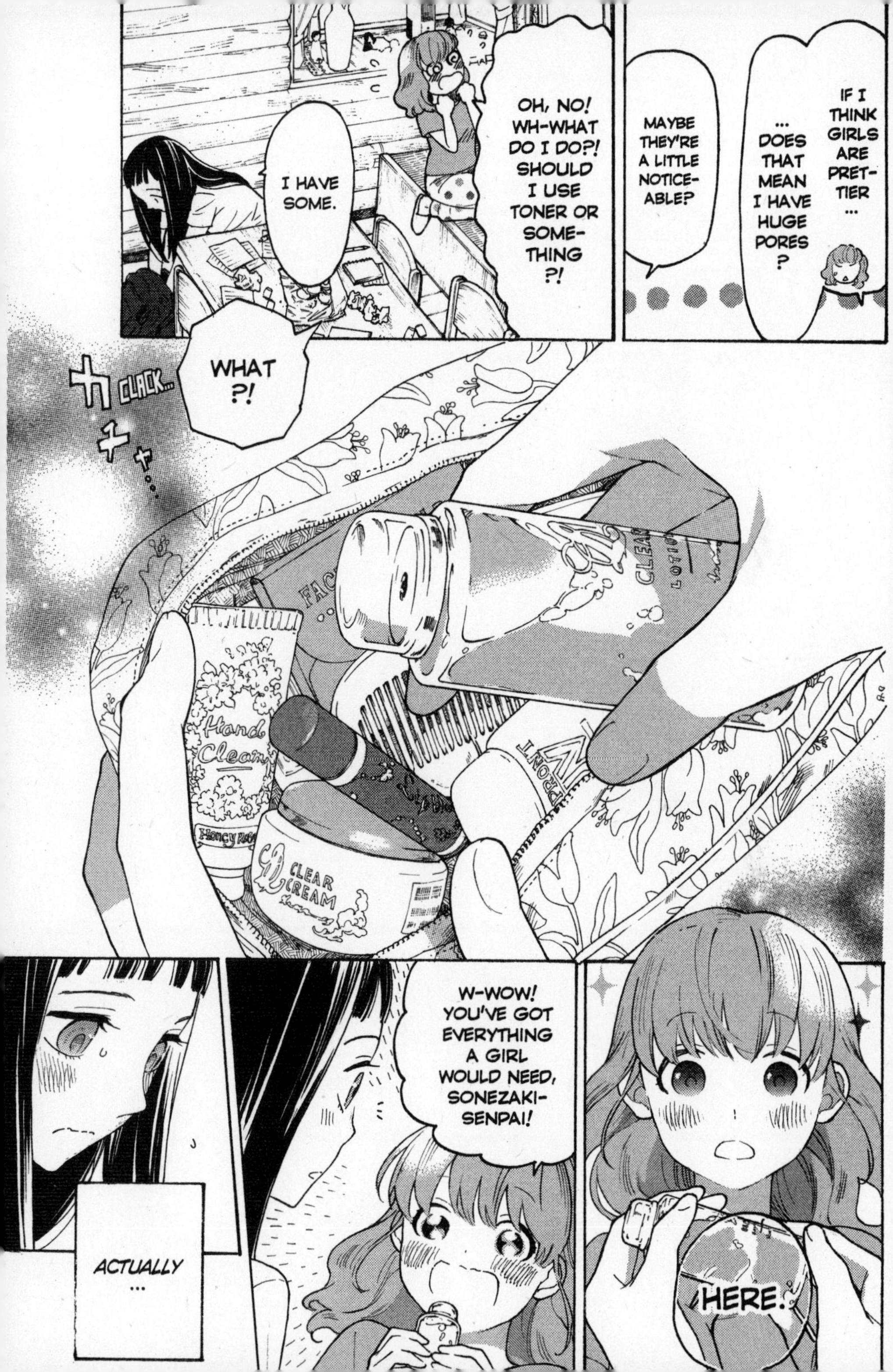
IF I THINK GIRLS ARE PRETTIER ...
... DOES THAT MEAN I HAVE HUGE PORES?
MAYBE THEY'RE A LITTLE NOTICEABLE?
OH, NO! WH-WHAT DO I DO?! SHOULD I USE TONER OR SOMETHING?!
I HAVE SOME.
WHAT?!
CLACK...
CLEAR LOTION
Hand Cream
CLEAR CREAM
HERE.
W-WOW! YOU'VE GOT EVERYTHING A GIRL WOULD NEED, SONEZAKI-SENPAI!
ACTUALLY ...

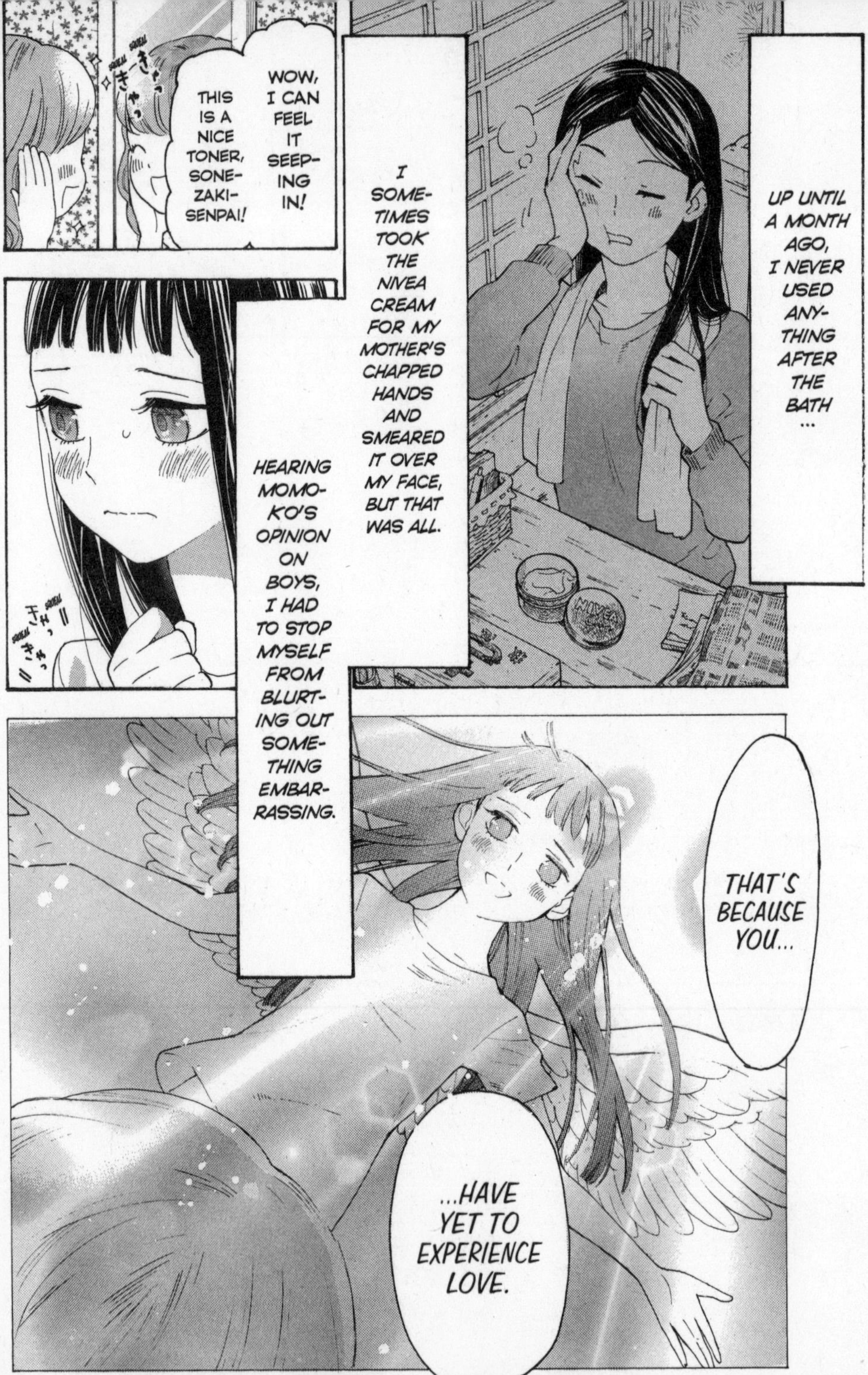

UP UNTIL A MONTH AGO, I NEVER USED ANYTHING AFTER THE BATH...
I SOMETIMES TOOK THE NIVEA CREAM FOR MY MOTHER'S CHAPPED HANDS AND SMEARED IT OVER MY FACE, BUT THAT WAS ALL.
NIVEA
WOW, I CAN FEEL IT SEEPING IN!
THIS IS A NICE TONER, SONEZAKI-SENPAI!
HEARING MOMOKO'S OPINION ON BOYS, I HAD TO STOP MYSELF FROM BLURTING OUT SOMETHING EMBARRASSING.
THAT'S BECAUSE YOU...
...HAVE YET TO EXPERIENCE LOVE.

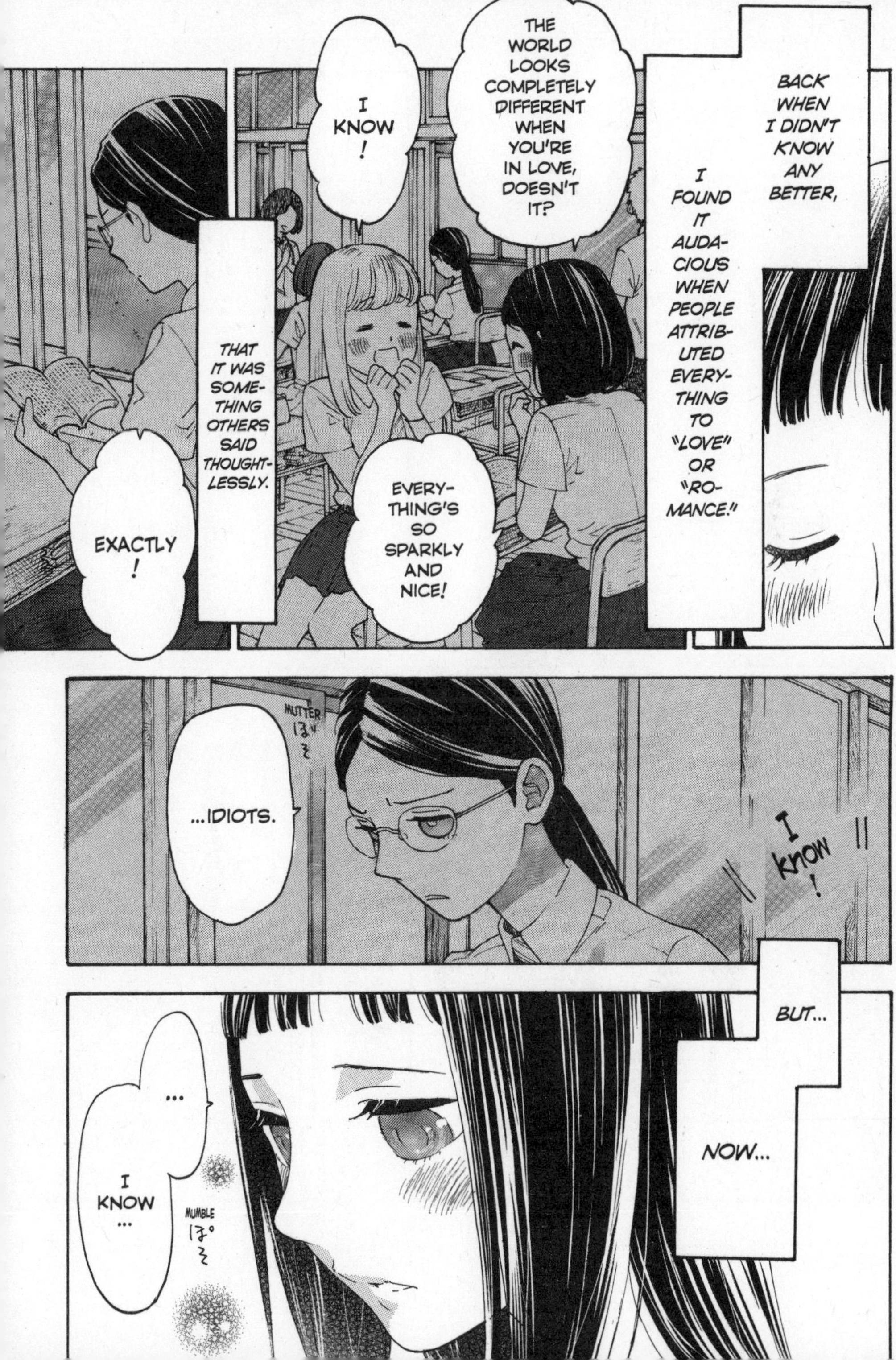
BACK WHEN I DIDN'T KNOW ANY BETTER,
I FOUND IT AUDACIOUS WHEN PEOPLE ATTRIBUTED EVERYTHING TO "LOVE" OR "ROMANCE."
THE WORLD LOOKS COMPLETELY DIFFERENT WHEN YOU'RE IN LOVE, DOESN'T IT?
I KNOW!
EVERYTHING'S SO SPARKLY AND NICE!
THAT IT WAS SOMETHING OTHERS SAID THOUGHTLESSLY.
EXACTLY!
I KNOW!
MUTTER ぼそ
...IDIOTS.
BUT...
NOW...
...
I KNOW...
MUMBLE ぼそ

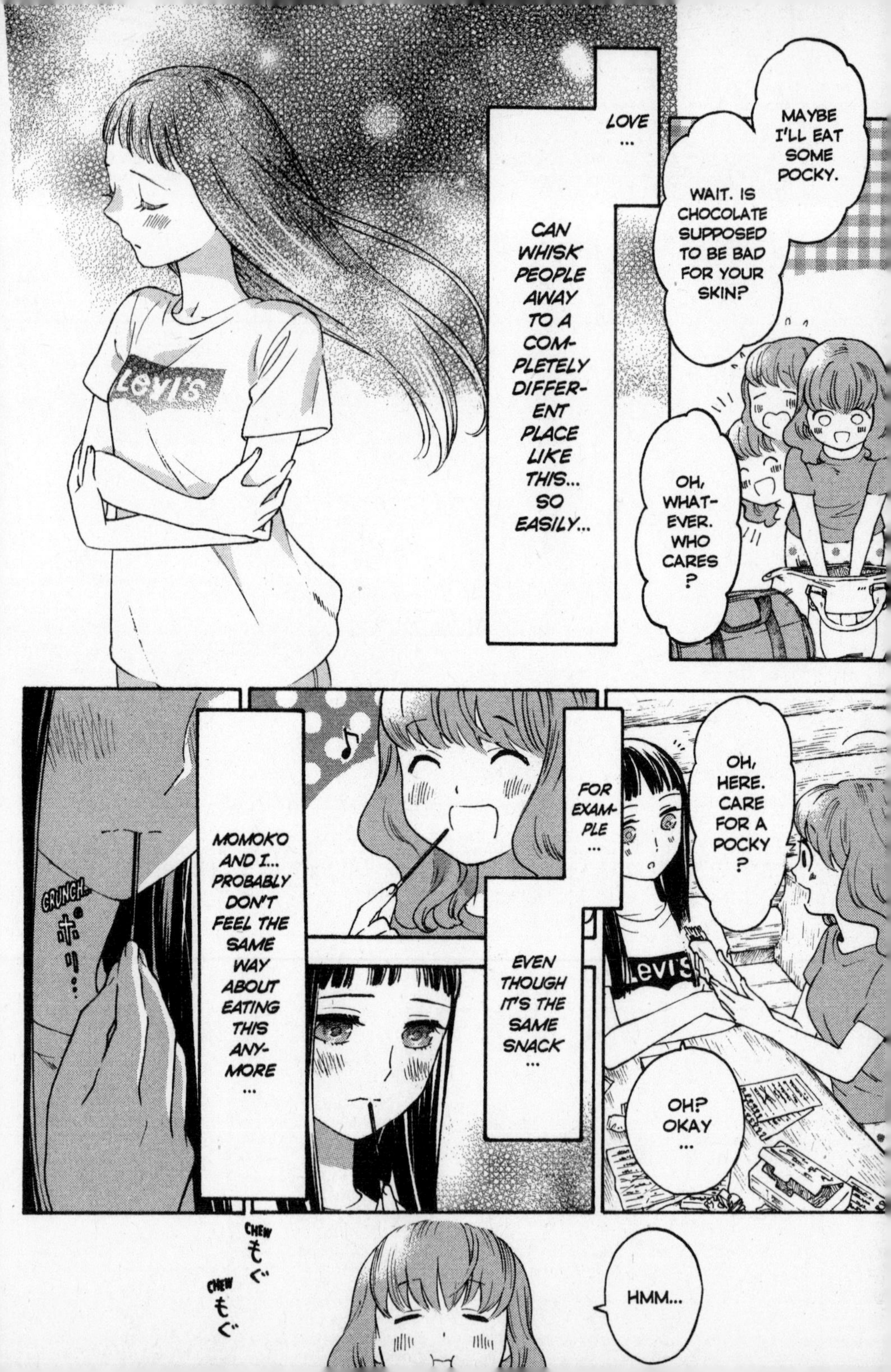
MAYBE I'LL EAT SOME POCKY.
WAIT. IS CHOCOLATE SUPPOSED TO BE BAD FOR YOUR SKIN?
OH, WHATEVER. WHO CARES?
LOVE ...
CAN WHISK PEOPLE AWAY TO A COMPLETELY DIFFERENT PLACE LIKE THIS... SO EASILY...
OH, HERE. CARE FOR A POCKY?
OH? OKAY ...
FOR EXAMPLE ...
EVEN THOUGH IT'S THE SAME SNACK ...
MOMOKO AND I... PROBABLY DON'T FEEL THE SAME WAY ABOUT EATING THIS ANYMORE ...
CRUNCH... ポリ...
HMM...
CHEW もぐ
CHEW もぐ

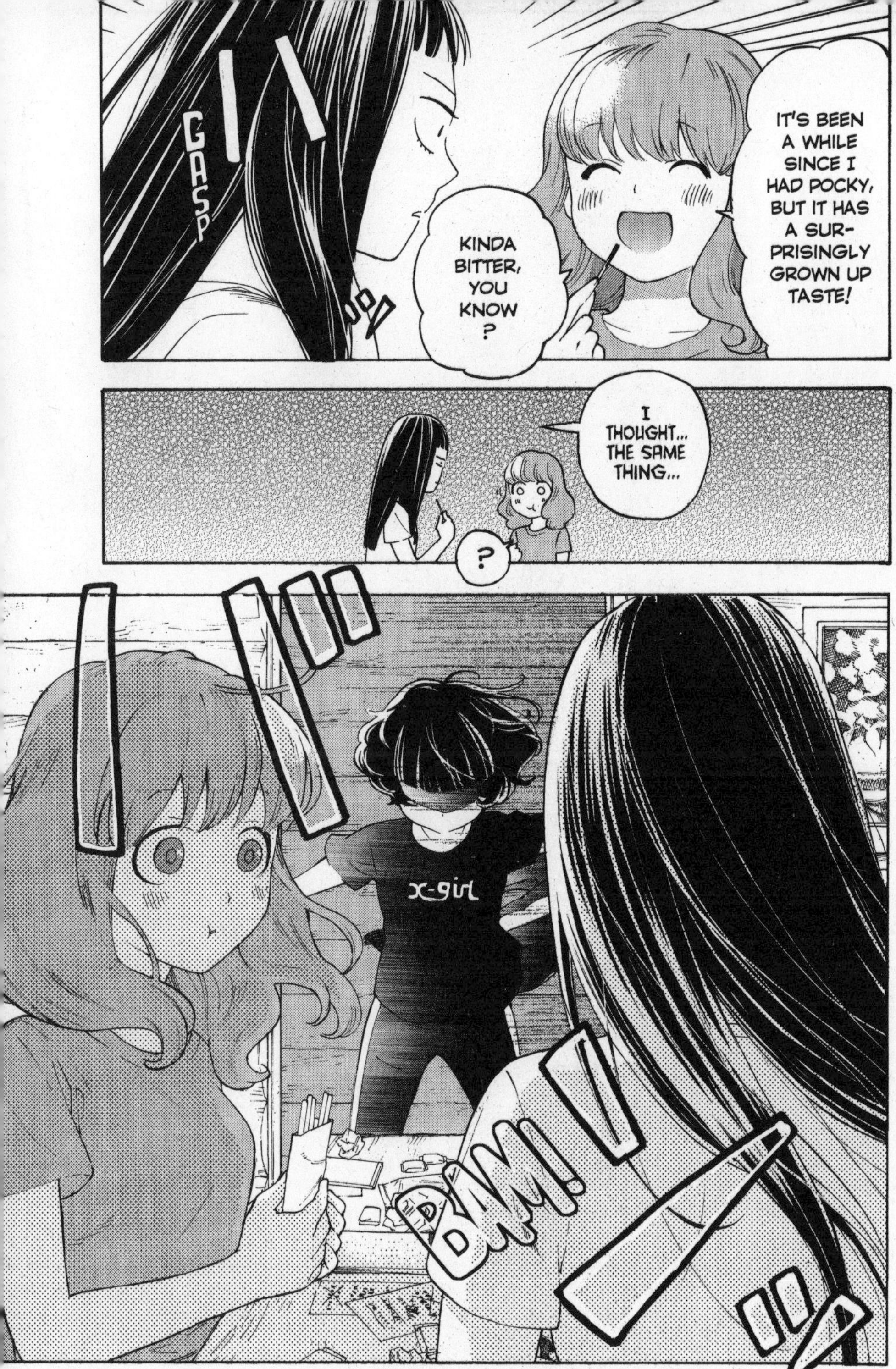
GASP
IT'S BEEN A WHILE SINCE I HAD POCKY, BUT IT HAS A SUR-PRISINGLY GROWN UP TASTE!
KINDA BITTER, YOU KNOW?
I THOUGHT... THE SAME THING...
?
x-girl
BAM!!

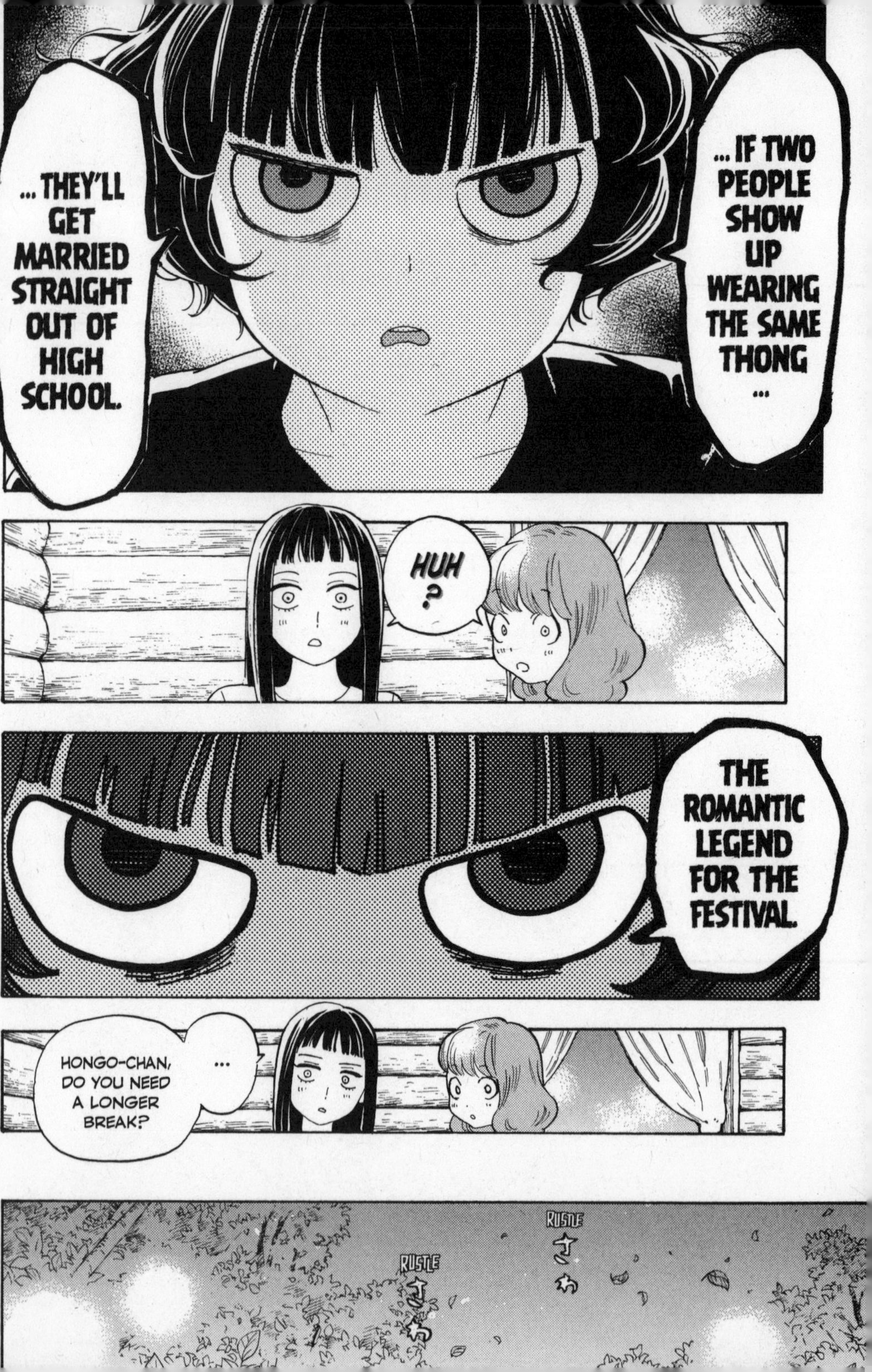
...IF TWO PEOPLE SHOW UP WEARING THE SAME THONG ...
...THEY'LL GET MARRIED STRAIGHT OUT OF HIGH SCHOOL.
HUH?
THE ROMANTIC LEGEND FOR THE FESTIVAL.
...
HONGO-CHAN, DO YOU NEED A LONGER BREAK?
RUSTLE
RUSTLE

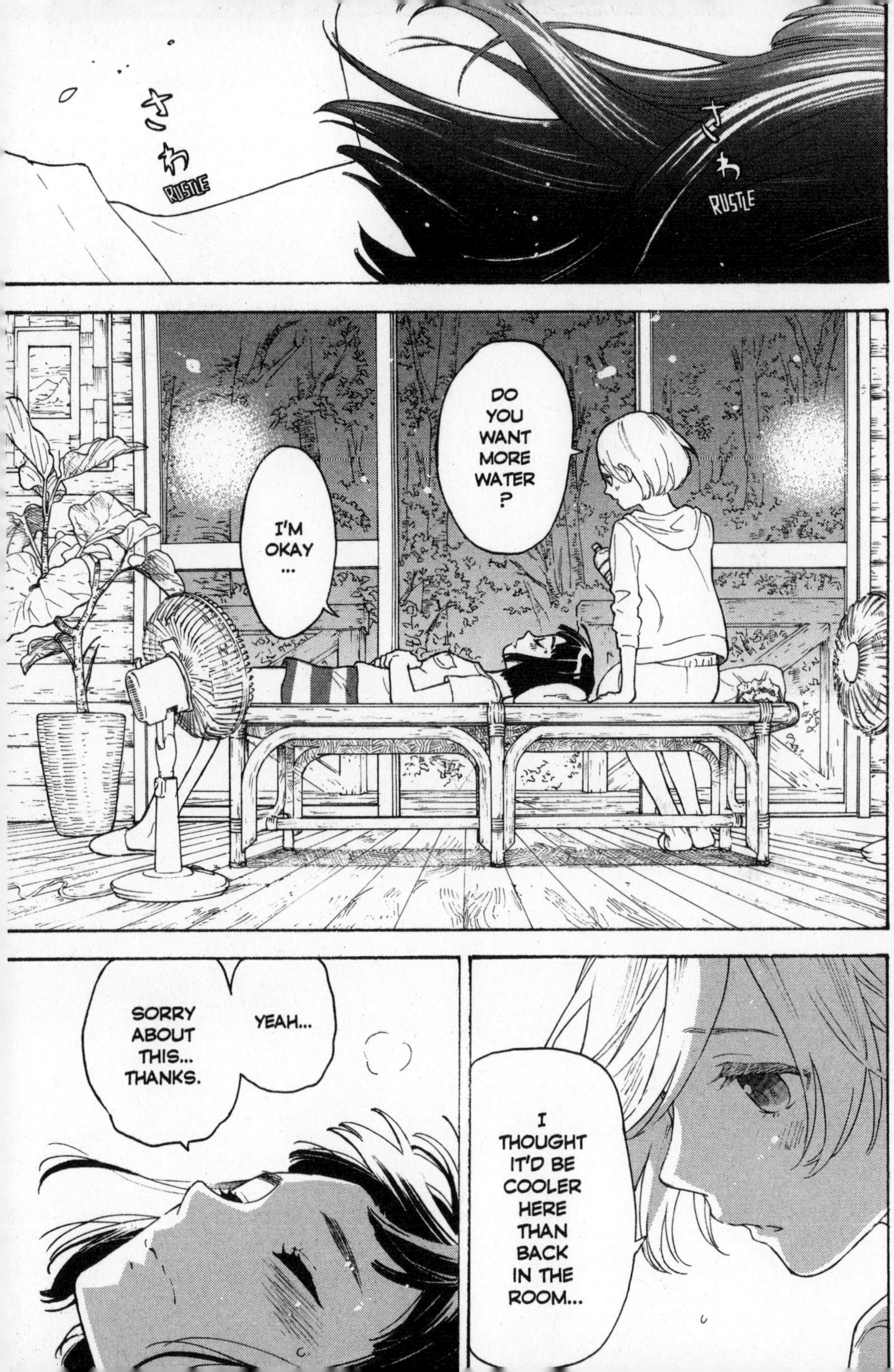
さわ
RUSTLE
さわ
RUSTLE
DO YOU WANT MORE WATER?
I'M OKAY...
I THOUGHT IT'D BE COOLER HERE THAN BACK IN THE ROOM...
YEAH...
SORRY ABOUT THIS... THANKS.

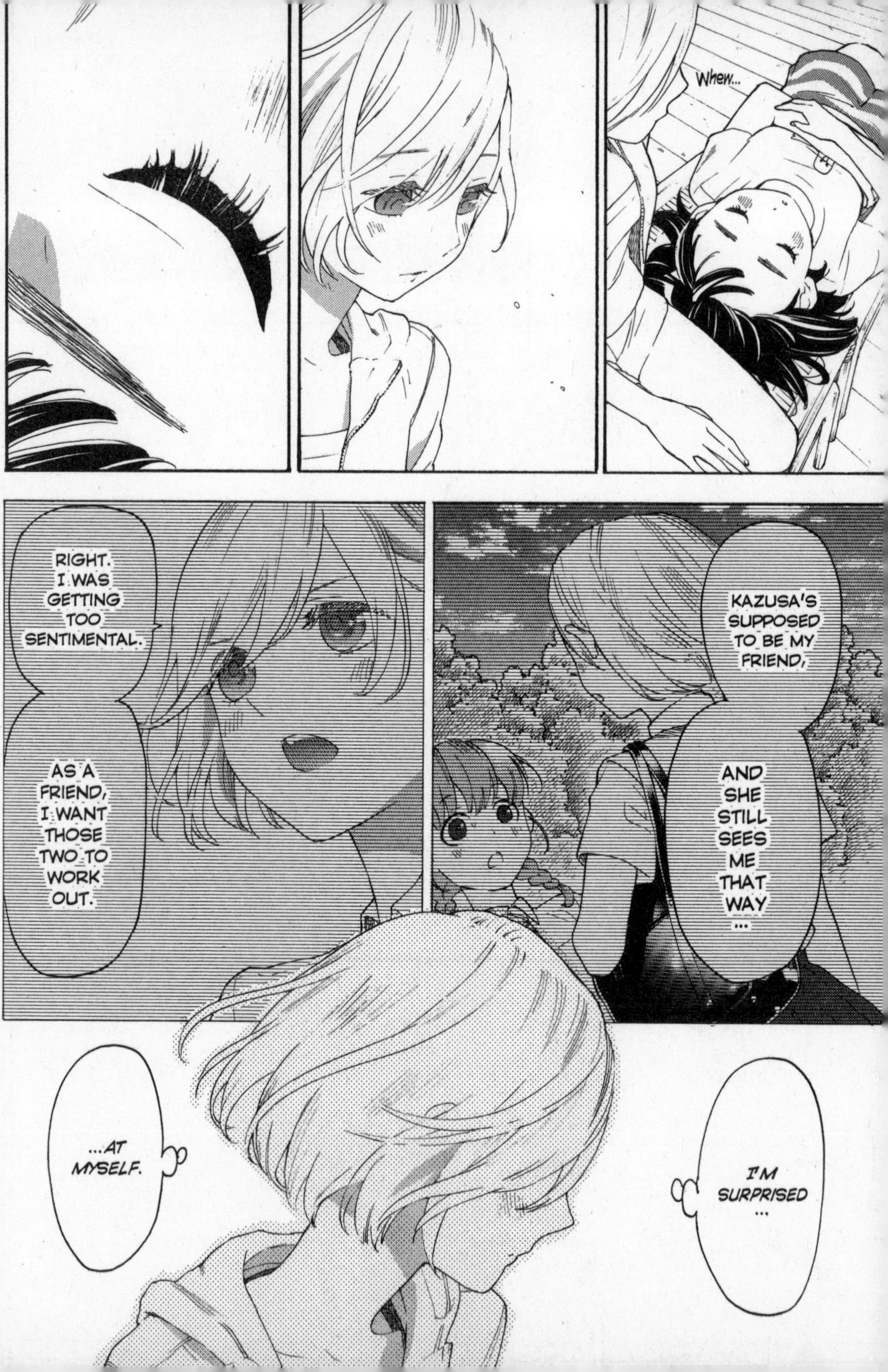
Whew...
KAZUSA'S SUPPOSED TO BE MY FRIEND,
AND SHE STILL SEES ME THAT WAY...
RIGHT. I WAS GETTING TOO SENTIMENTAL.
AS A FRIEND, I WANT THOSE TWO TO WORK OUT.
I'M SURPRISED...
...AT MYSELF.

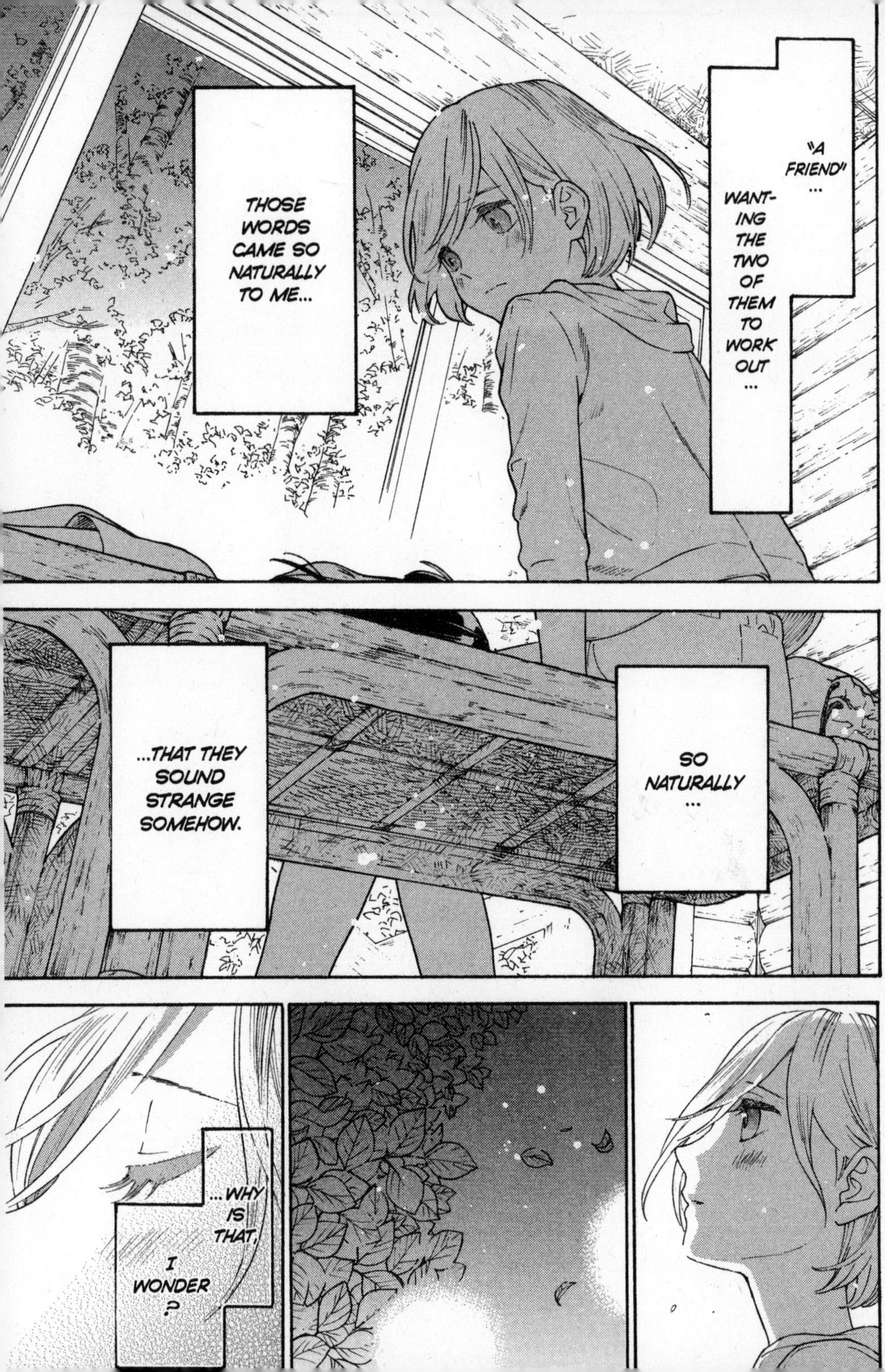
"A FRIEND"...
WANTING THE TWO OF THEM TO WORK OUT...
THOSE WORDS CAME SO NATURALLY TO ME...
SO NATURALLY...
...THAT THEY SOUND STRANGE SOMEHOW.
...WHY IS THAT, I WONDER?

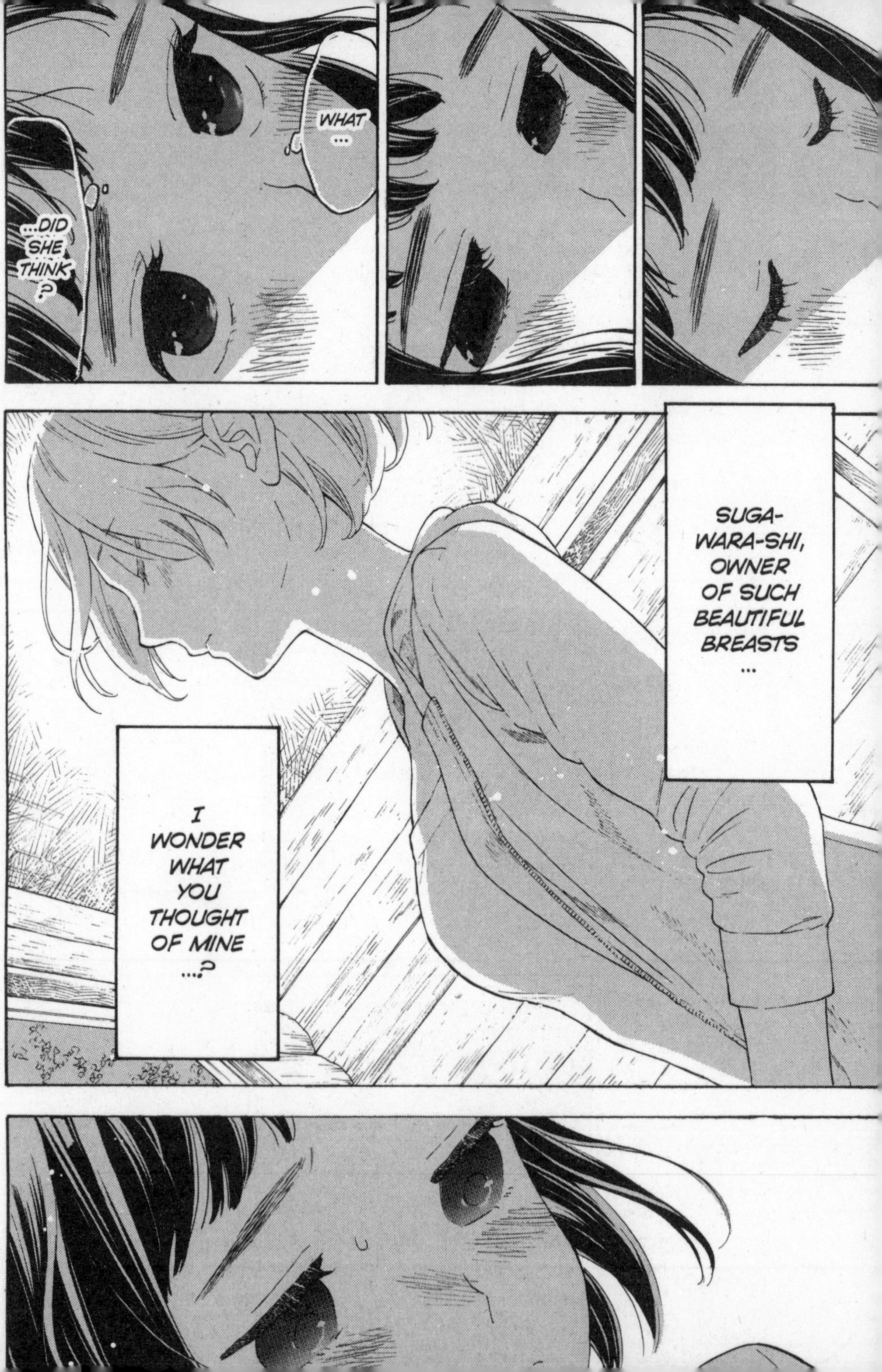
WHAT ...
...DID SHE THINK ?
SUGA-WARA-SHI, OWNER OF SUCH BEAUTIFUL BREASTS ...
I WONDER WHAT YOU THOUGHT OF MINE ...?

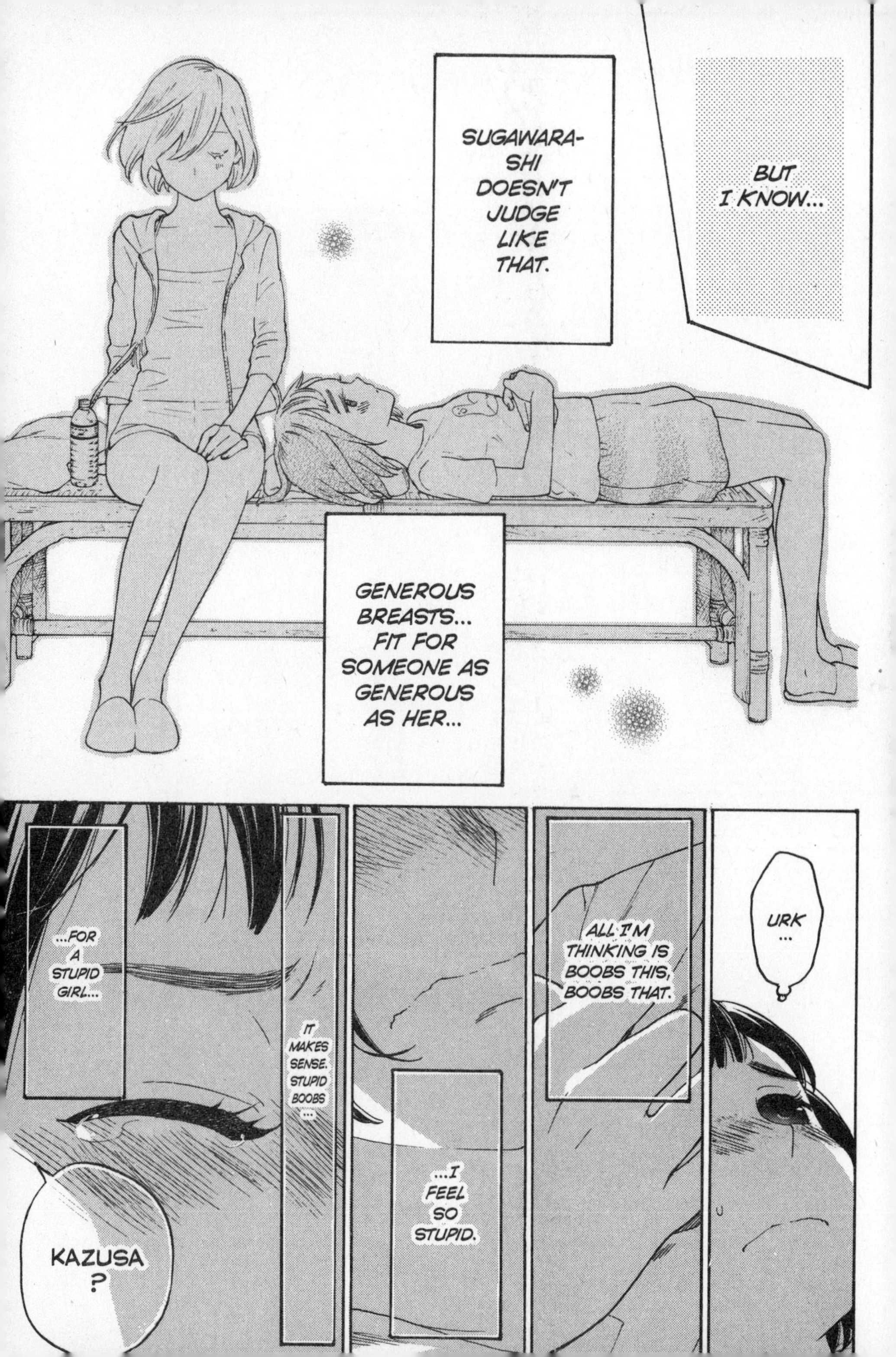
BUT I KNOW...
SUGAWARA-SHI DOESN'T JUDGE LIKE THAT.
GENEROUS BREASTS... FIT FOR SOMEONE AS GENEROUS AS HER...
URK ...
ALL I'M THINKING IS BOOBS THIS, BOOBS THAT.
...I FEEL SO STUPID.
IT MAKES SENSE. STUPID BOOBS ...
...FOR A STUPID GIRL...
KAZUSA ?

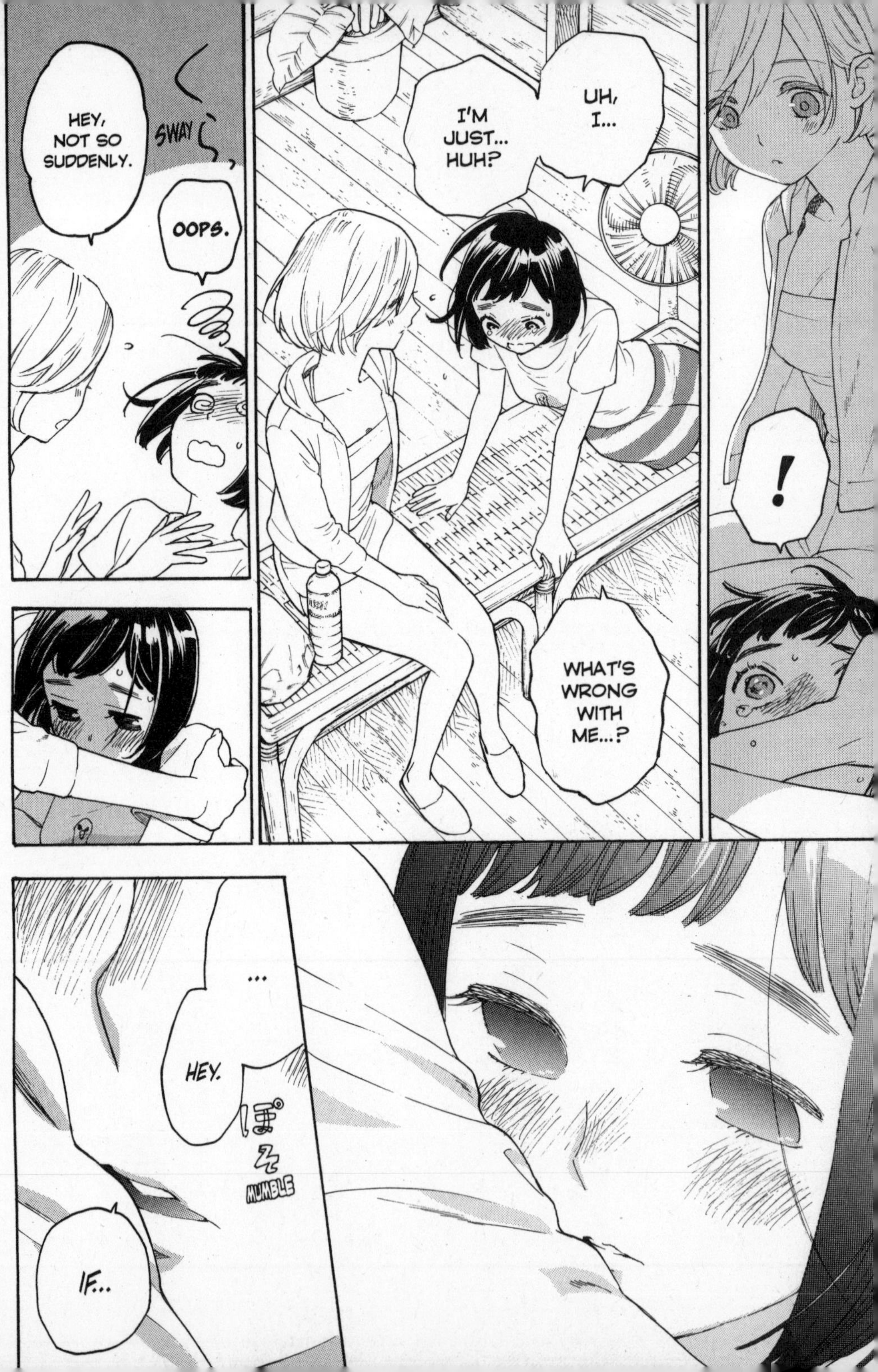
!
UH, I...
I'M JUST... HUH?
WHAT'S WRONG WITH ME...?
HEY, NOT SO SUDDENLY.
SWAY
OOPS.
...
HEY.
ぽそ
MUMBLE
IF...

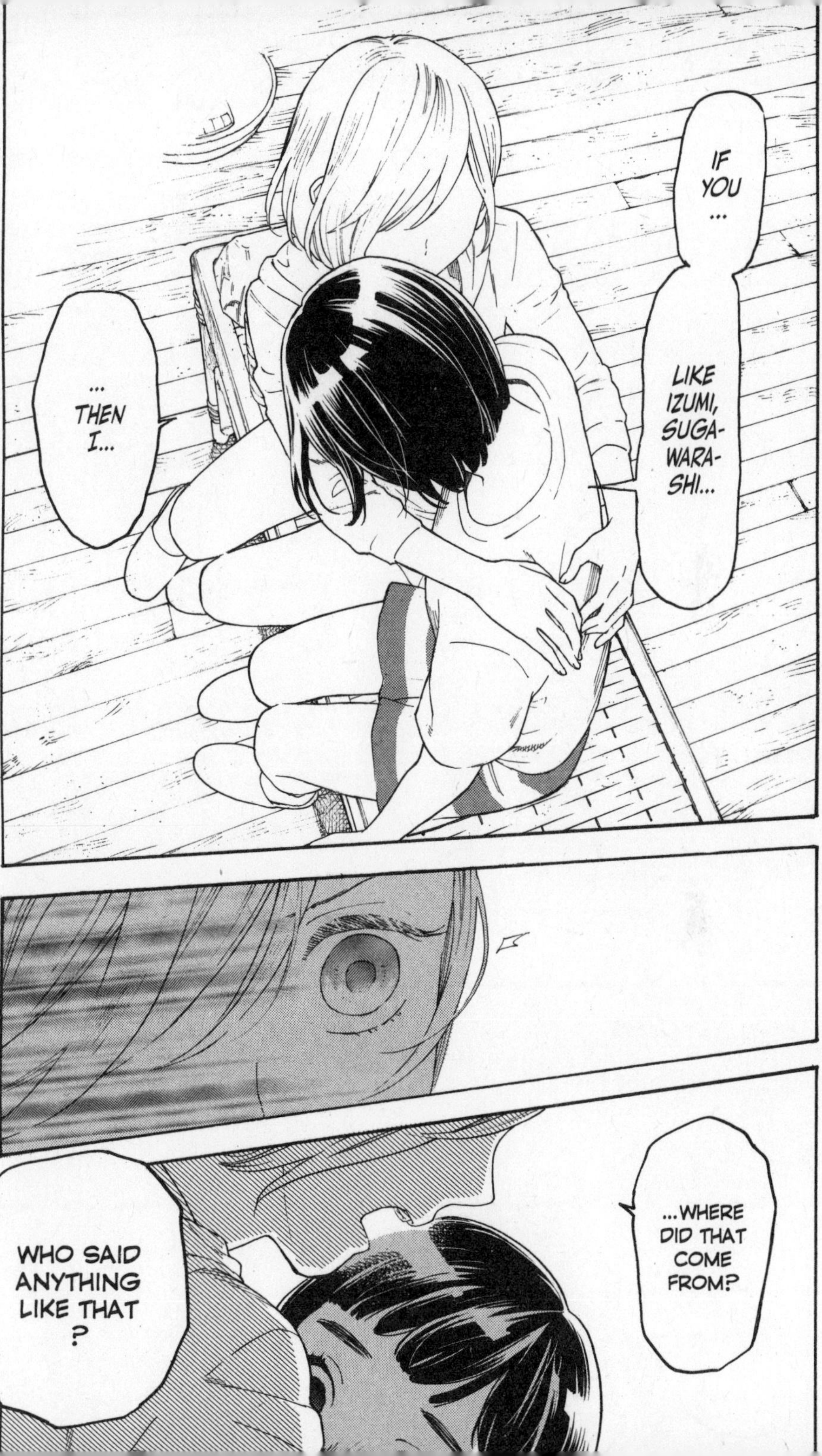
IF YOU ... LIKE IZUMI, SUGAWARA-SHI...
... THEN I...
...WHERE DID THAT COME FROM?
WHO SAID ANYTHING LIKE THAT?

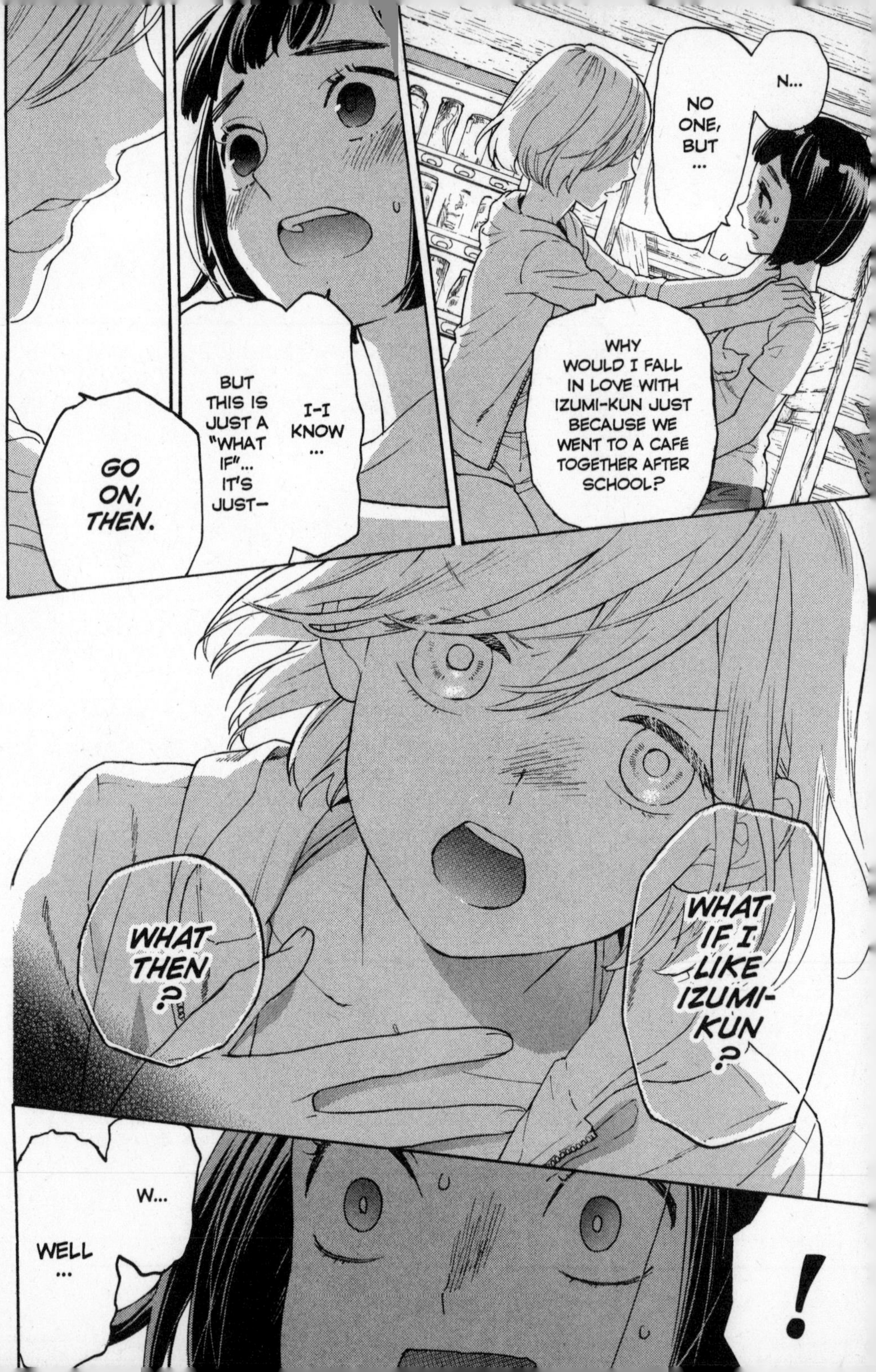
N...
NO ONE, BUT ...
WHY WOULD I FALL IN LOVE WITH IZUMI-KUN JUST BECAUSE WE WENT TO A CAFE TOGETHER AFTER SCHOOL?
I-I KNOW ...
BUT THIS IS JUST A "WHAT IF"... IT'S JUST—
GO ON, THEN.
WHAT IF I LIKE IZUMI-KUN?
WHAT THEN?
W...
WELL ...
!

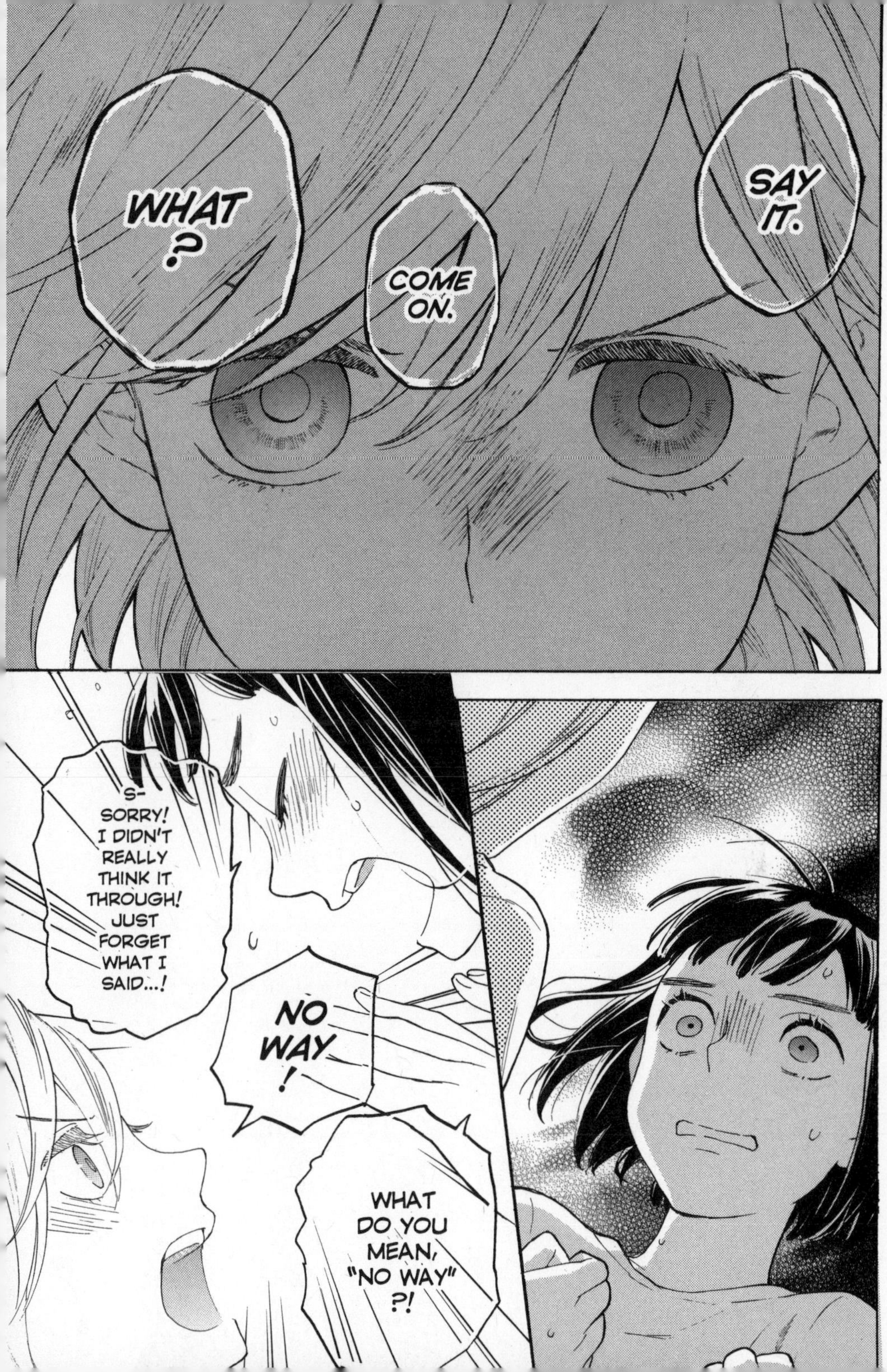
SAY IT.
COME ON.
WHAT?
S-SORRY! I DIDN'T REALLY THINK IT THROUGH! JUST FORGET WHAT I SAID...!
NO WAY!
WHAT DO YOU MEAN, "NO WAY"?!

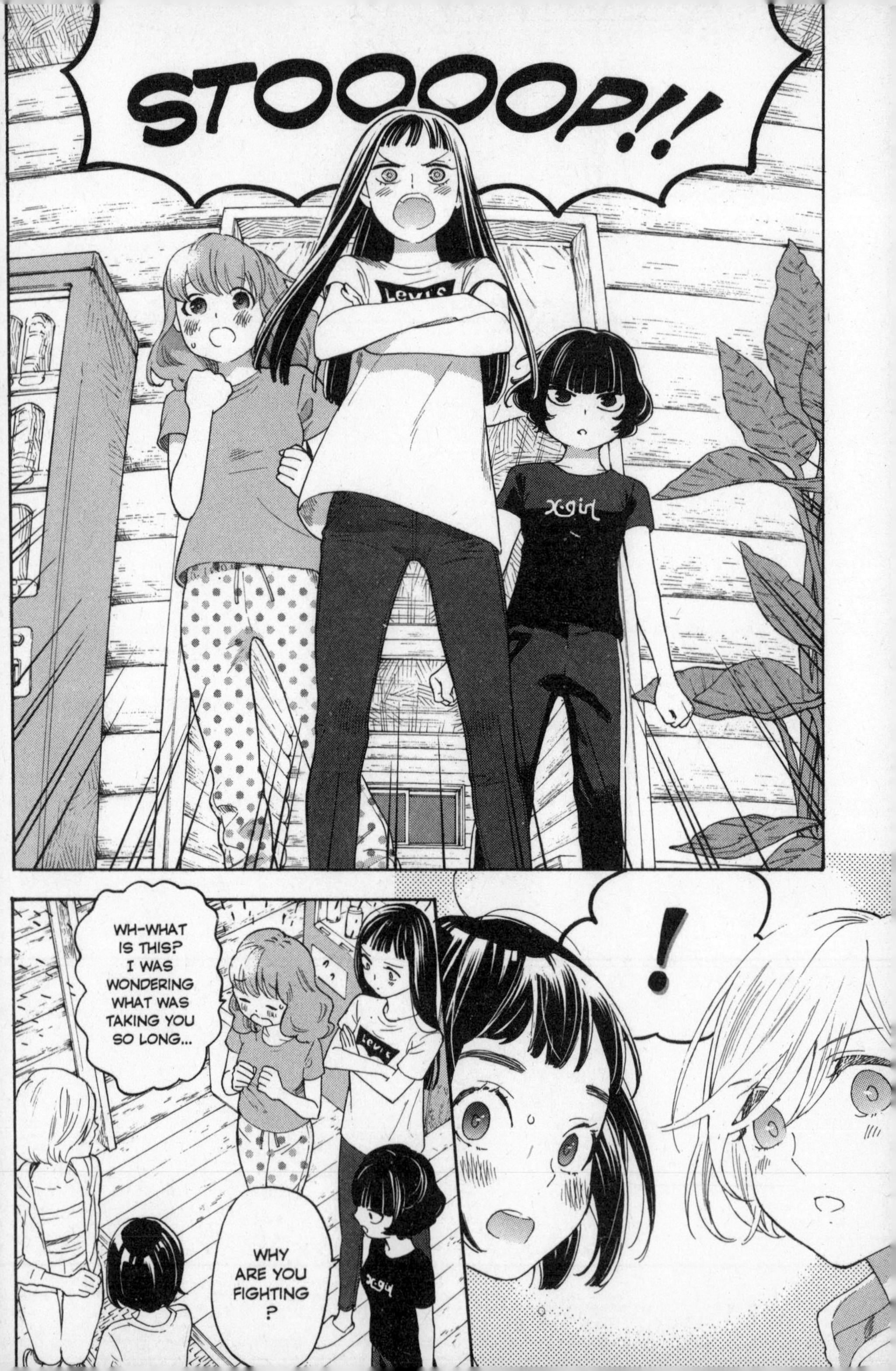
STOOOOP!!
!
WH-WHAT IS THIS? I WAS WONDERING WHAT WAS TAKING YOU SO LONG...
WHY ARE YOU FIGHTING?

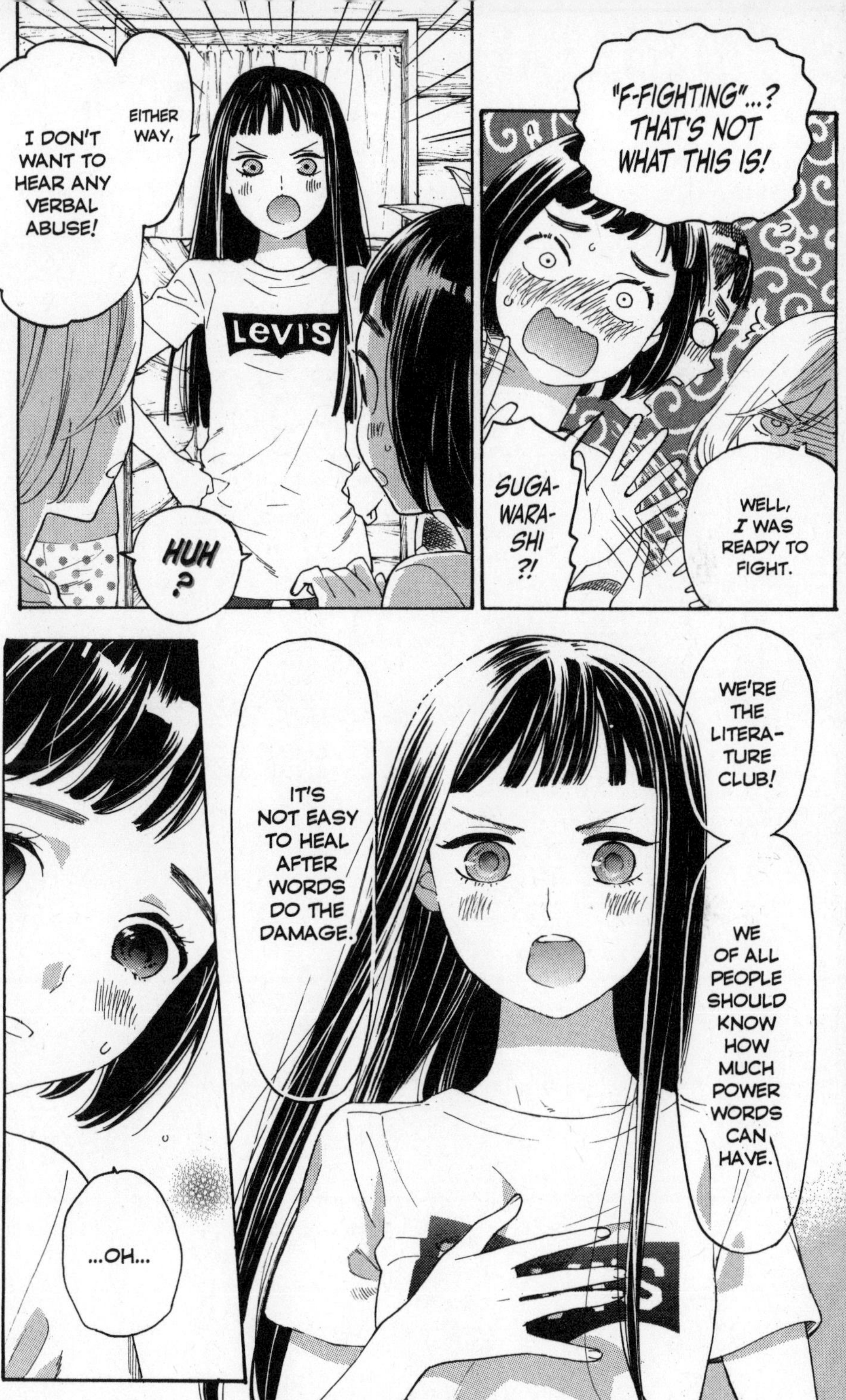
"F-FIGHTING"...? THAT'S NOT WHAT THIS IS!
WELL, I WAS READY TO FIGHT.
SUGA-WARA-SHI?!
EITHER WAY,
I DON'T WANT TO HEAR ANY VERBAL ABUSE!
HUH?
WE'RE THE LITERA-TURE CLUB!
WE OF ALL PEOPLE SHOULD KNOW HOW MUCH POWER WORDS CAN HAVE.
IT'S NOT EASY TO HEAL AFTER WORDS DO THE DAMAGE.
...OH...

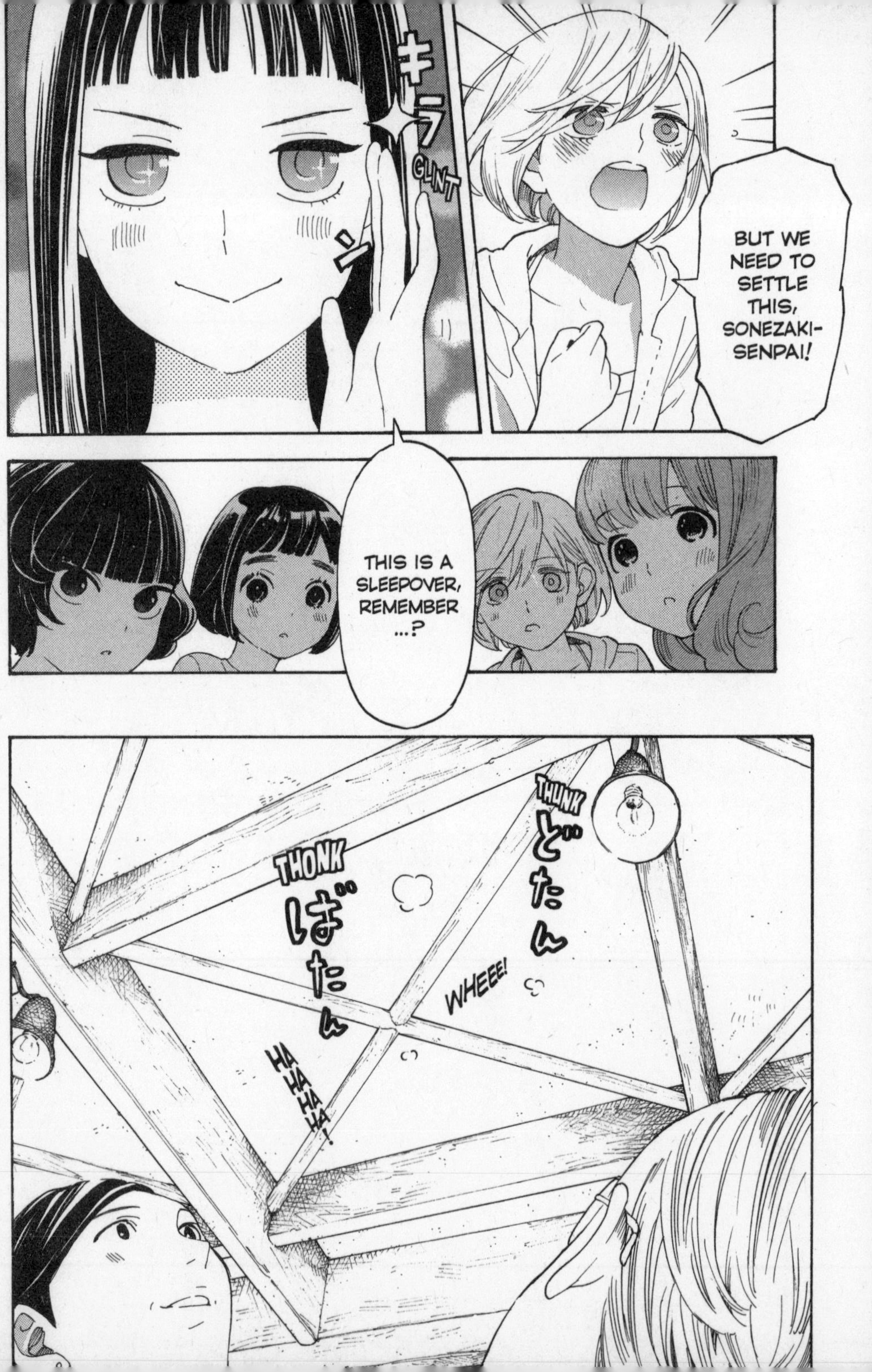
BUT WE NEED TO SETTLE THIS, SONEZAKI-SENPAI!
キラ
GLINT
THIS IS A SLEEPOVER, REMEMBER ...?
THUNK
どたん
THONK
ばたん
WHEEE!
HA HA HA HA!

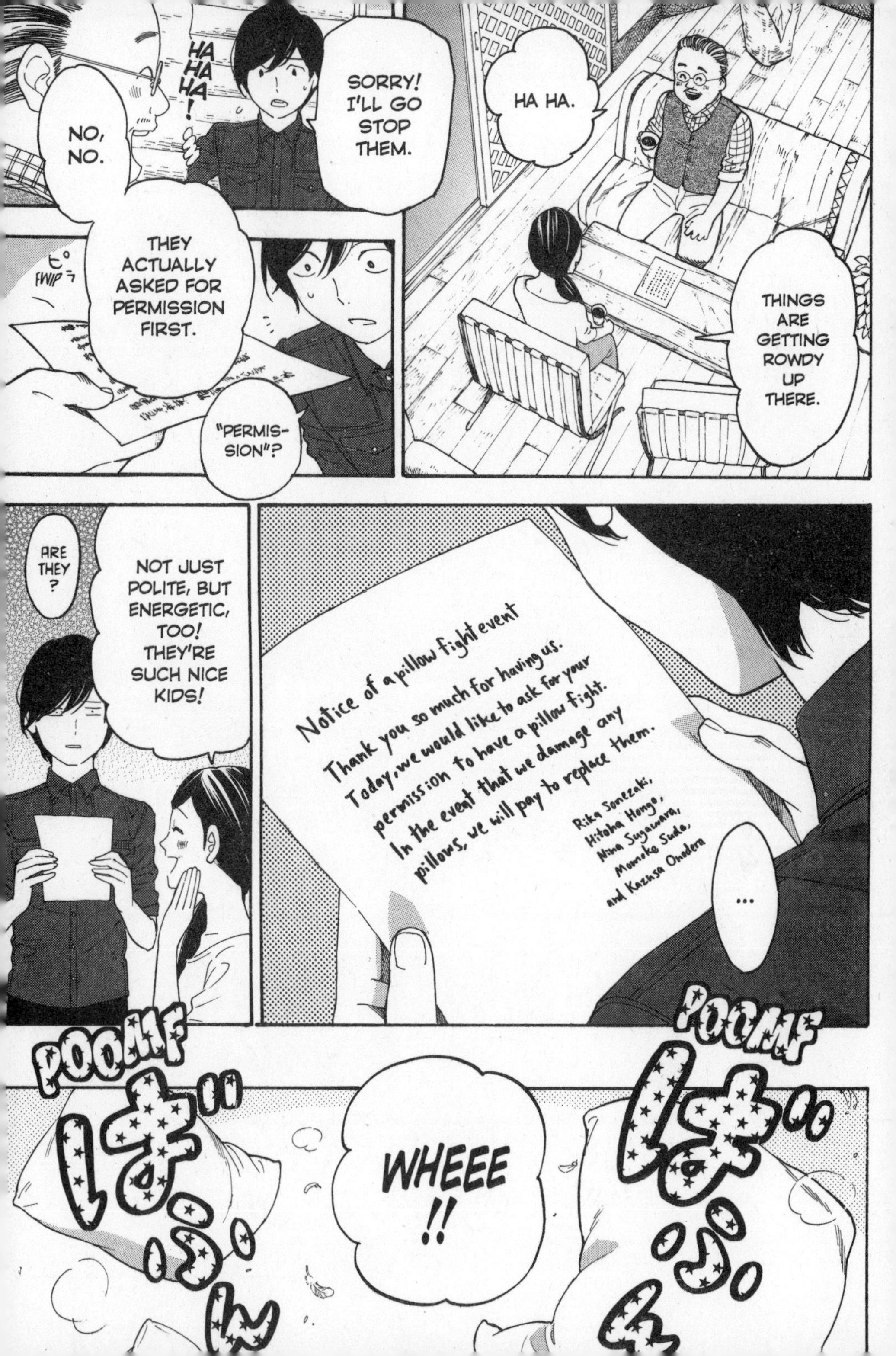
HA HA.
THINGS ARE GETTING ROWDY UP THERE.
SORRY! I'LL GO STOP THEM.
HA HA HA!
NO, NO.
THEY ACTUALLY ASKED FOR PERMISSION FIRST.
FWIP
"PERMIS-SION"?
Notice of a pillow fight event
Thank you so much for having us.
Today, we would like to ask for your permission to have a pillow fight.
In the event that we damage any pillows, we will pay to replace them.
Rika Sonezaki, Hitoha Hongo, Nina Sugawara, Momoko Sudo, and Kazusa Onodera
...
NOT JUST POLITE, BUT ENERGETIC, TOO! THEY'RE SUCH NICE KIDS!
ARE THEY?
POOMF
WHEEE!!
POOMF

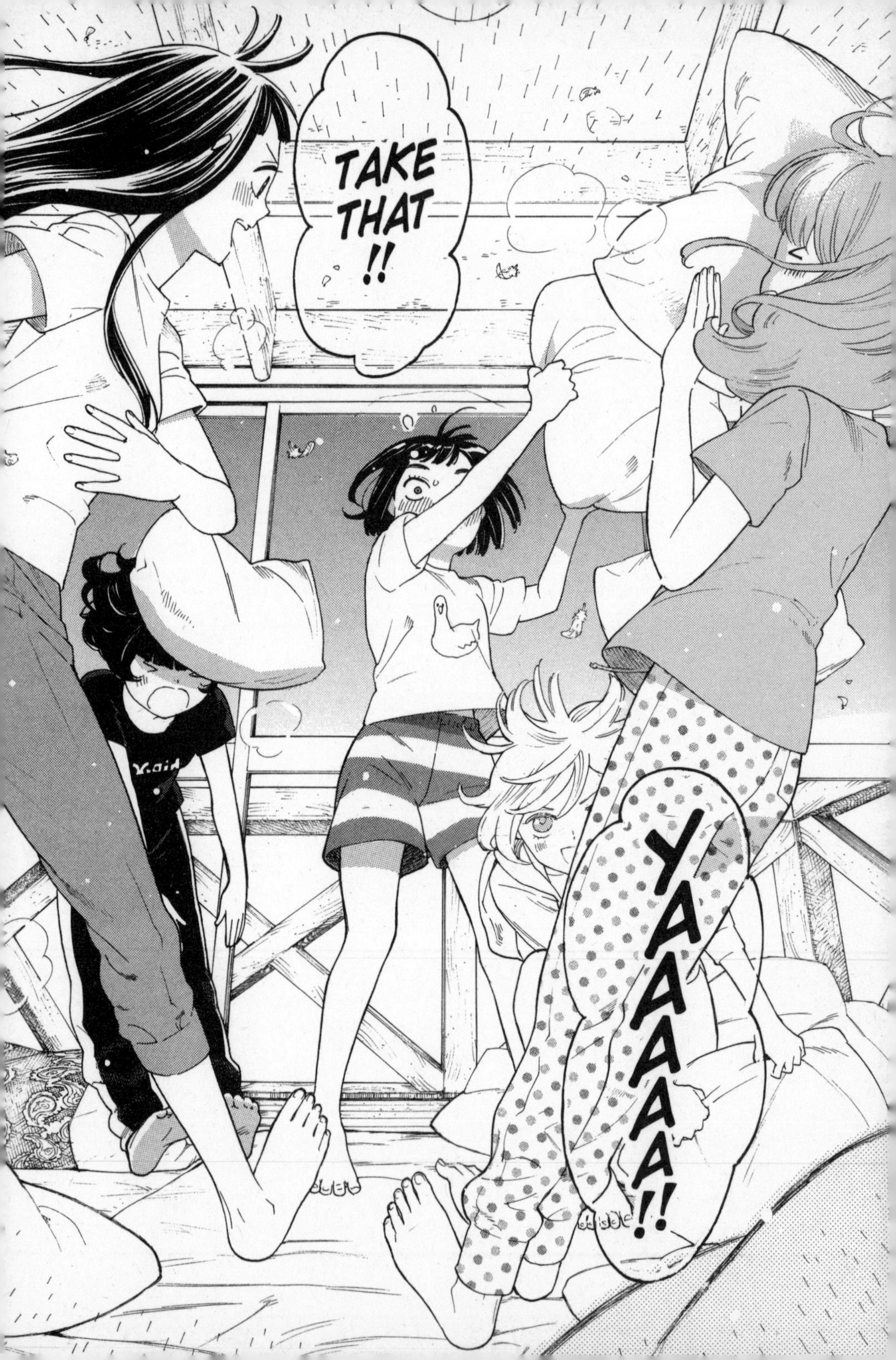
TAKE THAT !!
YAAAAA!!

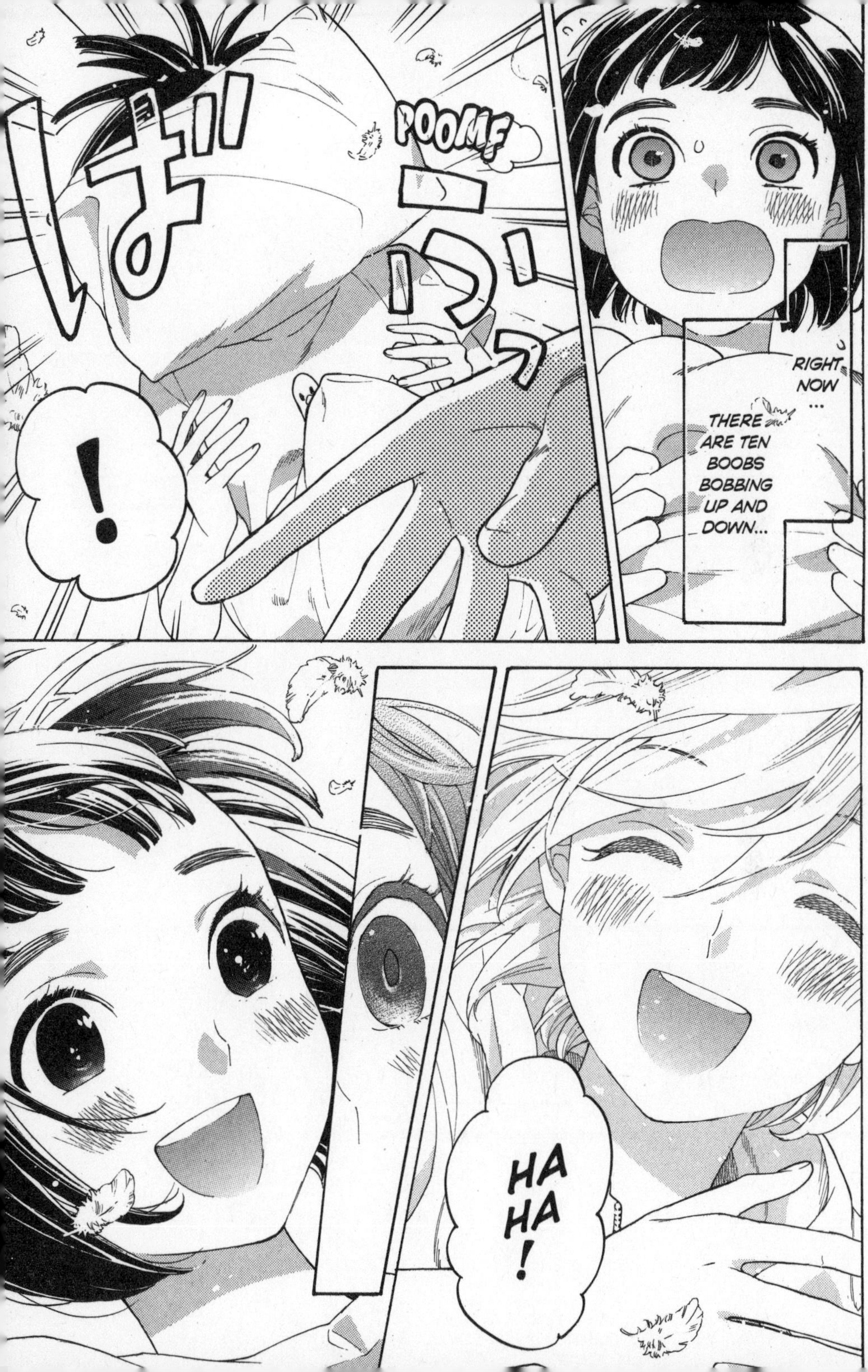

RIGHT NOW ... THERE ARE TEN BOOBS BOBBING UP AND DOWN...
POOMF
ばーっ
!
HA HA!

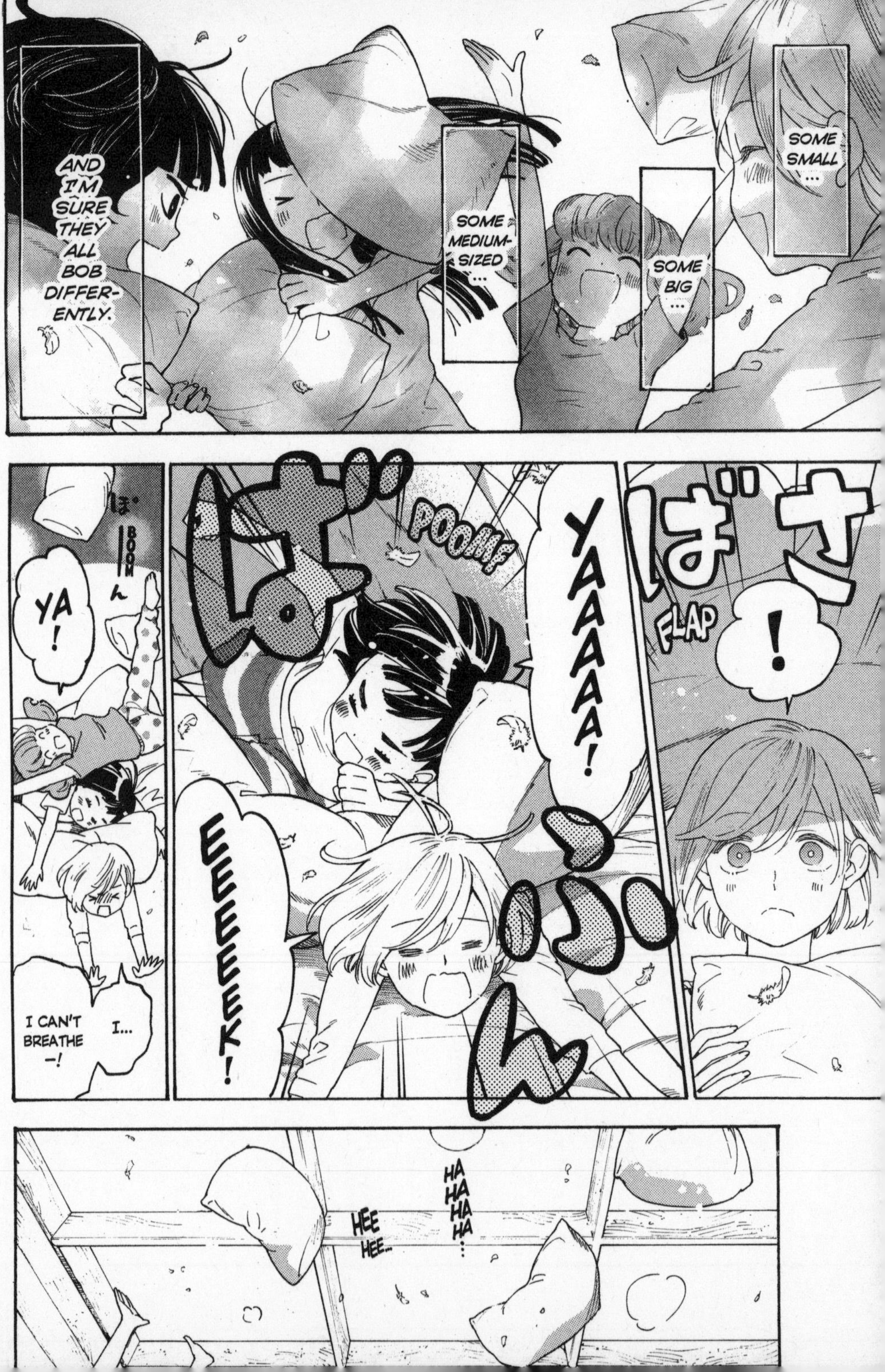
SOME SMALL...
SOME BIG...
SOME MEDIUM-SIZED...
AND I'M SURE THEY ALL BOB DIFFERENTLY.
ばさ
FLAP
!
POOMF
YAAAAAA!
EEEEEEK!
BOOM
YA!
I...
I CAN'T BREATHE—!
HA HA HA HA...
HEE HEE...

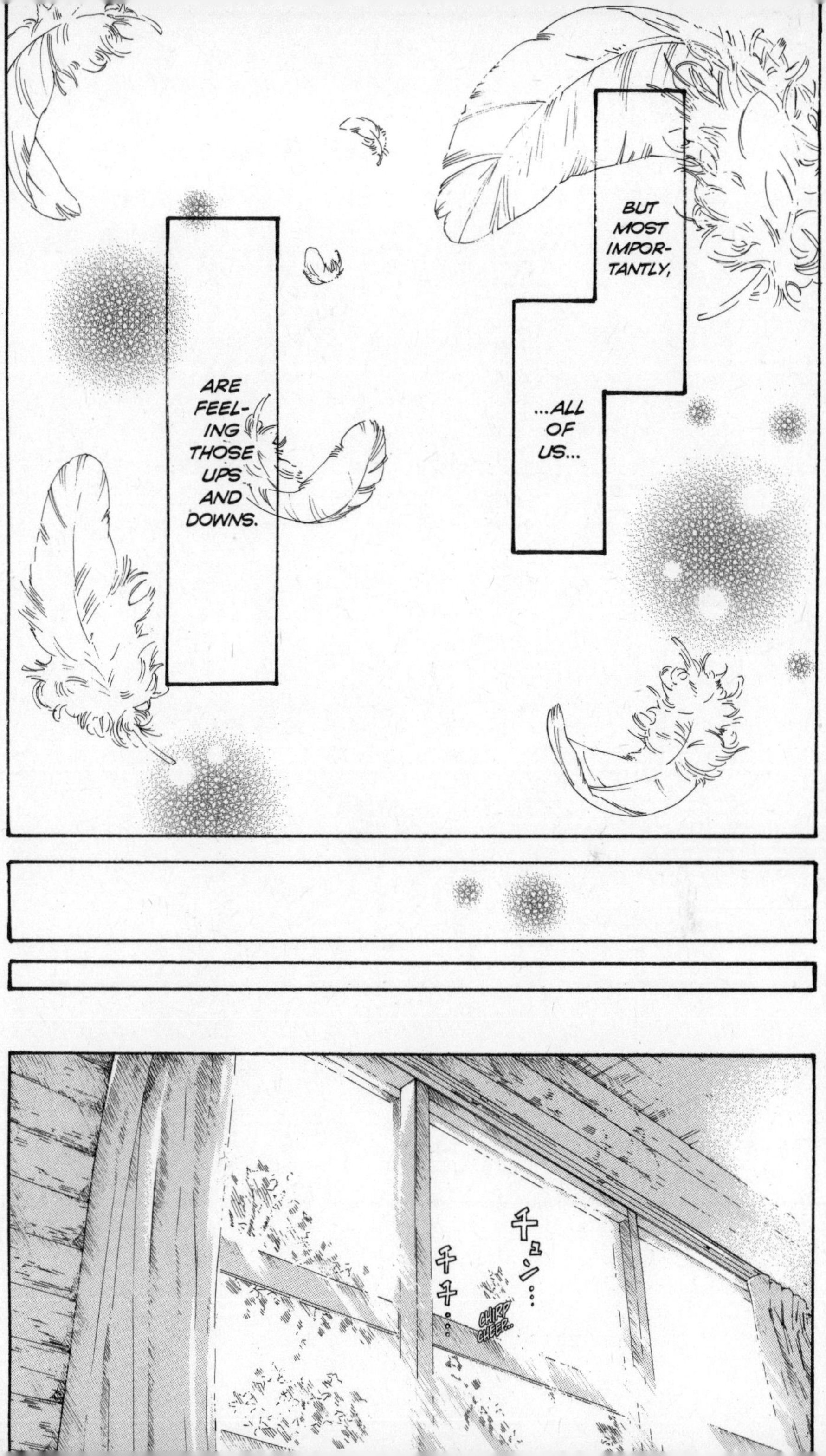
BUT MOST IMPOR-TANTLY,
...ALL OF US...
ARE FEEL-ING THOSE UPS AND DOWNS.
チュン…
チチ…
CHIRP CHEER...

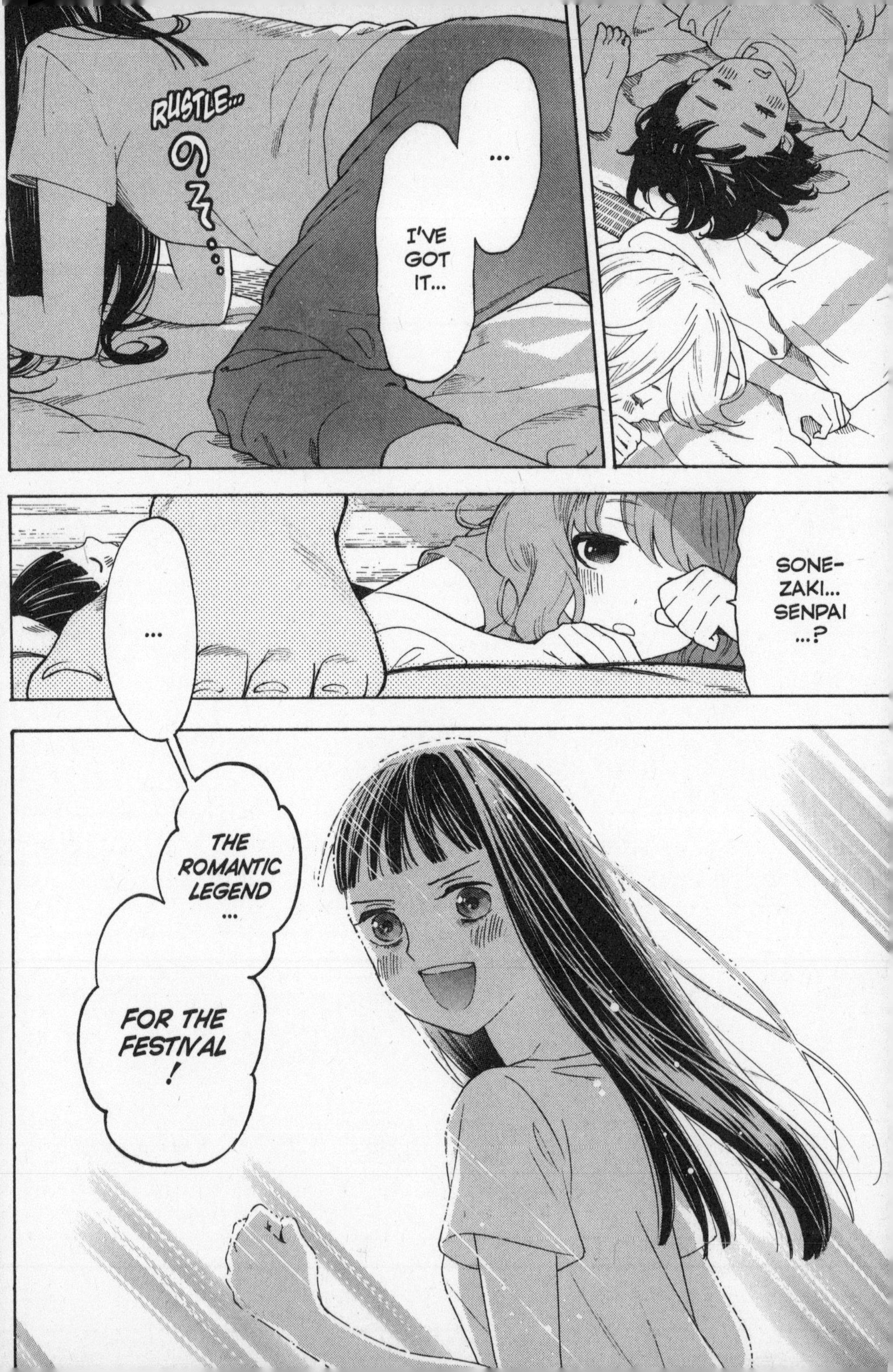
... I'VE GOT IT...
RUSTLE...
SONE-ZAKI... SENPAI...?
...
THE ROMANTIC LEGEND... FOR THE FESTIVAL!

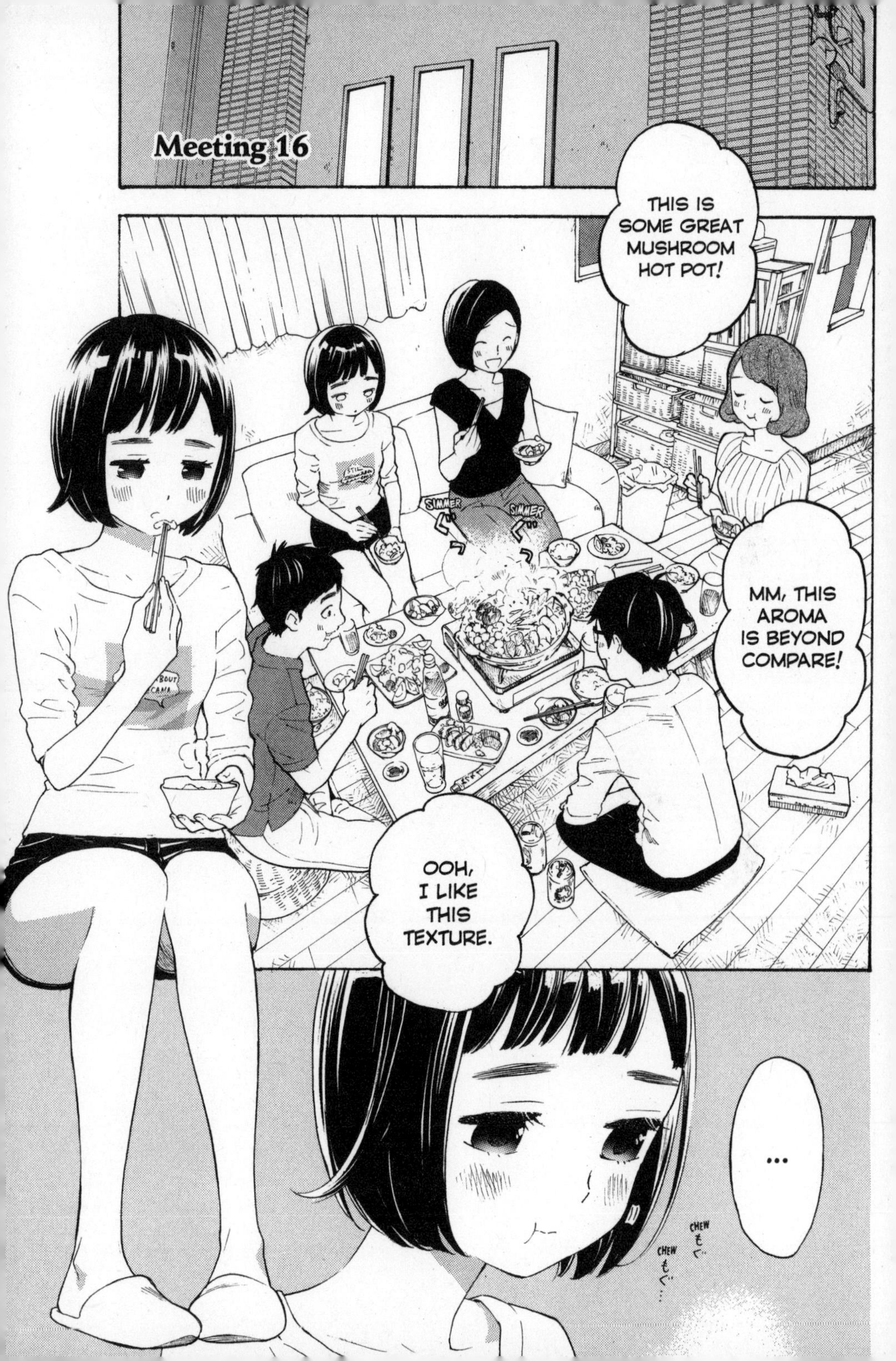
Meeting 16
THIS IS SOME GREAT MUSHROOM HOT POT!
MM, THIS AROMA IS BEYOND COMPARE!
SIMMER
SIMMER
OOH, I LIKE THIS TEXTURE.
...
CHEW もぐ
CHEW もぐ…

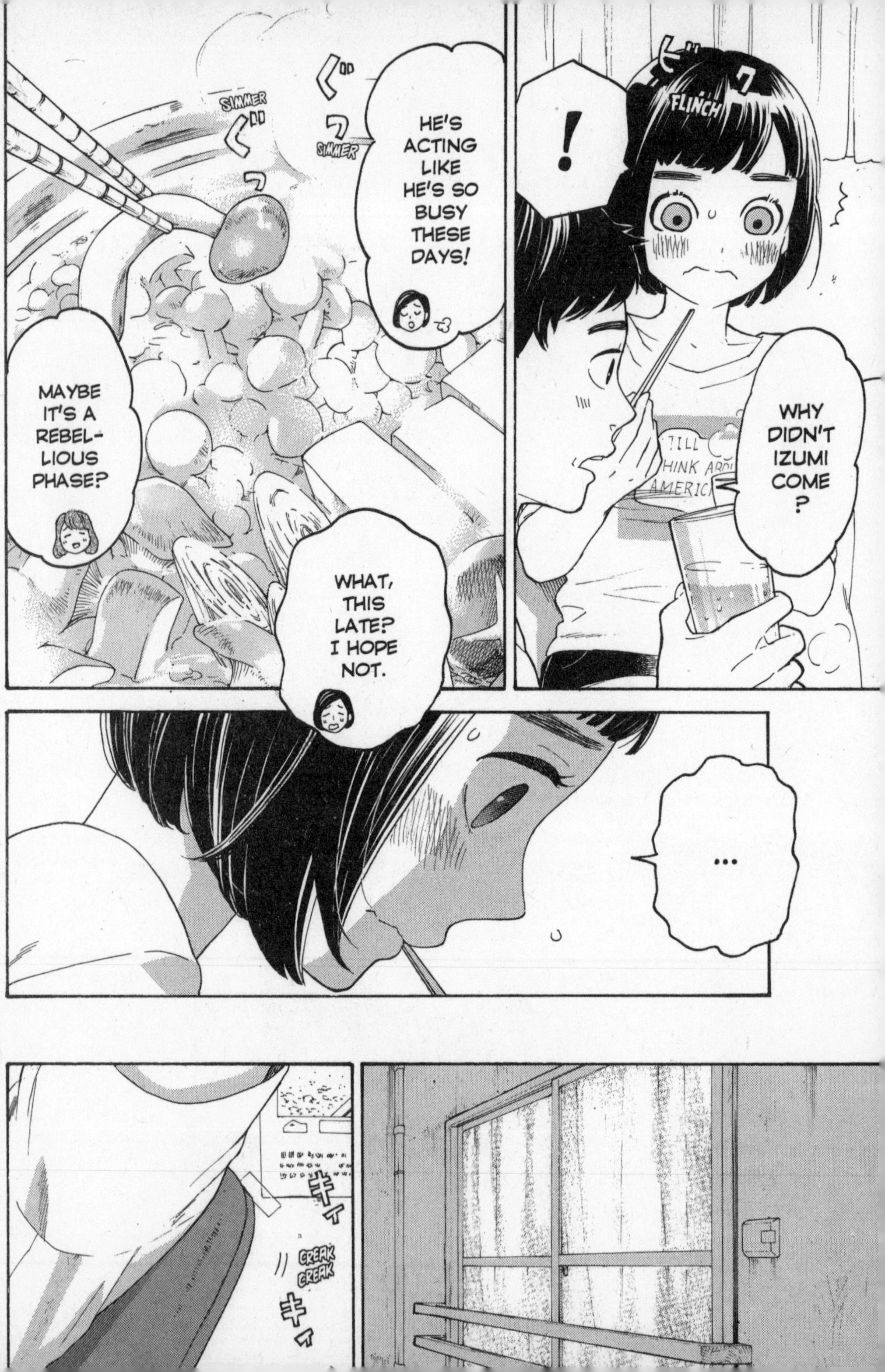
FLINCH
!
WHY DIDN'T IZUMI COME?
SIMMER
SIMMER
HE'S ACTING LIKE HE'S SO BUSY THESE DAYS!
MAYBE IT'S A REBEL-LIOUS PHASE?
WHAT, THIS LATE? I HOPE NOT.
...
CREAK CREAK

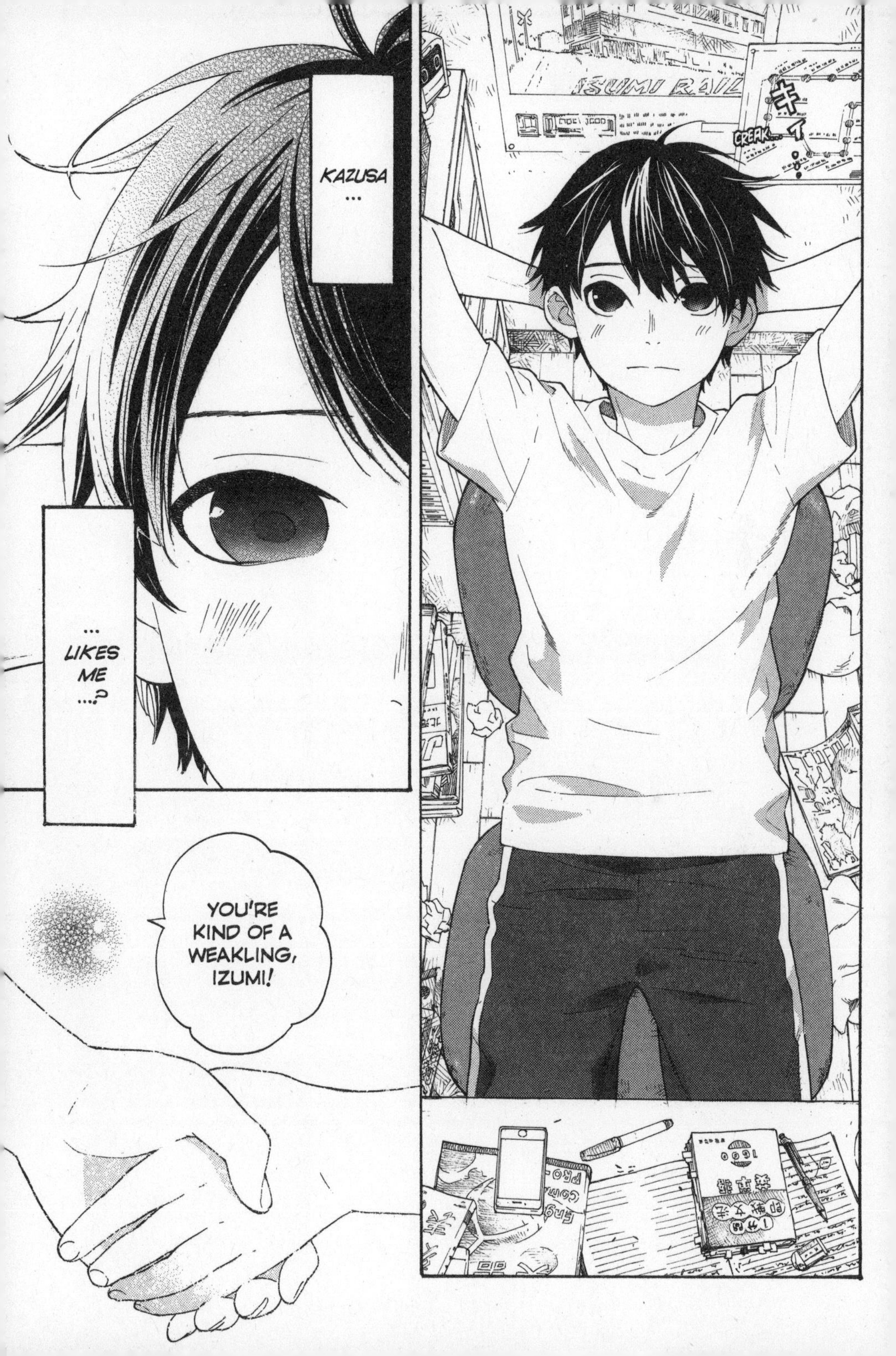
キィ
CREAK...
KAZUSA ...
... LIKES ME ...?
YOU'RE KIND OF A WEAKLING, IZUMI!

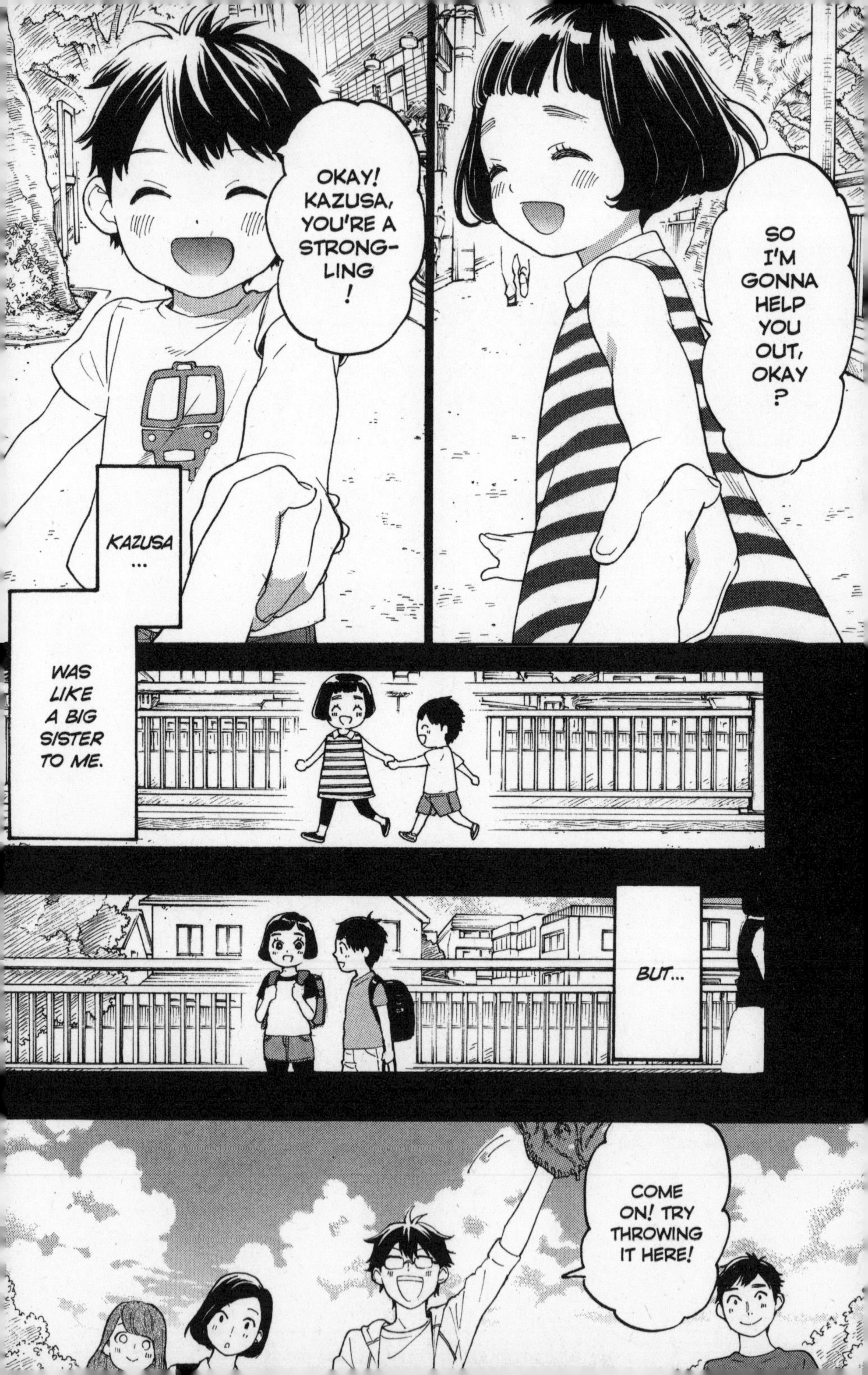
SO I'M GONNA HELP YOU OUT, OKAY?
OKAY! KAZUSA, YOU'RE A STRONG-LING!
KAZUSA...
WAS LIKE A BIG SISTER TO ME.
BUT...
COME ON! TRY THROWING IT HERE!

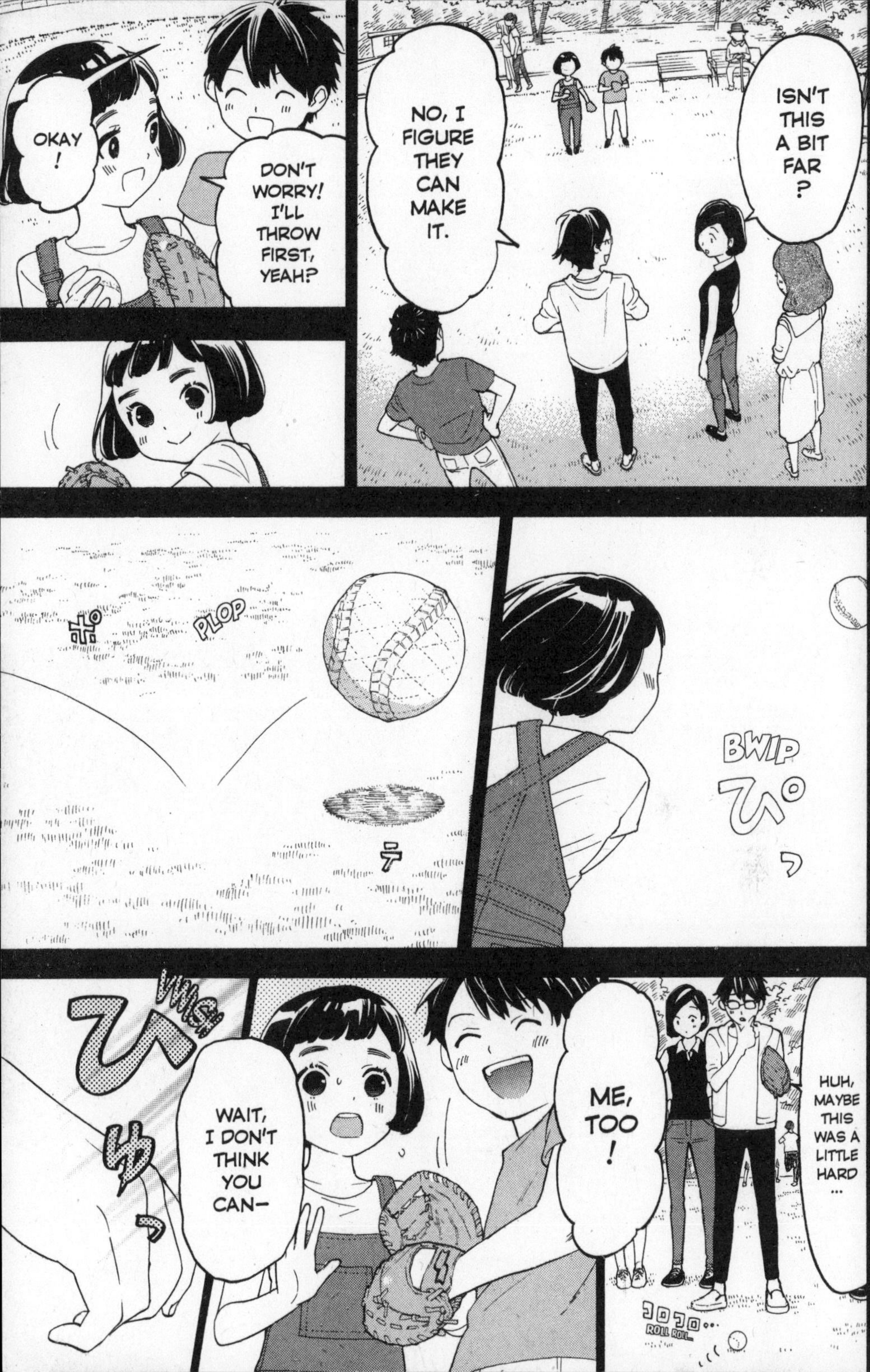

ISN'T THIS A BIT FAR?
NO, I FIGURE THEY CAN MAKE IT.
DON'T WORRY! I'LL THROW FIRST, YEAH?
OKAY!
BWIP
ひっ
ポテ
PLOP
HUH, MAYBE THIS WAS A LITTLE HARD...
ME, TOO!
WAIT, I DON'T THINK YOU CAN–
WHSH
ひゅっ
コロコロ..
ROLL ROLL..

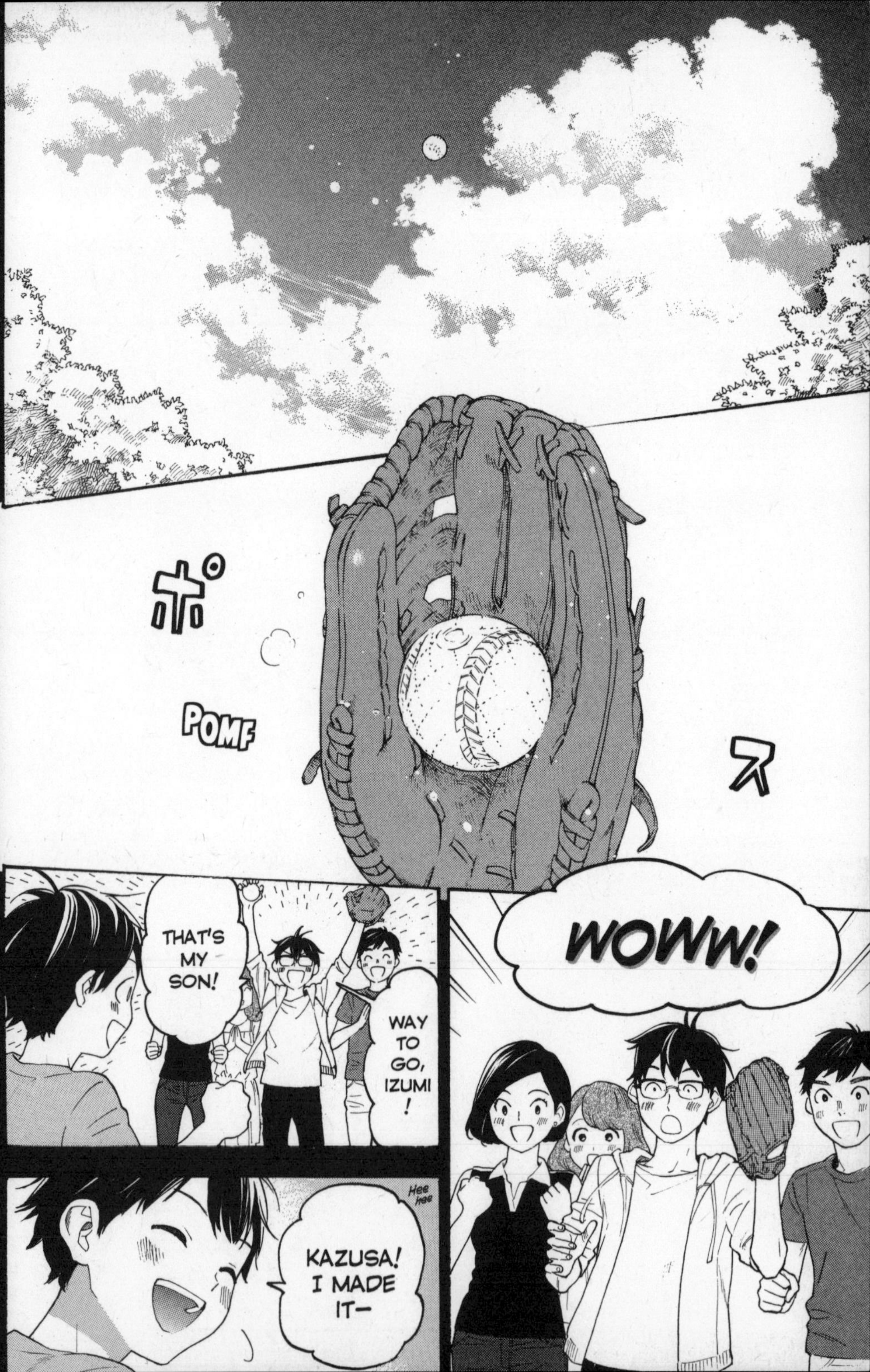
ポ
ス
POMF
WOWW!
THAT'S MY SON!
WAY TO GO, IZUMI!
Hee hee
KAZUSA! I MADE IT—

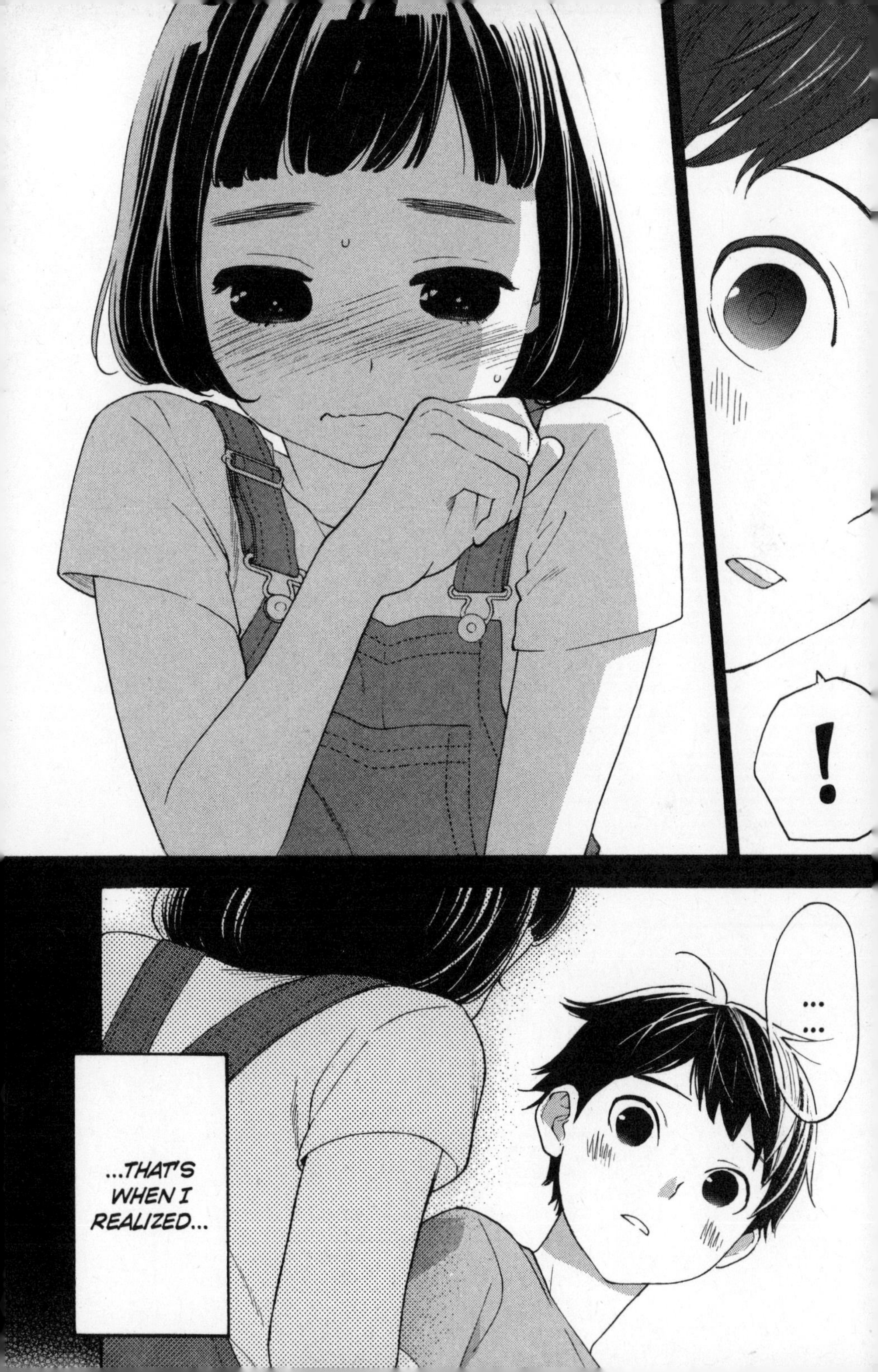
!
......
...THAT'S WHEN I REALIZED...

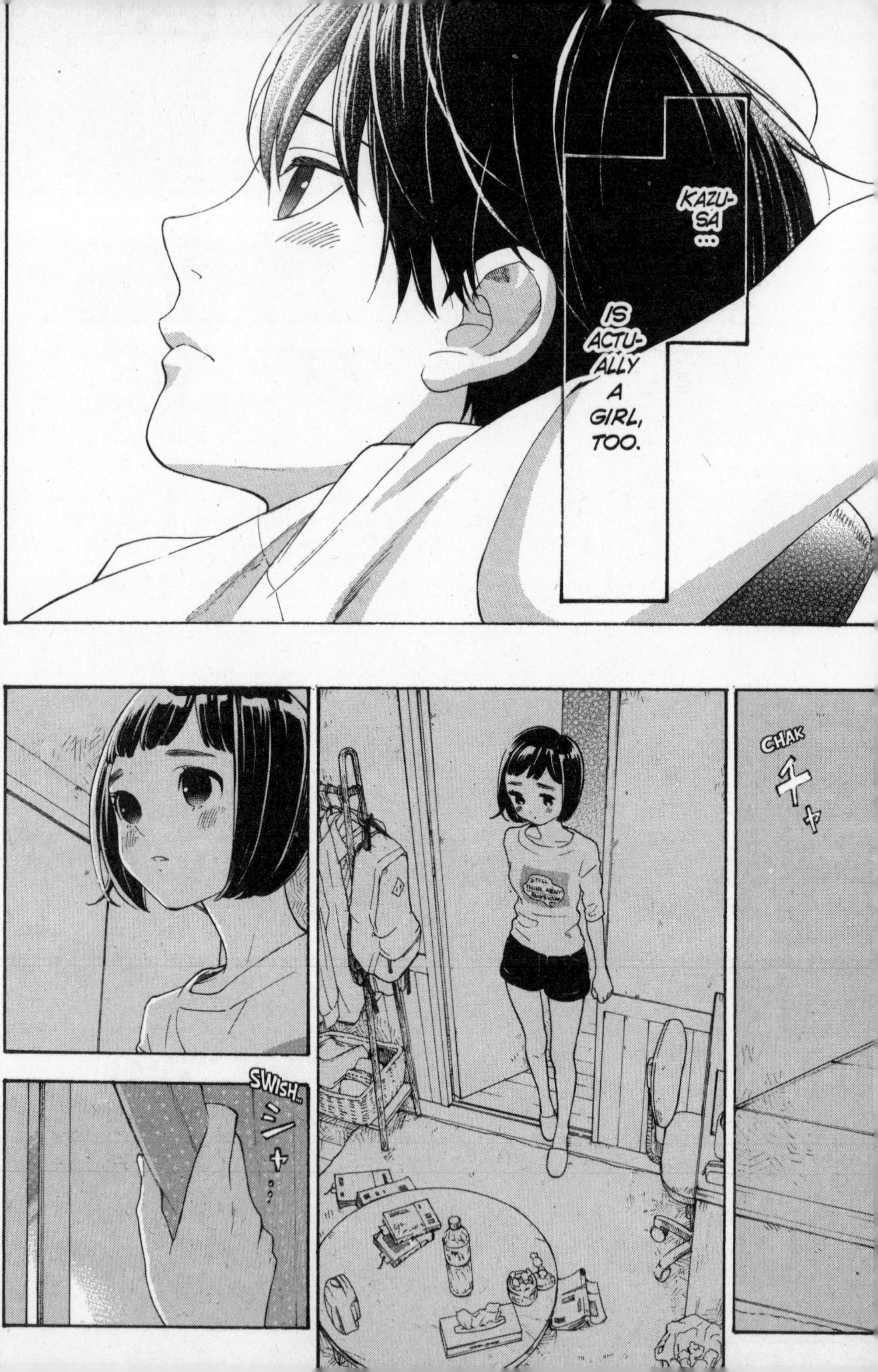
KAZUSA...
IS ACTUALLY A GIRL, TOO.
CHAK
SWISH...

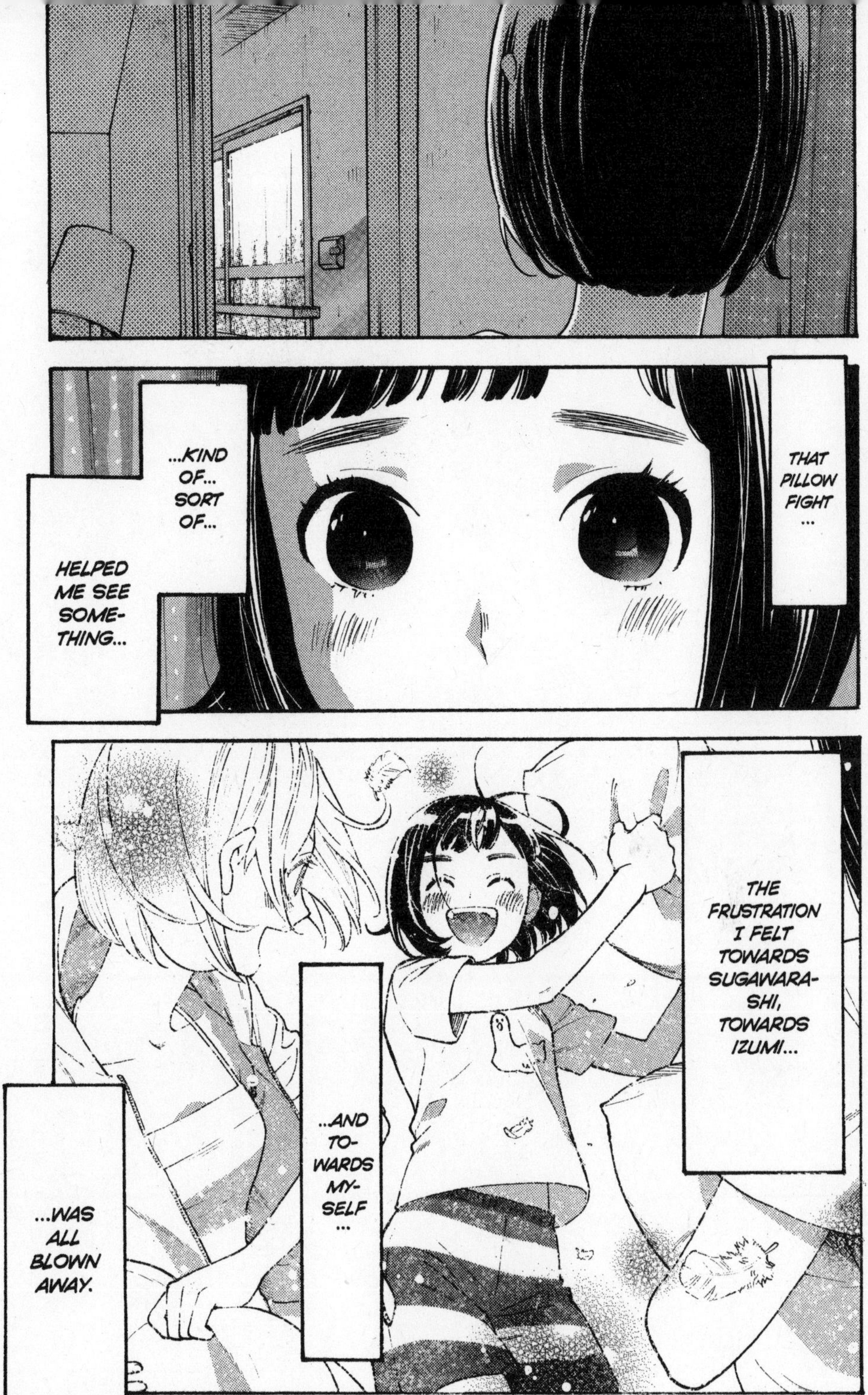
THAT PILLOW FIGHT...
...KIND OF... SORT OF...
HELPED ME SEE SOMETHING...
THE FRUSTRATION I FELT TOWARDS SUGAWARA-SHI, TOWARDS IZUMI...
...AND TOWARDS MYSELF...
...WAS ALL BLOWN AWAY.

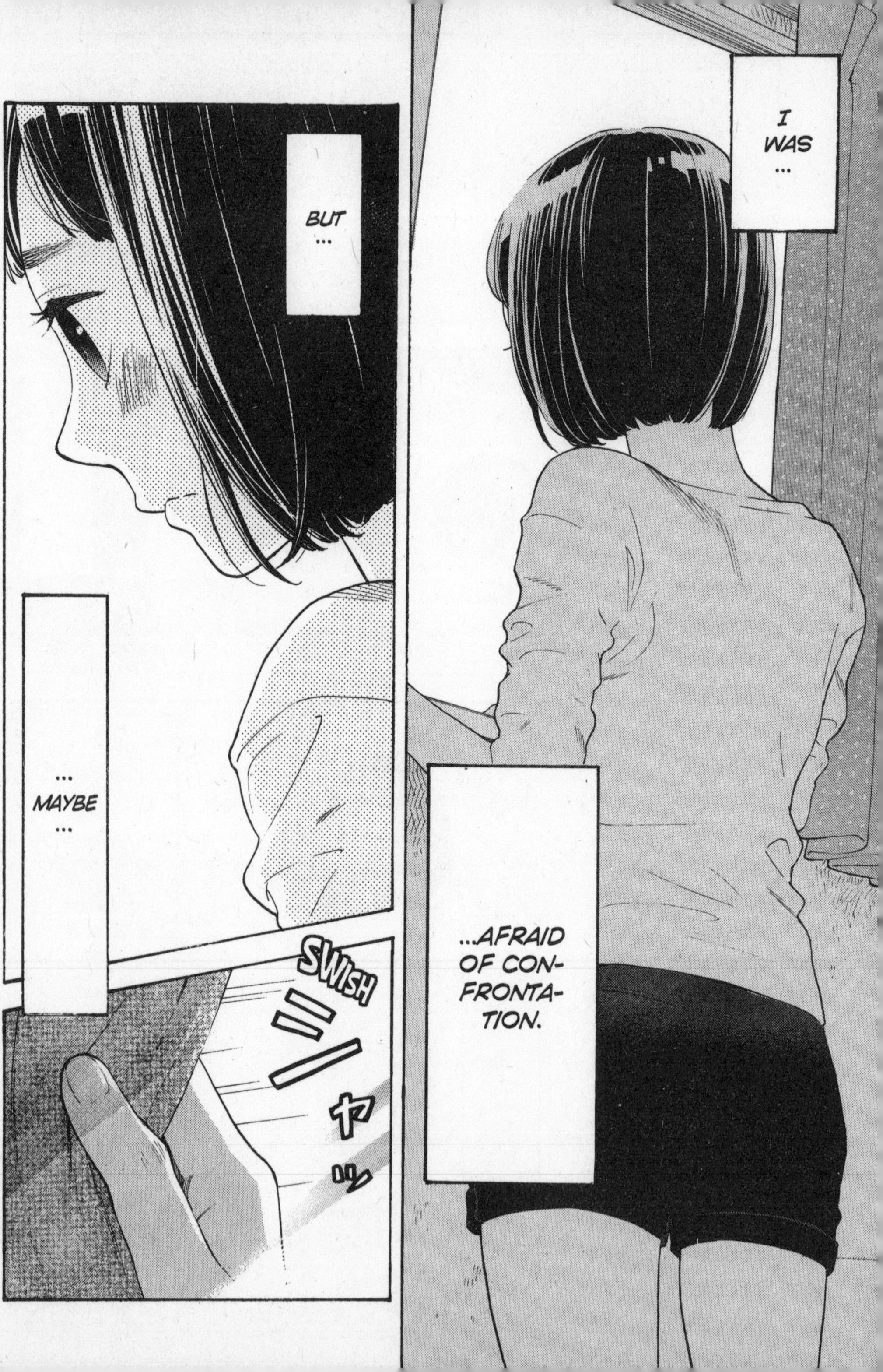
I WAS ...
...AFRAID OF CON-FRONTA-TION.
BUT ...
... MAYBE ...
SWISH

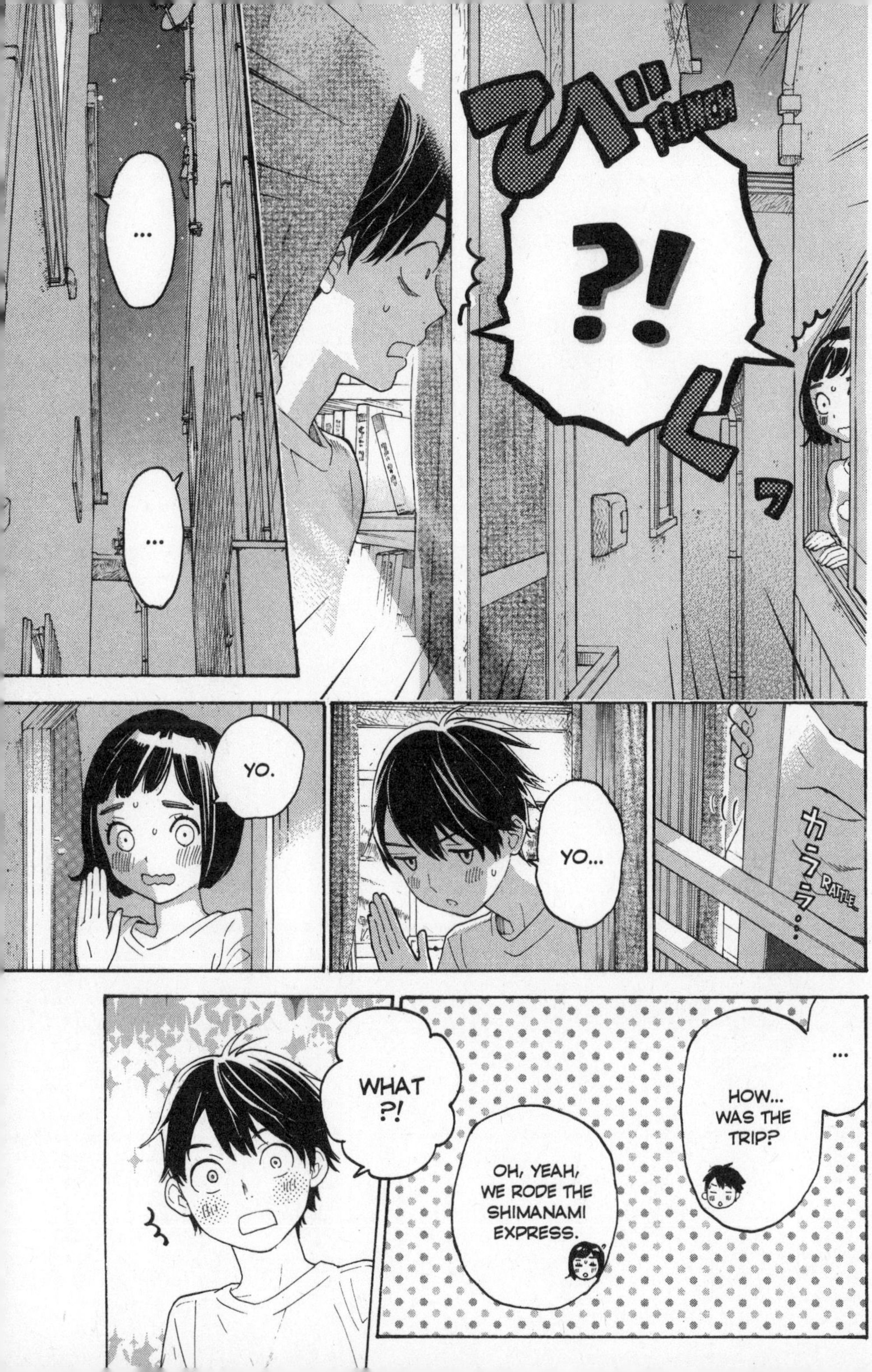
FLINCH
?!
...
...
RATTLE
YO...
YO.
...
HOW... WAS THE TRIP?
OH, YEAH, WE RODE THE SHIMANAMI EXPRESS.
WHAT ?!

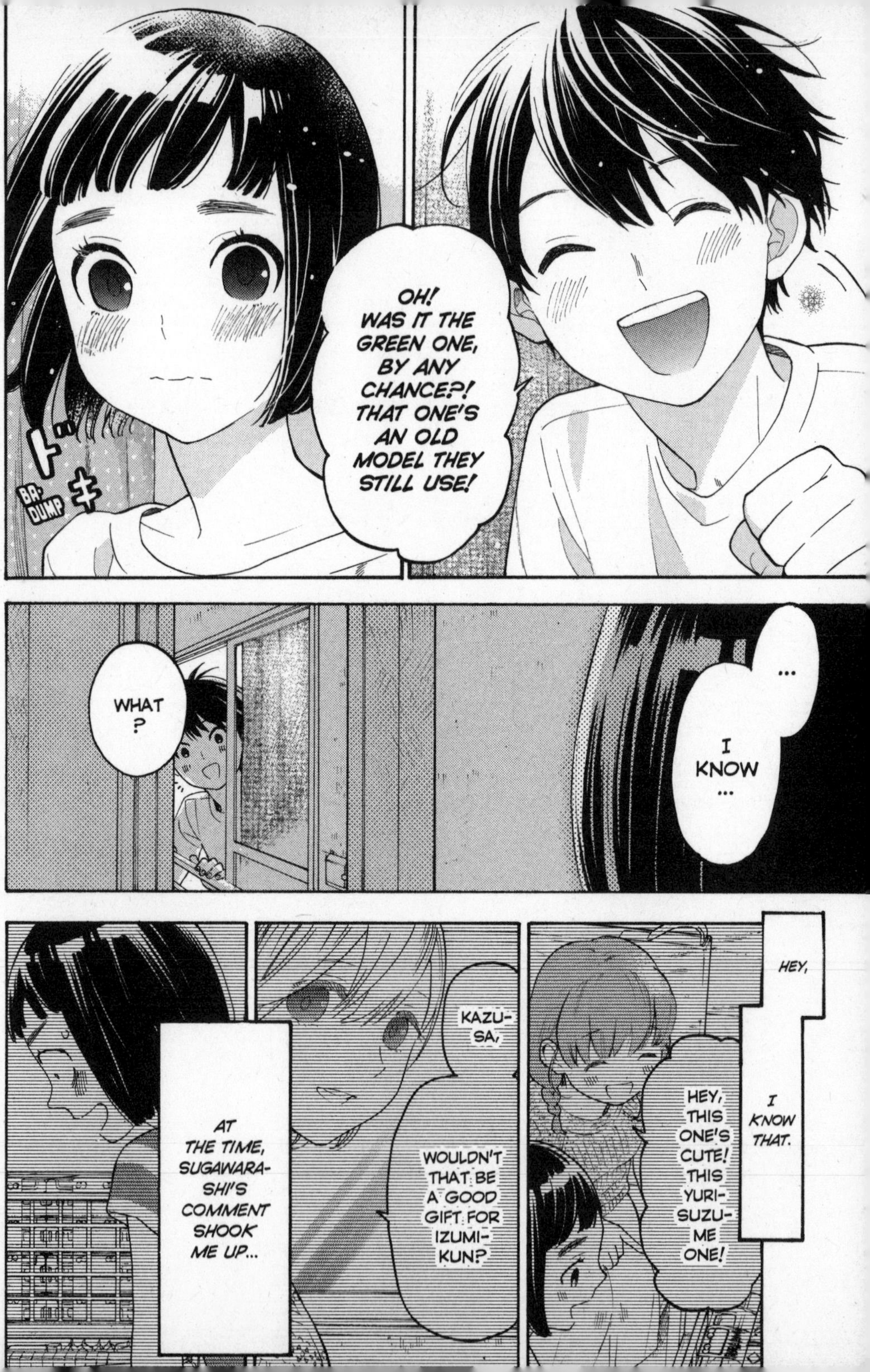
OH! WAS IT THE GREEN ONE, BY ANY CHANCE?! THAT ONE'S AN OLD MODEL THEY STILL USE!
ドキ
BA-DUMP
... I KNOW ...
WHAT?
HEY, I KNOW THAT.
HEY, THIS ONE'S CUTE! THIS YURI-SUZUME ONE!
KAZUSA,
WOULDN'T THAT BE A GOOD GIFT FOR IZUMI-KUN?
AT THE TIME, SUGAWARA-SHI'S COMMENT SHOOK ME UP...

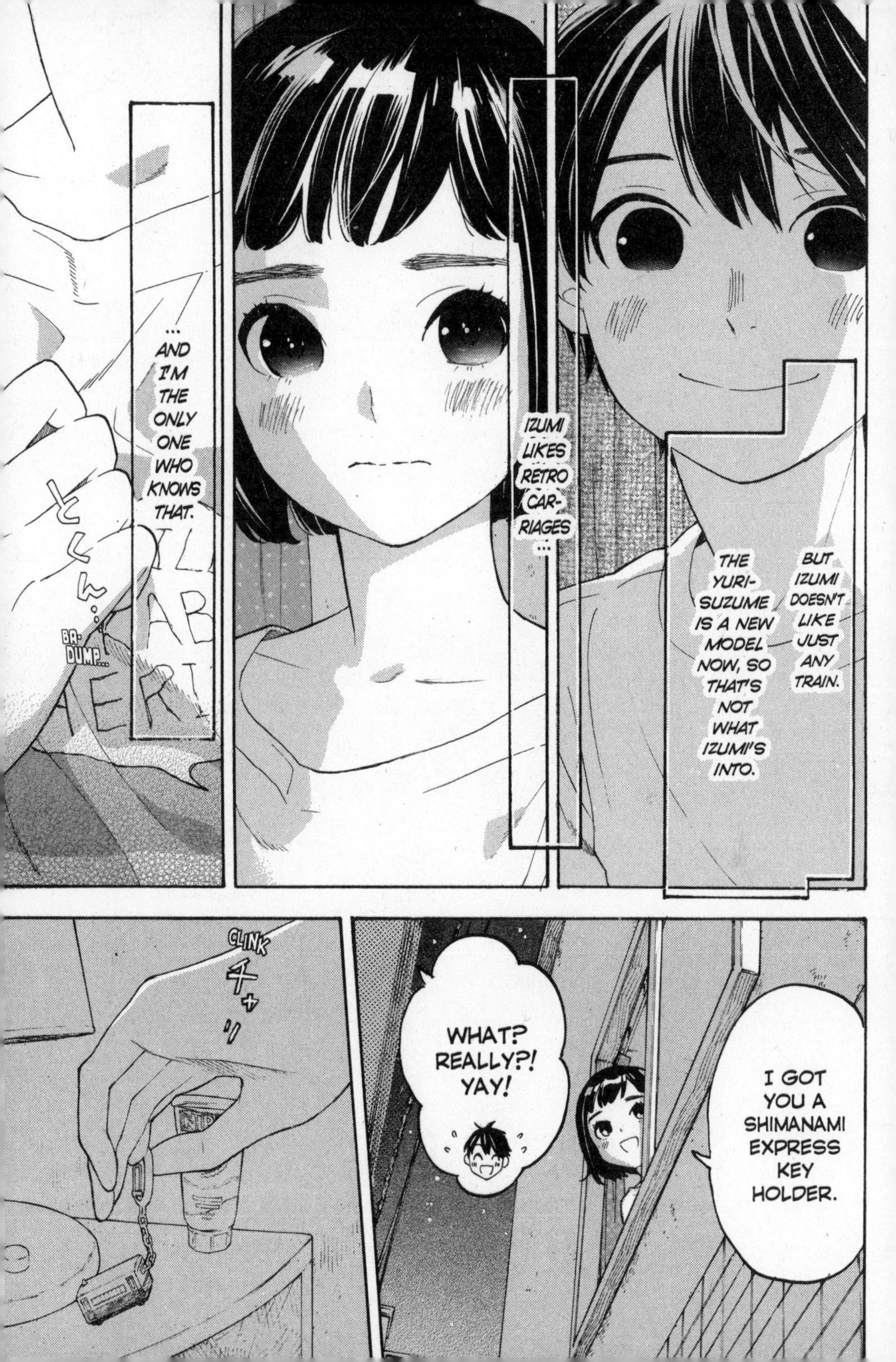
BUT IZUMI DOESN'T LIKE JUST ANY TRAIN.
THE YURI-SUZUME IS A NEW MODEL NOW, SO THAT'S NOT WHAT IZUMI'S INTO.
IZUMI LIKES RETRO CAR-RIAGES...
...AND I'M THE ONLY ONE WHO KNOWS THAT.
とくん…
BA-DUMP...
I GOT YOU A SHIMANAMI EXPRESS KEY HOLDER.
WHAT? REALLY?! YAY!
CLINK

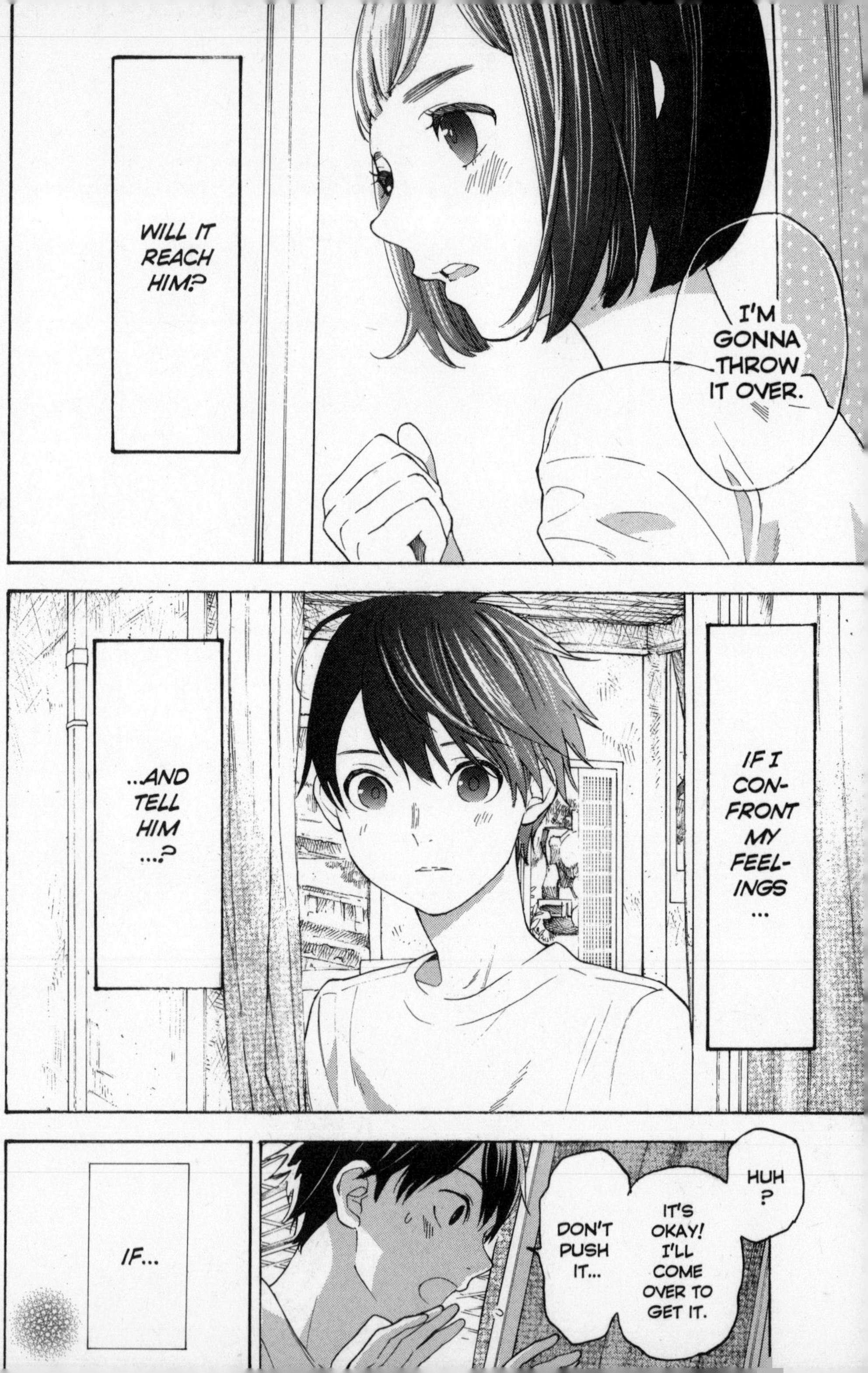
I'M GONNA THROW IT OVER.
WILL IT REACH HIM?
IF I CON-FRONT MY FEEL-INGS ...
...AND TELL HIM ...?
HUH ?
IT'S OKAY! I'LL COME OVER TO GET IT.
DON'T PUSH IT...
IF...

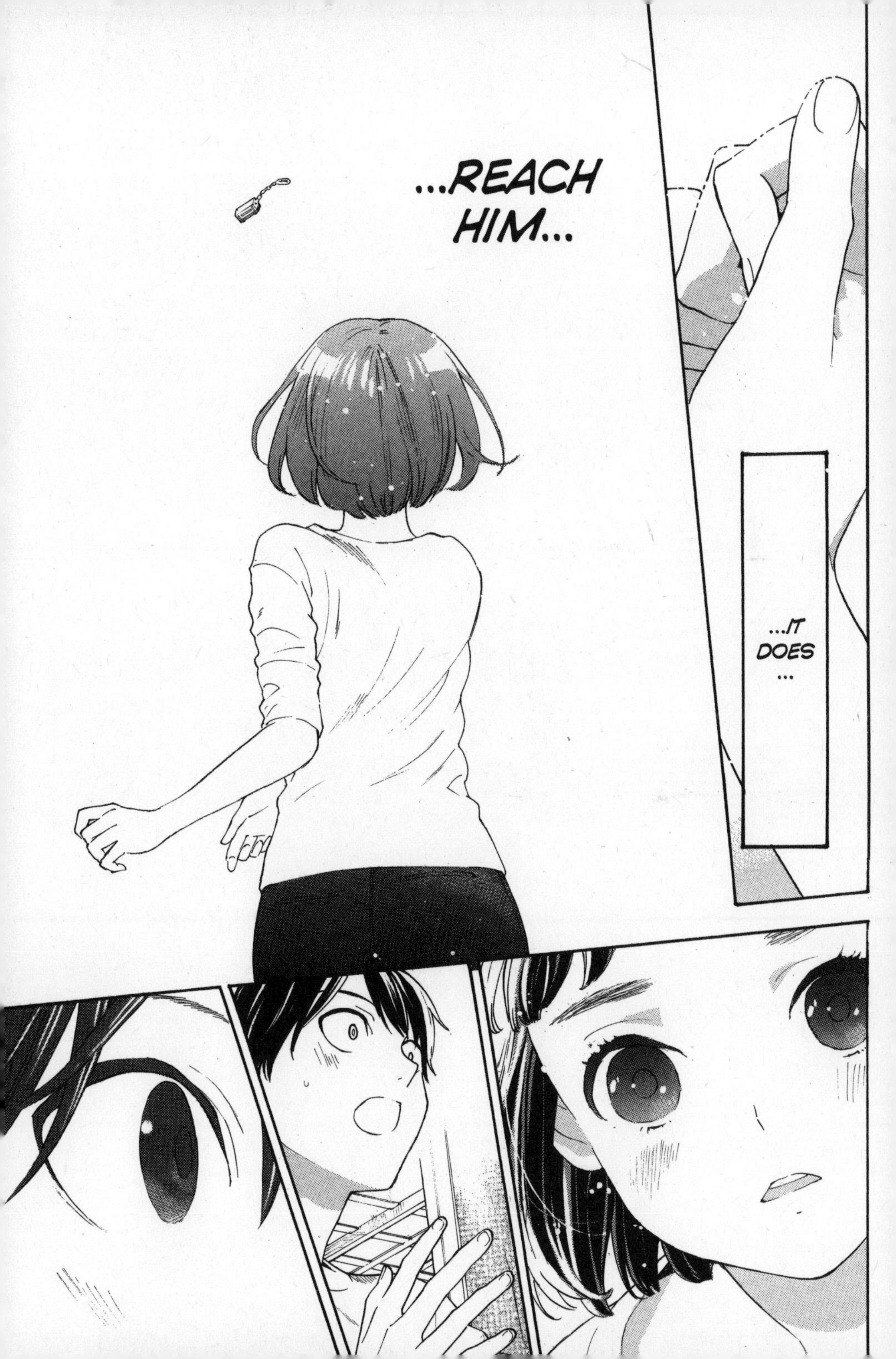
...IT DOES ...
...REACH HIM...

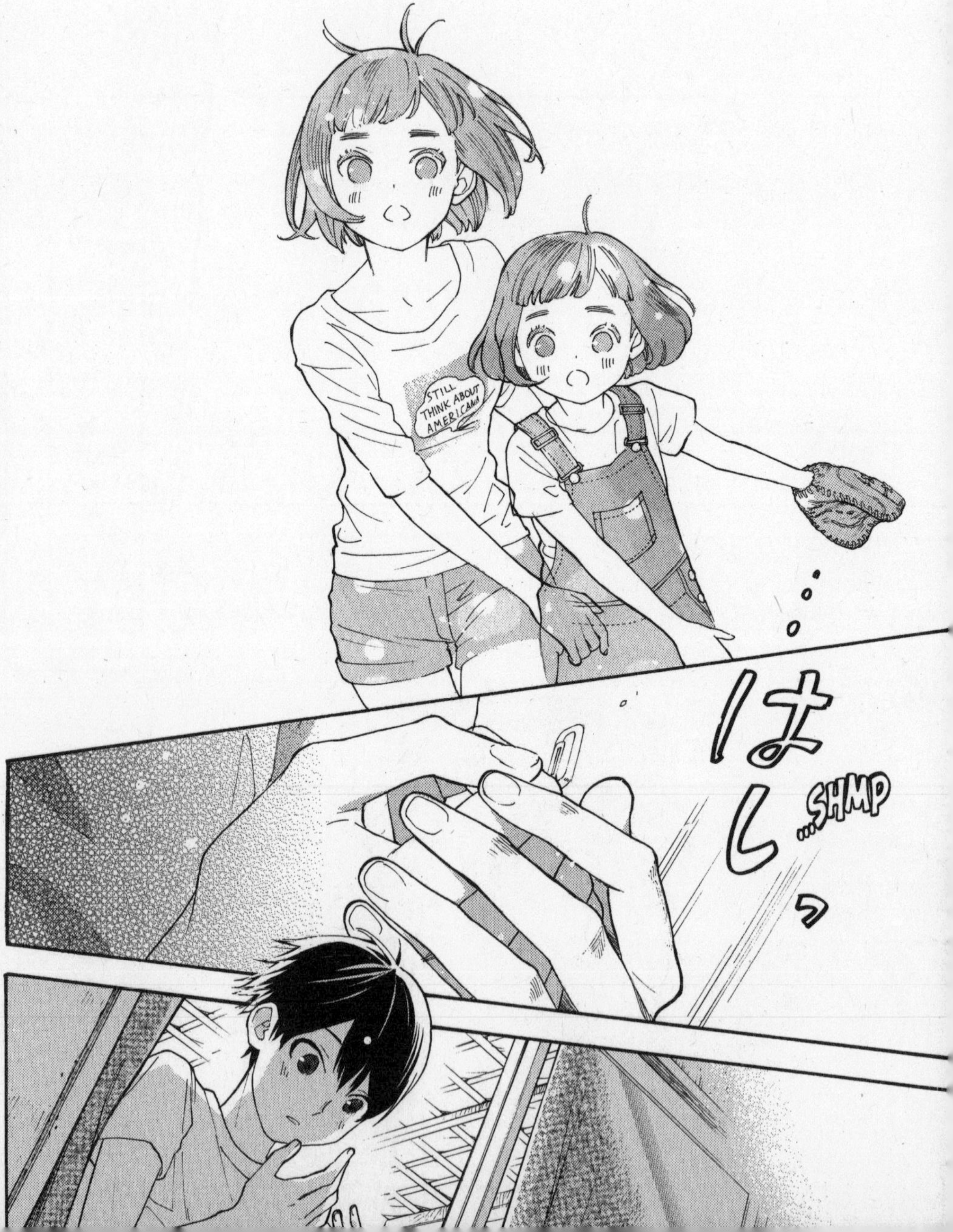
STILL THINK ABOUT AMERI.CANA
はしっ
...SHMP

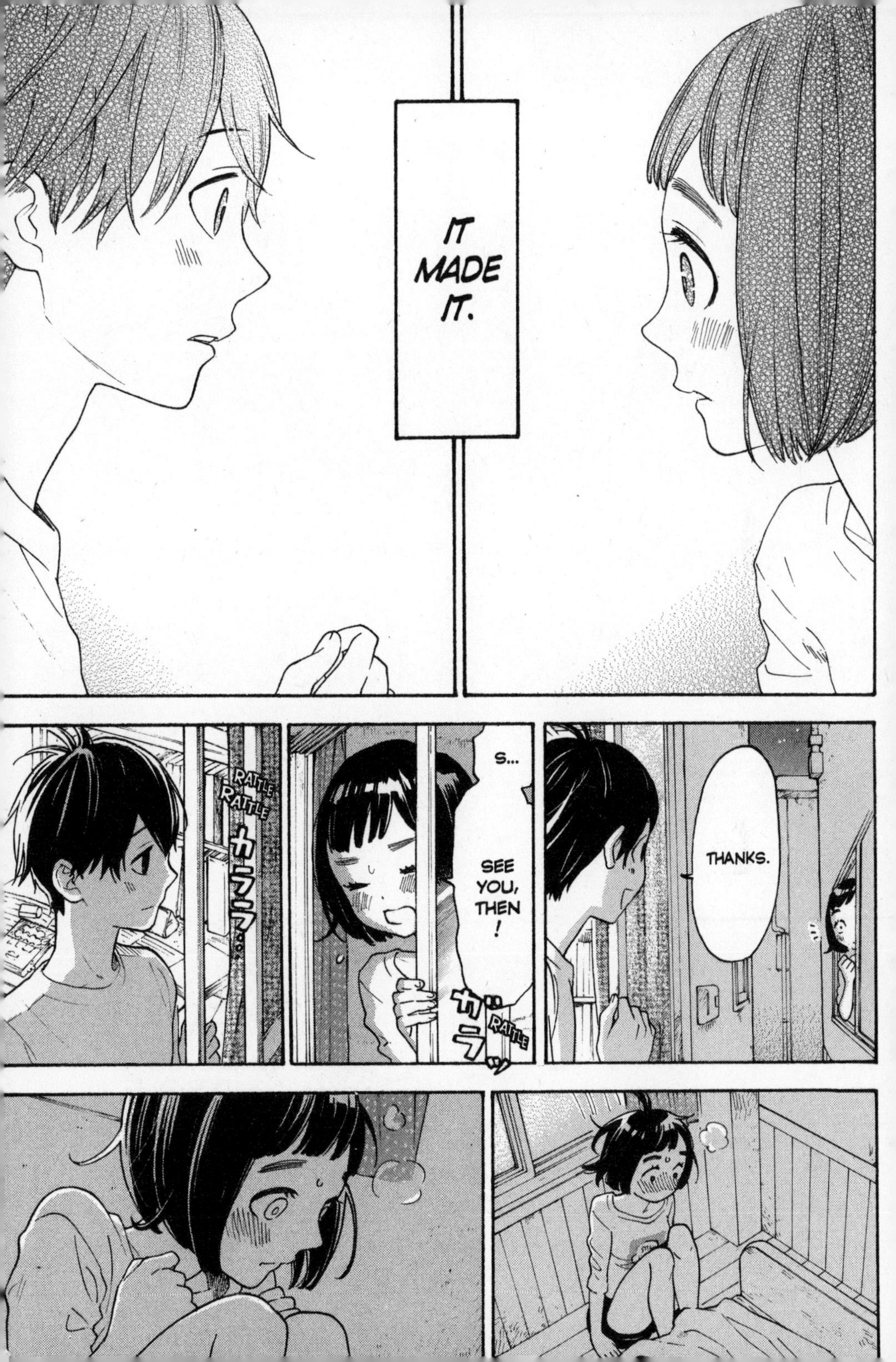
IT MADE IT.
THANKS.
S...
SEE YOU, THEN!
RATTLE
カラッ
RATTLE RATTLE
カラララ…

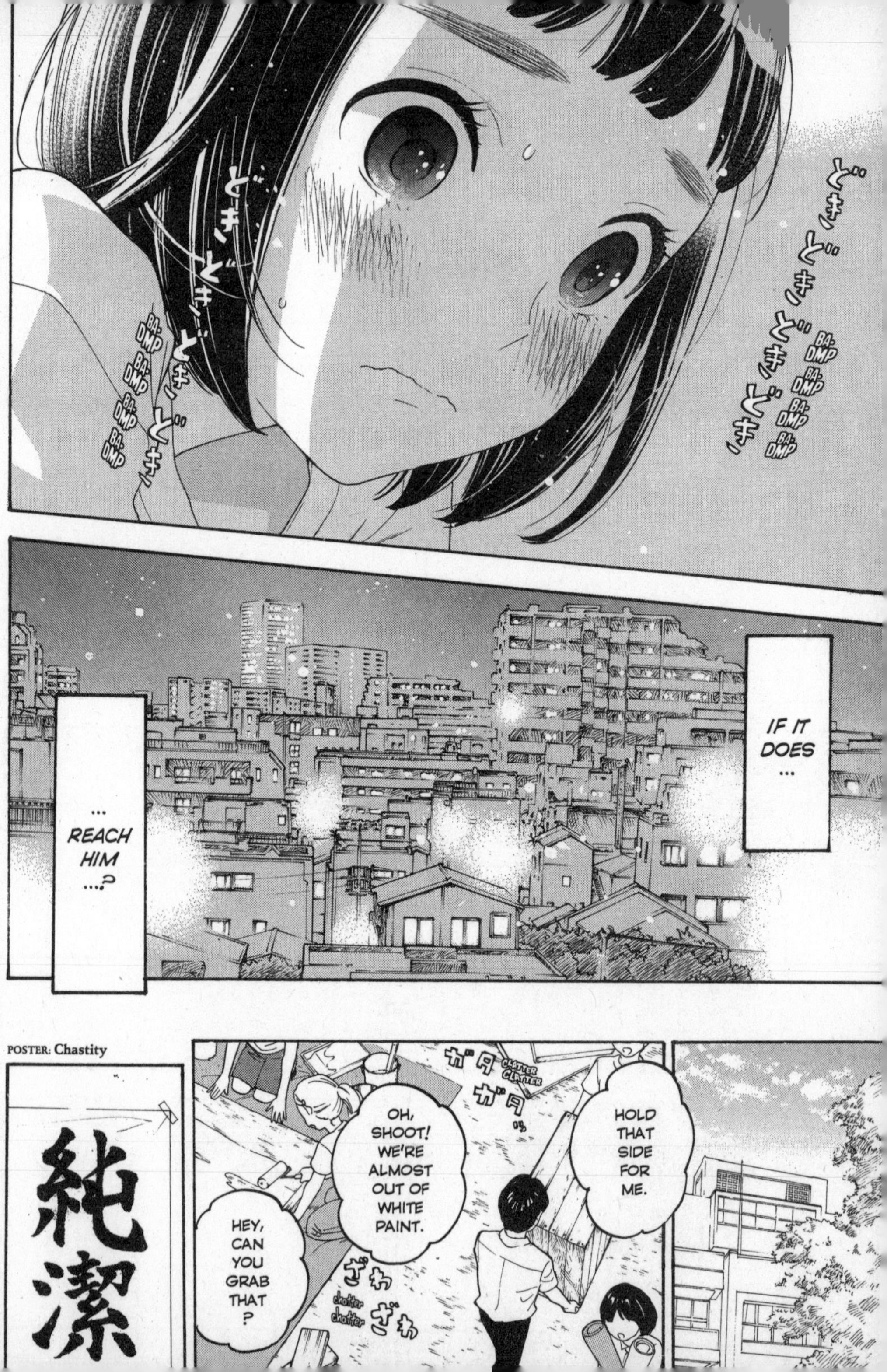
どきどきどきどき
BA-DMP BA-DMP BA-DMP BA-DMP
どきどきどきどき
BA-DMP BA-DMP BA-DMP BA-DMP
IF IT DOES ...
... REACH HIM ...?
HOLD THAT SIDE FOR ME.
ガタ ガタ
CLATTER CLATTER
OH, SHOOT! WE'RE ALMOST OUT OF WHITE PAINT.
HEY, CAN YOU GRAB THAT?
ざわ ざわ
chatter chatter
純潔
POSTER: Chastity

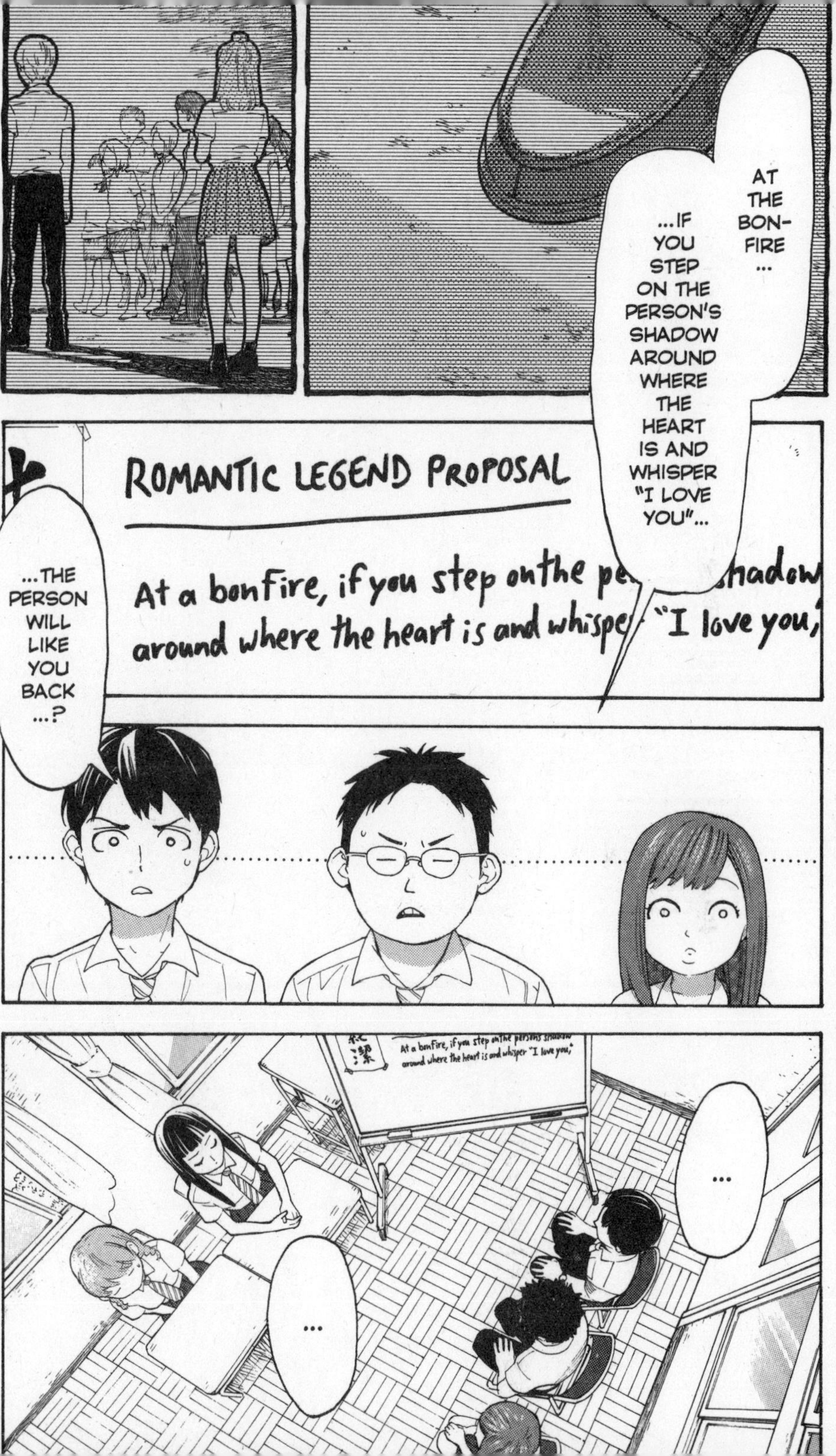
AT THE BON-FIRE...
...IF YOU STEP ON THE PERSON'S SHADOW AROUND WHERE THE HEART IS AND WHISPER "I LOVE YOU"...
ROMANTIC LEGEND PROPOSAL
At a bonfire, if you step onthe pe shadow
around where the heart is and whisper "I love you,"
...THE PERSON WILL LIKE YOU BACK...?
At a bonfire, if you step on the persons shadow around where the heart is and whisper "I love you,"
...
...

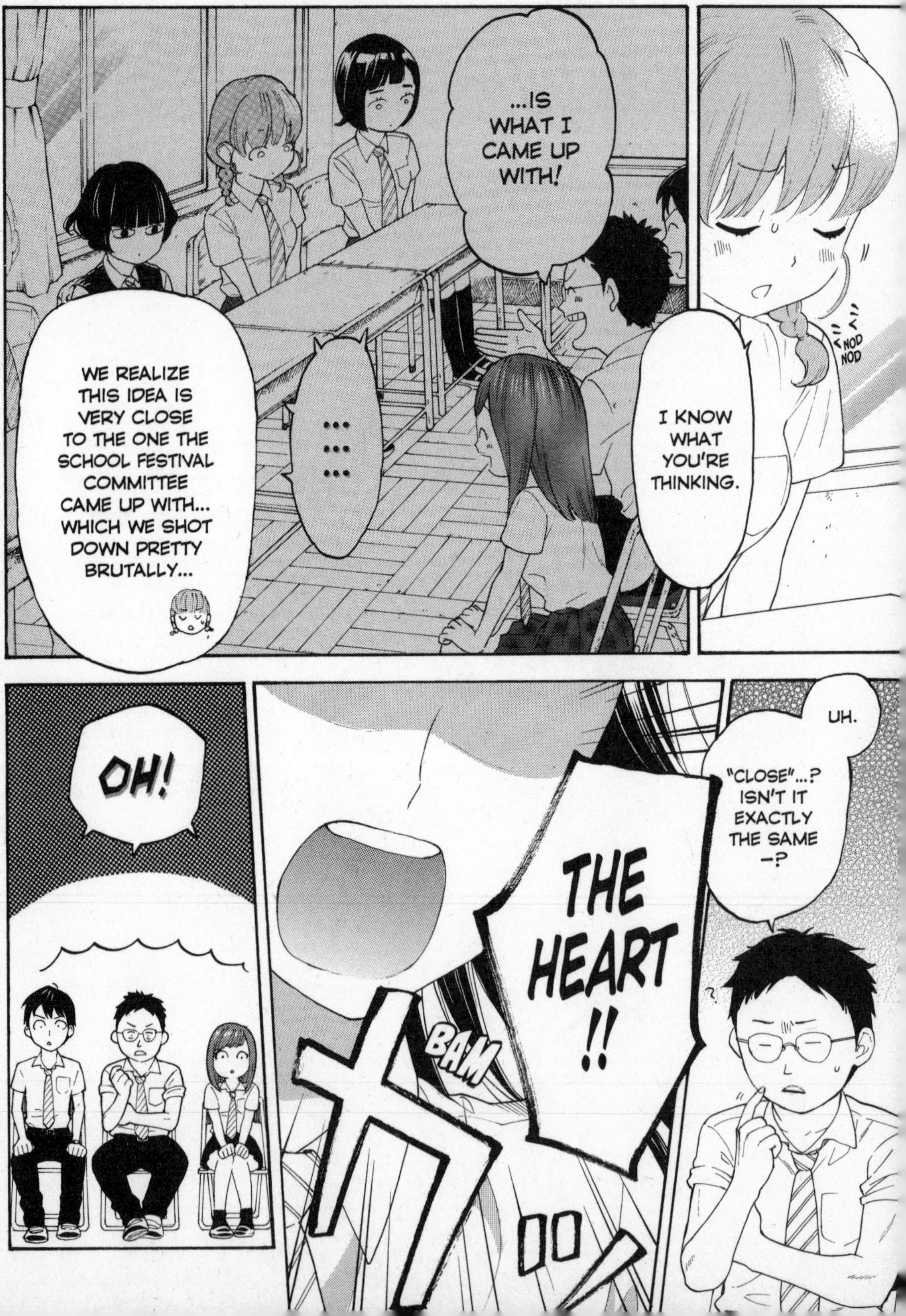
I KNOW WHAT YOU'RE THINKING.
NOD NOD
...IS WHAT I CAME UP WITH!
....
WE REALIZE THIS IDEA IS VERY CLOSE TO THE ONE THE SCHOOL FESTIVAL COMMITTEE CAME UP WITH... WHICH WE SHOT DOWN PRETTY BRUTALLY...
UH.
"CLOSE"...? ISN'T IT EXACTLY THE SAME —?
THE HEART!!
BAM
DO
OH!

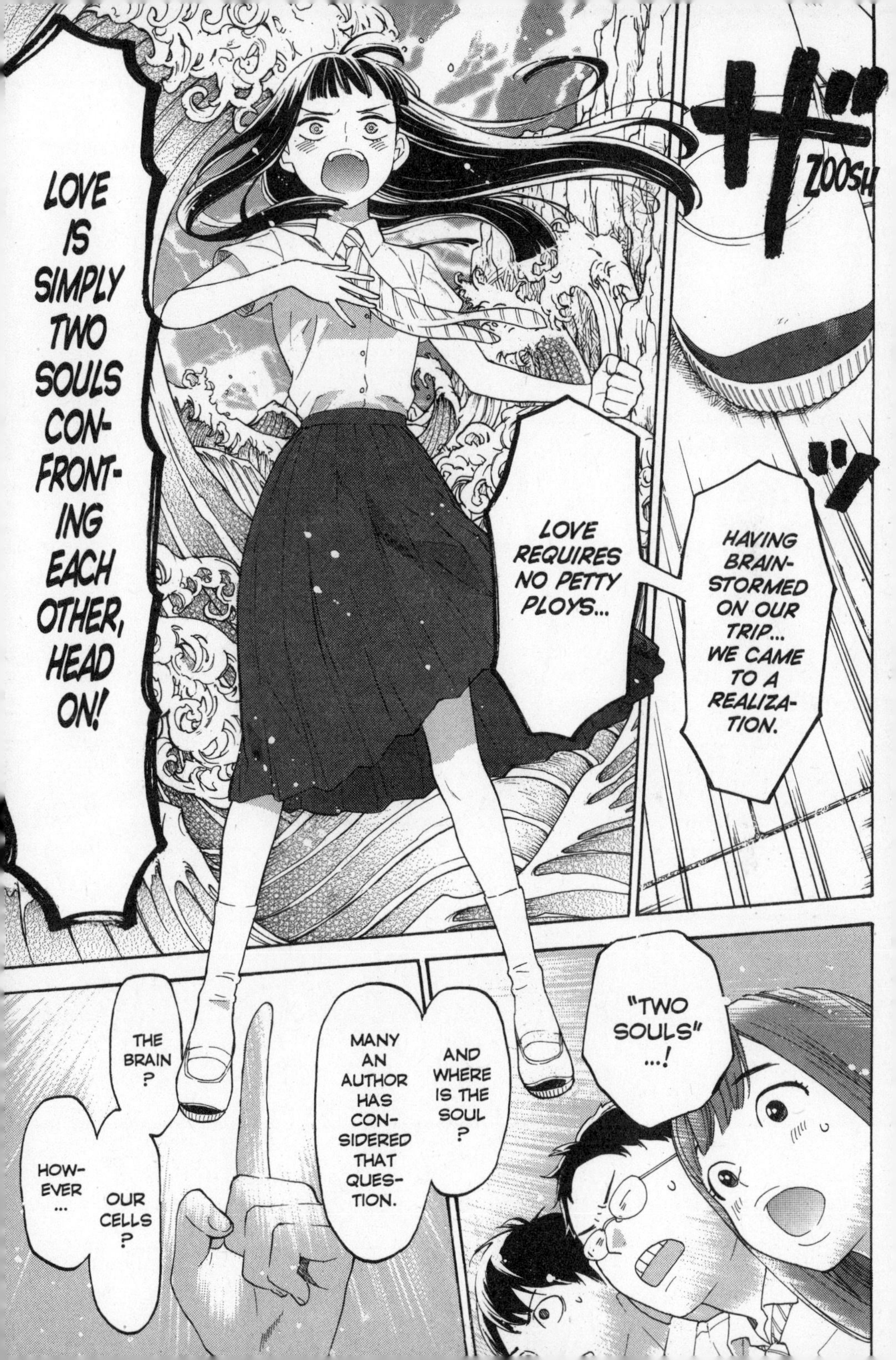
ZOOSH
HAVING BRAIN-STORMED ON OUR TRIP... WE CAME TO A REALIZA-TION.
LOVE REQUIRES NO PETTY PLOYS...
LOVE IS SIMPLY TWO SOULS CON-FRONT-ING EACH OTHER, HEAD ON!
"TWO SOULS" ...!
AND WHERE IS THE SOUL?
MANY AN AUTHOR HAS CON-SIDERED THAT QUES-TION.
THE BRAIN?
OUR CELLS?
HOW-EVER ...

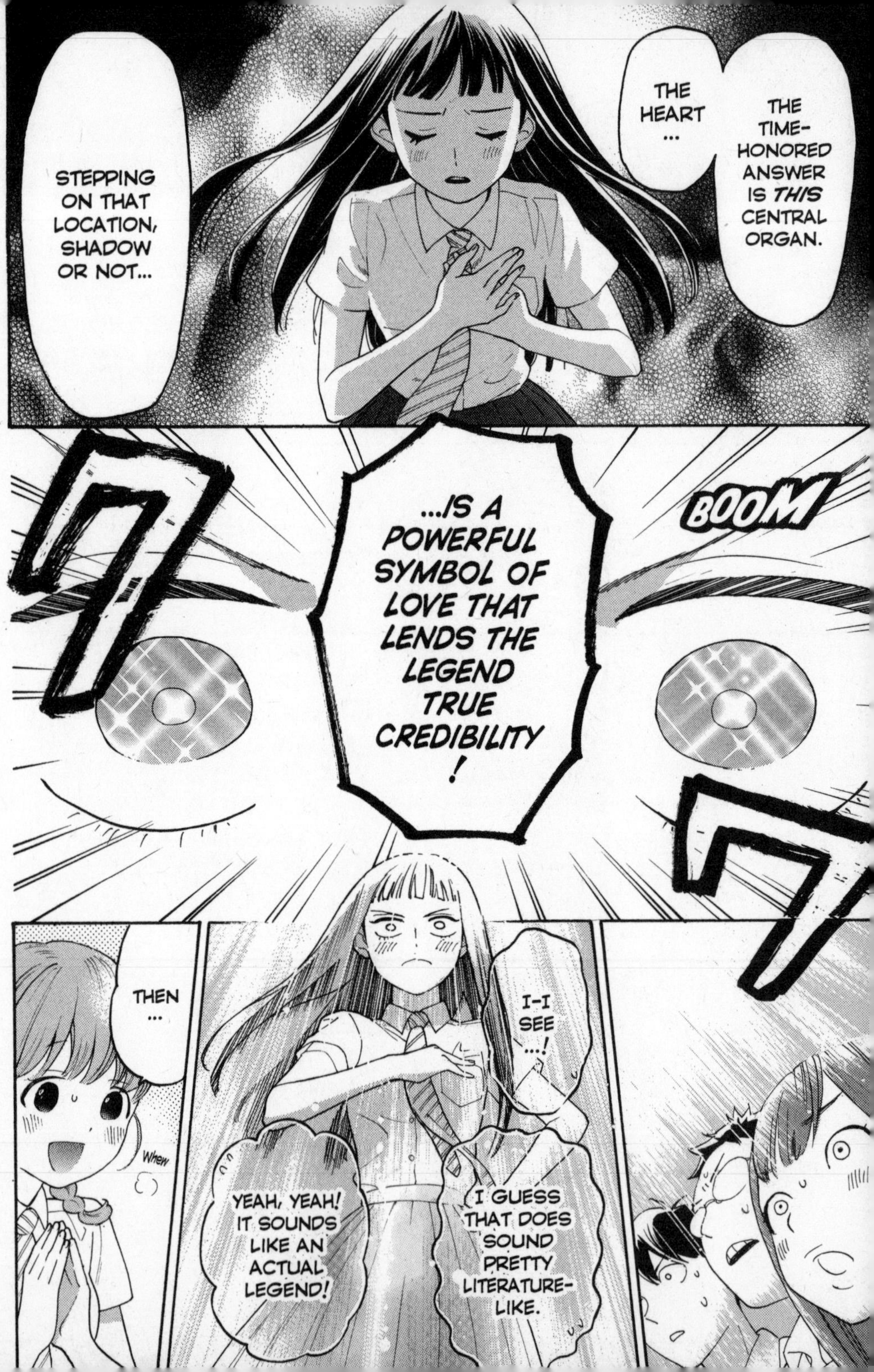
THE TIME-HONORED ANSWER IS *THIS* CENTRAL ORGAN.
THE HEART ...
STEPPING ON THAT LOCATION, SHADOW OR NOT...
BOOM
...IS A POWERFUL SYMBOL OF LOVE THAT LENDS THE LEGEND TRUE CREDIBILITY!
I-I SEE ...!
I GUESS THAT DOES SOUND PRETTY LITERATURE-LIKE.
YEAH, YEAH! IT SOUNDS LIKE AN ACTUAL LEGEND!
THEN ...
Whew

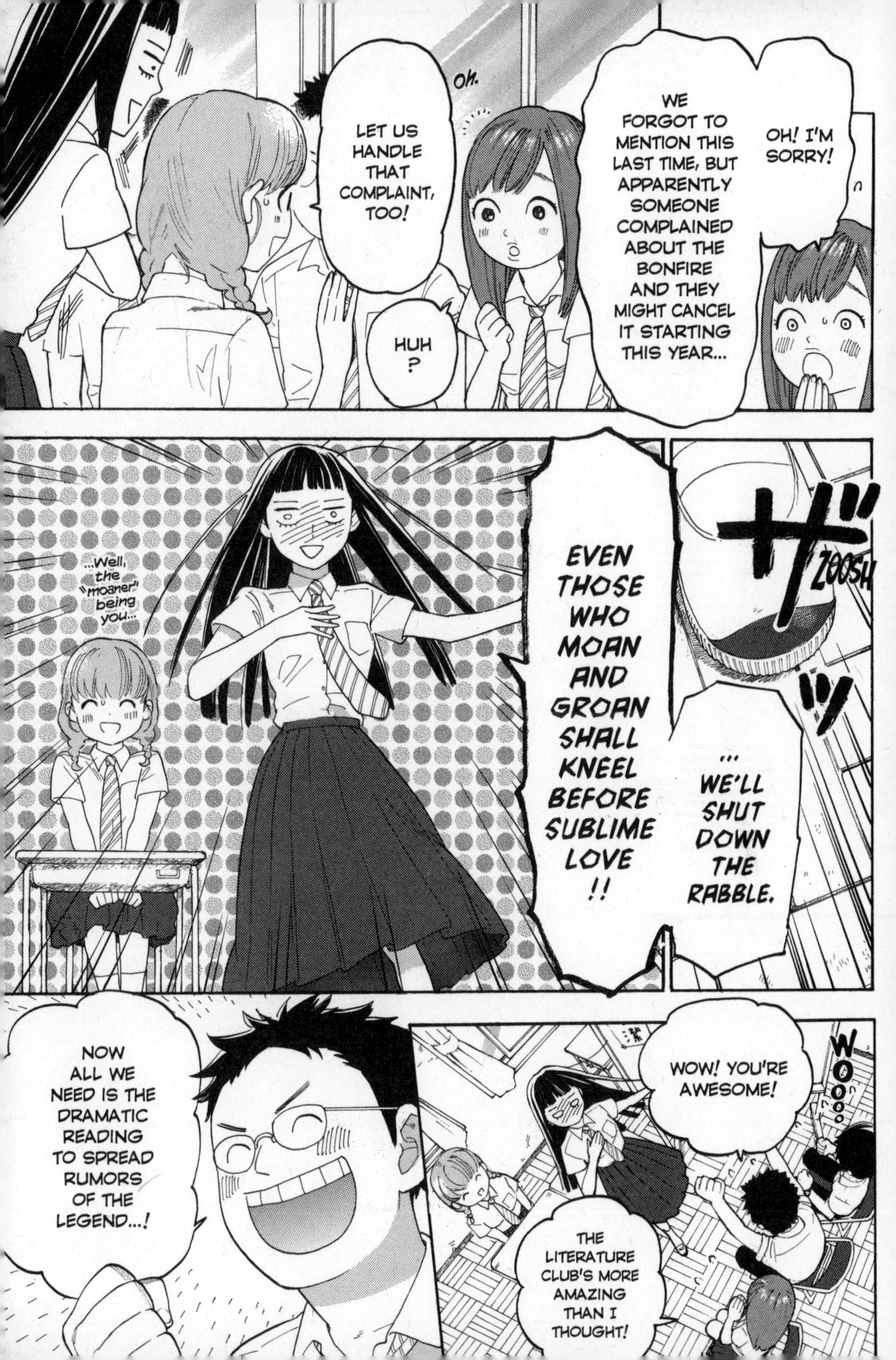
OH! I'M SORRY!
WE FORGOT TO MENTION THIS LAST TIME, BUT APPARENTLY SOMEONE COMPLAINED ABOUT THE BONFIRE AND THEY MIGHT CANCEL IT STARTING THIS YEAR...
oh.
LET US HANDLE THAT COMPLAINT, TOO!
HUH?
ZOOSH
... WE'LL SHUT DOWN THE RABBLE.
EVEN THOSE WHO MOAN AND GROAN SHALL KNEEL BEFORE SUBLIME LOVE!!
...Well, the "moaner" being you...
WOOOOO
WOW! YOU'RE AWESOME!
THE LITERATURE CLUB'S MORE AMAZING THAN I THOUGHT!
NOW ALL WE NEED IS THE DRAMATIC READING TO SPREAD RUMORS OF THE LEGEND...!

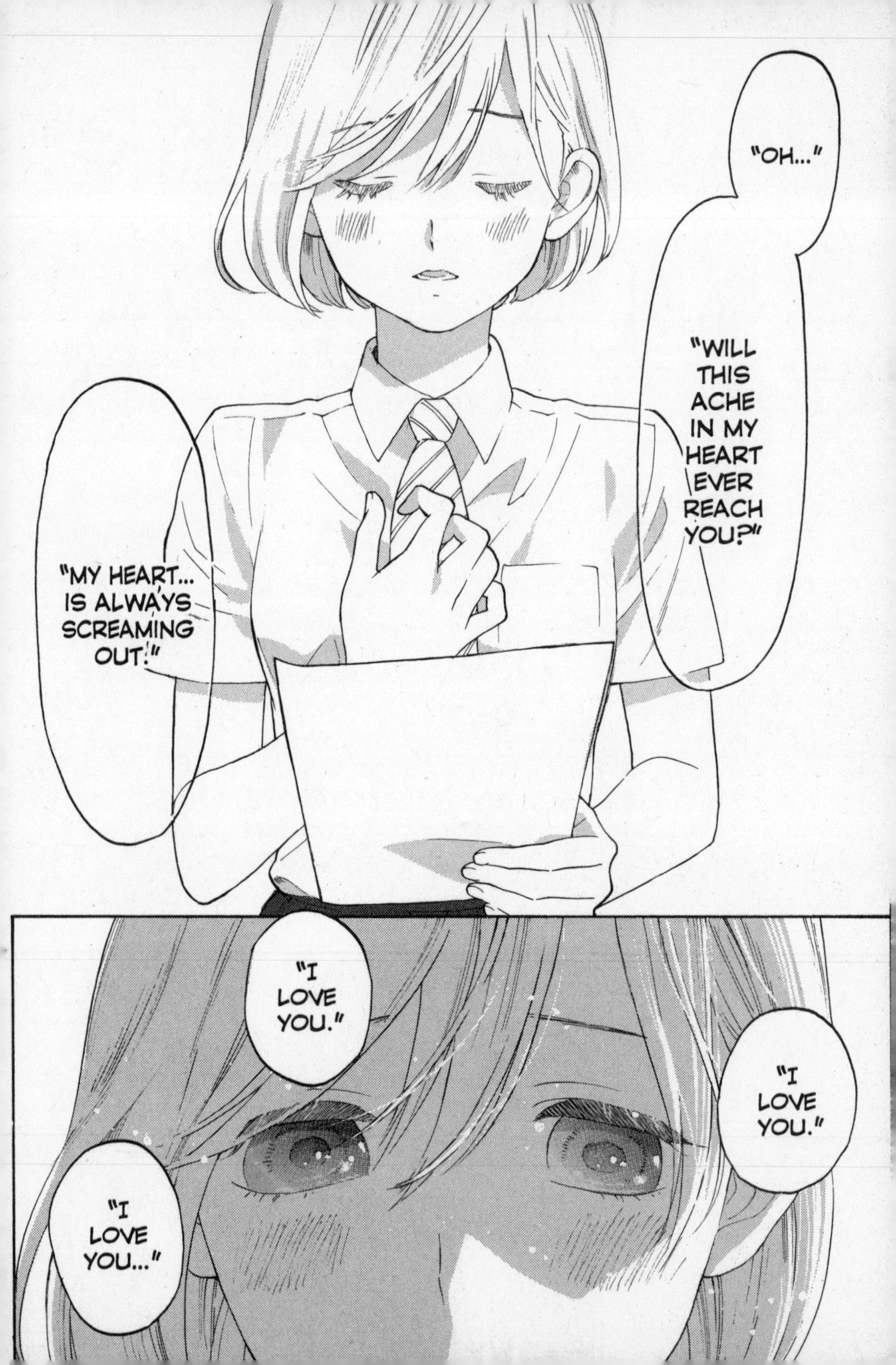
"OH..."
"WILL THIS ACHE IN MY HEART EVER REACH YOU?"
"MY HEART... IS ALWAYS SCREAMING OUT."
"I LOVE YOU."
"I LOVE YOU."
"I LOVE YOU..."

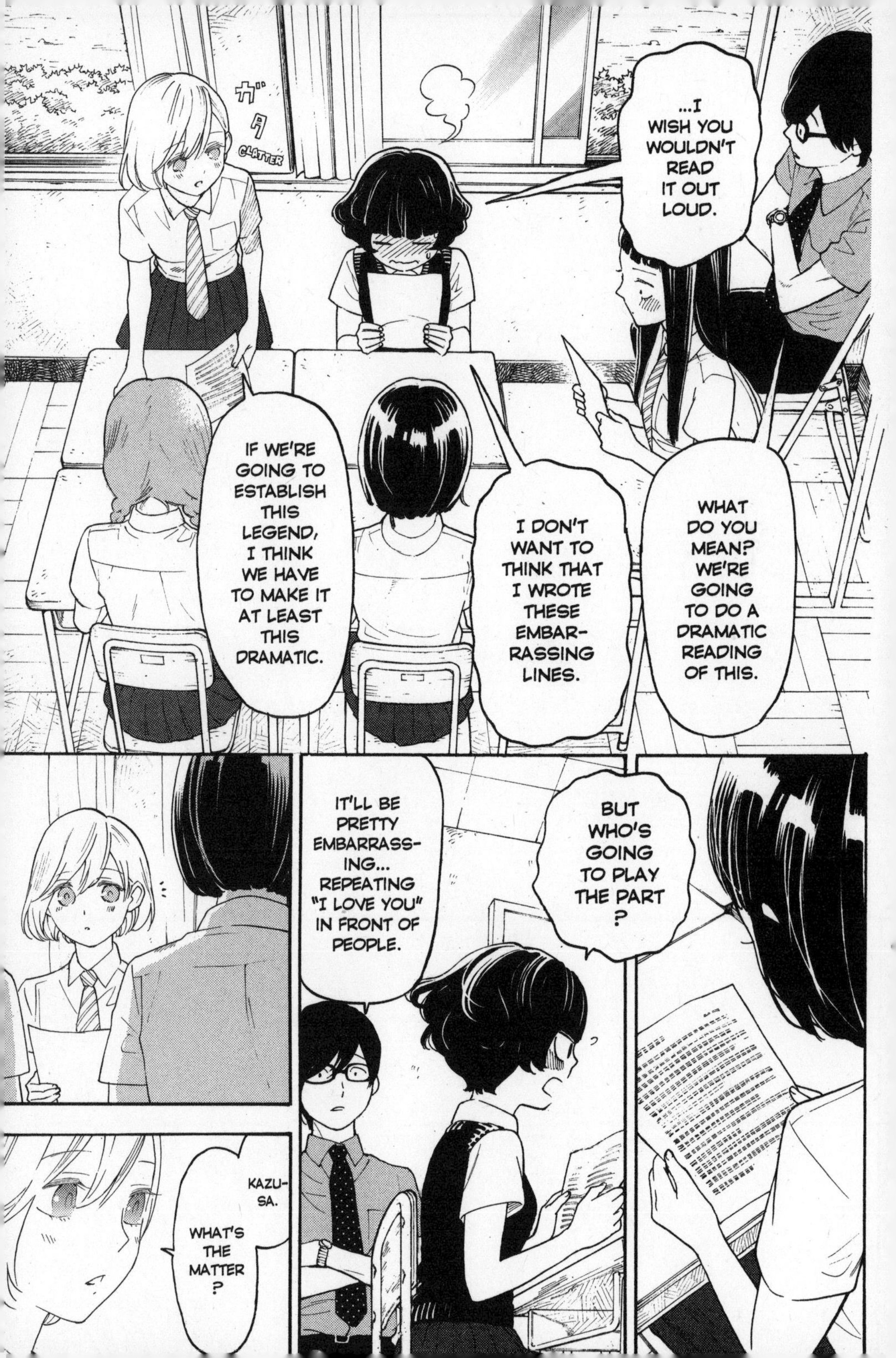
...I WISH YOU WOULDN'T READ IT OUT LOUD.
ガタ
CLATTER
WHAT DO YOU MEAN? WE'RE GOING TO DO A DRAMATIC READING OF THIS.
I DON'T WANT TO THINK THAT I WROTE THESE EMBARRASSING LINES.
IF WE'RE GOING TO ESTABLISH THIS LEGEND, I THINK WE HAVE TO MAKE IT AT LEAST THIS DRAMATIC.
BUT WHO'S GOING TO PLAY THE PART?
IT'LL BE PRETTY EMBARRASSING... REPEATING "I LOVE YOU" IN FRONT OF PEOPLE.
KAZUSA.
WHAT'S THE MATTER?

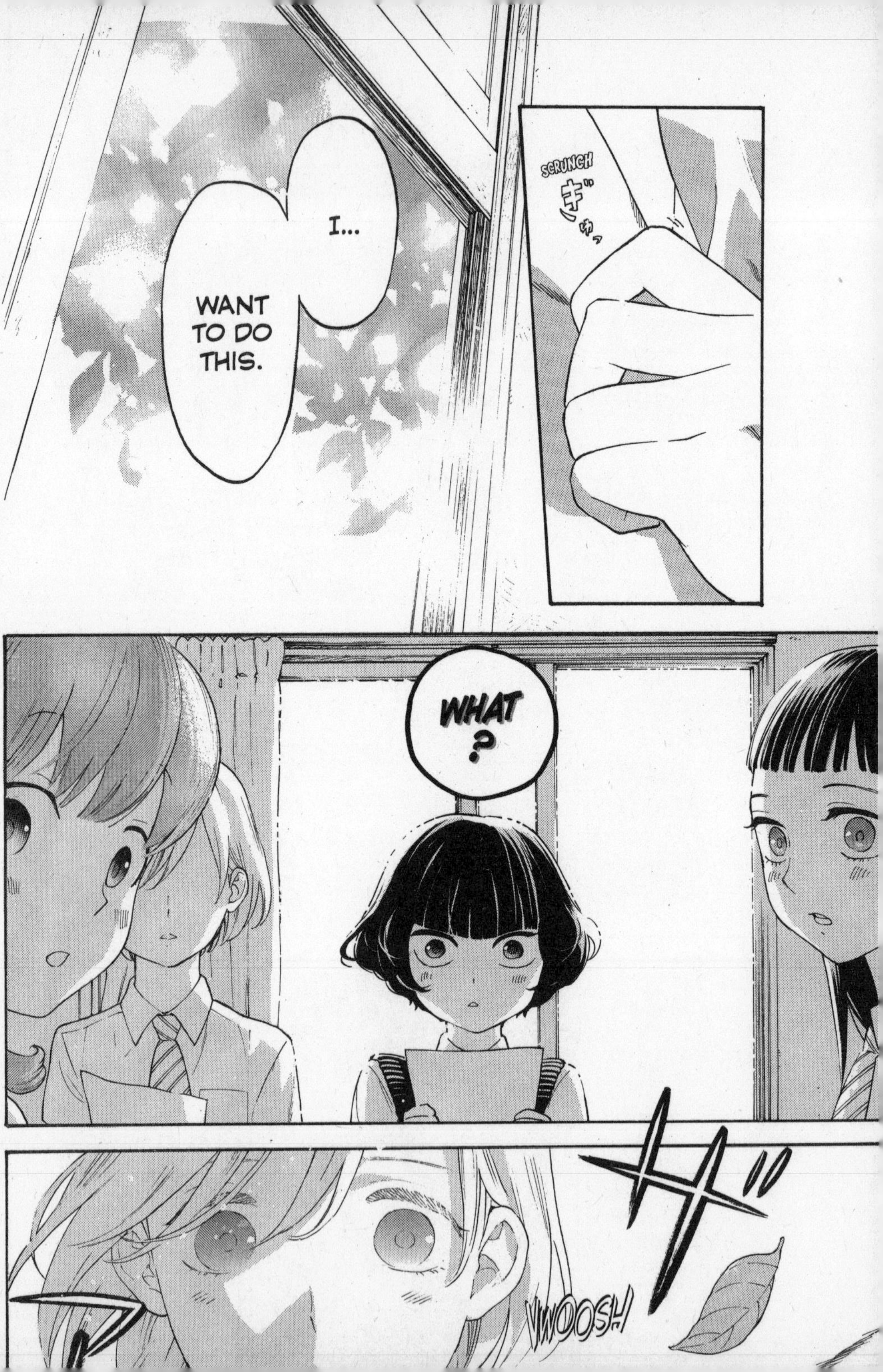
SCRUNCH
ぎゅっ
I...
WANT TO DO THIS.
WHAT?
ザッ
VWOOSH

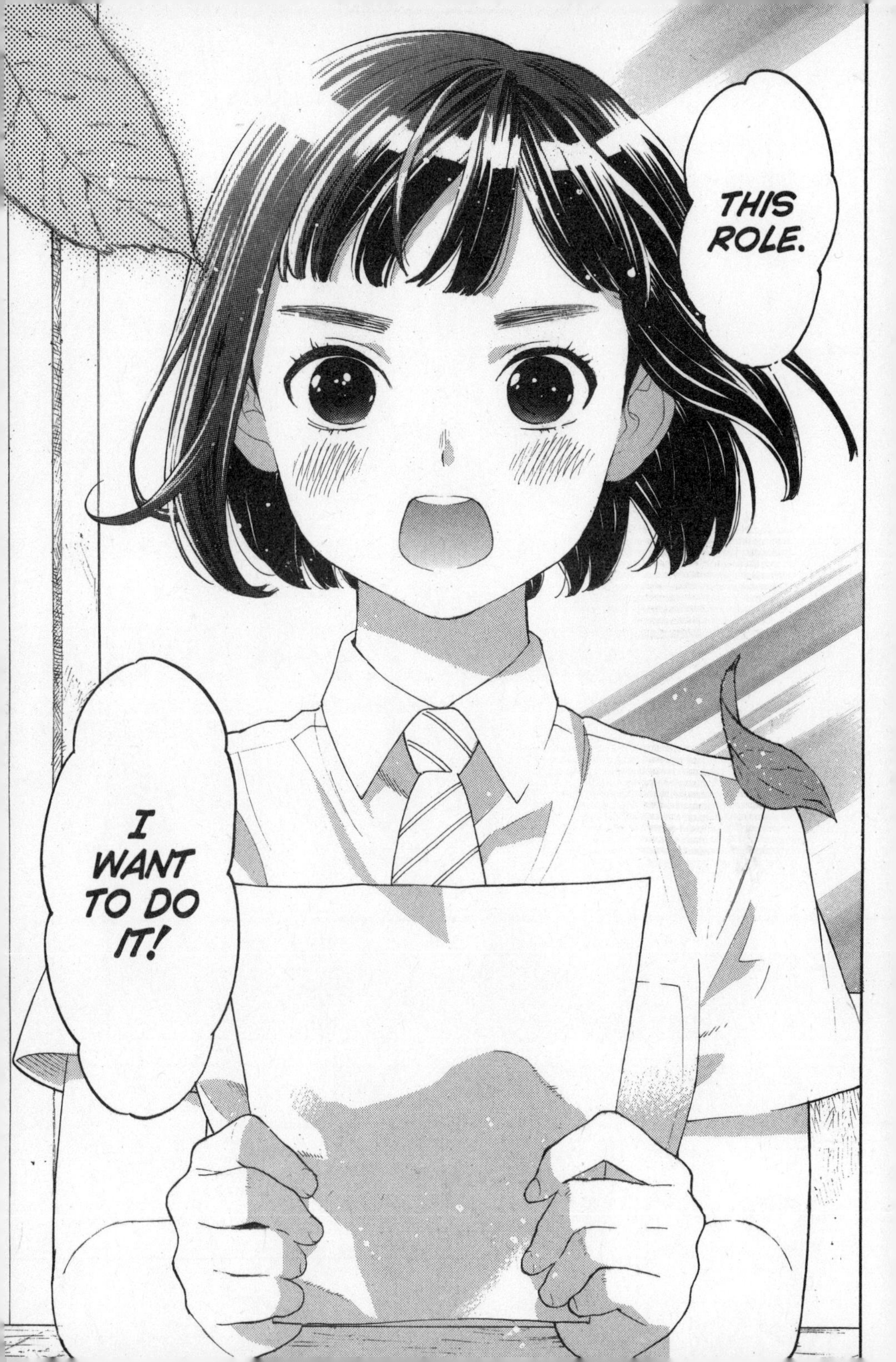
THIS ROLE.
I WANT TO DO IT!

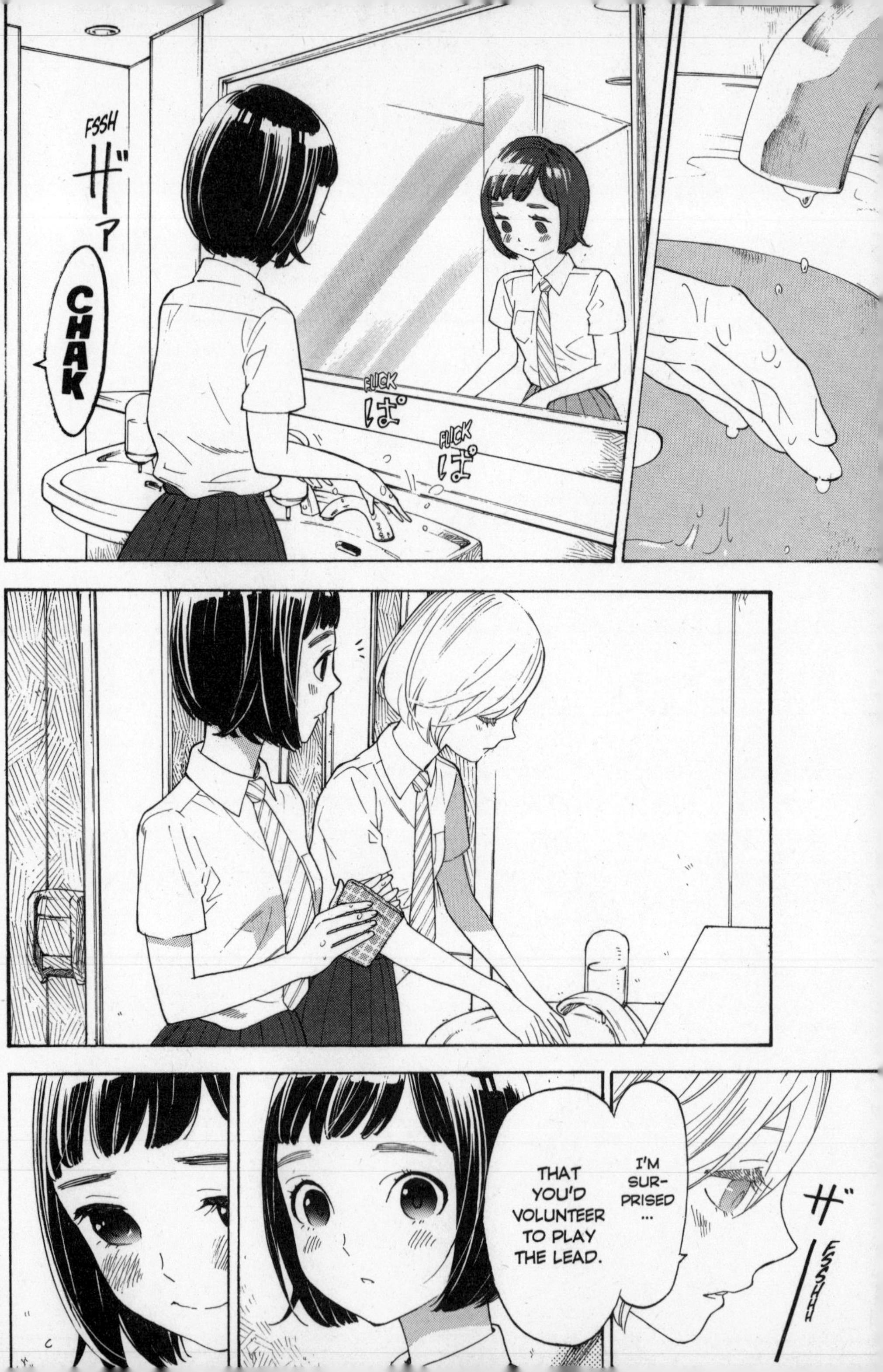
FSSH
ザァ
CHAK
FLICK
ぱ
FLICK
ぱ
I'M SURPRISED ...
THAT YOU'D VOLUNTEER TO PLAY THE LEAD.
ザ
FSSHHH

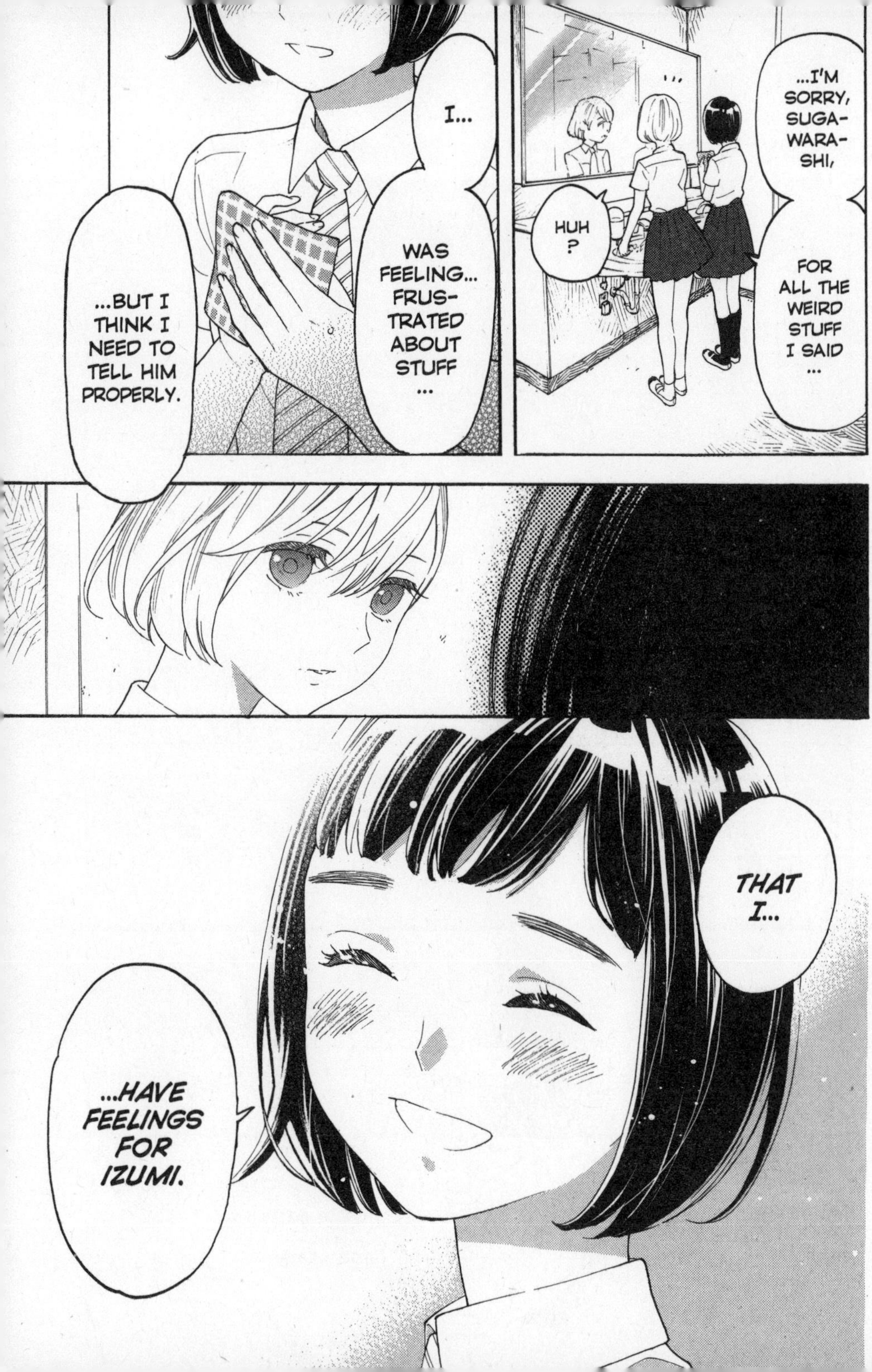
...I'M SORRY, SUGA-WARA-SHI,
FOR ALL THE WEIRD STUFF I SAID ...
HUH ?
I...
WAS FEELING... FRUS-TRATED ABOUT STUFF ...
...BUT I THINK I NEED TO TELL HIM PROPERLY.
THAT I...
...HAVE FEELINGS FOR IZUMI.

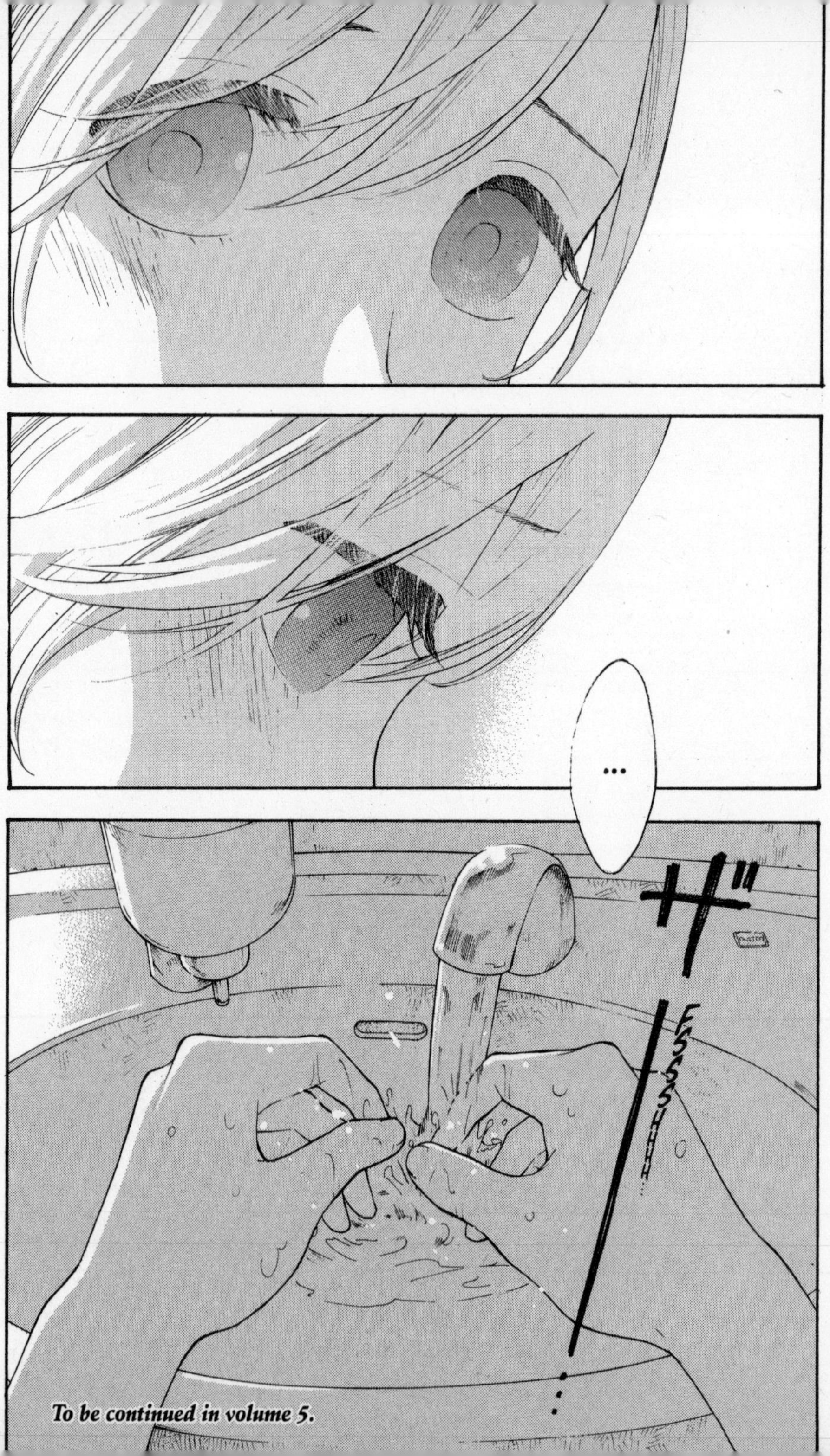
...
ザ"
FSSSSHHH...

To be continued in volume 5.

O Maidens in your Savage Season

Next volume preview

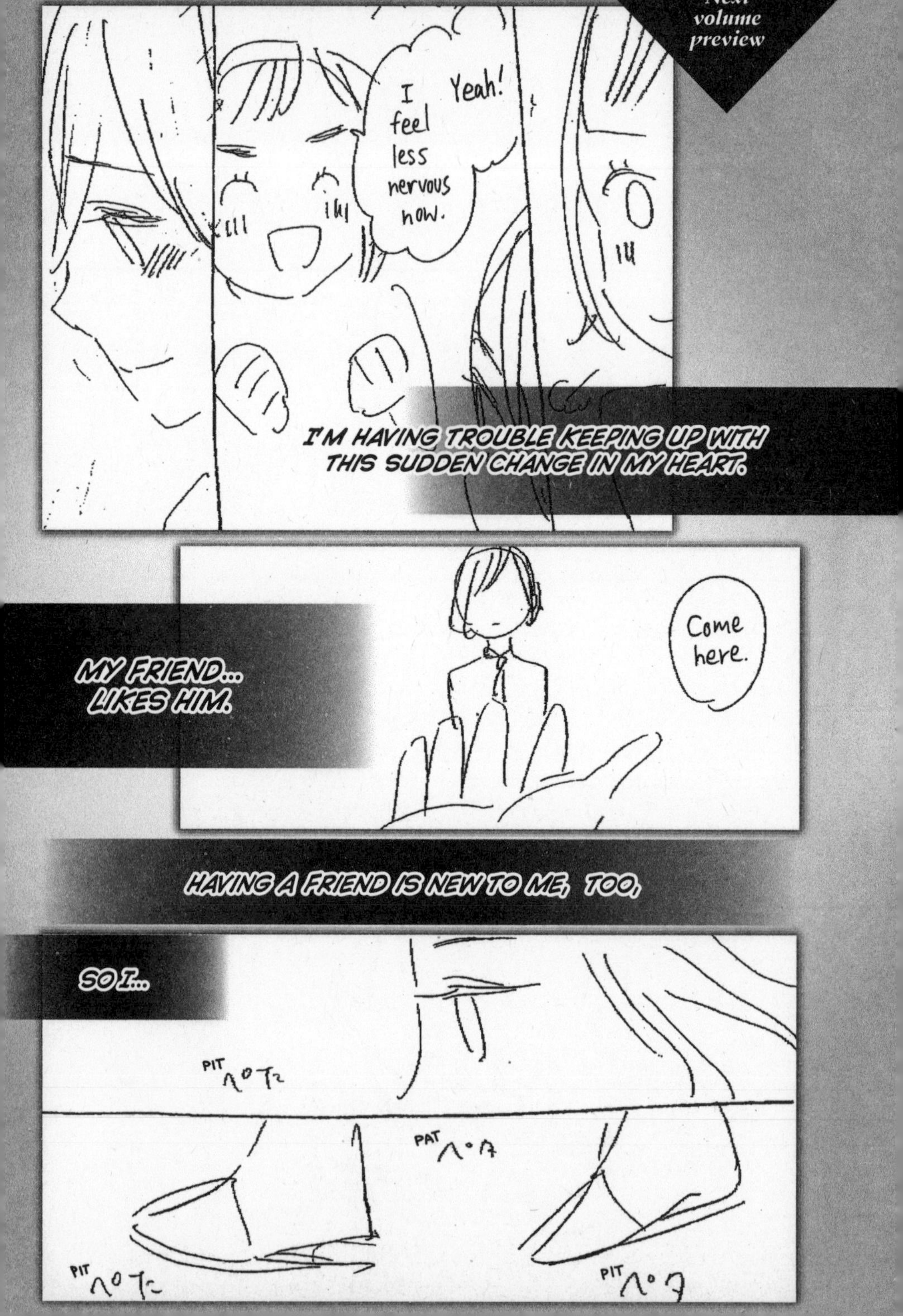
Yeah! I feel less nervous now.
I'M HAVING TROUBLE KEEPING UP WITH THIS SUDDEN CHANGE IN MY HEART.
Come here.
MY FRIEND... LIKES HIM.
HAVING A FRIEND IS NEW TO ME, TOO,
SO I...
PIT ぺた
PAT ペタ
PIT ペタ
PIT ぺた

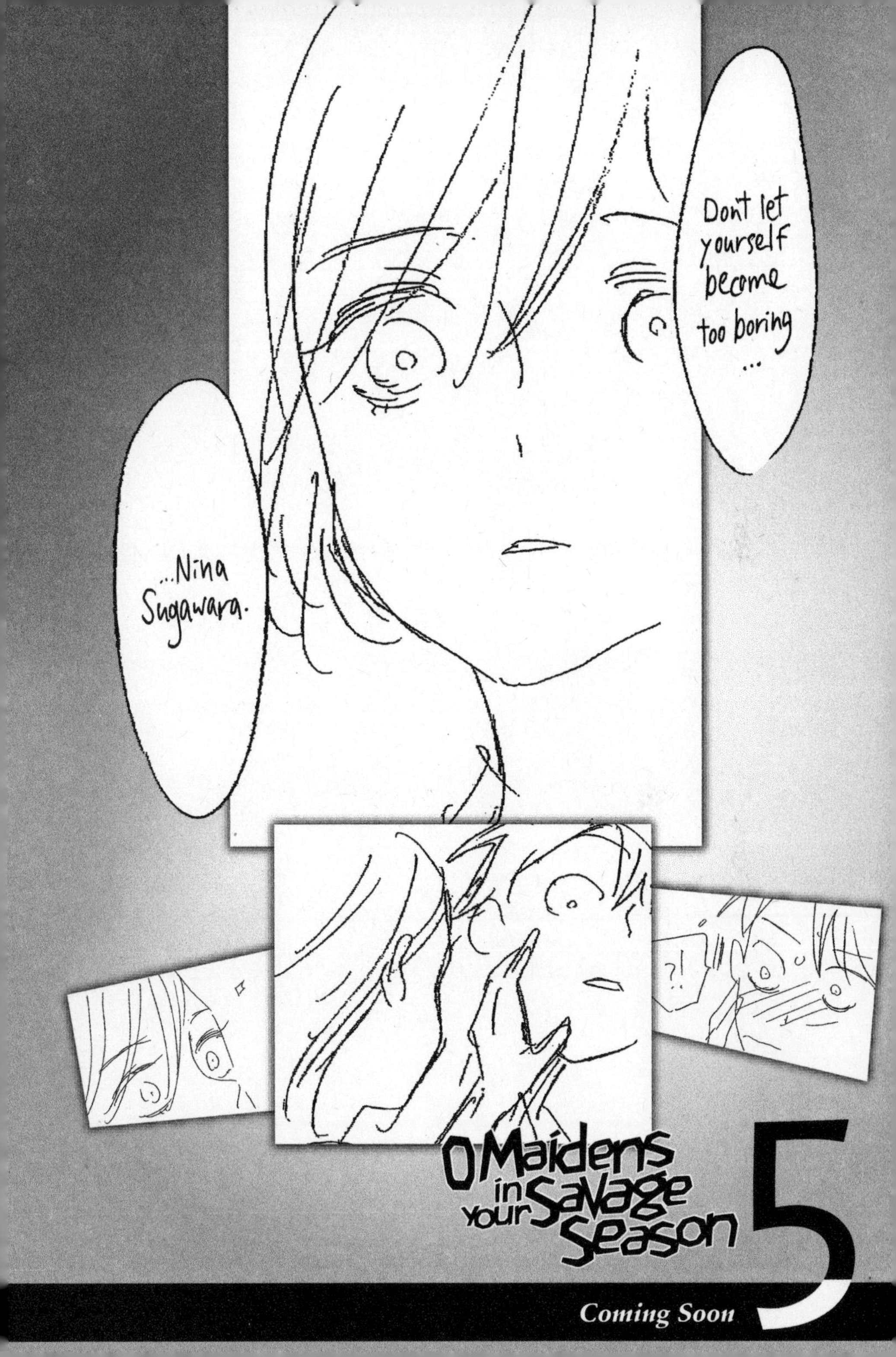
Don't let yourself become too boring ...
...Nina Sugawara.
?!
O Maidens in your Savage Season
5
Coming Soon

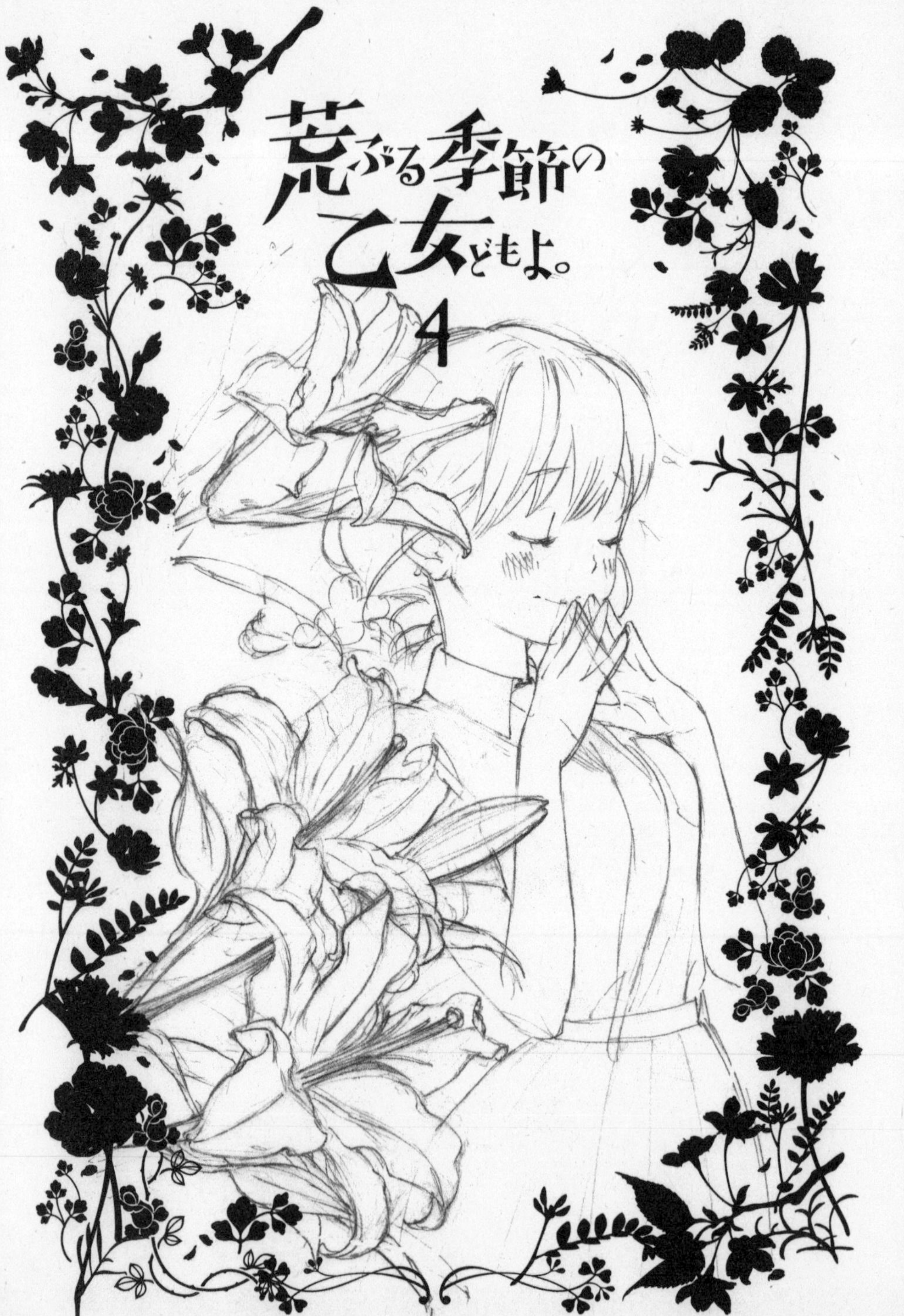
荒ぶる季節の乙女どもよ。
4

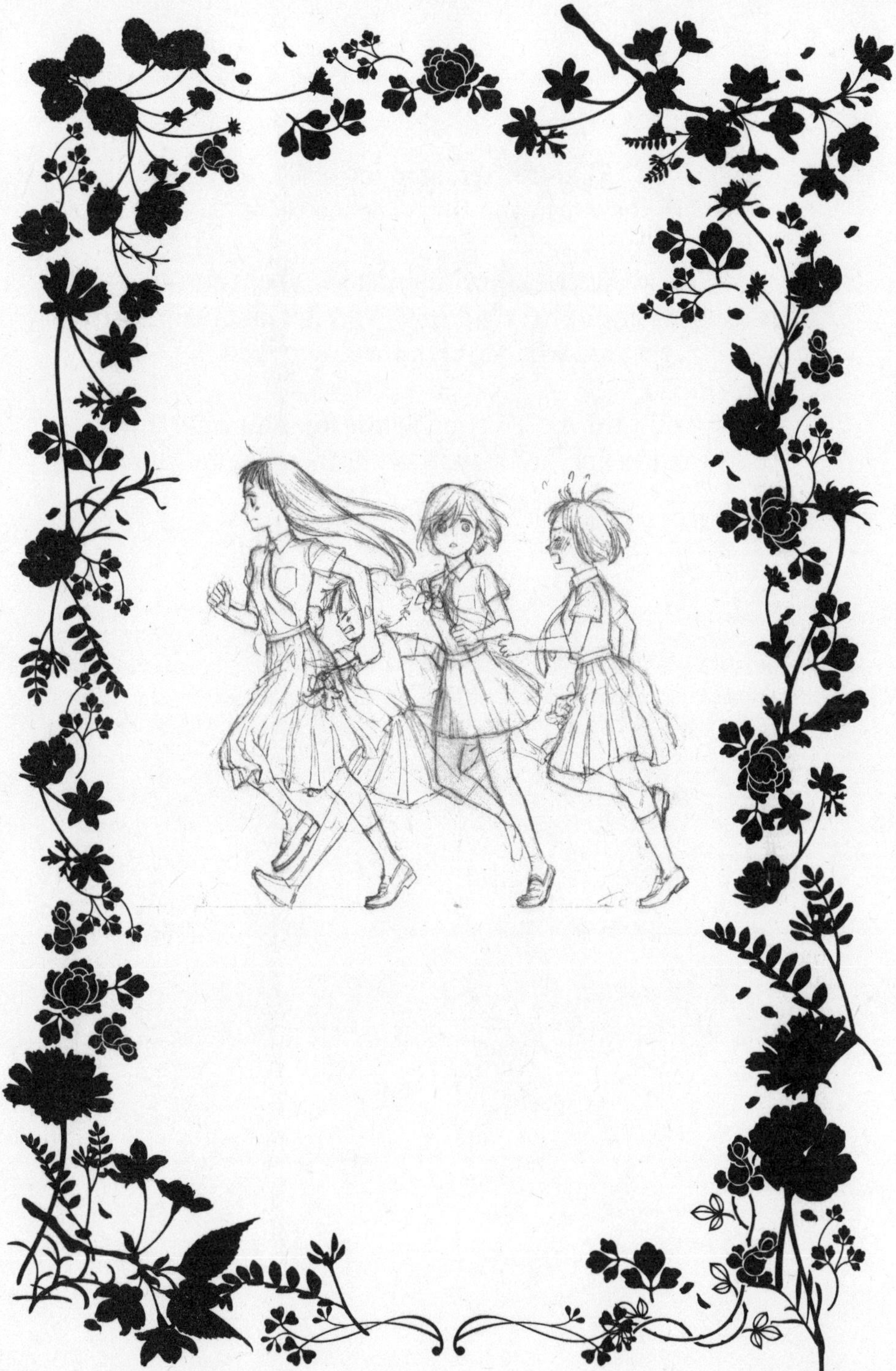

This fluttering in my chest,
the warm and fuzzy feeling there…

That wonderful inner monologue about chests
is really fitting of her right now—for her **and** her breasts
that are wonderful in their own way…

Meanwhile, the most fitting words for me are currently,
"a heavy feeling," or maybe a "tightness" in my chest.

Sigh!

Talk about heartache…

O Maidens in your Savage Season

O Maidens in Your Savage Season, volume 4

Translation Notes

page 12

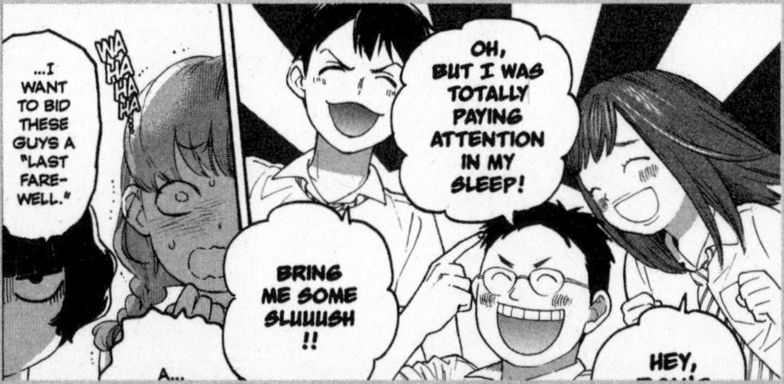
OH, BUT I WAS TOTALLY PAYING ATTENTION IN MY SLEEP!
HEY,
BRING ME SOME SLUUUSH !!
WAHAHAHA
...I WANT TO BID THESE GUYS A "LAST FAREWELL."
A...

A last farewell

The poem Hitoha was reading is "The Morning of the Last Farewell," written by Kenji Miyazawa about his sister lying on her deathbed, asking for a final taste of wet snow.

page 46

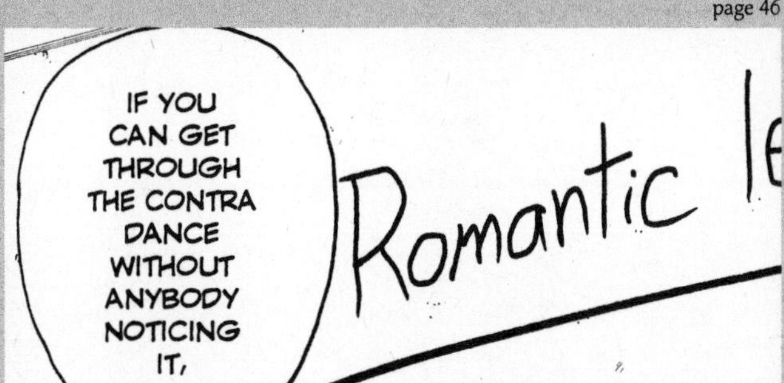
Romantic
IF YOU CAN GET THROUGH THE CONTRA DANCE WITHOUT ANYBODY NOTICING IT,

Contra dancing

The school festival's after party, usually reserved for students of the school, sometimes features contra dancing around the bonfire where boys and girls partner up.

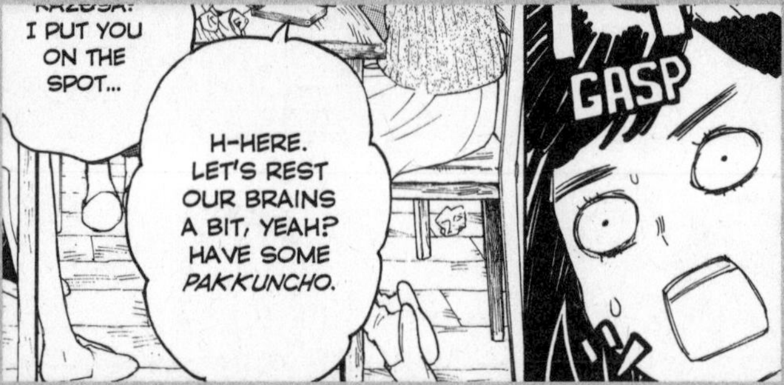
GASP
H-HERE. LET'S REST OUR BRAINS A BIT, YEAH? HAVE SOME *PAKKUNCHO.*
I PUT YOU ON THE SPOT...

Pakkuncho* and *Pie-no-Mi

Classic Japanese chocolate snacks that are reminiscent of childhood.

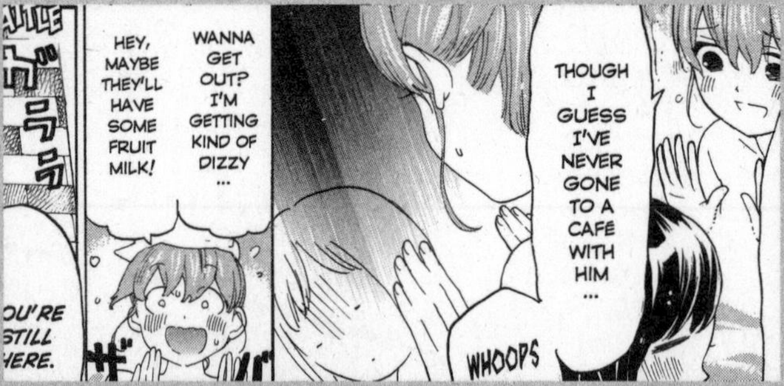
THOUGH I GUESS I'VE NEVER GONE TO A CAFE WITH HIM ...
WHOOPS
WANNA GET OUT? I'M GETTING KIND OF DIZZY ...
HEY, MAYBE THEY'LL HAVE SOME FRUIT MILK!

Fruit-flavored milk

Bathhouses commonly sell cold milk as an refreshing beverage after a bath. They come in various flavors such as fruit or coffee.

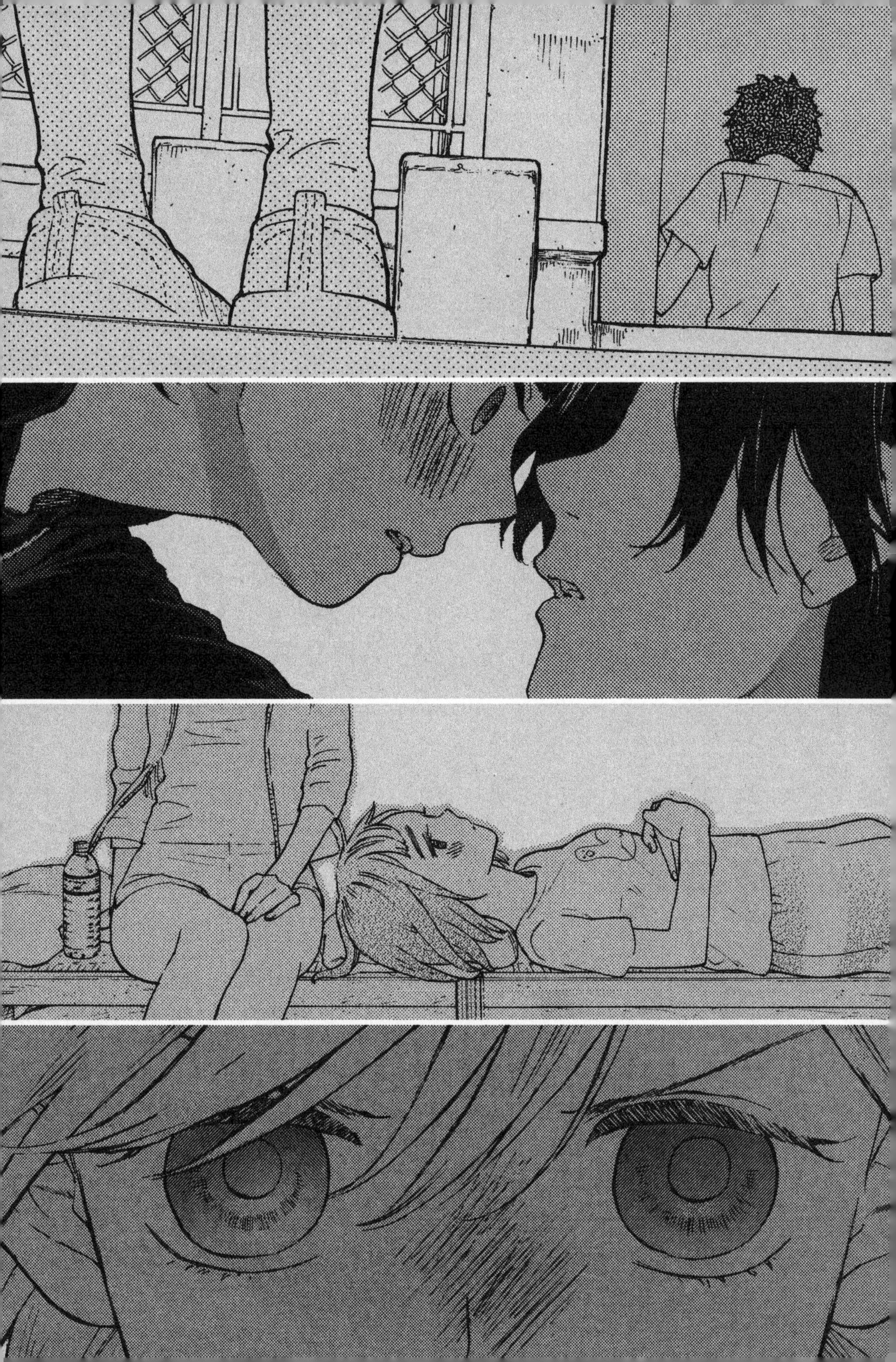

KAMOME SHIRAHAMA

Witch Hat Atelier

A magical manga adventure for fans of Disney and Studio Ghibli!

Witch Hat Atelier © Kamome Shirahama/Kodansha Ltd.

The magical adventure that took Japan by storm is finally here, from acclaimed DC and Marvel cover artist Kamome Shirahama!

In a world where everyone takes wonders like magic spells and dragons for granted, Coco is a girl with a simple dream: She wants to be a witch. But everybody knows magicians are born, not made, and Coco was not born with a gift for magic. Resigned to her un-magical life, Coco is about to give up on her dream to become a witch...until the day she meets Qifrey, a mysterious, traveling magician. After secretly seeing Qifrey perform magic in a way she's never seen before, Coco soon learns what everybody "knows" might not be the truth, and discovers that her magical dream may not be as far away as it may seem...

KC KODANSHA COMICS

Magus of the Library

Mitsu Izumi

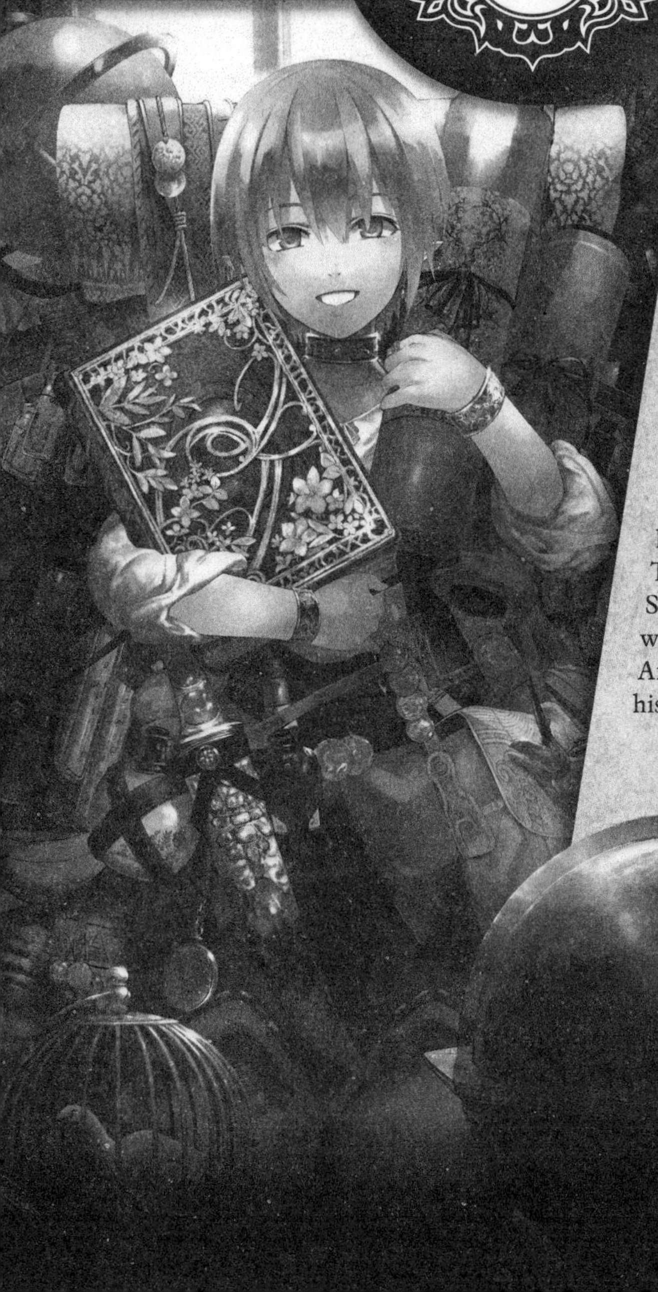

MITSU IZUMI'S STUNNING ARTWORK BRINGS A FANTASTICAL LITERARY ADVENTURE TO LUSH, THRILLING LIFE!

Young Theo adores books, but the prejudice and hatred of his village keeps them ever out of his reach. Then one day, he chances to meet Sedona, a traveling librarian who works for the great library of Aftzaak, City of Books, and his life changes forever...

KC KODANSHA COMICS

A picture-perfect shojo series from Yoko Nogiri, creator of the hit *That Wolf-Boy is Mine!*

Mako's always had a passion for photography. When she loses someone dear to her, she clings onto her art as a relic of the close relationship she once had... Luckily, her childhood best friend Kei encourages her to come to his high school and join their prestigious photo club. With nothing to lose, Mako grabs her camera and moves into the dorm where Kei and his classmates live. Soon, a fresh take on life, along with a mysterious new muse, begin to come into focus!

LOVE IN FOCUS

Praise for Yoko Nogiri's *That Wolf-Boy is Mine!*

KC KODANSHA COMICS

"Emotional squees...will-they-won't-they plot...[and a] pleasantly quick pace."
—Otaku USA Magazine

"A series that is pure shojo sugar—a cute love story about two nice people looking for their places in the world, and finding them with each other." —Anime News Network

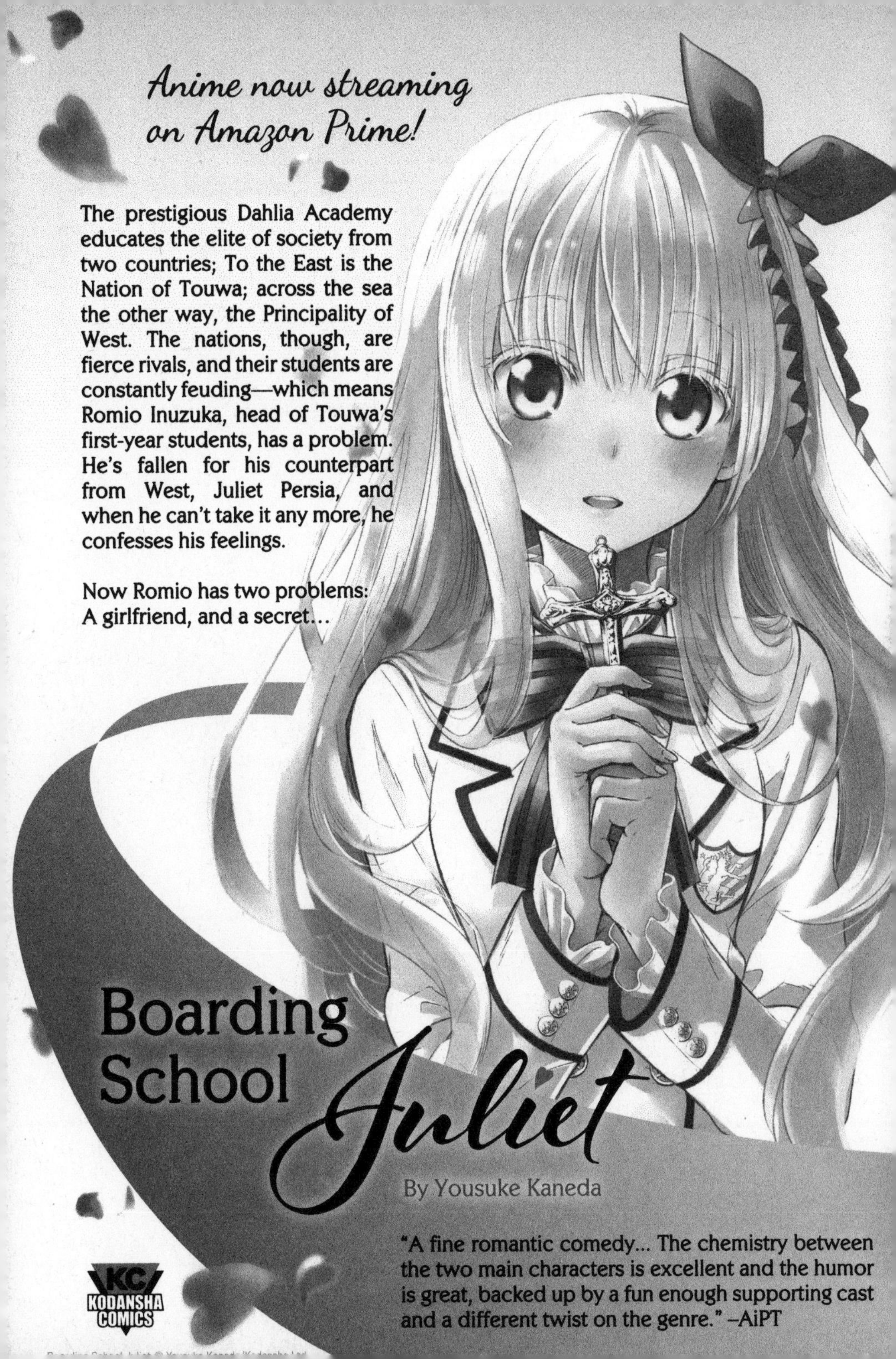
Anime now streaming on Amazon Prime!
The prestigious Dahlia Academy educates the elite of society from two countries; To the East is the Nation of Touwa; across the sea the other way, the Principality of West. The nations, though, are fierce rivals, and their students are constantly feuding—which means Romio Inuzuka, head of Touwa's first-year students, has a problem. He's fallen for his counterpart from West, Juliet Persia, and when he can't take it any more, he confesses his feelings.
Now Romio has two problems: A girlfriend, and a secret…
Boarding School Juliet
By Yousuke Kaneda
"A fine romantic comedy... The chemistry between the two main characters is excellent and the humor is great, backed up by a fun enough supporting cast and a different twist on the genre." –AiPT
KC KODANSHA COMICS

Princess Jellyfish

Akiko Higashimura

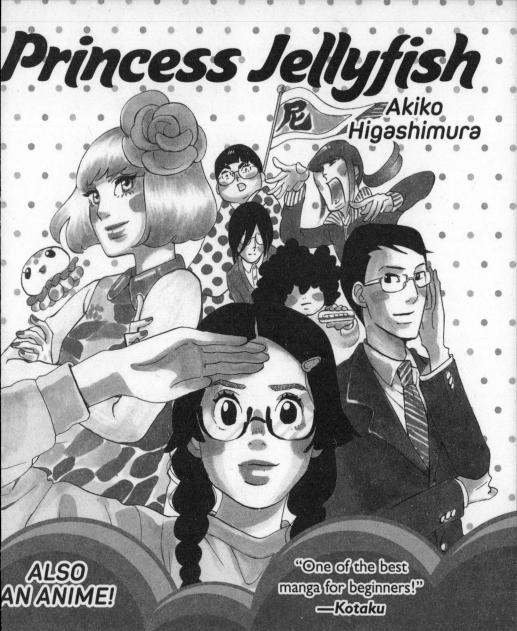

ALSO AN ANIME!

"One of the best manga for beginners!"
—*Kotaku*

Tsukimi Kurashita is fascinated with jellyfish. She's loved them from a young age and has carried that love with her to her new life in the big city of Tokyo. There, she resides in Amamizukan, a safe-haven for geek girls where no boys are allowed. One day, Tsukimi crosses paths with a beautiful and fashionable woman, but there's much more to this woman than her trendy clothes...!

The prince in his dark days

By **Hico Yamanaka**

A drunkard for a father, a household of poverty... For 17-year-old Atsuko, misfortune is all she knows and believes in. Until one day, a chance encounter with Itaru–the wealthy heir of a huge corporation–changes everything. The two look identical, uncannily so. When Itaru curiously goes missing, Atsuko is roped into being his stand-in. There, in his shoes, Atsuko must parade like a prince in a palace. She encounters many new experiences, but at what cost…?

A Kodansha Comics Trade Paperback Original
O Maidens in Your Savage Season 4 copyright © 2018 Mari Okada/Nao Emoto
English translation copyright © 2019 Mari Okada/Nao Emoto

Published in the United States by Kodansha Comics, an imprint of Kodansha USA Publishing, LLC, New York.

Publication rights for this English edition arranged through **Kodansha Ltd., Tokyo.**

First published in Japan in 2018 by Kodansha Ltd., Tokyo as *Araburu Kisetsu no Otomedomoyo* volume 4.

ISBN 978-1-63236-850-8

Printed in the United States of America.

www.kodanshacomics.com

9 8 7 6 5 4 3 2 1

Translation: **Sawa Matsueda Savage**
Lettering: **Evan Hayden**
Editing: **Haruko Hashimoto**
Kodansha Comics edition cover design by **Phil Balsman**

Publisher: Kiichiro Sugawara
Managing editor: Maya Rosewood
Vice president of marketing & publicity: Naho Yamada

Director of publishing services: Ben Applegate
Associate director of operations: Stephen Pakula
Publishing services managing editor: Noelle Webster
Assistant production manager: Emi Lotto